Ewelina Rogalska

Structures of European Civil Codes

Augsburger Schriften zur Rechtsgeschichte

Herausgegeben von

Dr. iur. utr. Christoph Becker
Universitätsprofessor
in Augsburg

Band 43

LIT

Ewelina Rogalska

Structures of European Civil Codes

LIT

This book is printed on acid-free paper.

Bibliographic information published by the Deutsche Nationalbibliothek
The Deutsche Nationalbibliothek lists this publication in the Deutsche Nationalbibliografie; detailed bibliographic data are available on the Internet at https://dnb.dnb.de.

ISBN 978-3-643-91680-8 (pb)
ISBN 978-3-643-96680-3 (PDF)
Zugl.:Augsburg, Univ., Diss., 2024

A catalogue record for this book is available from the British Library.

Contact:
Fresnostr. 2 D-48159 Münster
Tel. +49 (0) 2 51-62 03 20 Fax +49 (0) 2 51-23 19 72
e-Mail: lit@lit-verlag.de https://www.lit-verlag.de
Distribution:
In the UK: Global Book Marketing, e-mail: mo@centralbooks.com

In loving memory of my grandmother.

Thank you to my supervisor, Professor Dr. Christoph Becker,
for providing guidance and feedback throughout this project.

Table of contents

Introduction

Within the codification movement, since the mid-eighteenth century, a key question that arose concerned the form of civil codes. The systematization of a code is its plan. The aim of this monograph is to develop familiarity with the evolution of a code in the jurisdictions selected for this study. Due to the changes witnessed in Central and Eastern Europe, especially after the fall of the Soviet Union, new civil codes were adopted in Czechia, Hungary and Russia. Work on a new Polish civil code is also underway. The German *Bürgerliches Gesetzbuch* was reformed in 2002 and the French *Code civil* in 2016. There is also an ongoing discussion on the draft of a European civil code and its structure.

A research approach that compiles "old" and new codifications is necessary. All the codes mentioned above are connected to a single area, which is Central and Eastern Europe. The structure of the old codes influenced the systematization of the more current written laws in Central and Eastern Europe. My examination considers the Austrian, Czech, German, French, Hungarian, Polish, Russian and Swiss jurisdictions, as well as the drafts of a European civil code.

As the different models of arranging private law in legislation developed, nowadays while drafting a civil code, a lawmaker can enter the equivalent of a legal supermarket and choose among the available products. This study aims to fill a gap in the legal knowledge, and to offer readers possible ways of systematizing civil codes. These are the institutions of private law, not the precepts, which constitute its system. One of the conditions that a modern codification should meet is that of systematic order.

The first accessible model of arranging private law is systematization based on the Gaius model *(personae – res – actiones).* The first book regards persons[1]. The second site in the structure of the code is occupied by *res*[2]. The last factor in the arrangement of the code concerns *actiones*[3]. The Pandect model introduced the division into five books (general part – *ius in re* – obligations – family law – inheritance law). It was adopted in Germany and in other legal systems in Central

---

1 The first book of the CMBC (1756) concerns the legal rules in general and law of persons.
In the French *Code civil* (1804) the first book refers to persons.
In the ABGB (1811) the first book considers persons.

2 In the French CC (1804) the second book includes goods and different modifications of ownership.
In the ABGB (1811) the second book contains *ius rerum*.
In the CMBC (1756), the second book (on *ius in re*) and the third book (regarding inheritance law) constitute together *res*.

3 *Actiones* were reinterpreted differently in the structure of the researched codes.
In the CMBC (1756) those are obligations, situated in the last fourth book.
In the French CC (1804) the last third book deals with different ways of acquiring ownership.
In the ABGB (1811) the last third book comprises provisions common to personal rights and *ius in re*.

and Eastern Europe. Modifications of the Pandect structure enacted into the codes resulted in a field with multiple angles of interest from a comparative perspective.

The Pandect divisions, as well as the systematization of the German *Bürgerliches Gesetzbuch* (1896), determine the sequence of the chapters in this study. Following on from the introduction, the first chapter examines the possibilities for arranging the general part. The second chapter encompasses the law of obligations, and the third chapter *ius in re*. These are the longest chapters in the analysis. The fourth chapter considers the law of persons and family law (*personae*), whereas the final, fifth chapter addresses inheritance law. Following the introduction there are three sections, each serving as a foreword to the chapters. First, the history of editing civil codes. Here, readers have an opportunity to familiarise themselves with the basic problems connected with the systematization of civil codes. In the second section, I briefly consider the influence of legislative philosophy on the structure of the civil codes considered in this study. In the third section, I discuss the reception of the Pandect model with a general part in Central and Eastern Europe.

A) History of editing civil codes

I. The significance of the Gaius model for the study

As the only significant model available to lawyers up to this point has been the Gaius scheme, all analyses of the structure of civil codes are inseparably connected with it. The later evolution of the arrangement of civil codes results from the legislative reinterpretations of its nature. This section addresses the exterior divisions of the written laws in relation to the Gaius model. This builds the foundation for the ensuing analysis.

II. *Institutes* and applications of its system to the legislation

The first idea to explore concerning the structure of civil codes is the exact transposition of the Gaius scheme into legislation. The foundation of the analysis are the *Institutes*. Their shape could be introduced to civil codes in different ways. *Institutes* are based on three concepts: *personae – res – actiones*. In ancient Roman law, *persona* was a term used to designate a person and his rights. It is a subject of private law, and all that concerns the legal situation of a person. *Res* relates to what an individual could acquire, whereas *actio* is a right applying to the situation of a person and the legal possibility of claiming his rights by law.

According to Gaius, *personae* and *res* come under substantive private law, whereas *actiones* belong to civil procedure. For this study it is crucial to establish how those principles were reinterpreted in the structure of civil codes. *Res* encompasses all ways of acquiring property by an individual. They are *ius in re*, inheritance law, matrimonial property law and obligations. Currently, *res* is the equivalent of an object and a static element of the system. *Actiones* are a dynamic component of the system, inherently connected with the law of obligations. *Actio* is indispensable for the proper understanding of the Gaius scheme – without *actio* there are only *persona* and *res*; *actiones* are responsible for forming a connection between a person and his or her object[4]. The concepts with which Gaius provided lawyers constituted only the starting point. *Res* was not identical to that which is currently associated with *ius in re*; the same also applies to obligations. For the Romans, *obligatio* meant something different from its current sense, then relating to an obligation; in Rome *obligatio* was not a concept, but it would signify that something is legally effective[5]. An obligation is an example of a construct that derives from the Roman law, and which has had a predominant effect on modern legal systems and on our legal science. Not all the ideas pertaining to Roman law have been applicable in our time – for example, the case of the Roman *patria potestas* and guardianship[6]. The areas of Roman law mentioned here did not have the feature of universality – contrary to the Roman law of obligations or *ius in re*.

III. Transpositions of the Gaius scheme into legislation

The principles of the Gaius scheme have inspired lawyers who work on the arrangement of private law. As civil procedure was separated from substantive private law, the Gaius scheme needed to be adjusted to the current legal categories. In the 18th and 19th centuries, lawyers debated how the Gaius model could be introduced into legislation. As only three sites are accessible in the scheme, consequently private law in the civil codes had to be divided into three categories. The first position was allocated to the law of persons and family law (*personae*). The second place was given to *res*; *res* prevails in the composition of the oldest codifications. *Actiones* were reinterpreted differently in the codes. First, I will deal with the CMBC (1756), then with the French CC (1804) and finally with the ABGB (1811). Here only the original arrangement implemented in the civil codes is described.

1. Codex Maximilianeus Bavaricus Civilis (1756)

The first codification following the order of the *Institutes* is the CMBC. It is divided into four books: the legal rules in general and the law of persons (the first book), *ius in re* (the second book), inheritance law (the third book) and the law of obligations (the fourth book). The first book corresponds with *personae*. The second and third books together constitute *res*, where as the fourth book concerns

---

4 In the German BGB (1896) *actiones* are reinterpreted as juridical acts.
Conf. HATTENHAUER H., *Grundbegriffe des Bürgerlichen Rechts. Historisch-dogmatische Einführung*, München 2000, pp. 67 – 68.

5 *Ibidem*, pp. 87 – 88.

6 WESENBERG G., WESENER G., *Neuere deutsche Privatrechtsgeschichte im Rahmen der europäischen Rechtsentwicklung*, Lahr/Schwarzwald 1976, p. 123.

actiones. The systematic classifications introduced to the CMBC are the divisions of the branches of private law; in this aspect the Bavarian structure inspired the Pandect systematization.

2. French Code civil (1804)

The second civil code founded on the Gaius model is the French CC. The CC was a legal instrument for propagating the ideas of the French Revolution, and its shape needed to cohere with the new philosophy. A person and his ownership are crucial in the structure of the CC[7]. The first book includes *personae*. The second book concerns goods and different ways of modifying ownership (*res*). Regulations that did not fit into the first two books were assembled in the third book, which considers different ways of acquiring ownership (*actiones*). In such a context, most of the content of the substantive private law is classified among *actiones* instead of *res*. In the *Institutes* of Gaius *res* comprises *ius in re*, law of succession, matrimonial property law and the law of obligations.

The general provisions are located at the opening of the third book (Articles 711 – 717); they apply to the ways of acquiring ownership. The first title comprises successions. The second title, donations *inter vivos* and wills. The regulation of the general part of obligations subsequently follows: the third title of the third book deals with contracts and conventional obligations in general. The fourth title relates to commitments formed without an agreement: the non-contractual sources of obligations. The fifth title refers to prenuptial agreements and matrimonial regimes. Next in sequence are particular contracts (the sixth title: sales, the seventh title: exchange, the eighth title: lease, the ninth title: partnership contract, the tenth title: loan, the eleventh title: deposits and sequestrations, the twelfth title: aleatory contracts, the thirteenth title: mandate, the fourteenth title: guarantee, the fifteenth title: compromise). In the French composition, the entire volume of the law of obligations is located in one area. The sequence of the systematic components is: the general provisions on contracts – non-contractual sources of obligations – particular contracts.

This is the most significant difference between the composition of the law of obligations and *ius in re*. In the CC, *ius in re* are dispersed between two books. The second book concerning goods and different modifications of ownership comprises four titles (the first title: distinction of goods; the second title: ownership; the third title: usufruct, use and habitation; the fourth title: servitudes or land services). The institutions of *ius in re* that do not fit in the second book were placed at the end of the third book, on different ways of acquiring ownership. The sixteenth title concerns personal arrest in private law matters. The seventeenth title addres-

---

7 On the system of the French *Code civil* also here:
HUBE R., *Uwagi nad systematem Kodexu cywilnego francuzkiego* [The remarks on the system of the French *Code civil*], Warszawa 1829.

ses pledges. The eighteenth title, privileges and mortgages. The nineteenth title deals with forced expropriation and orders between creditors. The final, twentieth title considers prescription.

French legislators concentrated the system of the code on subjective legal categories[8]. The arrangement of the CC therefore foregrounds person and ownership. Those two concepts dominate the systematization of the written law. Since the adoption of the Pandect model, the French arrangement became anachronic. Nonetheless, that did not terminate the legislative career of the CC; the French code inspired lawyers attempting to find the most socialist arrangement of a civil code possible. They aimed to implement subjective elements in their codifications, of which the most crucial was ownership. Such an arrangement was based exclusively on the systematization of the CC, which mentions ownership in the titles of two among its three books.

3. Austrian Allgemeines bürgerliches Gesetzbuch (1811)

The ABGB is the last written law to involve the exact transposition of the Gaius model into legislation. Its first book regards personal rights (*personae*) [*von dem Personen-Rechte*], where as the second book concerns *ius rerum res*) [*von dem Sachenrechte*]. As with the Gaius scheme, almost all that relates to property is arranged in the second book (§§ 285 – 1341). The central construct of the second book is a thing, set in the opening of the second book, in the chapter on things and their legal classification (§§ 285 – 308). This content is set in front of the divisions of the ABGB.

The second book includes two divisions. The first division concerns *ius in re* [*von den dinglichen Rechten*], and the second division, personal rights [*von den persönlichen Sachenrechten*]. In the first division there are *ius in re* (chapters one to seven; § 309 – § 530) and inheritance law (chapters eight to fifteen; §§ 531 – 824). The final, sixteenth chapter of the second division considers the community of ownership (co-ownership) and other *ius in re* (§§ 825 – 858). In the systematization of the ABGB, the law of succession is a part of *ius in re*. The second division of the second book concerns personal rights (§§ 859 – 1341). The seventeenth chapter refers to contracts in general[9] (§§ 859 – 937). This is the general part of obligations. Particular obligations follow (chapters eighteen to thirty; §§ 938 – 1341). Matrimonial property law is located in the twenty-eighth chapter. The final, third book of the ABGB is dedicated to *actiones*, which are primarily obligations.

---

[8] Contrary to the CMBC (1756) and the ABGB (1811), founded on the objective and stable systematic classifications, the main systematic factor in the CC is ownership, a subjective concept.

[9] That was the original title of that chapter – now, the seventeenth chapter considers contracts and juridical acts in general *[von Verträgen und Rechtsgeschäften überhaupt]*.

Components that do not fit in the first two books are contained in the third book, which includes provisionscommonto personal rights and *ius in re* [*von Umänderung der Rechte und Verbindlichkeiten*]. Containing provisions from § 1342 to § 1502, the third book comprises around 10 % of the content of the ABGB. The first chapter (of the third book) considers the security of rights and obligations. The second chapter, modification of rights and obligations. The third chapter concerns cancellation of rights and obligations. The final, fourth chapter addresses prescription and usucaption. The titles of the chapters of the third book display the widest possible legal construct in private law – rights and obligations – but the content of the third book primarily involves the institutions of the law of obligations. In the ABGB, the law of obligations is split between two books.

The third book constitutes an attempt to find a common factor in private law. It can be viewed as what is common to *personae* and *res*, meaning that the last book should constitute what applies to the first two books, resulting from a relation of an individual (*persona*) towards his surroundings (*res*). Concurrently, the third book involves that which coheres with the two divisions of the second book on *ius rerum*; as the first division regards *ius in re* and the second division personal rights (obligations), then the third book can be perceived as concerning what is common to *ius in re* and the law of obligations. The main accomplishment of the Austrian systematization is an attempt to further systematize private law in a civil code. Even though the composition of the ABGB is evidently now outdated, it constitutes the passage between the codifications based on the Gaius scheme and the Pandect systematization. It could be stated that the system of the CC is closed whereas the systematization of the ABGB is "open". The third book of the ABGB, comprising provisions common to personal rights and *ius in re*, is an incentive for the further systematization of private law[10]. It seems that the lack of the general part is a main systematic deficit of the ABGB. One of the research fields covered in this study involves examining the impact of the Austrian structure on the codifications in Central and Eastern Europe, particularly in the 20th century[11].

---

[10] All codifications adopted in the German-speaking legal systems express the quest for the best possible arrangement of a civil code. That is visible in the CMBC (1756), in the Prussian *Landrecht* (1794), the ABGB (1811), the Saxon civil code (1863), the German BGB (1896) and the East German civil code (1975). The only exception is Switzerland with its civil code (1907) and the Code of obligations (1911). However, in Switzerland German is merely one of the official languages.

[11] The influence of the ABGB on the civil codes and their drafts in the 19th century is described here:

FROHNECKE E., *Die Rolle des ABGB in Gesetzgebung und Rechtswissenschaft des 19. Jahrhunderts*, Münster 2001.

In the publication the author compares the systematization of the codes and drafts with the arrangement of the ABGB.

The Austrian systematization is considered anachronic by Austrian scholars[12]; all the modern handbooks of the Austrian private law replicate the arrangement based on the Pandect model, instead of the arrangement of the ABGB[13]. In comparison to other codifications, the ABGB is rather short: it has 1502 provisions, whereas the CC (1804) at the moment of its adoption had 2281 provisions[14]. Contrary to the German BGB (1896), the ABGB is not an attempt towards to pursue perfection and legal precision[15]; for its authors it was clear that the gaps in the legislation would be fixed by legal practice[16].

IV. *Allgemeines Landrecht für die Preußischen Staaten* (1794)

Having established the codifications belonging to the Gaius scheme, we now move to considering the Prussian *Landrecht*. It also involves criminal law and administrative law, but the majority of its precepts concern private law. In the *Landrecht* the sequence is reversed, and instead of *personae – res*, there is *res – personae*. This perspective resulted in the Pandect systematization, where family law is considered after the main content[17] (general part – *ius in re* – law of obligations).

The *Landrecht* is divided into two parts. The majority of (the substantive) private law is arranged in the first part. The first part of *Landrecht* comprises the regulations that concern an individual and his rights[18]. The Gaius scheme *(personae – res – actiones)* is arranged in the opening section of the first part of the *Landrecht*[19]. After the (legal) actions constituting *actiones*, declarations of will[20] and contracts[21] are settled. Duties and rights, arising from illegal acts, subsequently follow[22]. Even though it is not isolated among the divisions of the *Landrecht*, the general part can be observed here. Next, there are further institutions, primarily connected to *res*. First, detention and possession, and then ownership[23]. After

---

12 POSCH W., *Grundzüge fremder Privatrechtssysteme*, Wien/Köln/Graz 1995, p. 6.

13 *Ibidem*, p. 6.

14 *Ibidem*, p. 6.

15 *Ibidem*, p. 7.

16 *Conf. Ibidem*, p. 7.

17 In the Saxon civil code (1863) the books are: a general part – *ius in re* – law of claims (obligations) – family law (including guardianship law) – inheritance law.
The German BGB (1896) contains: a general part – law of obligations – *ius in re* – family law – law of succession.

18 WESENBERG G., WESENER G., *Neuere deutsche Privatrechtsgeschichte im Rahmen der europäischen Rechtsentwicklung*, Lahr/Schwarzwald 1976, p. 146.

19 In the Prussian *Landrecht* (1794) the first title (of the first part) concerns persons and their rights in general. The second title: things and their rights in general. The third title: actions and thus originating rights.

20 The fourth title: declarations of will.

21 The fifth title: agreements.

22 The sixth title: duties and rights arising from unlawful acts.

23 The seventh title (of the first part) comprises detention and possession. The eighth title: ownership.

this follow the acquisition of ownership in general and the immediate methodsof acquisition in general (the ninth title). The eleventh title includes the titles of acquisition of ownership arising from contracts between living partners. The twelfth title comprises titles relating to acquiring ownership arising from dispositions in the case of death, which involves the regulation of the law of succession. The second part of the *Landrecht* addreses family law[24]. The second part also includes the regulations of different associations[25]. The original arrangement of the *Landrecht*, where the legal regulations were divided into two parts, was reinterpreted by the legal science which saw in this systematization two aspects of social life: one that perceives a person as an individual, and the other that considers a person as a member of a social group[26].

At the time when the *Landrecht* was adopted, it took into account all the scientific achievements of the epoch[27]. The most significant disadvantage of the *Landrecht* is its excessive casuistry[28]. Instead of attempting to find general rules and giving judges the possibility of reinterpreting private law if necessary, here the opposite approach was adopted. The most significant feature of the Prussian *Landrecht* is its attempt to settle all regulations in one written law. This is the last written law with such a supposition; from that point onward criminal law has been arranged in a criminal code, private law in a civil code, etc. Substantive private law is also isolated from the civil procedure. The assumptions mentioned here are an attribute of all codifications since the 19th century. In this aspect CMBC (1756) was ahead of its time.

V. Formation of the Pandect model

The preceding codes did not redistribute private law in a way that offered readers a quick and easy orientation in the text of the written law. In later codifications, divisions accordant with the branches of private law were introduced. As with the CMBC[29], in the Pandect model, the respective branches of private law are placed in separate books, with a division into five books: the general part, *ius in re*, the law of obligations, family law and succession law. Furthermore, substantial private law and civil procedure are fully separated from each other.

---

24 The first title of the second part deals with marriage. The second title: mutual rights and duties of parents and children. The third title: rights and duties of the remaining members of the family. The fourth title: common family rights in general.

25 WESENBERG G., WESENER G., *Neuere deutsche Privatrechtsgeschichte im Rahmen der europäischen Rechtsentwicklung*, Lahr/Schwarzwald 1976, p. 146.

26 *Conf. ibidem*, p. 146.

27 *Ibidem*, p. 146.

28 *Ibidem*, p. 146.

29 In the CMBC (1756) the first book includes the legal rules in general and the law of persons. The second book: *ius in re*. The third book: succession law. The last fourth book: the law of obligations.

The most distinctive feature of the Pandect model is the general part, with the Gaius scheme atits opening (*personae – res – actiones*). Institutions of private law that apply to all books of the code (e.g. an object) are situated in the general part. The most typical among them are persons, things and juridical acts. In the general part, juridical acts provide the grounding for the further compounds of the law of obligations: condition, representation and power of attorney. There may also be some provisions on contracts. Prescription is placed at the end of the general part. This arrangement is associated with the Pandect systematization. Concurrently, the branches of private law (law of obligations – *ius in re* – family law – law of succession) should be put in distinct books of the civil code.

The Pandect systematization derives from the system of legal handbooks elaborated by the German law professors. Alongside examining the structure of the civil codes, this study also concentrates on the systems of the handbooks in Central and Eastern Europe. The systematic categories implemented by legal scholars are verified. Further examination reveals that the Pandect systematization was rejected in the East German civil code (1975).

The German scholars whose work resulted in the establishment of the Pandect systematization believed their task to be elaborating private law and its concepts from the point of view of a systematically constructive, logical perspective. The Roman law from *Digesta Iustiniani*, considered by them a closed system, had to be elaborated once again. In their reasoning and reflections there was only place for positive law; natural law or any other extralegal factors could not be taken into account. The formal logic of their system was defined as the legal philosophy of concepts (*Begriffsjurisprudenz*). The approach discussed here dominated the German and Austrian scholarship[30].

The first civil code that adopted the Pandect systematization is the Saxon civil code (1863). Its first book contains the general part. The second book: *ius in re*. The third book: the law of claims (obligations). The fourth book: family law (including guardianship law). The final, fifth book: inheritance law. *Ius in re* immediately follows the general part; the emphasis on this branch of private law in the divisions of the Saxon code is connected with the impact of the Gaius model, which prefers *res*. The third book considers the law of claims – a visible sign of the lack of a clear distinction between substantive private law and civil procedure.

The second civil code, and the best known for the Pandect structure, is the German *Bürgerliches Gesetzbuch* (1896). Its first book is the general part. The law of obligations (*actiones*) is set directly after the general part, in the second book. *Ius in re* (*res*) occupies the third book. The fourth book includes family law and the final, fifth book, inheritance law. Arranging the law of obligations immediately

---

30 FLOSSMANN U., KALB H., NEUWIRTH K., *Österreichische Privatrechtgschichte*, Wien 2014, p. 21.

after the general part results from foregrounding obligations (*actiones*) instead of *ius in re* (*res*) in the structure of the code.

In the Pandect structure, the code is composed of legal concepts (*Begriffe*), acting rather like the bricks of the system. They are embedded in the general part. If a concept is defined in the general part, then this setting also applies to other books. The Pandect systematization provides multiple systematic opportunities. The essence of a written law may vary significantly. As the general part acts as the superstructure for the code, new books can be added (e.g. private international law, copyright law or patent law[31]) without disturbing its functioning. The general part also applies to private law, which is not included in the code.

The abstract nature of the Pandect model lends ita certain aloof and inorganic character. The achievements of 19th century German legal science were introduced into legislation, resulting in a highly abstract and logical construction. The legislative interference is written into the core of the German code. The French CC was supposed to "make itself on its own"[32]. That was also the case in the ABGB (1811). Nonetheless, despite the passage of over 100 years, the structure of the BGB (1896) did not become anachronic. It was necessary to amend the German law of obligations, and for this reason in 2001 the reform of the BGB was adopted (it entered in force on 1st January 2002), but the most crucial systematic compound of the structure of the BGB did not become outdated. Most of the values of its interior systematization are still relevant; the freedom and equality of individuals have been crucial for the German legislator. Of the elements mentioned above, freedom of contract, freedom of ownership and the testamentary freedom are prominent; these are the values of a liberal codification[33]. The issue which was not sufficiently dealt with in the BGB has been a social issue among *ius in re*, the law of obligations and inheritance law[34]. In addition, the solutions adopted in family law with in the German BGB at the moment of its adoption were characterized by patriarchal and conservative ideas[35].

---

[31] This is the case in the Russian civil codes (1964 and 1994–2006).

In the second socialist Russian civil code (1964) there are: general part–ownership–obligations–copyright law–right of discovery–patent law–succession law–international private law.

In the current Russian civil code (1994–2006) the books are: general provisions–right of ownership and other rights to estate–general part of obligations–particular kinds of obligations–inheritance law–international private law–rights to results of intellectual activities and means of individualisation.

[32] *« Les codes des peuples se font avec le temps; mais, à proprement parler, on ne le fait pas ».*

FENET P.-A., *Recueil complet des travaux préparatoires du Code civil. Tome premier*, Paris 1836, p. 476.

[33] KÖHLER H., *BGB. Allgemeiner Teil. Ein Studienbuch*, München 2005, pp. 10–11.

[34] *Ibidem*, p. 11.

The author uses here the term of *Vermögensrecht*.

[35] *Ibidem*, p. 11.

VI. Divisions accordant with the branches of private law and without a general part

After the German BGB (1896), an aspiration for an arrangement without a general part and with the sequence of the Gaius model emerged. The books of the code are in accordance with the branches of private law. The composition discussed here obtains in Switzerland and Hungary.

1. Switzerland

The Swiss civil code (1907) consists of four books: law of persons, family law, inheritance law and *ius in re*. The law of persons and family law comprise *personae*, whereas succession law and *ius in re*, *res*. The law of obligations is placed in a separate Code of obligations (1911); despite the fact that from the formal point of view the Code of obligations constitutes a distinct bill, simultaneously it is treated as the last and fifth book of the civil code[36]. It needs to be mentioned that the distinction of obligations emphasises its position of *actiones*. The Swiss systematization as a whole expresses the preference for the Gaius model and the refusal to include in its structure a derivation from the German general part. Its clear and concise provisions vary from the extensive provisions of the German BGB (1896). One of the most significant features of the Swiss systematization was implementing the unity of private law[37], at a time when a commercial code was standard[38]. The proportions are now different; the unity of a civil code is a feature of the Polish civil code (1964), Russian civil code (1994 – 2006), Czech civil code (2012) and Hungarian civil code (2013).

2. Hungary

In Hungary there is no general part, and the Gaius scheme is visible in the exterior divisions of the codes. It is present in the Hungarian draft (1928), in the socialist Hungarian civil code (1959) and the current Hungarian civil code[39] (2013). In Hungary the sequence of the systematic components is: *personae – res (ius in re) – actiones* (law of obligations and inheritance law). The Hungarian draft (1928) includes: law of persons and family law – *ius in re* – law of obligations – law of

---

36 POSCH W., *Grundzüge fremder Privatrechtssysteme*, Wien/Köln/Graz 1995, p. 57.

37 BUCHER E., *Schweizerisches Obligationenrecht. Allgemeiner Teil ohne Deliktsrecht*, Zürich 1988, p. 12.

38 GÓRNICKI L., *Zagadnienia systematyki kodyfikacji prawa cywilnego i handlowego w pracach Komisji Kodyfikacyjnej (1918 – 1939)* [The issues of the systematization of the codification of private and commercial law in the works of the Codification Committee (1918 – 1939)], Kwartalnik Prawa Prywatnego [The Quarterly of Private Law] 2004 vol. 3, p. 633.
The author states that in the interwar period a commercial code was the most wide-spread systematization of a civil code.

39 About the current Hungarian civil code (2013) here:
MENYHÁRD A., VERESS E. (ed.), *New Civil Codes in Hungary and Romania*, Budapest/Cluj Napoca 2017.

succession. In the socialist Hungarian civil code[40] (1959) there are: introductory provisions – persons – right of ownership – law of obligations – inheritance law. Like in all socialist codes, family law is set in separate legislation.

The current Hungarian civil code[41] (2013) contains: introductory provisions – individual as a subject of law – legal entity – family law – *ius in re* – law of obligations – succession law. In the current Hungarian code, the first four books constitute *personae*. *Ius in re* is *res*. Law of obligations and inheritance law are an equivalent of *actiones*. The most distinctive feature of the Hungarian systematization is that the law of obligations and the law of succession together constitute *actiones*; among the sources translated into foreign languages, the Hungarian systematization was visible from the period of the Hungarian draft in 1901 onward[42]. The Hungarian composition is the result of the compromise between the connection to German legal science and the German BGB (1896), as well as the ABGB (1811).

One of the issues verified in this study are the divisions implemented in legal handbooks. Hungarian legal science replicates the scheme visible in the legislation: first, the general principles of private law, then law of persons, family law, *ius in re*, law of obligations and finally succession law[43]. Besides the general part, all other divisions adopted by Pandect German legal science are also present in Hungary. *Ius in re*, the law of obligations and inheritance law are constant elements of the Hungarian systematization; in the socialist Hungarian civil code (1959) the impact of socialism is evident in the replacement of *ius in re* with the book concerning ownership. *Personae* prevail in the Hungarian arrangement and there are more opportunities of settling the issue. It may be situated in a single book in the opening of the code[44] or it can be distributed between more books[45].

VII. Order of the *Institutes* adopted in the Pandect structure with a general part

The standard Pandect code includes five books and results in the separation of the general part (*persona*) from family law. In order to prevent such a division, the books can be arranged following the sequence of the *Institutes*. This classification

---

40 For more about the socialist Hungarian civil code (1959), see:
EÖRSI G., *Das ungarische Zivilgesetzbuch in fünf Studien*, Budapest 1963.

41 About the Hungarian private law also here:
KÜPPER H., *Einführung in das ungarische Recht*, München 2011.

42 *Entwurf eines ungarischen allgemeinen bürgerliches Gesetzbuches*, Budapest 1901.

43 KÜPPER H., *Einführung in das ungarische Recht*, München 2011.

44 In the Hungarian draft (1928) the first book concerns the law of persons and family law.

45 In the current Hungarian civil code (2013), the second book considers individual as subject of law. The third book: legal entity. The fourth book: family law.

is present in the Russian draft[46] (1905) and the Czech civil code[47] (2012). In both written laws, the first two books (general part and family law) are the equivalent of *personae*. Next in the arrangement is *res* (*ius in re* and inheritance law), and finally, obligations (*actiones*). Such an outline can be implemented only in a bourgeois civil code; in socialist civil codes, family law is external to the civil code.

VIII. The Pandect structure in the socialist civil codes including a general part

The Pandect model is a feature of the majority of the socialist civil codes researched in this study. The socialist codifications do not contain family law. The most typical arrangement in a socialist civil code is: general part – *res* – obligations (*actiones*) – inheritance law. *Res (ius in re* or ownership) representing socialist ownership is underlined in the structure of the socialist civil codes and is set out after the general part. That is the order in the socialist Russian civil codes and in the current Russian civil code[48] (1922, 1964, 1994 – 2006), the socialist Czechoslovak civil codes[49] (1950, 1964) and the Polish civil code[50] (1964), which were shaped by socialism.

IX. Civil codes arranged according to the needs of the socialist citizens

Another systematic possibility for systematizing a socialist civil code is arranging it according to the needs of socialist citizens. This structure is present in

---

46 The Russian draft (1905) contains: general part – family law – inheritance law – *ius in re* – law of obligations.

The first two books (general part and family law) are the equivalent of *personae*. Inheritance law and *ius in re* constitute together *res*. Obligations are *actiones*.

47 In the current Czech civil code, the sequence of books is: general part – family law – absolute property rights (*ius in re* and succession law) – relative property rights (obligations).

The general part and family law compose *personae*. In the third book, referring to absolute property rights *(res) ius in re* and law of succession are arranged together. The last fourth book considering relative property rights (obligations) comprises *actiones*.

In Czechia, such an arrangement is the effect of the attachment to the Austrian systematization.

48 In the first socialist Russian civil code (1922) the sequence of books is: general part – *ius in re* – law of obligations – inheritance law.

In the second socialist Russian civil code (1964) the order is: general part – ownership – obligations – copyright law – right of discovery – patent law – succession law – international private law.

The current Russian civil code (1994 – 2006) encompasses: general provisions – right of ownership and other rights to estate – general part of obligations – particular kinds of obligations – inheritance law – international private law – rights to results of intellectual activities and means of individualisation.

49 In the first socialist Czechoslovak civil code (1950) the books are: introductory provisions – general provisions – *ius in re* – law of obligations – succession law.

50 The sequence of books in the Polish civil code (1964) is: general part – ownership and other *ius in re* – obligations – law of succession.

the Czechoslovak (1964) and East German (1975) civil codes. Both codifications are the most significant attempts to break with the bourgeois systematization of private law. The result of the rupture with the traditional arrangement is that the structure was aimed at socialist citizens and their needs. The scope of the civil codes was restricted, and did not include the economic transactions between socialist organizations[51]. The civil codes comprise what is necessary for citizens and their daily functioning. Among the traditional contracts sales feature, but the civil code is concentrated on the needs of the citizens; for this reason instead of universal sales, applying to all legal subjects, there is the purchase of goods by citizens.

Given that, in socialist jurisdictions, the rights of individuals were limited and they were not allowed to own the means of production (such as land), it is not surprising that the concept of a codification was fully coherent with socialist ideology. The East German civil code (1975), just as the German *Bürgerliches Gesetzbuch* (1896), implements the particular contracts, but their arrangement is different, dictated by daily needs; for instance, the lease of flats is positioned as the first contract, before sales. According to East German lawyers, due to its significance lease of flats is the most important contract, more relevant for socialist

[51] "Section 1 In the domain of the satisfaction of material and cultural needs, civil law relationships arise between citizens and socialist organizations, and among the citizens themselves. Those relationships are primarily regulated by the Civil Code.

The present section attempts to delimit the scope of the Civil Code and to that end employs two inseparable criteria. According to one criterion the Code governs legal relationships belonging to civil law, in particular those relationships which are entered into voluntarily in order to satisfy the citizens' material and cultural needs. Accordingly, a citizen needing housing may enter into a private law contract to purchase a family home or to lease it; if he needs furniture, he may order the manufacture of such household effects; if he wants to enjoy an artistic performance, he may procure a ticket from the theater concerned; if he wants to make a will, he may do so under the requirements of the Code. Apart from such relationships entered into voluntarily, others may lay civil law duties at the citizen's door; if he inflicts damage, he may be forced to pay damages where he is at fault; if he has profited from unjust enrichment, he may be forced to surrender the profit. And where his privacy is invaded, he may seek an injunction or perpetual redress. (...)

The Civil Code does not govern relationships regulated by the Family Law or relationships covered by the Labor Code. (...)

The relationships arising among socialist organizations are governed by the Economic Code. In this province, the Civil Code may not be applied even where the Economic Code shows gaps and the Civil Code could fill them easily. Economic law is seen as a fully independent branch of law. In the province of foreign or international trade, the Code of International Trade applies."

VONDRACEK Th. J., *Commentary on the Czechoslovak civil code*, Dordrecht/Boston/ Lancaster 1988, pp. 11 – 12.

"Das ZGB der ČSSR regelt – wie das ZGB der DDR – grundsätzlich nur die Versorgungsbeziehungen der Bürger. Die Kooperationsbeziehungen der Betriebe werden mittels des Wirtschaftsrechts geleitet, in dessen Rahmen spezielle Regelungen ergangen sind".

GÖHRING J. (ed.), *Grundfragen des sozialistischen Zivilrechts*, Berlin 1978, p. 42.

citizens than sales, which are usually placed at the beginning of the particular contracts in bourgeois civil codes[52].

The Pandect model was used as a legislative instrument to implement these ideas in written law. Constituting state ideology, socialism needed a tool to introduce its assumptions into private law. The learnedness of the Pandect systematization made it highly suitable for attaining that end. In the civil codes, two kinds of foundational material were employed. The first was the Gaius model, which makes use of the naturalness and simplicity of the composition introduced in the *Institutes*. Codes that belong to such an arrangement (and that do not have a general part) adhere to the sequencing of the Gaius model. Its systematization does not cooperate well with socialism. Socialism triggers the reinforcement of *res* (socialist ownership) at the expense of *personae*, which prevails in the composition of Gaius. For this reason, introducing the Gaius scheme into the exterior divisions is not appropriate for a complete socialist civil code. The socialist Hungarian civil code (1959) follows the Gaius model, but it simultaneously preserves numerous bourgeois institutions, such as the freedom of contract or possession. It is a socialist codification with bourgeois features.

Apart from the Gaius model, the second possible material for structuring a civil code pertains to the general part. With its theoretical and abstract background, it can serve different purposes and be remodelled in many ways. Using this superstructure, the socialist legislators could easily fulfil the spirit of the code, depending on their preferences. In this aspect, the Pandect structure is much more flexible than the codes based on the Gaius model. The Gaius model was perfect for the French *Code civil* (1804), but both Gaius and the French Revolution placed focus on an individual and his rights. In this field, the Pandect systematization turns out to be much more resilient than the codifications founded on the Gaius scheme. The composition of the second socialist Czechoslovak civil code (1964) and the East German civil code (1975) are discussed below.

1. Czechoslovak civil code (1964)

The systematization of the Czechoslovak civil code of 1964 adopts a slightly modified Pandect structure with the sequence: general part – *ius in re* – obligations – inheritance law. The first book is the general part. The second book considers socialist communal ownership and personal ownership, whereas the third book covers the personal use of dwelling units, other living spaces, and tracts of land. These two books include the volume accordant with *ius in re*. The subsequent three books contain content relevant to the law of obligations. The fourth book

[52] In the East German civil code (1975) sales is settled in the third chapter of the third book (including contracts relating to material and cultural life).

The first chapter (of the third book): general provisions regarding agreements. The second chapter: lease of flats. The third chapter: sales.

refers to services. The fifth book covers rights and duties from other juridical acts. The sixth book addresses responsibility for damage and unjust enrichment. The seventh book concerns the inheritance of property as personal ownership.

2. East German civil code (1975)

In the East German civil code, the first book includes the fundamental principles of socialist private law. The second book refers to socialist ownership and personal ownership. The third book considers contracts relating to material and cultural life. The fourth book encompasses the use of real estate and buildings for residential and recreational purposes. The fifth book covers the protection of life, health and property (*Eigentum*) from damage. The sixth book is concerned with inheritance law. The final, seventh book includes the specific provisions of the respective relationships of private law.

3. Common features of the arrangement of the Czechoslovak (1964) and East German (1975) civil codes

This section considers the common features of both codifications. Ownership is a prominent component in both codes' systematization, included in the second book. A separate book addresses the housing needs of citizens, which in the Czechoslovak civil code is the third book (on the personal use of dwelling units, other living spaces, and tracts of land) while in the East German civil code it is located in the fourth book (on the use of real estate and buildings for residential and recreational purposes). In both codes, *res* dominates in their structure, and two books include content relevant to *ius in re*.

The notion of or terminology belonging to "obligation" is not visible in the systems of either code. In the Czechoslovak code we can identify services (the fourth book), rights and duties from other juridical acts (the fifth book) and the responsibility for damage and unjust enrichment (the sixth book). In the East German code, the third book comprises contracts relating to material and cultural life. The fifth book addresses protection of life, health and property from damage. The final, seventh book, concerning the specific provisions of the respective relationships of private law, contains some institutions of the law of obligations[53].

To summarize briefly: two books contain *ius in re* and three books the law of obligations. The non-contractual sources of obligations are given a separate book; in the Czechoslovak code, they are situated in the fifth book (responsibility for damage and unjust enrichment), and they are also in the fifth book in the East German code (concerning the protection of life, health and property from damage). As with all socialist civil codes, family law is set outside the civil code,

[53] The first chapter (of the seventh book) deals with the specific features of performing contractual obligations. The second chapter: participation of some contractors in a contract. The third chapter: securing claims.

and succession law is placed at the end (or very close to the end) of the written law. Both codifications are the socialist civil codes of consumer protection. They cannot follow the unity of private law, because that choice of system would result in incorporating a volume into the civil codes that would be irrelevant to socialist citizens.

B) Influence of legislative philosophy on the structure of civil codes

While drafting a written law, a legislator can shape a new reality. Private law does not constitute an area distinct from state ideology, and it may serve as an instrument for implementing the principles promoted by the state[54]. This claim applies both to the content of the civil codes and their systematization. Depending on the values promoted by a lawmaker, the divisions of the code may vary. Each code is an image of the social and economic reality formed by the legislator; it is a reflection of human life in a certain legal system. In this section, the French *Code civil* is first considered, followed by the socialist civil codes. The most significant feature of the codifications impacted by the legislative philosophy is that a considerable focus is given to ownership in each system. That emphasis might seem unusual in current systems, but previously it was the case that the entire system of private law was concentrated on ownership[55].

I. French *Code civil* (1804)

The *Code civil des français* (1804) was one of the tools used to introduce the principles of the French Revolution into the lives of individuals. Its overall structure promotes the glorification of the Revolution's ideals. The French Revolution elevated the individual, and the potential for him to own and to acquire goods. For this reason, the first book is concerned with persons. The second book considers goods and different modelsof ownership. The final, third, book comprises different ways of acquiring ownership. In the CC, the system of private law is reduced to a person and his ownership, recalled in the titles of two of the three books of the written law.

II. Socialist civil codes

The aim of the socialist revolution was to spread socialist ideas. National legislators could decide on the structure of the codes independently, provided that they followed socialist principles. For this reason, the socialist civil codes in Central and Eastern Europe were built on different structures. The content of private law

[54] EISENHARDT U., *Allgemeiner Teil des BGB*, Heidelberg 1989, p. 29 and the following pages.

[55] HAFERKAMP H.-P., *Wege zur Rechtsgeschichte: Das BGB*, Köln/Wien 2022, p. 64.
MICHAELS R., *vor § 241. Systemfragen des Schuldrechts*, in: ZIMMERMANN R. (ed.), *Historisch-kritischer Kommentar zum BGB. Band II Schuldrecht: Allgemeiner Teil §§ 241–432*, Tübingen 2007, pp. 32–34.

(especially of *ius in re*) was strongly affected by socialism. The catalogue of *ius in re* was reduced, and most typically, instead of *ius in re* the second book considers (socialist) ownership. Another feature of the socialist civil codes is regulating family law in separate statutes. In socialist civil codes with a general part, the most typical systematization is: general part – *res* – obligations – succession law. It is also possible to establish a civil code arranged according to the needs of socialist citizens. In addition, the Pandect model with a general part has proved to be useful to the construction of socialist legal systems.

One feature of the socialist systematization could also involve isolating different areas of private law. The most obvious example is evidently family law, which is not included in any of the socialist codifications researched for this study. In the last socialist civil codes to have been established (Russia – 1964, Czechoslovakia – 1964, East Germany – 1975), so-called land law is extracted and placed outside a civil code[56]. That may lead to the conclusion that the most particular feature of a civil code impacted by the legislative ideology may involve arranging different branches of private law outside a civil code. It could be a way of manifesting the unique character of a civil code. In the case of the ultimate socialist civil codes, the foundation for elaborating new systematizations concerned the needs of socialist citizens. This approach was present in Czechoslovakia (1964) and East Germany (1975). Among the socialist codifications that was the only scientific basis for introducing new concepts in private law.

C) Reception of the Pandect model with a general part

This section informs readers about the adoption of the Pandect model with a general part in Russia, Czechoslovakia and Poland. The general part was never adopted in Hungary. The divisions are in line with those of jurisdictions. Russia is discussed first, followed by Czechoslovakia, Poland and East Germany respectively.

I. Russia

Here, four Russian codes are analyzed: the pre-revolutionary draft of 1905 (the first division), the first socialist Russian civil code of 1922 (the second division), the second socialist Russian civil code of 1964 (the third division) and the current Russian civil code, 1994 – 2006 (the fourth division).

---

56 About the Sovietmodel in the isolation oflandlaw:
SCHELLE K., VESELÁ R., VOJÁČEK L., TAUCHEN J., *Europäischer Kontext der Entwicklung des Privatrechts auf dem Gebiet der Tschechischen Republik (Ausgewählte Kapitel aus der Geschichte der Rechtsangleichung in Europa)*, Brno 2009, pp. 131 – 137.

1. The pre-revolutionary draft (1905)

The adoption of the Pandect scheme in Russia was the legacy of the strong influence of German legal science, resulting in the draft of 1905, which incorporated the Pandect systematization. The draft did not enter into force due to the outbreak of the First World War, and to the Revolution in Russia[57]. In the draft, the order of books follows the Gaius sequence. The first two books (general part and family law) together constitute *personae*. The third book (inheritance law) and the fourth book (*ius in re*) are the equivalent of *res*. Obligations (*actiones*) are settled in the final, fifth book[58].

2. First socialist Russian civil code (1922)

The Russian civil code of 1922 was inspired by the pre-revolutionary model. It was prepared by a single author in a short period of time. Unnecessary parts were removed from the draft, and some provisions based on the socialist principles were introduced instead[59]. The books are: general part – *ius in re* – law of obligations – inheritance law. As with all later socialist codifications, family law is arranged in separate statutes. The sequence of the books in the code modifies the typical arrangement[60]. The most striking feature of the system of the code is that family law, labour law and the legal relationships relevant to land are isolated outside the civil code. This principle is expressed in Article 3 of the first socialist Russian civil code[61].

---

57 The Russian Codification Committee was established in 1882 and the code was almost ready at the end of the $19^t h$ century. The overall situation in Russia, also the revolution in 1905 and the war with Japan, caused the lack of adoption of the civil code.

58 The mentioned structure looks like an intersection of the German and Swiss arrangement. There is the classical Pandect systematization with a general part in the opening of the code, but at the same time, the Gaius scheme was introduced into the exterior divisions of the draft.

59 Nolde B., *Le code civil de la République des Soviets*, Bulletin de la Société de Législation Comparée 1923 nos. 7–8–9, p. 235. Just checking whether these two words should be lower case.

60 In the German BGB (1896) the order is: general part – law of obligations – *ius in re* – family law – inheritance law, whereas in prior to it, the Saxon civil code the books are: general part – *ius in re* – law of claims (law of obligations) – family law (including guardianship law) – succession law.

The general part is put in the beginning of the code. Underlining *res* is typical for the socialist codifications. Due to this reason, *ius in re* is arranged directly after the general part. Family law is settled outside the civil code. The remaining books are the law of obligations and inheritance law. Obligations come in the third book. Just like in the German BGB (1896), the succession law is situated at the end of the code.

61 *Article 3 Les rapports agraires, les rapports nés de la location de la force ouvrière et les rapports familiaux sont réglés par des codes particuliers.*

3. Second socialist Russian civil code (1964)

The Pandect structure, due to its complexity and high level of legal abstraction, could be used as an instrument to implement socialist ideas. Socialist concepts were embedded in the structure of the second socialist Russian civil code (1964), the last socialist Russian codification[62]. The books in the code are: general part – right of ownership – law of obligations – copyright law – right of discovery – patent law – succession law – international private law. Apart from the typical volumes in the code, there are also supplementary books. The code does not include family law and *ius in re* is replaced by ownership, which is better suited to the ideas of socialism.

While considering the systematization of the second socialist Russian civil code (1964), we can clearly see that before it was adopted its composition was elaborated in the legal science. The most significant issue was replacing *ius in re* with ownership[63]. The sequence of the content in the legal handbooks is: general part – right of ownership – law of obligations – copyright law – family law – inheritance law. Family law is described in this volume, even though in socialist legal science, family law was treated as an area distinct from private law and it was settled in separate statutes. Most probably, family law was introduced into Gienkin's handbook for practical reasons[64].

Here the source of the systematization of the second socialist Russian civil code (1964) needs to be discussed. Introducing the regulation of copyright into the system of the code is not a socialist invention; before the October Revolution, in pre-revolutionary Russia, there were already claims that the main disadvantage of the German Pandect model was that it restricts itself to the main areas of private law (the general part, the law of obligations, *ius in re*, family law and inheritance law) and that it does not address intellectual property law [65]. Shershenievich nevertheless claimed that although the German Pandect systematization has its disadvantages, it is the best among the models available, and that it surpasses the arrangement based on the Gaius model[66].

---

62 NOWICKI I. B., ŁUNC Ł. A., *Ogólna nauka o zobowiązaniach* [The general science of the law of obligations], Warszawa 1954.
That is the handbook to the socialist Russian law of obligations.

63 The ideological framework of socialist ownership is the well-known monograph: WIENIEDIKTOW A.W., *Państwowa własność socjalistyczna* [Socialist state ownership], Warszawa 1952.

64 I analyzed the table of contents of: GIENKIN D. M, *Radzieckie prawo cywilne. Tom I* [Soviet private law. Volume I], Warszawa 1955 and GIENKIN D. M., *Radzieckie prawo cywilne. Tom II* [Soviet private law. Volume II], Warszawa 1955.

65 Шершеневич Г.Ф., Учебник русскаго гражданского права. Том I, Москва 1914, p. 80.
Shershenevich G.F., *Uchebnik russkago grazhdanskogo prava. Tom I*, Moskva 1914, p. 80. [Shershenevich G.F., Textbook of Russian private law. Volume I, Moskva 1914, p. 80].

66 *Ibidem*, p. 79.

This indicates that systematic choices concerning the shape of the Russian civil codes were taken before the October Revolution. The German Pandect model was preferred by Russian lawyers, but contrary to their German counterparts, they believed that a civil code should include more areas of private law than a standard codification[67]. This viewpoint is convergent with the systematization that can be later observed in the Russian legislation – additional branches of private law were implemented in both the second socialist Russian civil code (1964) and the current Russian civil code[68] (1994 – 2006).

Furthermore, all Russian codifications (1905, 1922, 1964, 1994 – 2006) follow the unity of private law. Here, the inspiration from Switzerland is discernible in the quest pursued by pre-revolutionary Russian lawyers to find legislative solutions that would be most appropriate to Russia. Their work was not a mere replication of the foreign conclusions.

The draft of the Russian civil code of 1948 was translated into Polish, and the explanation appended to it constitutes a valuable source concerning the Russian systematization[69]. It explains the passage between the first socialist Russian civil code (1922) and its successor of 1964. The books in the draft are: the general part – right of ownership – the law of obligations – copyright law – inheritance law[70]. The main difference between the draft and the hitherto existing civil codes of the Soviet Republics is that multiple capitalist institutions that could be found in the valid legislation were removed[71]. The unity of a civil code was one of the basic assumptions of the draft; it regulates the legal relationships between socialist organisations, between socialist organisations and citizens, and also between citizens themselves[72]. Family law constitutes an area distinct from private law and it so, it was argued, it should be settled in separate statutes[73]. The regulation of

[67] The standard Pandect systematization puts stress on the core branches of private law and this approach automatically reduces the areas of private law.
von Lewinski K., *Deutschrechtliche Systembildung im 19. Jahrhundert*, Frankfurt am Main/ Berlin/ Bern/ Bruxelles/ New York/ Oxford/ Wien 2001, p. 30.

[68] The current Russian civil code (1994 – 2006) includes: general provisions – right of ownership and other rights to estate – general part of obligations – particular kinds of obligations – inheritance law – international private law – rights to results of intellectual activities and means of individualization.

[69] Opracowywanie Kodeksu cywilnego. Materiały pomocnicze. Projekt Kodeksu cywilnego ZSRR, objaśnienia do projektu 1948 – 1950. [Development of the Civil Code. Supporting materials. Draft civil code of the USSR, explanations to the draft 1948 – 1950].
Archiwum Akt Nowych, Ministerstwo Sprawiedliwości, Departament Ustawodawczy, WydziałPrawa Cywilnego, sygnatura: 2/285/0/4.2/2201. [Archive of New Files, Ministry of Justice, Legislative Department, Private Law Department, reference number: 2/285/0/4.2/2201].

[70] If whenever the discussed document from the archive is used, it is necessary to know that its content is not properly organized; the general part is put after inheritance law.

[71] *Ibidem*, p. 157 (of the archive document).

[72] *Ibidem*, p. 158.

[73] *Ibidem*, p. 159.

patents is situated outside the draft[74], whereas copyright law is arranged in the draft[75].

"The draft of a civil code of the USSR includes, in comparison to other binding civil codes of the Soviet Republics, some new institutions which partially developed in the court practice and the regulation of which results from the real-life practice"[76]. Those include, for example, deposit, management without mandate or the public promise of reward[77]. That was the official justification for introducing institutions omitted in the first socialist Russian civil code (1922).

4. Current Russian civil code (1994 – 2006)

The current Russian civil code also follows the Pandect model. In its formulation, both the socialist and capitalist concepts were now taken into account. It was not possible to with draw completely from socialist concepts, but the separation from Soviet values was one of the pillars of the codification[78]. The new codification presented an evolutionary break with socialism[79]. The structure of the 1964 code was the starting point. Family law is not included in the civil code. The order of the books in the current Russian codification is: general provisions – right of ownership and other rights to estate – general part of obligations – particular kinds of obligations – inheritance law – international private law – rights to the results of intellectual activities and the means of individualisation. The main difference between the socialist model and the current code is that the law of obligations is split into two distinct books, containing the general part of obligations and particular kinds of obligations. Following its predecessor model, the final book of the current Russian civil code comprises the rights to results of intellectual activities and the means of individualisation.

Sukhanov, one of the authors of the current Russian civil code, published a handbook of private law in two volumes. The first volume contains, in sequence: content corresponding with the general issues in private law, *ius in re*, inheritance

---

74 *Ibidem*, p. 160.
75 *Ibidem*, p. 162.
76 *Ibidem,* pp. 160 – 161.
77 *Ibidem*, p. 161.
78 NUSSBERGER A., *Einführung in das russische Recht*, München 2010, p. 119.
79 *Conf.* OSAKWE C., *Russian civil code annotated*, Moscow 2000, p. 27.

law and copyright law[80]. The second volume covers the law of obligations[81]. In Russian private law (*Privatrecht*) there are four segments: civil law (*Zivilrecht*), family law, labour law and international private law[82].

Some features of the Russian arrangement are clearly distinguishable. First, the Russian model favours the Pandect systematization[83], which needed to be adapted to suit local requirements – since the implementation of socialism, these involve the isolation of family law outside a civil code. Second, the Russian system does not appear to display an urgent requirement to restructure or to develop the civil code or to invent something new. Such an approach was probably to be found in jurisdictions operating with in socialist legal systems. In Hungary a new arrangement of the civil code was elaborated, and has now been a feature of Hungarian private law for over 100 years. Czechoslovak and East German lawyers aspired to draft a definitive socialist civil code, expressing the new legislative ideology most effectively. Polish lawyers in the interwar period developed the subjective – objective systematization, described in the section concerning freedom of contract in the chapter on the law of obligations. They subsesequently succeeded in establishing a bourgeois civil code in the socialist reality.

II. Czechoslovakia

This section addresses the systematic development of the codes in Czechoslovakia. For the period following the division of Czechoslovakia the term Czechia is used; Slovakia is not covered in this study. After a short introduction, this section examines the codes. The interwar Czechoslovak draft (1937) replicates the struc-

---

80 Суханов Е.А. (ed.), *Российское гражданское право: Учебник: В 2-х томах. Том I. Общая часть. Вещное право. Наследственное право. Интеллектуальные права. Личные неимущественные права, Москва 2009.*

Sukhanov E.A. (ed.), *Rossiyskoye grazhdanskoye pravo: Uchebnik: V 2-kh tomakh. Tom I. Obshchaya Chast. Veshchnoyepravo. Nasledstvennoyepravo. Intellektualnye prava. Lichnyyeprava*, Moskva 2009.

[Sukhanov E.A. (ed.), *Russian private law. Handbook in two volumes. Volume I. General part.* Ius in re . *Inheritance law. Intellectual rights. Personal non-property rights*, Moskva 2009.]

81 Суханов Е.А. (ed.) *Российское гражданское право: Учебник: В 2-х томах. Том II. Обязательственное право*, Москва. 2011.

Sukhanov E.A., *Rossiyskoye grazhdanskoye pravo: Uchebnik: V 2-kh tomakh. Tom II. Obyazatelnojepravo*, Moskva 2011.

[Sukhanov E.A., *Russian private law. Handbook in two volumes. Volume II. The law of obligations*, Moskva 2011.]

82 Sukhanov E.A. (ed.), *Russian private law. Handbook in two volumes. Volume I. General part.* Ius in re . *Inheritance law. Intellectual rights. Personal non-property rights*, Moskva 2009, pp. 61 – 62.

83 About the Russian systematization also here:

Raskazova Y. N., *Russian Law of Obligations: Structure, Positioning and Connection with Supra national Law*, in: Schulze R., Zoll F. (ed.), *The Law of Obligations in Europe. A New Wave of Codifications*, Munich 2013, pp. 139 – 140.

ture of the ABGB (1811), binding in Czechia until 1950[84]. In the draft there are: rights and persons – property law – common provisions of property law. All three later codes (1950, 1964, 2012) include a general part. This section first considers the introduction of the Pandect systematization with a general part, while referring to the first socialist Czechoslovak civil code from 1950. The second socialist Czechoslovak civil code of 1964 is subsequently described. Finally, the current Czech civil code of 2012 is analyzed.

1. Introducing the Pandect systematization with a general part – code from 1950

The order of books in the first socialist Czechoslovak civil code is: introductory provisions – general part – *ius in re* – law of obligations – law of succession. The application of the general part in Czechoslovakia is a continuation of the Austrian legal tradition. The ABGB is the product of a further systematization beyond the CC (1804). Its final book, including provisions common to personal rights and *ius in re*, is an incentive for the further categorization of private law. In the fifties, Czechoslovak lawyers maintained the fundamental divisions deriving from bourgeois legal science in their handbooks. In order to preserve the clarity of the system, they arranged private law and family law together, but the title (handbook of private law and family law) suggests that these are two distinct branches of law. The content of the volumes and the sequence reflect the system of the first socialist Czechoslovak civil code. In the first volume, there are the general part and *ius in re*[85]. The second volume comprises the law of obligations[86]. The third volume concerns inheritance law and family law[87].

2. Socialist Czechoslovak civil code from 1964

In the Czechoslovak civil code of 1964, the Pandect model was an instrument for the implementation of socialist ideas in legislation[88]. Socialist legal engineering was much further advanced in Czechoslovakia than in Russia. The sequence is

---

84 For further discussion concerning the legislative works in Czechoslovakia in the interwar period: BAZOVSKÝ J., *La codification du droit civil en Tchéco-Slovaquie*, Paris 1927.

85 KNAPP V., BEDŘICH A., *Učebnice občanského a rodinného práva: celostátní vysokoš kolskáučebnice. Svazek 1. Obecná část – Práva věcná* [Textbook of private and family law: national university textbook. Volume 1. General part – *Ius in re*], Praha 1955.

86 KNAPP V., LUBY Š., BLAŽKE J., *Učebnice občanského a rodinného práva: celostátní vysokoškolská učebnice. Sv. 2 – Závazkové právo* [Textbook of private and family law: national university textbook. Volume 2 – Law of obligations], Praha 1954.

87 KNAPP V., LUBY Š., BLAŽ KE J., *Učebnice občanského a rodinného práva: celostátní vysokoškolská učebnice. Sv. 3 – Dědické právo. Rodinné právo* [Textbook of private and family law: national university textbook. Volume 3 – Inheritance law. Family law], Praha 1954.

88 About the system of the second socialist Czechoslovak civil code:
KNAPP V., *Předmet a systém československého socialistického práva občanského* [Subject and system of the Czechoslovak socialist private law], Praha 1959.

the same as in the code of 1950 (general part – *ius in re* – obligations – inheritance law), but private law was separated in a greater number of books, consonant with the needs of socialist citizens. The first book is the general part. The second book (regarding socialist communal ownership and personal ownership) and the third book (concerning the personal use of dwelling units, other living spaces, and tracts of land) contain *ius in re*. The fourth book (services), the fifth book (rights and duties from other juridical acts) as well as the sixth book (responsibility for damage and unjust enrichment) comprise the law of obligations. The seventh book considers the inheritance of property as personal ownership.

Czechoslovak legal science reconciles the systematic categories of bourgeois and socialist law. The first volume contains: general part, ownership and other *ius in re* as well as personal use (*osobní užívání*). There is a concluding reference to the law of obligations[89]. The law of obligations is also considered in the second volume. As with the second socialist Czechoslovak civil code, the legal science distinguishes the obligations arising from damage and unjust enrichment in the table of contents. The law of succession is located at the end of the second volume[90].

3. Current Czech civil code (2012)

The first book of the current Czech civil code of 2012 (which entered into force in 2014) is the general part. The second book covers family law. These two books are equivalent to *personae*. The third book (including *ius in re* and the law of succession) considers absolute property rights (*res*). The final, fourth book deals with relative property rights (obligations); it is the equivalent of *actiones*.

The impact of Austrian private law in Czechia is extensive, and remains so to the present day; when the ABGB was abolished after the Second World War in Czechia, it had been in force for almost 150 years. Current Czech legislation constitutes an attempt to reform the Austrian solutions. The Austrian impact is particularly visible in the interwar Czechoslovak draft of a civil code of 1937, by which means the ABGB continues to affect Czech private law[91]. The current

---

[89] KNAPP V., LUBY Š., *Československé občanské právo. Druhé př epracované a doplněné vydání Schváleno výnosem ministerstva školství ČSR čj. 8.153/74-31 ze dne 26. února 1974 jako vysokoš kolska učebnice. Svazek 1* [Czechoslovak private law. Second, revised and extended edition. Approved by ordinance of the Ministry of Education of the Czechoslovak Socialist Republic, no. 8.153/74-31 from the 26th February 1974 as a university textbook. Volume 1], Praha 1974.

[90] KNAPP V., LUBY Š., *Československé občanské právo. Československé občanské právo. Druhé př epracované a doplněné vydání Schváleno výnosem ministerstva školství ČSR čj. 8.153/74-31 ze dne 26. ú nora 1974 jakovysokoš kolskaučebnice. Svazek 2* [Czechoslovak private law. Second, revised and extended edition. Approved by ordinance of the Ministry of Education of the Czechoslovak Socialist Republic, no. 8.153/74-31 from the 26th February 1974 as a university-textbook. Volume 2], Praha 1974.

[91] *Conf.* TICHÝ L., *Czech and European Law of Obligations at a Turning Point*, in: SCHULZE R., ZOLL F. (ed.), *The Law of Obligations in Europe. A New Wave of Codifications*, Munich 2013,

Czech civil code is an effort to find a golden mean between the Austrian legal tradition (the Gaius scheme) and the Pandect systematization. Taking into account that Czech scholars consider the ABGB the best civil code among those that are binding in their land[92], it is not surprising that it still acts as the main model for private law in Czechia.

III. Poland

1. Interwar period

When Poland regained independence in 1918, the Austrian, French and German civil codes were applied across its territories, alongside pre-revolutionary Russian law. Having knowledge of those systems and willing to be innovative, Polish lawyers established a new autonomous system of private law. The main accomplishment of the interwar Codification Committee is the Polish Code of obligations[93] (1933). It was mainly inspired by the form of the Swiss Code of obligations (1911). The Code of obligations was the only part of the interwar Polish civil code which was adopted in legislation.

Ludwik Domański proposed a division into five books (general part, *ius in re*, law of obligations, family law and inheritance law) which was typical for the Pandect structure, but their exact sequence was not determined[94]. The most innovative element of the system of the Code of obligations was its interior, not exterior, structure[95]. Apart from drafting the code, the aim of Polish lawyers in

---

pp. 31 – 33.

92 SCHELLEOVÁ I., SCHELLE K., *Vývoj kodifikace občanského prava* [The evolution of the codification of private law], in: SCHELLE K. (ed.), *Vývoj právních kodifikací. Sborník z mezinárod nívedecké konference* [The development of legal codifications. Proceedings of an international scientific conference], Brno 2004, p. 21.

93 LONGCHAMPS DE BÉRIER Roman, *Zobowiązania* [Obligations], Lwów 1939.
That is the most important handbook to the Polish Code of obligations (1933).

94 Ludwik Domański proposed the division of Polish civil code into five books:
Of private law relationships in general – the first book.
Of property law relationships (or obligations) – the second book.
Of the relationships concerning the law of obligations (or *ius in re*) – the third book.
Of the family relationships – the fourth book.
Of the inheritance relationships – the fifth book.
DOMAŃSKI L, *O systemie przyszłego Kodeksu Cywilnego Polskiego* [About the future system of the Polish Civil Code], Dziennik Urzędowy Ministerstwa Sprawiedliwości [Official Gazette of the Polish Ministry of Justice], Year II (1921), Dział Nieurzędowy [Unofficial Part], no. 4 – 8, p. 173.

95 KOSCHEMBAHR-ŁYSKOWSKI I., *W sprawie kodyfikacji naszego prawa cywilnego* [In the subject of codification of our private law], Warszawa 1925.
DE KOSCHEMBAHR-LYSKOWSKI I., *Quelques dispositions générales d'un projet de Code civil polonais*, Revue trimestrielle de droit civil, n°3 juillet – septembre 1928, Paris 1928.
DE KOSCHEMBAHR-LYSKOWSKI I., *Les règles de la loi et le droit en droit civil. Ėtude de droit comparé*, Varsovie 1933.

the interwar period was to elaborate high-quality legislation, which could be later transformed in numerous ways.

2. After the Second World War

After the Second World War, the Pandect systematization was chosen for the Polish civil code – all the published drafts of the Polish civil code after the Second World War include a general part. As a result, the Polish civil code became similar to the German BGB. The first legislative steps towards the adoption of the Pandect scheme in Poland were undertaken in 1950, when the written law containing the general provisions of private law was adopted. Polish lawyers were resentful towards of the need to abandon the interwar Code of obligations (1933), theoutstand ingachievement of Polish legal science[96]. Around two thirds of the content of the Code of obligations were incorporated into the Polish civil code (1964). The flexible provisions of the Code of obligations were organized in a rigid Pandect form.

The doctrine of the interwar code was adapted to the civil code and to the new reality; the substance of the Polish civil code was derived from the concepts belonging to the Code of obligations, built in a way that gave many opportunities for legal interpretation. The high level of legal abstraction in the Pandect systematization enabled the inclusion of bourgeois ideas in the general part. The most particular feature of the Polish civil code has been the system of two layers. The written law contained socialist provisions, at the same time preserving a deeply bourgeois spirit[97]. The specific systematization of the code was connected with the legal doctrine of the socialist period, written in a way that was also appropriate to capitalism. The socialist formulations (written in a peculiar, almost unnatural and

---

96 This argument was put forward by Jan Wasilkowski, the author of the Polish civil code, and an important member of the Codification Committee of Private Law in the interwar period.

In a paper published in 1947, Wasilkowski claims that the problem of the general part of the code cannot be viewed as indisputable. Numerous codifications (among others the Swiss civil code, the *code-modèle*, the form of which he compliments) do not contain a general part.

If there is no general part in the code, a preliminary title or an introductory part must be introduced to the code. The law of obligations, inheritance law and *ius in re* constitute the strictly separated areas of private law.

If a code were to comprise a general part, then, according to Wasilkowski, the sequence of books should be: general part (the first book) – family law (the second book) – succession law (the third book) – law of obligations (the fourth book) – *ius in re* (the fifth book).

Wasilkowski also suggests the isolation of a book on immaterial goods in the code.

WASILKOWSKI J., *Zagadnienie kodyfikacji jednolitego prawa cywilnego* [The problem of the codification of the unified private law], Demokratyczny Przegląd Prawniczy [Democratic Law Journal] 1947 no. 1 – 2, pp. 63 – 64.

97 This potential dual structure only exists thanks to the complexity of the Pandect model with the general part. It provides legislators with the possibility of realising different aims.

In Russia, the Pandect model enabled the introduction of socialism in private law, whereas in Poland, it facilitated the preservation of the fundamental concepts of bourgeois law.

artificial way) were introduced into the code. They paralysed the capitalist core of the code, but could be deleted at any point.

Finally, this section deals with the systematization of the legal handbooks of private law in Poland. In the System of Private Law, the first volume comprises the general part[98]. The second volume concerns ownership and other *ius in re*[99]. The third volume addresses the law of obligations, published in two parts, including in sequence the general part of obligations and the particular obligations[100]. The final, fourth volume comprises inheritance law[101]. The sequence of the volumes replicates the order of the books of the Polish civil code of 1964. The series does not cover family law, which is covered in a separate volume[102].

IV. East Germany

The system of the East German civil code was inspired by the arrangement of the German BGB (1896) and the second socialist Czechoslovak civil code (1964). It was adopted much later than other socialist codifications researched for this study; the East German lawyers considered which arrangement would be most appropriate to the creation of a definitive socialist civil code, and whether they should choose the unity of private law or place the regulation of economic law in separate statutes[103]. It was eventually decided that the East German civil code (1975) should only include those areas of private law that concern a citizen or the activities in which citizens participate[104]. As a result economic law was placed in separate statutes[105]. This concept is different from the Russian (1922, 1964), Hungarian (1959) and Polish (1964) civil codes. The East German civil code is short in comparison to other civil codes – it comprises only 480 provisions[106]. That

---

98 GRZYBOWSKI S., *System Prawa Cywilnego. (Tom I) Część ogólna* [System of Private law. (Volume I) General part], Wrocław/ Warszawa/ Kraków/ Gdańsk 1974.

99 IGNATOWICZ J., *System Prawa Cywilnego. (Volume II) Prawo własności i inne prawa rzeczowe* [System of Private Law. (Volume II) The right of ownership and other *ius in re*], Wrocław/ Warszawa/ Kraków/Gdańsk 1977.

100 RADWAŃSKI Z., *System Prawa Cywilnego. (Tom III, Część 1) Prawo zobowiązań – Część ogólna* [System of Private Law. (Volume III, part 1) The law of obligations – general part], Wrocław/ Warszawa/ Kraków/Gdańsk/ Łódź 1981.

GRZYBOWSKI S., *System Prawa Cywilnego. (Tom III, Część 2) Prawo zobowiązań – Część szczegółowa* [System of Private Law. (Volume III, part 2) The law of obligations – particular part], Wrocław/ Warszawa/ Kraków/Gdańsk 1976.

101 PIĄTOWSKI S.J., *System Prawa Cywilnego (Tom IV). Prawos padkowe* [System of Private Law (Volume IV). Inheritance law], Wrocław/ Warszawa/ Kraków/ Gdańsk/ Łódź 1986.

102 PIĄTOWSKI S.J., *System prawa rodzinnego i opiekuńczego* [System of Family and Guardianship Law], Wrocław/ Warszawa/ Kraków/ Gdańsk/ Łódź 1985.

103 WESTEN K. (ed.), *Das neue Zivilrecht der DDR nach dem Zivilgesetzbuch von 1975*, Berlin 1977, p. 17.

104 *Ibidem*, p. 19.

105 *Ibidem*, pp. 19 – 20.

106 *Ibidem*, p. 18.

brevity results from isolating much of the content that is usually arranged in civil codes (e.g. family law or legal transactions with in the socialist economy) outside the civil code[107].

The East German civil code contains more books than its predecessors. The content of the general part was divided between the first book (on the fundamental principles of socialist private law) and the final, seventh book (comprising the specific provisions of the respective relationships of private law). The second book (including socialist ownership and personal ownership) is an equivalent of *res* in the system of the code. The third book (dealing with contracts relating to material and cultural life) contains the law of obligations, but it is based on a contract instead of an obligation. The third book takes the function of *actiones* in the code. The fourth book (considering the use of real estate for residential and recreational purposes) comprises the volume relevant to *ius in re*. The fifth book (referring to the protection of life, health and property from damage) encompasses the non-contractual sources of obligations[108]. The sixth book concerns succession law.

The systematization discussed here results from breaking with the Pandect model, and it is therefore the arrangement that can be found in the majority of socialist codifications. The East German lawyers followed a new path, designated by the second socialist Czechoslovak civil code (1964). The basis for the divisions in the East German codification concerns the aspects of the life of a citizen[109] (such as ownership, contracts or the use of real estate). The fifth book, which considers the protection of life, health and property from damage, was borrowed from the second socialist Czechoslovak civil code of 1964; including such a book in a civil code is also the inevitable consequence of abandoning the German Pandect model, in which *actiones* prevail[110].

The exterior divisions of the East German civil code are the result of a compromise between the typical sequence of books in the socialist civil codes (general part – ownership – law of obligations – law of succession) as well as the systematization of the German BGB (general part – law of obligations – *ius in re* – family law – inheritance law). The location of the book including *ius in re* resembles the German BGB. Consisting of five books, the German code places it in the third book, whereas in the East German civil code, constituted of seven books, it is in the fourth book, on the use of real estate for residential and recreational purposes.

---

[107] *Ibidem*, pp. 18 – 19.

[108] The fifth book includes: prevention of damage (the first chapter) – reparation of damage (the second chapter) – duty of returning unjustifiably obtained benefits (the third chapter) – duty of returning found objects (the fourth chapter).

[109] Westen K. (ed.), *Das neue Zivilrecht der DDR nach dem Zivilgesetzbuch von 1975*, Berlin 1977, pp. 21 – 22.

[110] *Ibidem*, p. 238.

The arrangement of legal handbooks in East Germany is the final point examined in this section. The first volume concerns the basic problems of socialist private law[111]; it is equivalent to the first book, which considers the fundamental principles of socialist private law. The second volume corresponds with the law of ownership as well as the use of real estate and buildings for residential and recreational purposes[112]. The content of the second volume represents the second book (socialist ownership and personal ownership) and the fourth book (use of real estate for residential and recreational purposes). The third volume deals with general contract law[113], followed by particular contracts. The fourth volume covers leases[114], and the fifth volume, sales[115]. The sixth volume deals with services, the communities of citizens, mutual assistance and gifts[116]. The seventh volume addresses accounts, savings accounts, credit and loan agreements and insurance[117]. The eighth volume comprises non-contractual sources of obligations; its title is identical to that of the fifth book of the East German civil code, which considers the protection of life, health and property from damage[118]. The ninth volume refers to inheritance law[119]. The final, tenth volume covers the content not present in the code: civil law relationships and international contacts[120]. The system of handbooks in East Germany occupies a middle ground between the system of books in the civil code and the fundamental legal categories. The sequence of the content is: general problems of private law – *ius in re* – law of obligations – succession law.

D) *Lex imperat, sed non docet* or *lex imperat et docet*?

This section considers the principle of *lex imperat, sed non docet* in socialist civil codes with reference to the Polish legal system. The meaning of this Latin expression is: a (written) law rules, but does not teach. This policy was questioned in the socialist reality, because socialism aims at creating a new reality, whereas the bourgeois civil codes concentrate on preserving the status quo. In the socialist

---

111 GÖHRING J. (ed.), *Grundfragen des sozialistischen Zivilrechts* (Grundriß Zivilrecht. Heft 1), Berlin 1978.

112 KLINKERT J., OEHLER E., ROHDE G., *Eigentumsrecht. Nutzung von Grundstücken und Gebäuden zum Wohnen und zur Erholung* (Grundriß Zivilrecht. Heft 2), Berlin 1977.

113 POSCH M., *Allgemeines Vertragsrecht* (Grundriß Zivilrecht. Heft 3), Berlin 1977.

114 MÜHLMANN M., *Miete* (Grundriß Zivilrecht. Heft 4), Berlin 1977.

115 GÖHRING J., KURZHALS P., *Kauf* (Grundriß Zivilrecht. Heft 5), Berlin 1977.

116 GÖHRING J., *Dienstleistungen, Gemeinschaften von Bürgern, Gegenseitige Hilfe und Schenkung* (Grundriß Zivilrecht. Heft 6), Berlin 1977.

117 GOLDHAHN E., SCHMIDT H., *Konto-, Sparkonto-, Kredit – und Darlehnsverträge, Versicherungen* (Grundriß Zivilrecht. Heft 7), Berlin 1977.

118 POSCH M., *Schutz des Lebens, der Gesundheit und des Eigentums vor Schadenszufügung* (Grundriß Zivilrecht. Heft 8), Berlin 1977.

119 DREWS W., HALGASCH R., *Erbrecht* (Grundriß Zivilrecht. Heft 9), Berlin 1978.

120 LÜBCHEN G.-A., POSCH M., *Zivilrechtsverhältnisse mit Auslandsberührung* (Grundriß Zivilrecht. Heft 10), Berlin 1978.

civil codes, the written laws both rule and teach. The best example of such an approach is the East German civil code (1975). Many of its precepts have a purely educational character[121].

Influenced by the socialist background, Polish lawyers were obliged to discuss this principle. This section includes some fragments from *Materiały dyskusyjne do projektu kodeksu cywilnego Polskiej Rzeczypospolitej Ludowej. Materiały sesji naukowej 8–10 grudnia 1954 r.* (Discursive materials for the draft of the civil code of the People's Republic of Poland. Materials for the scientific session 8th – 10th December 1954) to provide background information. The arguments cited are taken from translations or reformulations of the lawyers' viewpoints.

While deliberating on the utility of *lex imperat, sed non docet* for the socialist civil codes, Jerzy Wiszniewski expressed his opinion: "The reporter agrees with prof. Szpunar, regarding the need to eliminate from the draft those provisions that do not have the character of legal precepts. A socialist civil code should be a set of legal precepts. Introducing the provisions that do not have the character of legal precepts does not seem purposeful and may lead to misunderstandings. The thesis that in a socialist society the principle *lex imperat, sed non docet* is not binding should be understood in such a way that a socialist bill teaches by its normative content how the members of a socialist society should act. On the other hand, a bourgeois bill does not teach the masses, but forces the comportment beneficial for the bourgeoisie. The precepts of the socialist law are simultaneously moral precepts, and for this reason the principle *lex imperat, sed non docet* is foreign to the socialist law, which at the same time holds *imperat et docet*. From this, however, it should not be deduced that the sources of socialist law should also comprise other precepts, apart from the legal precepts"[122].

---

[121] E.g. *§ 9. (1) Die umfassende Mitwirkung der Bürger und ihrer Kollektive an der Entwicklung des polit ischen, -wirtschaftlichen und kulturellen Lebens ist Ausdruck der sozialistischen Demokratie. In Wahrnehmung ihres demokratischen Rechts auf Mitgestaltung der Arbeits- und Lebensbedingungen wirken die Bürger insbesondere bei der Erhaltung; dem Um- und Ausbau und der Modernisierung von Wohnraum, der Verbesserung der Handelstätigkeit und der Versorgung mit Konsumgütern und Dienstleistungen mit. Die Mitwirkung der Bürger gilt ebenso der Ausnutzung aller Möglichkeiten zur Erholung und Freizeitgestaltung sowie dem -sozialistischen Gemeinschaftsleben im Wohngebiet.*

(2) Die örtlichen Staatsorgane, die Handels- und Dienstleistungsbetriebe sowie die Betriebe der Gebäude- und Wohnungswirtschaft haben entsprechende Organisationsformen für die Einbeziehung der Bevölkerung zur Lösung ihrer Aufgaben zu schaffen und die Mitwirkung der Bürger zu fördern.

[122] WISZNIEWSKI J., *System projektu kodeksu cywilnego Polskiej Rzeczypospolitej Ludowej* (System of the draft of the civil code of the People's Republic of Poland), in: *Materiały dyskusyjne do projektu kodeksu cywilnego Polskiej Rzeczypospolitej Ludowej. Materiały sesji naukowej 8–10 grudnia 1954 r.* [Discursive materials for the draft of the civil code of the People's Republic of Poland. Materials for the scientific session 8th – 10th December 1954], Warszawa 1955, p. 67.

The extreme consicion of this statement is typical of the first socialist civil codes (Russia – 1922, Czechoslovakia – 1950). In Poland, such a systematization was criticised by lawyers, with reference to the draft of the Polish civil code. Shortening a civil code does not result in the simplification of life regulated by a written law. The omission of unsocialist institutions seems to be a necessary resolution, but the excessive abbreviation of the provisions preserved in the code causes a lack of regulation in many fundamental issues, which induces many unnecessary procedures, incurring a loss of time and money for the parties involved, and an unnecessary encumbrance for the courts. Superfluous concision also triggers trouble in the interpretation of the written law. The Supreme Court could deal with these problems, but it does not recognize these cases in the first instance; many cases would never reach the Supreme Court. Provisions in the draft that are too short and too general would result in the divergence of courts in the second instance. The legal measures foreseen in the legal system could not solve those issues[123]. Jerzy Wiszniewski's comments confirm that in Poland, the traditional viewpoints prevailed.

Legal scholars use different kinds of legal argumentation to express their thoughts. The principle *lex imperat, sed non docet* was defended. In order to draft a bourgeois civil code in socialist reality, it was necessary to use newspeak. The cited extracts are typical of Polish legal science in the socialist era, especially during the 1950s. Due to censorship the bourgeois stance had to be camouflaged. The ambiguity of legal science may serve as a legal instrument for the preservation of bourgeois ideas. A capitalist solution may be criticized and then admitted a few sentences later.

---

[123] *Ibidem*, pp. 42 – 43.
The arguments were mentioned in the discussion after the presentation by Jan Gwiazdomorski.

Chapter 1: General Part

The first chapter of this study considers the possibilities for arranging the general part, based on analysis of the civil codes. The general part in the structure of the civil codes is deliberated first, followed by the origin of the general part. The arrangement of the systematic components placed in the general part is subsequently adressed, then the modifications of the general part among the researched jurisdictions. The chapter closes with conclusions drawn from the preceding analysis.

A) General part in the structure of the civil codes

The general part is an identification mark of Pandect systematization. It is a superstructure for the system of private law, present from the beginning of the code. The general part is a product of considerations of the arrangement based on the *Institutes*. It was devised to avoid repetitions in the code, and it includes institutions that apply to all branches of private law. Constructs settled in the general part are used in the same way in other books. Just as students' handbooks contain fundamental issues for a particular branch, so the same general part is supposed to incorporate what is a common factor for other books of the code. In addition, private law set outside the civil code in separate statutes must be compliant with the general part. The first book acts as a bridge between the code and separate legislation. The general part was primarily conceived of by legal scholars and later introduced into multiple codifications. Arnold Heise, a German professor who published his book *Grundriss eines Systems des gemeinen Civilrechts. Zum Behuf von Pandecten-Vorlesungen* in Heidelberg in 1816, famously proposed a new structure for private law, which placed the general part at the beginning. In the arrangement of the general part the impact of legal science is much more significant than in other branches of private law.

The general part was first introduced in the Saxon civil code (1863). Later, it was included into the German BGB (1896). Under German influence, it became an inherent element of every Russian civil code (1905, 1922, 1964, 1994 – 2006). It is present also in Czechia (1950, 1964, 2012) and in Poland (1964).

B) Origin of the general part

This section approaches the origin of the general part in the systems of the civil codes and the legal science. The main focus of the study is the research that has been conducted regarding written laws; it is for this reason that this issue comes first. However, the general part was primarily developed by legal scholars whose work reflected on the possibilities of systematizing private law. The analysis here does not concentrate on the achievements of these respective scholars; instead, its purpose is to portray the legal discussion concerning the general part and the German Pandect systematization respectively:as the general part serves as a distinguishing mark of the Pandect model, these two issues cannot be separated[124].

The manifestations of the general part are visible in the previous codifications deriving from German-speaking legal systems. The civil codes are listed here in chronological order. The first codification is the *Codex Maximilianeus Bavaricus Civilis* (CMBC; 1756). In the CMBC, the first book comprises the legal rules in general and the law of persons. In this code, the general principles were placed at the beginning of the code and recalled in its division into books.

The second codification is the Prussian *Allgemeines Landrecht* (1794). It constitutes an attempt to arrange the content of private law from the most general to the most specific. Just as in later codes with a general part, the Gaius model (*personae – res – actiones*) was introduced at the beginning of the *Landrecht*[125]. Even if the general part is not extracted in the structure of the *Landrecht*, it is discernible at its beginning[126].What remained to be done involved amending the arrangement that can be found in *Allgemeines Landrecht* and isolating it in a distinct book of a civil code. The main systematic compounds present in the opening sections of *Landrecht* are: persons[127], things[128], legal actions[129], declarations of will[130] and con-

[124] The allegations towards the general part can be found e.g. here:
HÜBNER H., *Allgemeiner Teil des Bürgerlichen Gesetzbuches*, Berlin/ New York 1985, p. 44.

[125] In the *Allgemeines Landrecht* (1794) the first title (of the first part) includes persons and their rights in general. The second title: things and their rights in general (*von Sachen und deren Rechten überhaupt*). The third title: legal actions [of individuals] and therefore arising rights (*von Handlungen und den daraus enstehenden Rechten*).

[126] Firstly, in the opening of the *Landrecht* (1794) there is a preliminary title, including laws in general and general principles of law.
The first title (of the first part) regards persons and their rights in general. The second title: things and their rights in general. The third title refers to legal actions and therefore arising rights. The fourth title concerns declarations of will. The fifth title: contracts. The sixth title: duties and rights, arising from unlawful acts.

[127] In the *Landrecht* (1794) the first title (of the first part) includes persons and their rights in general.

[128] The second title (of the first part) concerns things and their rights in general.

[129] The third title (of the first part) comprises legal actions and therefore arising rights.

[130] The fourth title (of the first part) regards declarations of will.

tracts[131]. This systematization strongly resembles the arrangement of the general part in the German *Bürgerliches Gesetzbuch* (BGB; 1896).

The final codification which contributed to the systematization of the general part was the Austrian *Allgemeines Bürgerliches Gesetzbuch* (ABGB; 1811); the Saxon civil code (1863) already contained a well-formed general part. In the ABGB, the final, third book (*actiones*) includes provisions common to personal rights and *ius in re*. It is an attempt to extract a mutual factor in the code and to isolate it in a distinct book. One of the institutions settled in the third book is prescription[132], typical for the general part. The last book of the ABGB principally includes the institutions of the law of obligations[133], but it evokes a wider perspective: it applies the widest possible construct, rights and obligations. The systematic position of a preliminary title could also have inspired the general part[134]. If some provisions already apply to private law in its entirety, why not extend this idea and establish a separate book of the code with a similar systematic function?

Elaborating the arrangement of the systematic components in the general part was only one of the stages in the formation of the general part and the Pandect systematization. The general part was first implemented in the Saxon civil code of 1863. As previously mentioned, the general part is principally the result of the work of legal scholars, among whom the most remarkable was Bernhard Windscheid, author of *Lehrbuch des Pandektenrechts*[135]. Without their contribution and the conclusions they drew, which were aimed at establishing new constructs, it would not have been possible to introduce the general part to the German *Bür-*

---

131 The fifth title (of the first part) deals with contracts.

132 In the ABGB (1811), the fourth chapter (of the third book) considers prescription and usucaption.

133 In the ABGB, in the last third book there are: security of rights and obligations (the first chapter), modification of rights and obligations (the second chapter), cancellation of rights and obligations (the third chapter) as well as prescription and usucaption (the fourth chapter).

134 The preliminary title is present in the French *Code civil* (1804), the Prussian *Landrecht* (1794) and the ABGB (1811).

The preliminary titles are a feature of the natural law codifications and they would primarily occupy themselves with the institution of a written law.

SIMON T., *Inhalt und rechtspolitische Bedeutung der "Einleitung" des ABGB im Kontext der Kodifikationsgesetzgebung des frühen 19. Jahrhunderts*, in: DÖLEMEYER B., MOHNHAUPT H. (ed.), *200 Jahre ABGB (1811 – 2011): Die österreichische Kodifikation im internationalen Kontext*, Frankfurt am Main 2012, pp. 41 – 42.

More about the preliminary titles in the natural law codifications: *Ibidem*, p. 41 and the following pages.

135 WINDSCHEID B., *Lehrbuch des Pandektenrechts. Erster Band*, Düsseldorf 1862.

WINDSCHEID B., *Lehrbuch des Pandektenrechts. Zweiter Band. Erste Abtheilung*, Düsseldorf 1865.

WINDSCHEID B., *Lehrbuch des Pandektenrechts. Zweiter Band. Zweite Abtheilung*, Düsseldorf 1866.

WINDSCHEID B., *Lehrbuch des Pandektenrechts. Dritter Band*, Düsseldorf 1870.

gerliches Gesetzbuch (1896). Windscheid published his notable works after the establishment of the Saxon civil code; for this reason, his ideas were implemented in the German BGB (1896) in the final decades of the nineteenth century.

The creation of the general part is the accomplishment of the lawyers who elaborated the structure of the civil codes, which can be observed in the adopted statutes. The scientific foundation of the general part is a juridical act, supported by the theory of the declaration of will[136]. The method the legal scholars developed enabled finding a balance between the functioning of a system as a whole and the implementation of the legal principles in the legal precepts[137]. Simultaneously the construct of juridical acts forms the core of the general part and of the Pandect systematization[138].

As the general part and the Pandect systematization are primarily the product of legal science, the scientific discussion on this issue must be summarized here[139]. The specific legislative method applied in the German BGB (1896) involves placing the most general components in the opening section of the written law. For this reason, the general part constitutes the high level of the code. The structure resembles a pyramid, in which the various areas of private law are arranged from top to bottom. The general part remains at the top (the first book), followed by the law of obligations (the second book), *ius in re* (the third book), family law (the fourth book) and inheritance law (the fifth book). This approach and systematization enable the avoidance of repetitions in the code[140]. In the German arrangement the general part is the general book, whereas the further books (obligations, *ius in re*, family law and inheritance law) are described as the special books[141]. The general part comprises the common principles and the designations of the relationships of private law, whereas the task of the special books is to configure particular legal relationships[142]. In the arrangement of a civil code the function of a general part can be compared to the head of a human body.

---

[136] RANIERI F., *Europäisches Obligationenrecht. Ein Handbuch mit Texten und Materialien*, Wien 2003, pp. 16 – 17.

[137] SCHULZE R., *Allgemeine Rechtsgrundsätze und europäisches Privatrecht*, in: Zeitschrift für Europäisches Privatrecht 1993, p. 461.

[138] DANNEMANN G., SCHULZE R., *German Civil Code. Bürgerliches Gesetzbuch (BGB). Volume I. Books 1 – 3: §§ 1 – 1296. Article-by-Article Commentary*, München 2020, p. 11.

[139] The most general principles of the Pandect systematization are provided here:
HAFERKAMP H.-P., *Wege zur Rechtsgeschichte: Das BGB*, Köln/ Wien 2022, pp. 47 – 54.

[140] SCHMIDT R., *Familienrecht (Ehe, Verwandtschaft, Vormundschaft, Betreuung, Pflegschaft)*, Hannover 2018, p. 3.
In German this legislative method is designated as "*Vor-die-Klammer-Ziehen*".

[141] LIPP M., *Die Bedeutung des Naturrechts für die Ausbildung der Allgemeinen Lehren des deutschen Privatrechts*, Berlin 1980, p. 41.

[142] LEHMANN H., HÜBNER H., *Allgemeiner Teil des Bürgerlichen Gesetzbuches*, Berlin 1966, p. 30.

The main inspiration for the establishment of the general part came from the ABGB (1811); the Prussian *Landrecht* (1794) was too anachronic to satisfy the desired objective. A notable Austrian lawyer, Joseph Unger, stated that the absence of the general part constitutes a fault in the ABGB[143]. The concept of the general part presents as effective, but it is also risky. An incorrectly constructed general part poses a danger, because it may result in incorrect decisions made by the courts. A fault in the first book of the code may affect the entire system of private law, which is why lawyers working on a civil code should pay special attention to this area of the code. Furthermore, the content of the general part needs to be harmonized with the other books of the code[144]. It must be stressed that the concepts defined in the general part do not need to be regulated in the other books, unless there is a divergence[145]. Nonetheless, the specifics of the general part and its high level of legal abstraction provoked the criticism of numerous scholars[146]. However, that is a legislative aspect specific to the Pandect systematization: the high level of legal abstraction results from the fact that the more general the regulation, the more abstract its formulation must be[147]. An advantage of assembling the general principles of private law in a single place, in a general part, is that they can be applied to private law in its entirety, and to that which is arranged outside a civil code – e.g. provisions on entering into agreements settled in the general part are also valid for contracts in the areas of commercial law and employment law[148].

In the BGB (1896), the general part determines the set of general rules that are binding for the entire code; in the remaining four books multiple exceptions are formulated based on the principles included in the general part[149]. For instance, the application of the provisions concerning representation from the general part is excluded in the case of marriage ceremonies or in the creation of a testament[150]. The BGB is constructed in such a way that a more specific rule is always applied; in this way, a more general precept is superseded by that which more appropriately fits a particular case[151]. The German code was supposed to be able to deal with all legal cases. The general part acts as a functional element of this system, and it is only a summary of the wider general theory of German private law[152]. The task

143 SCHMOECKEL M., *Der Allgemeine Teil in der Ordnung des BGB*, in: SCHMOECKEL M., RÜCKERT J., ZIMMERMANN R. (ed.), *Historisch-kritischer Kommentar zum BGB. Band I Allgemeiner Teil §§ 1 – 240*, Tübingen 2003, p. 152.

144 *Ibidem*, p. 154.

145 *Ibidem*, p. 156.

146 More in: *Ibidem*, pp. 156 – 162.

147 BORK R., *Allgemeiner Teil des Bürgerlichen Gesetzbuchs*, Tübingen 2016, p. 36.

148 EISENHARDT U., *Allgemeiner Teil des BGB*, Heidelberg 1989, p. 3.

149 More in: BORK R., *Allgemeiner Teil des Bürgerlichen Gesetzbuchs*, Tübingen 2016, p. 36.

150 WERTENBRUCH J., *BGB. Allgemeiner Teil*, München 2021, p. 7.

151 MEDICUS D., *Schuldrecht I. Allgemeiner Teil*, München 2006, p. 14.

152 *Conf.*LIPP M., *Die Bedeutung des Naturrechts für die Ausbildung der Allgemeinen Lehren des deutschen Privatrechts*, Berlin 1980, p. 31.

of the general part is solely to provide the general concepts and the construction material for a civil code[153].

C) Arrangement of the systematic elements placed in the general part

The arrangement of the systematic components placed in the general part is now considered in this section. The first systematic segment introduced in the general part are persons[154]. After persons, *res*, the static element of the system, is arranged. *Res* can be encompassed in the codes as things[155], objects of civil rights[156], things and rights[157] or property[158]. After *res*, there are juridical acts[159] (*actiones*).

---

[153] HATTENHAUER H., *Grundbegriffe des Bürgerlichen Rechts. Historisch-dogmatische Einführung*, München 2000, p. 86.

[154] In the Saxon civil code (1863) the second division of the general part refers to persons.

In the German BGB (1896) the first chapter of the general part considers persons.

In the Russian draft (1905) the first division of the general part deals with persons.

In the first socialist Russian civil code (1922) the second chapter of the general part includes subjects of rights (persons).

In the second socialist Russian civil code (1964) the second chapter of the general part contains persons.

In the current Russian civil code (1994 – 2006) the second subsection of the general part deals with persons.

In the first socialist Czechoslovak civil code (1950) the first chapter of the general part regards persons.

In the second socialist Czechoslovak civil code (1964) the second division of the general part concerns the participants of private law relationships.

In the current Czech civil code (2012) the second title of the general part encompasses persons.

In the Polish civil code (1964) the second title of the general part comprises persons.

[155] In the Saxon civil code (1863) the third division of the general part regards things *(von den Sachen)*.

In the German BGB the second chapter of the general part refers to things *(Sachen)*.

In the Russian draft (1905) the second division of the general part considers things *(Sachen)*.

In the current Czech civil code (2012) the fourth title of general part concerns things and their division.

[156] In the first socialist Russian civil code (1922) the third chapter of the general part includes objects of rights (goods).

In the current Russian civil code (1994 – 2006) the third subsection of the general part contains objects of civil rights.

[157] In the first socialist Czechoslovak civil code (1950) the second chapter of the general part comprises things and rights.

[158] In the Polish civil code (1964) the third title of general part deals with property.

[159] In the German BGB (1896) the third chapter of the general part considers juridical acts.

In the first socialist Russian civil code (1922) the fourth chapter of the general part embraces juridical acts.

In the second socialist Russian civil code (1964) the third chapter of the general part refers to juridical acts.

In the current Russian civil code (1994 – 2006) the fourth subsection of the general part considers deals (juridical acts) and representation.

In the oldest codifications, the actions of individuals are included, rather than juridical acts[160] (*Handlungen*). The introduction of juridical acts to the civil codes is connected with the separation of substantive private law from civil procedure. Condition might be positioned among provisions relevant to juridical acts[161] or in a separate section, falling underjuridical acts[162]. Representation and power of attorney might act as a systematic subset of juridical acts[163] or they can be placed in a separate systematic section after juridical acts[164]. Prescription is placed at the end of the general part[165].

The general part is concentrated around five problem areas: the status of a person, subjective rights, juridical acts and legal actions, representation, and the

In the Polish civil code (1964) the fourth title of the general part deals with juridical acts.

In the first socialist Czechoslovak civil code (1950) the third chapter of the general part considers juridical acts.

160 In the Prussian *Landrecht* (1794) the third title (of the first part) contains actions and thus originating rights *(von den Handlungen und den daraus enstehenden Rechten)*.

In the Saxon civil code (1863) the fourth division of the general part refers to actions *(von den Handlungen)*.

161 E.g. in the second socialist Russian civil code (1964) condition is placed in Article 61 (regarding juridical acts performed under a condition), the last provision of the third chapter on juridical acts (in the general part).

In the first socialist Czechoslovak civil code (1950) condition is situated at the end of the third chapter considering juridical acts, in Articles 53 – 55. The third chapter contains Articles 30 – 55.

162 In the German BGB (1896) the fourth title (of the third chapter on juridical acts, in the general part) concerns condition and fixing of time.

In the Polish civil code (1964) the fifth division (of the fourth title on juridical acts, in the general part) deals with condition.

163 In the German BGB (1896) the third chapter of the general part considers juridical acts. The fifth title of the third chapter concerns agency and power of attorney.

In the Polish civil code (1964) the fourth title of the general part contains juridical acts. The sixth division of the fourth title comprises representation.

164 In the first socialist Czechoslovak civil code (1950) the third chapter of the general part refers to juridical acts. The fourth chapter: representation and power of attorney.

In the second socialist Russian civil code (1964) the third chapter of the general part deals with juridical acts. The fourth chapter: representation and power of attorney.

165 In the German BGB (1896) the fifth chapter of the general part contains prescription. The sixth chapter: exercise of rights, self-defense, self-help. The last seventh chapter: giving of security.

In the first socialist Russian civil code (1922) the last fifth chapter of the general part considers the prescription of actions.

In the second socialist Russian civil code (1964) the last sixth chapter of the general part includes the prescription of claims.

In the current Russian civil code (1994 – 2006) the last twelfth chapter of the general part comprises the limitation of actions.

In the first socialist Czechoslovak civil code (1950) the last sixth chapter of the general part deals with prescription.

In the Polish civil code (1964) the last sixth title of the general part encompasses prescription of claims.

execution of rights[166]. The institutions placed in the general part constitute a special set, which were first present in the Saxon civil code (1863) and the German BGB (1896). The initial arrangement may have been slightly modified in later codifications, but in the majority the general parts of the various codes are very similar. Persons, things and juridical acts evidently apply to all branches of private law. Accordingly, terms found in the general part are valid for the entirety of private law[167]. The regulation of prescription in the general part applies to all books of the code, but it is only a shortened version; for other institutions there may be more precise periods of prescription, which therefore exclude the general period of prescription which results from the general part[168].

D) Modification of the general part

Finally, this section presents alterations to the general part, which involves verifying whether a general part can be successfully reformulated and modified. Is it possible to go further? The analysis is founed on the systematizations adopted in the legal systems examined. The first area of analysis addresses the composition of the first division of the sixth book on obligations in the current Hungarian civil code (2013) – even though there is no general part in Hungary, its code clearly displays inspiration drawn from the general part. This indicates how the arrangement of the general part can inspire the structuring of the general part of the law of obligations in a civil code that does not comprise a general part. The Hungarian composition replicates the arrangement of a general part in many of its aspects.

The socialist civil codes are subsequently discussed: first, the second socialist Czechoslovak civil code (1964), followed by the East German civil code (1975). In both codifications legal scholars struggled to adapt the general part to the requirements of their legislative ideology; their conclusion was an attempt to establish an ultimate socialist civil code. There are multiple references to the composition of the general part in the second socialist Czechoslovak civil code (1964) and in the East German civil code (1975) in the chapter on the law of obligations.

I. Hungarian civil code (2013)

The sixth book of the current Hungarian civil code, on obligations, is organized in two systematic divisions. The first division includes the common provisions relating to obligations, and the second division the general provisions on contracts. In the first division, the first title contains the general provisions. The second title concerns multi-party obligations. The final, third title (of the first division) addresses the settlement of an obligation. In the first title, which includes the gene-

---

166 PAWLOWSKI H.-M., *Allgemeiner Teil des BGB. Grundlehren des bürgerlichen Rechts*, Heidelberg 2000, p. 45.
167 MEDICUS D., *Allgemeiner Teil des BGB. Ein Lehrbuch*, Heidelberg 2002, p. 14.
168 *Ibidem*, p. 14.

ral provisions, there are five chapters. In sequence, these are: obligation (the first chapter), legal statements (the second chapter), representation (the third chapter), the statute of limitations (the fourth chapter) and acknowledgement of debt and composition (the fifth chapter). The first and fifth chapters include content typical only for the law of obligations, whereas in the second, third and fourth chapters, there are also institutions classified in the general part. They are arranged in the order that can be found in the general part: legal statements, representation and the statute of limitations.

II. Czechoslovakia (1964)

The second socialist Czechoslovak civil code of 1964 does not contain the general part of obligations[169]. The first division of the general part encompasses private law relationships and their protection. The second division concerns the participants of private law relationships. The third division addresses representation. The fourth division, juridical acts. This content is typical for the general part. Subsequently, institutions representative of the general part of obligations follow. The fifth division refers to securing rights and duties[170]. The sixth division concerns the transition of rights and duties[171]. The seventh division regards the extinction of rights and duties[172]. The eighth division includes prescription, and the final, ninth division the explanation of certain (legal) concepts[173].

Th. J. Vondracek stated of the arrangement of the general provisions that: "The General Provisions (Sections 1 to 122) may also be termed the Civil Code's General Part and consist of those provisions which are applicable to all civil law relationships (...). The General Part is a comparative latecomer in the historical

---

169 The second socialist Czechoslovak civil code (1964) contains: general provisions – socialist collective ownership and personal ownership – personal use of dwelling units, other living space, and tracts of land – services – rights and obligations from other juridical acts – responsibility for damage and unjust enrichment – inheritance of property constituting personal ownership.

170 The fifth division of the general part deals with securing rights and duties (§§ 52 – 62). First guarantee is situated (§§ 52 – 56), then contract for set-off from the remuneration and other revenues (§ 57), the limitation of the transfer of ownership (§§ 58 – 61) and making a deposit (§ 62).

171 The sixth division of the general part considers the transition of rights and duties (§§ 63 – 70). In the beginning the assignment of (a) claim is located (§§ 63 – 67), after that assumption of debt (§§ 68 – 69) and finally joining the debt (§ 70).

172 The seventh division of the general part deals with the extinction of rights and duties (§§ 71 – 99). In the opening the performance of an obligation (§§ 71 – 89), subsequently settlement agreement (§§ 90 – 92), impossibility of performance (§ 93), passage of time (§ 94), death of a debtor or a creditor (§ 95), set-off (§§ 96 – 98) and at the end failure to pursue a right (§ 99).

173 The last ninth division of the general part comprising a dictionary (§§ 115 – 122) includes: a household (§ 115), close persons (§§ 116 – 117), things and rights (§§ 118 – 121) and the calculation of dates (§ 122).

Things and rights as well as the calculation of dates are the institutions typical for the general part.

development of civil law and old codifications do not have one. It is the laborious product of meticulously balanced and experienced scholarship. As a creation for general application in civil law, the General Part deals with the "subjects" of civil law (Persons), the "objects" of civil law (Things), juridical acts including the general law of contract, the statute of limitation, and other institutions and notions of a general nature spread out over nine Chapters. This comes to almost one quarter of the Code, a record compared with other civil law codifications. The legal impact of the General Part is felt throughout the entire Code, including its subsidiary legislation, and in many other instances"[174].

III. East Germany (1975)

In the East German civil code, the content of the general part is divided between two books[175]: the first book[176] (which considers the fundamental principles of socialist private law) and the final, seventh, book[177] (which includes the specific provisions of the respective relationships of private law). The first chapter of the first book designates the tasks of private law. The second chapter deals with the status of citizens in private law, whereas the third addresses the status of enterprises in private law. The final, fourth chapter encompasses the rules of cooperation between citizens and enterprises. The first book of the East German civil code contains the theoretical and abstract aspects of the general part and precepts relevant to *personae*.

The seventh book refers to the specific provisions of the respective relationships of private law[178]. Instead of comprising what is most general, it includes what is particular. The first chapter of the seventh book concerns the specific features of performing contractual obligations. The second chapter considers the partici-

---

174 VONDRACEK Th. J., *Commentary on the Czechoslovak civil code*, Dordrecht/ Boston/ Lancaster 1988, p. 11.

175 The books in the East German civil code (1975) are: fundamental principles of the socialist private law – socialist ownership and personal ownership – contracts relating to material and cultural life – use of real estate for residential and recreational purposes – protection of life, health and property from damage – inheritance law – specific provisions of the respective relationships of private law.

176 *Grundsätze des sozialistischen Zivilrechts.*

177 *Besondere Bestimmungen über einzelne Zivilrechtsverhältnisse.*

178 The East German legal science expressed its opinion on the systematization of the seventh book: "Damit ist jedoch wiederum nicht gesagt, daß etwa auch der Siebente Teil des ZGB (Besondere Bestimmungen für einzelne Zivilrechtsverhältnisse) in der Systematisierung des Zivilrechts Ausdruck finden muß. Für die Ausgliederung des Siebenten Teils waren andere Gesichtspunkte ausschlaggebend. Sie ermöglichte es, im Rahmen der Gesetzgebung die Regelung der einzelnen gesellschaftlichen Beziehungen bzw. die Gestaltung der Rechtsinstitute auf wesentliche Erscheinungsformen zu konzentrieren und damit die Kodifikation überschaubarer zu machen. Bei der Betrachtung des Rechtszweiges in seiner Gesamtheit müssen folglich die Bestimmungen des Siebenten Teils des ZGB im jeweiligen sachlichen Zusammenhang gesehen werden".
GÖHRING J. (ed.), *Grundfragen des sozialistischen Zivilrechts*, Berlin 1978, p. 38.

pation of some contractors in a contract. The third chapter addresses the securing of claims. The fourth chapter deals with incapacitation, death in absentia and cancellation of instruments. The fifth chapter provides an explanation of legislative terms. The last sixth chapter discusses prescription.

The first and seventh books comprise two sides of the general part in the East German civil code. The first book is successful, consolidating the abstract principles of the general part as well as the regulation of *personae*. Meanwhile, the final, seventh book includes those compounds that cannot be accommodated in the other books, resembling an attic where unwanted items can be stored[179]. The seventh book of the East German civil code has much in common with the third and final book of the ABGB (1811). Both books are arranged at the end of the codifications, and they include the regulation of prescription[180] and a chapter on securing obligations[181].

E) Conclusions

The arrangement of the general part does not vary significantly between the examined codes. The major shifts (Czechoslovakia – 1964, East Germany – 1975) did not result in a successful systematization. The model elaborated by German lawyers in the 19th century is also valid nowadays. The newer civil codes demonstrate progress in their arrangement: the general part includes fewer systematic components, resulting in a simpler and clearer arrangement[182]. The most significant elements of the systematization of the general part are, in sequence: persons,

179 The arrangement of the seventh book of the East German civil code (1975) was negatively commented by the East German legal science:

WESTEN K. (ed.), *Das neue Zivilrecht der DDR nach dem Zivilgesetzbuch von 1975*, Berlin 1977, pp. 293 – 294.

180 In the ABGB (1811) prescription is included in the final, fourth chapter of the third book. In the East German civil code (1975) the sixth and final chapter of the seventh book refers to prescription.

181 In the ABGB that is the first chapter of the third book, regarding the security of rights and obligations, whereas in the East German civil code the third chapter of the seventh book composes securing claims.

182 The systematic categories in the German BGB (1896) are: the persons (the first chapter), the things (the second chapter), the juridical acts (the third chapter), the periods of time and time limits (the fourth chapter), prescription (the fifth chapter), the exercise of rights, self-defence and self-help (the sixth chapter) and the giving of security (the seventh chapter).

In the general part in the Polish civil code (1964) there are: the preliminary provisions (the first title), the persons (the second title), property (the third title), the juridical acts (the fourth title), the calculation of time (the fifth title) and the limitation of claims (the sixth title).

The general part in the current Russian civil code (1994 – 2006) includes: the basic provisions (the first subsection), the persons (the second subsection), the objects of civil rights (the third subsection), the deals and the representation (the fourth subsection), the term and the limtation of actions (the fifth subsection).

things, juridical acts, representation and prescription. They can be found in the majority of the general parts in the researched codifications.

Some elements can be put either in the general part or in later books of the code. In the German BGB (1896), for instance, capacity in delictual relationships is placed in the second book on obligations[183]. The sixth chapter of the general part of the German BGB includes exercise of rights[184], self-defence and self-help, whereas the seventh chapter concerns the assurance of security[185]. The German arrangement is currently less common, but it can be found in some other codifications[186]. Nonetheless, most civil codes that include a general part do not distinguish the exercise of rights in a separate systematic unit.

In relation to the general part, the most relevant legislative dilemma is whether the institutions classified in the general part in the Pandect German model should be situated in the general part or among the law of obligations. This demonstrates that there are two main solutions between which a lawmaker may choose. In Switzerland there is no general part, and for this reason those institutions are arranged in the Swiss Code of obligations (1911). If a new civil code with a general part were to be adopted in Switzerland, then that volume would have to be transferred to the general part. Swiss legal science justifies the Swiss systematization, stating that from a practical point of view those institutions are the most crucial for the law of obligations and that is why they should be settled in that location[187].

---

[183] *§ 827 Ausschluss und Minderung der Verantwortlichkeit.*
Wer im Zustand der Bewusstlosigkeit oder in einem die freie Willensbestimmung ausschließenden Zustand krankhafter Störung der Geistestätigkeit einem anderen Schaden zufügt, ist für den Schaden nicht verantwortlich.

[184] More in: MEDICUS D., *Allgemeiner Teil des BGB. Ein Lehrbuch*, Heidelberg 2002, p. 14.

[185] The arrangement of the general part in the German BGB (1896) was criticized here: *Ibidem*, p. 14.

[186] In the general part of the Greek civil code (1940) there are: the legal precepts in general (the first chapter), international private law (the second chapter), natural persons (the third chapter), legal persons (the fourth chapter), juridical acts (the fifth chapter), conditions and terms (the sixth chapter), representation and power of attorney (the seventh chapter), compromise and authorization (the eighth chapter), terms (the ninth chapter), prescription and deadlines (the tenth chapter) as well as the exercise of rights, self-help, self-defence and state of emergency (the eleventh chapter).

In the part I (including the general principles) of the Chinese civil code (1929) there are: application rules (the first chapter), persons (the second chapter), things (the third chapter), juridical acts (the fourth chapter), dates and periods (the fifth chapter), extinctive prescription (the sixth chapter) and exercise of rights (the seventh chapter).

[187] SCHULIN H., VOGT N. P., *Einleitung zum Obligationenrecht*, in: *Schweizerisches Obligationenrecht*, Basel 2018, p. XXXII.

About the Swiss systematization also here: KUNDERT W., HOLTHÖFER E., DÖLEMEYER B., *Schweiz*, in: COING H. (ed.), *Handbuch der Quellen und Literatur der Neueren Europäischen Privatrechtsgeschichte. Dritter Band. Zweiter Teilband: Gesetzgebung zum allgemeinen Privatrecht und zum Verfahrensrecht. Allgemeines Privatrecht: Mitteleuropa (Abschnitte 8 bis 14). Landesberichte: England, Rußland (Abschnitte 15, 16). Verfahrensrecht*, München 1982,

It seems that there is no one universal reply to whether a civil code should include a general part or not; this issue depends on the systematization initially chosen in a jurisdiction, which later becomes an integral part of private law in each legal system. Legal scholars consolidate the systematization with which they have been familiar from the outset of their legal studies in the arrangement they subsequently implement in their handbooks.

However, the scientific foundation introduced in the general part of the German BGB (1896) over 100 years ago is still valid and does not require reform[188]. The Pandect systematization with the general part, elaborated by German legal scholars, has become one of the most significant systematic models for legislators in Central and Eastern Europe[189].

---

pp. 1995 – 1996.

188 BORK R., *Allgemeiner Teil des Bürgerlichen Gesetzbuchs*, Tübingen 2016, p. 23.

189 *Conf.* RANIERI F., *Europäisches Obligationenrecht. Ein Handbuch mit Texten und Materialien*, Wien 2003, p. 17.

Chapter 2: Obligations

A) Introduction

This chapter analyzes the systematization of the law of obligations in the civil codes researched for this study, from the end of the 18th century to the present day. Obligations are the broadest branch of private law and the most significant from the point of view of structuring a civil code. Even though multiple institutions of the general part (such as representation or condition) are strongly (but not exclusively) connected to the law of obligations, this chapter principally focuses on the issues primarily related to the systematization of the general part. The intersection between both branches of private law requires such an arrangement.

As a result, it was necessary to refer to the issues related to the general part in other chapters of this monograph (just as the systematization of a thing is discussed in the chapter concerning *ius in re*). The content settled in the general part and connected to other branches of private law is described in subsequent chapters. Following initial remarks this chapter returns to considering the arrangement of the law of obligations. The framework of this study corresponds to the systematization of the German BGB (1896), where obligations are located in the second book, immediately after the general part.

The most relevant aspects of the system concerning the law of obligations are identifiedand described here. As Roman Longchamps de Berier stated: "The law of obligations is the least dependent on other areas of private law among the branches of private law, as well as being distinctive in its historical and territorial attributes; concurrently it is an area where the laws of different countries interact with each other in the simplest and most effective way, which gradually facilitates its internationalization"[190].

In the arrangement of the law of obligations, the location of many institutions does not seem to have particular significance for the functioning of the system of a

---

[190] LONGCHAMPS DE BÉRIER R., *Zasada wolności umów w projektach polskiego prawa o zobowiązaniach* [The principle of freedom of contract in the drafts of the Polish law of obligations], Lwów 1930, p. 1.

The same reasoning is visible in legislative works in Czechoslovakia in the interwar period: BAZOVSKÝ J., *La codification du droit civil en Tchéco-Slovaquie*, Paris 1927, p. 195.

Czechoslovak lawyers aimed to find a middle ground between the ABGB (1811), which was binding in Czechia, and Hungarian customary law, which applies in Slovakia.

civil code as a single whole. The systematization of *ius in re* is determined by rigid rules, resembling lines in which each system should fit. The law of obligations is different, more reminiscent of floating elements (or islands) which can freely move on the surface of water. The positioning of islands is determined by the natural currents of water (with in the law of obligations, these are the principles of logic), affecting the arrangement of the institutions. In this study, the main islands are distinguished. Their possible placement is checked, often in relation to other compounds of the system.

The systematization of the civil codes can be presented according to two aspects. Either we consider the external structure – that is, the distribution of institutions and books in the system of a civil code, the issue with which this monograph is principally concerned. We might also deliberate the internal systematization of the civil codes; in mentioning this point we refer to the principles of the systems of the civil codes, their rules as well as their justifications – that is their soul, their spirit. However, evidently the content and the exterior shape of the written laws are closely interconnected, and cannot be fully separated from each other. In terms of freedom of contract, this study's research elaborates on the internal structure of the civil codes.

Following these introductory remarks, the chapter on the law of obligations is structured as follows. First, obligations in the external divisions of the researched civil codes are considered. This is an expanded section, intended to lay the groundwork for the chapter's subsequent sections. The chapter then addresses the problems arising from the arrangement of obligations in the systems of the civil codes (the hierarchy of legal concepts). This section is followed by an analysis of the arrangement of the general part of obligations, and then of freedom of contract in the structure of the civil codes. Subsequently, this chapter addresses cause in the researched civil codes. The systematization of the particular obligations is next discussed, involving both the composition of particular contracts and the non-contractual sources of obligations. Finally, conclusions from the analysis are presented.

B) Obligations in the external divisions of the researched civil codes

The first issue to be considered is the arrangement of obligations in the external divisions of the civil codes. Initially, the problem is described in codes prior to the Pandect structure. Those are the codes founded on the Gaius model (the CMBC – 1756, the CC – 1804, the ABGB – 1811) and the Prussian *Landrecht* (1794). The Pandect codes are subsequently analyzed.

I. Obligations in the systematization of *Institutes* of Gaius

In *Institutes* of Gaius private law is divided in three categories: *personae*, *res* and *actiones*. *Personae* contain the non-property regulations of the law of persons, whereas *res* include different ways of acquiring ownership. Gaius divided things (*res*) into material and immaterial objects, stating: "Immaterial [objects] are those which cannot be touched, so these are the ones which are a right, such as inheritance, usufruct or obligations committed in any way[191]". *Actiones* are an ancient equivalent of the current civil procedure. Obligations are classified in the second site of the scheme: *res*. *Res* is a broad concept covering law referring to property. Currently, most legislators view obligations as *actiones* in the structure of the codes. That is a consequence of the systematic choices applied in the German BGB (1896).

II. Obligations in the structure of the codes founded on the Gaius model

This concept, stemming from antiquity, was also relevant in the 18th century, but the lawmakers only had three areas with in the scheme that could be distributed in different ways. The French CC (1804), the CMBC (1756) and the ABGB (1811) follow the Gaius model. Each provides a different vision of the same concept. Their common feature is maintaining the order in which the obligations are placed at the end of the code. In his listing of things (*res*) Gaius placed obligations at the end.

1. CMBC (1756)

The CMBC follows the simplest possible systematization by positioning obligations in the fourth and final book on obligations. Obligations replace *actiones*. Before obligations come legal rules in general and the law of persons (the first book), *ius in re* (the second book) and inheritance law (the third book). The greatest systematic accomplishment of the CMBC is condensing the law of obligations in a single book. Furthermore, the divisions accordant with the branches of private law are visible in the CMBC. The divisions of the fourth book on obligations are mainly the systematic categories copied from Roman law[192].

---

[191] *Quaedam praeterea res corporales sunt, quaedam incorporales. <Corporales> hae<sunt>, quae tangi possunt, veluti fundus homo vestis aurum argentum et denique aliae res innumerabiles. Incorporales sunt quae tangi non possunt, qualia sunt ea quae <in> iure consistunt, sicut hereditas ususfructus obligationes quoquo modo contractae.*

Gai Institutiones. Instytucje Gaiusa, Poznań 2003, p. 42.

[192] In the CMBC (1756) the divisions of the book on obligations are fairly simple. There is also no division into general and particular obligations. Finding a better way of classifying the law of obligations was the task for later codifications.

In the fourth book on obligations there are: contracts and therefrom arising duties in general (the first chapter); nominate contracts (*benannten Vertragen*) and contracts which come by means of actual delivery of a thing (the second chapter); consensual contracts, in particular sa-

All codes prior to the Pandect systematization (the Prussian *Landrecht* – 1794, the CC – 1804, the ABGB – 1811) follow an arrangement that differs from the CMBC. The lawyers probably needed time to appreciate the Bavarian composition. Nonetheless, the simpler (and more usual) the structure of a civil code, the better it is; there is a limited amount of clear and "successful" systematic patterns. If the arrangement is successful, then it is often copied into other codifications. This point of view is drawn from the monograph of Gérard Cornu, which is used in the description of the French systematization.

2. French *Code civil* (1804)

The CC is focused on ownership; the third book (*actiones*) is dedicated to addressing all methodsof acquiring ownership. The second book concerns property (goods – *des biens*) and different modifications of ownership. Obligations are classified in the third book, among *actiones*. Such an approach reduces the entire volume of the law of obligations (also the law of damages) to being a tool for acquiring ownership. In the CC, property, ownership and contract cannot be separated from each other. As a contract is the main legal instrument for obtaining new goods, it is glorified in the structure of the code.

---

le (the third chapter); particular [kinds of] sales (the fourth chapter); entry (the fifth chapter); lease and tenancy (the sixth chapter); emphytheusis and superficies (the seventh chapter); partnership (the eighth chapter); mandate and power of attorney (the ninth chapter); guarantee (the tenth chapter); literal contracts (*von Literal-Verträgen*; the eleventh chapter); innominate contracts (*von unbenannten Verträgen*; the twelfth chapter); claim rights from grounds similar to contracts (quasi-contracts; the thirteenth chapter); performance of obligations, particularly payment (the fourteenth chapter); other kinds of cancellation of obligations (the fifteenth chapter); claims arising from offenses (the sixteenth chapter); defamation (the seventeenth chapter) and finally feudal law (the eighteenth chapter).

The content of the seventh chapter (emphytheusis and superficies) should be placed among *ius in re* instead of the law of obligations.

Some issues can be noted after browsing the table of contents. The concept underpinning the divisions in the fourth book on obligations are contracts; an obligation is a central construct, appearing in the system of books, but the perception of this branch of private law is focused on agreements. In the first chapter there is the volume of the general part of obligations – the first chapter includes contracts and therefrom arising duties in general. Subsequently, the contents concern either particular contracts (chapters from the second to twelfth) or institutions strongly related to contracts (quasi-contracts in the thirteenth chapter).

Then, there are: performance of obligations particularly payment (the fourteenth chapter) and other kinds of cancellation of obligations (the fifteenth chapter). Those are the institutions of the general part of obligations, but in Bavaria, in terms of the system, the focus is on chronology. The idea of separating the general and particular obligations is not yet implemented in the divisions of the fourth book on obligations.

There follow the non-contractual sources of obligations (claims arising from offenses in the sixteenth chapter as well as defamation in the seventeenth chapter) and finally feudal law in the eighteenth chapter. Situating the feudal law at the end is a logical choice; if the legal reality changes and the regulations of feudal law are no longer necessary, then they can be removed from the code, without changing the numeration of divisions.

In the CC the provisions of the general part of obligations are assembled in the third title (of the third book on different ways of acquiring ownership) considering contracts and conventional obligations in general. In this composition a contract and the agreement of the parties (*convention*) prevail in the system of the code[193]. The fourth title of the third book comprises the commitments formed without an agreement. The fifth title considers prenuptial agreements and matrimonial regimes. After matrimonial property law the particular contracts follow.

In reference to the French systematization, this section cites some extracts concerning the structure of the civil codes taken from the monograph of Gérard Cornu[194]. First, the French *Code civil* puts atits centre the definition of a contract, visible in Article 1101, rather than an obligation[195]. In Roman law the main construct was an obligation (*"Vinculum juris quo necessitate astringimur alicujus solvendae rei, secundum nostrae civitatis jura"*). In France this concept was amended to suit the needs of the French structure:instead of an obligation, a contract is the primary determinant of the system of the law of obligations[196]. The next innovation introduced in the French *Code civil* was that a contract is sufficient to transfer ownership[197]. This formulation is contradictory to the principles of Roman law and to pre-revolutionary French legal science (*ancienne jurisprudence*), where a contract itself did not have such force[198]. Furthermore, the third title regarding contracts and conventional obligations in general was drafted on the basis of the works of French lawyers, especially Domat and Pothier[199]. Cornu is also not satisfied with Article 1131 and how it expresses cause[200].

---

193 The general part of obligations in the CC after the reform of 2016 has a new structure.
From now on the third title (of the third book on different ways of acquiring ownership) regards the sources of obligations. Among the sources of obligations there are contract (the first sub-title), extra-contractual liability (the second sub-title) and other sources of obligations (the third sub-title).
The fourth title considers the general regime of obligations. There is also a fourth title, B (IV b), comprising the proof of obligations.

194 CORNU G., *Regards sur le titre III du livre III du Code civil « contrats ou des obligations conventionnelles en général » (Essai de lecture d'un titre du Code)*, Paris 1976.

195 *Article 1101 Le contrat est une convention par laquelle une ou plusieurs personnes s'obligent, envers une ou plusieurs autres, à donner, à faire ou à ne pas faire quelque chose.*

196 CORNU G., *Regards sur le titre III du livre III du Code civil « contrats ou des obligations conventionnelles en général » (Essai de lecture d'un titre du Code)*, Paris 1976, p. 32.

197 *Article 1138 l'obligation de livrer la chose est parfaite par le seul consentement des parties contractantes.*
Elle rend le créancier propriétaire (…).

198 CORNU G., *Regards sur le titre III du livre III du Code civil « contrats ou des obligations conventionnelles en général » (Essai de lecture d'un titre du Code)* , Paris 1976, p. 36.

199 *Ibidem* , p. 37.

200 *Article 1131 l'obligation sans cause, ou sur une fausse cause, ou sur une cause illicite, ne peut avoir aucun effet.*
Ibidem, p. 48.

In the subsequent part of his work, Cornu evaluates the structure of the third title. He decides to abandon the typical French perspective, replacing it with a comparative one. He asks himself how the modern codifications comprehend and arrange the content, which in the CC is placed in the third title[201]. In his study, Cornu refers to other codifications more extensively than the author of this monograph, but the conclusions are similar. Cornu states that all civil codes formulate the general theory of contracts – that is their common feature with the CC[202]. The codifications distinguish the series of particular rules, special for each kind of contract (*Autre point commun, ces règles générales à tous les contrats se distinguent de la série des règles particulières à chaque espèce du contrat*). The distinction of the general law of contracts (*droit commun des contrats*) from particular contracts is internationally accepted[203].

The main difference is that in all other codifications, the general theory of contracts becomes part of the theory of obligations. In other words, contracts become an element of a certain whole[204]. In all other systems, a contract is a systematic subset of obligations. The French codification is the only one that links a contract and an obligation to ownership (*propriété*). Among the codifications, Cornu verifies that no other code would posita contract as a way of acquiring ownership[205]. According to Cornu, the general part formulated by the German lawyers constitutes scientific progress[206]. Additionally, Cornu claims that in other codifications the general theory of contracts becomes part of the law of obligations. Contract is just one of the sources of obligations. The law of obligations comprises a number of rules common to all other sources of obligations[207]. One idea belonging to the source of obligations is strongly connected with their formation[208]. Subsequently, Cornu presents the significance of the declaration of will[209]. Finally, a cause being a condition of the validity of a contract is eliminated in other jurisdictions[210].

Gérard Cornu's remarks gave direction to the reform of the French law of contracts and obligations. Lawyers working on the reform of contracts and obligations found a happy medium between the need to modernize the CC and their legal traditions. Prior to Cornu's book there already existed a French-Italian draft of 1927, which to a certain extent was also an amended version of the CC. Its composition is portrayed among the drafts of a European civil code. My study is

201 *Ibidem*, p. 162.
202 *Ibidem*, p. 171.
203 *Ibidem*, p. 171.
204 *Ibidem*, p. 172.
205 *Ibidem*, pp. 172 – 173.
206 *Ibidem*, p. 176.
207 *Ibidem*, p. 177.
208 *Ibidem*, p. 179.
209 *Ibidem*, p. 183 and the subsequent pages.
210 *Ibidem*, p. 192.

necessarily limited in its scope; for this reason, the structure of the French law of contracts and obligations is presented concisely. Currently the third title (of the third book, on different ways of acquiring ownership) concerns the sources of obligations. Here Cornu's suggestion was realized. The third title lists the sources of obligations, which are: contract (the first sub-title), extra-contractual liability (the second sub-title) and other sources of obligations (the third sub-title). This arrangement is neutral, but a contract prevails in the composition of the general part of obligations. Just as Cornu postulated, there are also provisions common to all other obligations. That is the fourth title, concerning the general regime of obligations. In the French hierarchy of legal concepts, a contract comes before an obligation. Title IV b follows after the reform in the CC, which includes the proof of obligations. That is a remnant of the original French arrangement; the sixth chapter (of the third title on contracts and conventional obligations in general, in the third book on different ways of acquiring ownership) deals with the proof of obligations and payment.

3. Austrian *Allgemeines bürgerliches Gesetzbuch* (1811)

In the ABGB, obligations are mentioned in the second division (personal rights) of the second book on *ius rerum*. The second book includes private law regarding property: *ius in re*, succession law, obligations and matrimonial property law[211]. The second book of the code (*res*) is separated into two divisions. The first division concerns *ius in re*, while the second involves personal rights (obligations). The third book (*actiones*) includes the provisions common to personal rights and those concerning things (*ius in re*). The second book (on *ius rerum*) is split into the first division (on *ius in re*), which could be considered as *res*, and the second division, on personal rights (obligations), which may be perceived as *actiones*[212].

In the ABGB, provisions relevant to obligations are almost hidden in the second book on *ius rerum (res)*. The seventeenth chapter (the first chapter in the second division on personal rights) concerns contracts in general. Subsequently, there are particular obligations (chapters eighteen to thirty). More particular institutions of the law of obligations are also contained in the last third book (*actiones*),

---

211 In the ABGB (1811), the first division (of the second book on *ius rerum*) regards *ius in re* and it comprises *ius in re* (chapters from first to seventh) and succession law (chapters from eighth to fifteenth). The second division of the second book comprises personal rights. That is the law of obligations (chapters from seventeenth to thirtieth). Matrimonial property law is put in the twenty-eighth chapter of the second division, among the particular contracts.

212 This distinction is the foundation of private law. The classification of the content of the substantive private law in the terms on *res (ius in re)* and personal rights (obligations), reformulated into *actiones*, dominated the later codifications. Since the German BGB (1896) was adopted, *ius in re* is perceived as *res* and obligations as *actiones*.

This classification evidently also has origins in the CMBC (1756), where *ius in re* (the second book) and law of succession (the third book) together compose *res* while obligations (the fourth book) are *actiones*.

including provisions common to *personae* and *res*[213]. The division of some aspects of the general part of obligations between two books in the ABGB necessarily hinders the possibilities of reform; according to newer tendencies, all provisions of the general part of obligations should be combined or transferred to the general part. That would require the near-simultaneous amendment of the entire code; the entire codification would have to be written almost anew. Dividing the general part of obligations between two books seems to be the most particular feature of how obligations are arranged in the ABGB. The Czechoslovak draft (1937) adopted the Austrian systematization[214]. This review merely considers the original arrangement of the ABGB; in order to acquire more up-to-date data it is necessary to read into the section on the composition of the legal concepts in the verified jurisdictions, where the ABGB is also described.

III. Obligations in the structure of the *Code civil* and the ABGB

Before proceeding to discuss the Pandect systematization, we must consider the specifics of the composition of the law of obligations in the *Code civil* and the ABGB. Both codes are still in force. In both codifications obligations were not separated in the divisions into books. The Pandect model was elaborated to remedy systematic problems in the previous codifications; as the CC applied to Germany, the modernization of its structure was also of significant interest to German lawyers. The arrangement of the law of obligations in the CC and the ABGB requires a separate reference[215]. In the CC the law of obligations is not distinguished

---

[213] In the ABGB (1811), the first chapter (of the third book) considers the security of rights and obligations. The second chapter: modification of rights and obligations. The third chapter: cancellation of rights and obligations. The fourth chapter: prescription and usucaption.

[214] In the Czechoslovak draft (1937) the second book regards the property law (*droits patrimoniaux*). The second book of the Czechoslovak draft consists of two divisions. The first division considers *ius in re* while the second division claims *(Ansprüche)*. The first section (the twenty-fifth section) in the second division on claims concerns contracts and juridical acts. Afterwards there are particular obligations (sections from twenty-sixth to forty-second).

Just as with the ABGB (1811), in the third book there are provisions common to personal rights and *ius in re* (*les dispositions communes des droits patrimoniaux*). In the final, third book of the Czechoslovak draft (1937) are security for rights and obligations (the forty-third section), modification of rights and obligations (the forty-fourth section), change of a creditor or a debtor (the forty-fifth section), extinction of rights and obligations (the forty-sixth section) and finally prescription (the forty-seventh section).

[215] Among 2281 Articles of the CC in 1804 obligations were regulated from Article 1101 until 2058. The first two books include 710 Articles – that is less than one third of its content.

The second book of the ABGB (1811), at the moment of its adoption, contained provisions from § 285 until § 1341. Code included 1502 provisions. Obligations are settled from § 859 until § 1502.

Here it needs to be underlined that those numerations should not in any case be treated as the the exact divisions of branches of private law into books in both codifications.

In the CC, as the last institution of the law of obligations in the third book (on different ways

from any other area of private law, whereas in the ABGB it is divided between two books. Here we can see the foundation of the two basic ways of structuring the law of obligations in later codes. Either obligations are settled in one area of the code (the CC) or they are distributed between two books (the ABGB).

IV. Prussian *Landrecht* (1794)

Before the Pandect structure is examined, the composition of the Prussian *Landrecht* (1794) must be determined. The Prussian *Landrecht* represents an attempt to arrange the content of private law from the most general to the most specific. These efforts were related to the particularly significant attention given to *res*, which in Prussia was perceived in the context of the relation of an institution to ownership, prevailing in its divisions.

The *Landrecht* consists of two parts. The law of obligations is situated in the first part. Here we can observe all institutions of private law that cannot be reorganizedinto *personae* or family law. After some general remarks, this section will describe the composition of the law of obligations in the *Landrecht*. The Gaius scheme was introduced in the beginning of the first part[216]; an equivalent of *actiones* are all legal actions that an individual might take in private law (*Handlungen*). The sequence of the systematic components is: legal actions, declarations of will, agreements and rights arising from unlawful acts[217]. The institutions mentioned here constitute a certain systematic whole, not divided into the sections of the *Landrecht*, but later recognized by lawyers who elaborated upon the Pandect systematization. This volume is a predecessor of the general part[218].

---

of acquiring ownership), compromise was chosen, found in the fifteenth title. I assumed that this what is further is the part of *ius in re*. In the ABGB prescription and usucaptionwere treated as the part of the law of obligations. In the first codifications the systematic divisions were not full.

For this study, the most important conclusion from this computation points to the lack of systematic balance in the CC and the ABGB. Even though in those codifications the law of obligations occupies a considerable amount of space, none of them features a book on obligations.

216 In the Prussian *Landrecht* (1794) the first title (of the first part) involves persons and their rights in general. The second title: things and their rights in general. The third title: actions and thus originating rights.

217 The third title considers actions and thus originating rights *(von Handlungen und den daraus enstehenden Rechten)*. The fourth title: declarations of will *(von Willensklärungen)*. The fifth title: agreements. The sixth title: duties and rights arising from unlawful acts *(von den Pflichten und Rechten, die aus unerlaubten Handlungen enstehen)*.

218 The resemblance of the arrangement in the Prussian *Landrecht* to the general part in the German BGB (1896) is mentioned here:

BECKER C., *Systembildung in Europas Kodifikationen*, in: *Naturrecht in Antike und früher Neuzeit. Symposium aus Anlass des 75. Geburstages von Klaus Luig*, ARMGARDT M., REPGEN T. (ed.) Tübingen 2014, p. 48.

Detention, possession and ownership follow later[219]. Those institutions serve as an opening to the wider content of private law, viewed in terms of the acquisition of ownership. Particular contracts are arranged among the titles of the acquisition of ownership resulting from contracts between living partners[220]. The institutions of the law of obligations are also perceived in the context of the acquisition of ownership of things and rights by a third party[221] or the conservation of ownership and rights[222]. The regulation of the expiration of rights and obligations is subsequently settled[223].

The Prussian *Landrecht* is the second oldest codification. The development of the structure of the law of obligations was yet to come: the Pandect systematization was later elaborated, for which the Prussian achievements were foundational. Without the *Landrecht* there would have been no further progress. The features that were lacking in the arrangement of the *Landrecht*, but which could be found in other codifications, were introduced in codes that followed the Pandect structure.

V. Pandect systematization in the bourgeois codifications (Saxony – 1863, Germany – 1896, Russia – 1905, Czechia – 2012)

After outlining the arrangement of the law of obligations in the prior codifications, this section establishes the composition of obligations in the codes following the Pandect model. In the Pandect systematization there is a book containing obliga-

219 The seventh title (of the first part) includes detention and possession. The eighth title: ownership.

220 The eleventh title (of the first part) considers titles of acquisition of ownership arising from contracts between living partners *(von den Titeln zur Erwerbung des Eigenthums, welche sich in Verträgen unter Lebendigen gründen)*. Here there are some particular contracts.

These include sales (the first chapter), exchange (the second chapter), transfer of rights (the third chapter), purchase of a total inheritance (the fourth chapter), jumble contract (the fifth chapter), aleatory contracts and uncertain expectations (the sixth chapter), loan (the seventh chapter), contracts by which are promised things versus things and actions versus actions (the eighth chapter) and finally donation (the ninth chapter).

221 The thirteenth title (of the first part) regards the acquisition of things and rights by a third party. In the thirteenth title there are attorney's mandate (the first chapter), spontaneous agency without mandate and lastly useful outlay (the third chapter).

222 The fourteenth title (of the first part) concerning the conservation of ownership and rights there are deposit (the first chapter), managing of things and goods belonging to another (the second chapter), security deposits and guarantees (the third chapter), seizures (the fourth chapter) and finally protests (the fifth chapter).

223 The sixteenth title (of the first part) regulates the expiration of rights and obligations *(Rechte und Verbindlichkeiten)*. The sixteenth title comprises ten chapters.

The first chapter: performance of obligations in general. The second chapter: payment. The third chapter: deposit. The fourth chapter: delivery in lieu of payment. The fifth chapter: order. The sixth chapter: set-off. The seventh chapter: waiving rights. The eighth chapter: settlement. The ninth chapter: cancellation of rights and obligations by their novation. The tenth chapter: cancellation of rights and obligations by their consolidation.

tions[224]. Obligations are divided between a general part and a book on obligations. The most general content, also relevant to other books, is found in the general part. The CMBC isolated the law of obligations in a single book, whereas the *Landrecht* introduced new thinking regarding the system of private law: which institutions are more general and which more specific? Those features of both codifications are visible in the arrangement of the German BGB (1896). That can be ascertained by analyzing the arrangement of the civil codes, but the role of legal scholars in elaborating the Pandect systematization cannot be ignored.

Obligations are an equivalent of *actiones* and *ius in re* of *res*. This arrangement was promoted by the German BGB[225] (1896). The general part is established at the beginning of the code, as the first book. It contains institutions of the law of persons, *ius in re* and obligations. The general part is an instrument that distributes obligations and is a factor common to all books. This is the next stage in the development of the systematization based on the *Institutes* of Gaius. The location of the general part at the beginning of a civil code resembles the positioning of some general precepts before *personae* in the *Institutes*, but the general part is much more extensive than the content situated before *personae*.

Having provided this background, this section now proceeds to present the divisions visible in the codifications. Here only the bourgeois civil codes are considered; the modifications implemented in socialist codes require a separate analysis. In the first code comprising a general part – the Saxon civil code (1863) – the sequence of books is: the general part – *ius in re* – the law of claims (law of obligations) – family law (including guardianship law) – inheritance law. In such an arrangement, *res* (*ius in re*) dominates the system of the code. This systematic pattern results from the inspiration provided by codes founded on the Gaius scheme, which underline *res* in their composition.

The second option is discernible in the German BGB (1896). In the BGB there are: the general part – law of obligations (*actiones*) – *ius in re* (*res*) – family law – succession law. This systematization results from opposition to the Gaius model. In Germany the dynamic element of private law (*actiones*) prevails in the

224 In this aspect, the CMBC (1756) acted as a model – its fourth and last book includes the law of obligations. It is the only code prior to the Pandect structure in which obligations are separated in the system of the books.

225 *Actiones* were reinterpreted differently in codes prior to Pandect structure.
In the CMBC (1756) those are obligations, in the CC (1804) different ways of acquiring ownership, whereas in the ABGB (1811) the provisions are common to personal rights and *ius in re*.
Both in the CMBC and in the CC obligations are classified among *actiones*; only in the ABGB they are included among *res*. In the Pandect model the simplest and clearest solution was associating *actiones* with the law of obligations.

arrangement of the code[226]. The significant volume of the law of obligations is placed in the general part, with the result being that in such a composition all the regulations of obligations are positioned next to each other. In the German arrangement the law of obligations is isolated between two books (the general part and the law of obligations); in addition, a significant volume of the law of obligations is transposed to the commercial code[227].

In both codifications (Saxony – 1863, Germany – 1896) family law and the general part are situated at a remove from each other. Being part of *personae*, family law is detached from the general part. This can be considered as a disadvantage, acting as an incentive for a new arrangement; in bourgeois civil codes, the general part and family law may be placed in the first two books of the code. As a result, family law (in the codes set on the Gaius scheme that is the part of *personae*) and the general part (in the Pandect systematization perceived as *persona*) form a certain systematic whole. After *personae* comes *res* (*ius in re* and inheritance law) and finally *actiones* (law of obligations), found in the last book of the code. This composition is visible in the Russian draft (1905) and in the current Czech civil code (2012)[228]. Interestingly, it is possible to include a general part and the Gaius modelin the same codification. As, in socialist codifications, family law is extracted from the civil code, none of the systematic patterns mentioned above can be found in the socialist civil codes.

VI. Codes with a distinct book on obligations and without a general part

If a general part is not adopted in the structure of the code, then lawmakers return to their main inspiration: the Gaius scheme[229]. Two principal ways of arranging a civil code can be observed in the codes: establishing the structure of the code according to the Gaius model or the general part. If the Gaius model is introduced

---

226 HATTENHAUER H., *Grundbegriffe des Bürgerlichen Rechts. Historisch-dogmatische Einführung*, München 2000, pp. 86 – 87.

227 MICHAELS R., *vor § 241. Systemfragen des Schuldrechts*, in: ZIMMERMANN R. (ed.), *Historisch-kritischer Kommentar zum BGB. Band II Schuldrecht: Allgemeiner Teil §§ 241 – 432*, Tübingen 2007, pp. 12 – 13.
More about the arrangement of the law of obligations in Germany:
Ibidem, pp. 12 – 20.

228 In the Russian draft (1905), the order of the books is: general part – family law – succession law – *ius in re* – law of obligations.
The current Czech civil code (2012) contains a general part – family law – absolute property rights (*ius in re* and inheritance law) – relative property rights (obligations).
In the mentioned codes the first two books (general part and family law) constitute *personae*. Inheritance law and *ius in re* are together an equivalent of *res*. The last book on obligations implies *actiones*.

229 At the same time institutions applying to all branches of private law are placed among obligations, arranged in a sole book. Those are the institutions of the law of obligations, such as declaration of will, condition, representation, power of attorney and prescription.

in the exterior divisions of a civil code, then accordingly *personae* go first, followed by *res* and finally *actiones*. This shape is visible in Switzerland and Hungary. Replicating the arrangement of the *Institutes* ensures the balance of the codifications. Contrary to the first codifications based on the Gaius scheme, in Switzerland and Hungary the substantive private law is isolated from the civil procedure and *actiones* are associated with the law of obligations.

In both legal systems, *res* and *actiones* have concurrently been reinterpreted differently; in Switzerland both succession law and *ius in re* constitute *res*, whereas in Hungary *res* is perceived as *ius in re*. In Switzerland, the law of obligations are *actiones*, while in Hungary the law of obligations and the law of succession constitute together *actiones*. This appears to be an inspiration from the CMBC (1756) and the German BGB (1896), both identifying obligations with *actiones*. This is an example of the interaction between different codifications; the codes including a general part may be inspired by codifications not including a general part and vice versa. Obviously, we do not address the arrangement discussed above as the Pandect systematization; this term designates the codifications containing a general part. But the Swiss and Hungarian arrangement is nevertheless the outcome of both the Pandect model and of German legal science.

1. Switzerland

The Swiss Code of obligations (1911) is treated as the fifth and final book of the Swiss civil code (1907). The Swiss civil code includes the law of persons, family law, inheritance law and *ius in re*. In Switzerland obligations constitute *actiones*. The exterior shell of the Swiss codification is similar to the CMBC (1756). Just asin the CMBC, in Switzerland *actiones* are arranged at the end of the code. The only difference is that in Switzerland private law is included in two written laws instead of one.

2. Hungary

The Hungarian structure is very similar to the Swiss arrangement, but in Hungary the law of obligations, together with succession law, comprise *actiones*. The sequence in Hungary is: *personae* – *res* (*ius in re*) – *actiones* (obligations and inheritance law)[230]. The law of obligations is found in the second to last book of the civil code. The Hungarian composition can be considered in the terms of a person (*personae*) who can take legal actions (*actiones*) in relaiton to his property (*ius in re*/ *res*). Primarily, the law of obligations is associated with *actiones*, but in Hun-

[230] In the Hungarian draft (1928), there are: law of persons and family law – *ius in re* – law of obligations – law of succession.

In the socialist Hungarian civil code (1959), the sequence of books is: introductory provisions – persons – right of ownership – law of obligations – inheritance law.

The current Hungarian civil code (2013) includes: introductory provisions – individual as subject of law – legal entity – family law – *ius in re* – law of obligations – succession law.

gary inheritance law is also perceived as part of *actiones*; such a systematization does not change the balance of the code, because the law of succession is purely a systematic detail that can be included almost anywhere.

VII. Obligations in the structure of the socialist civil codes

This section considers the arrangement of obligations in the systems of the socialist civil codes. Family law is isolated in a separate code. In socialist civil codes containing a general part the most typical sequence is: the general part – *res (ius in re* / ownership) – law of obligations (*actiones*) – inheritance law. It seems that such an arrangement gives a socialist civil code the best possible equilibrium. If a significant area (family law) is removed from a civil code, then it is necessary to find a systematization that best suits the new ideology. The general part stabilizes the composition of the code; the system does not fluctuate, because it is built on a firm foundation of legal science and concepts.

Furthermore, to adapt a civil code to socialism, *res* (*ius in re* or ownership), representing socialist ownership, dominates the system of a civil code. *Res* must be situated directly after the general part. As a result, in examining a socialist civil code its goals and assumptions are clear. Socialist ownership is the central principle of socialist civil codes. Obligations (*actiones*) are situated after *res*. In the Pandect structure the general part acts as *persona*, *ius in re* as *res,* and the law of obligations as *actiones*. Three crucial compounds (*persona* – *res* – *actiones*) can be found next to each other, maintaining the system of a socialist codification. Removing family law from a similarly arranged civil code does not disturb the balance of the codification.

The rules of the systematization mentioned above concern the majority of socialist civil codes, apart from the socialist Hungarian civil code (1959) and the East German civil code (1975). The socialist Hungarian civil code (1959) retains the original Hungarian arrangement (without a general part), whereas East German lawyers have worked for many years to elaborate a structure that introduces variations to the German BGB (1896).

First, the socialist Hungarian civil code (1959) is discussed here, because it does not contain a general part. The most typical arrangement is subsequently considered (the general part – *res* – law of obligations – law of succession). It can be found in the majority of socialist civil codes. The discussion then proceeds to more extensive issues: the systematization of the second socialist Czechoslovak civil code (1964) and of the East German civil code (1975). So as to open upfurther analysis in the chapter on obligations, those codifications are discussed very precisely here. The systematic patterns applied in both civil codes vary too greatly from the traditional arrangement.

1. Hungarian civil code (1959) – a socialist civil code without a general part

The socialist Hungarian civil code (1959) does not contain a general part and follows the Gaius model. The arrangement is the same as in the Hungarian draft (1928), where obligations together with the succession law constitute *actiones*[231]. The Hungarian arrangement is discussed more thoroughly in the next section, with reference to the composition of the legal concepts in the verified codes.

2. Arrangement of the law of obligations in the socialist civil codes with a general part

Other socialist civil codes include a general part. The first book is the general part. *Res* (*ius in re* or ownership) is placed immediately after the general part and it is underlined in the system of the code. The law of obligations (*actiones*) and the law of succession follow. This arrangement is a modified version of the composition discernible in the Saxon civil code (1863), comprising sections in the following order: general part – *ius in re* – law of claims (obligations) – family law (including guardianship law) – succession law. This sequence in present in Russia[232] (1922, 1964, 1994 – 2006), Czechoslovakia[233] (1950, 1964) and Poland[234] (1964).

In Russia supplementary books were added later (1964, 1994 – 2006)[235]; nonetheless, the additional content does not affect the systematization of the law of obligations[236]. In the current Russian civil code (1994 – 2006), the law of obligations is extracted in the general part of the law of obligations and the particular kinds of obligations, but that is solely a technical division, and it does not modify the sequence of the compounds in the civil code.

---

231 The sequence in the socialist Hungarian civil code (1959) is: introductory provisions – persons – right of ownership – law of obligations – inheritance law.

In the Hungarian draft (1928), there are four books: law of persons and family law – *ius in re* – law of obligations – succession law.

232 In the first socialist Russian civil code (1922) there are: general part – *ius in re* – law of obligations – law of succession.

233 In Czechoslovakia (1950) the order of books is: introductory provisions – general part – *ius in re* – obligations – inheritance law.

234 In Poland (1964) the sequence is: general part – ownership and other *ius in re* – obligations – succession law.

235 The sequence in the second socialist Russian civil code from 1964 is: general part – ownership – obligations – copyright law – right of discovery – patent law – succession law – international private law.

The order in the current Russian civil code (1994 – 2006) is: general provisions – right of ownership and other rights to estate – general part of obligations – particular kinds of obligations – inheritance law – international private law – rights to results of intellectual activities and means of individualisation.

236 In the current Russian civil code (1994 – 2006), the law of obligations is divided into two separate books. The third book regards the general part of obligations and the fourth book includes the particular kinds of obligations.

3. Czechoslovakia (1964)

In the second socialist Czechoslovak civil code (1964), the sequence of the systematic components follows that of other socialist civil codes, but obligations are divided between three books. (This section of the discussion considers what a reader of the code can initially discern from glancing at the table of contents of the code.) The fourth book contains services. The fifth book comprises rights and duties from other juridical acts, whereas the sixth book deals with damage and unjust enrichment. To comprehend the Czechoslovak systematization more fully, we must delve moredeeply into the structure of the civil code. The first book includes the general provisions. The second book deals with socialist collective ownership and personal ownership, whereas the third book regulates the personal use of dwelling units, other living spaces, and tracts of land. These constitute the general part and *ius in re*; the legal category of *ius in re* is isolated between two books, positioned next to each other. The law of obligations follows (the fourth book, containing services; the fifth book, rights and duties from other juridical acts; and the sixth book, responsibility for damage and unjust enrichment). The seventh book concerns the inheritance of property as personal ownership. The final provisions are located in the concluding eighth book.

The first impression this codification provides is almost identical to that gained of other socialist civil codes containing a general part and following the sequence of *ius in re*, law of obligations and law of succession. If we read more deeply in the Czechoslovak code, then we learn more and notice the modifications introduced in its structure. The general part of the Czechoslovak code comprises numerous institutions of the general part of obligations[237]. Adopting the content of the general part of obligations with in the general part changes the balance of the code and makes it an equivalent of the general part of obligations. As a result, in the Czechoslovak code obligations are divided between four books. The fourth, fifth and sixth books are accordant with the particular obligations. The sixth book, concerning the responsibility for damage and unjust enrichment, includes the non-

[237] The sixth chapter (§§ 63 – 70) of the general part of Czechoslovak civil code (1964) considers the transition of rights and duties (obligations). First (§§ 63 – 67), the assignment of a claim is set. Then assumption of debt (§§ 68 – 69). In § 70 accession to debt is arranged.

The seventh chapter (§§ 71 – 99) deals with the extinction of rights and duties (obligations). In the beginning (§§ 71 – 89) the performance of an obligation is placed. Subsequently, there is settlement (§§ 90 – 92), the impossibility of performance *[Unmöglichkeit der Leistung]* (§ 93), passage of time (§ 94), death of a debtor or a creditor (§ 95), set-off (§§ 96 – 98) and lack of enforcing a right (§ 99).

The eighth chapter includes prescription.

Here primarily the institutions not typical for the general part are mentioned. More about the arrangement of the general part in the Czechoslovak code can be found in the chapter on the systematization of the general part.

contractual sources of obligations[238]. The fourth and fifth books contain particular contracts. The fourth book concerns services, whereas the fifth book deals with the rights and duties drawn from other juridical acts. The criterion for distinguishing between the contracts of both books concerns the subjects of an agreement; the fourth book considers services – the agreements concluded between citizens and socialist organizations. The citizens are the receivers of the performances *(Leistungen)* provided by the socialist organizations[239]. In accordance with part 2 of § 2, the participants in private law relationships are equal. The footnote reference discusses the arrangement of contracts included in the fourth book[240]. As

---

238 The sixth book (referring to the responsibility for damage and unjust enrichment) includes the prevention of impending damage and unjust enrichment (the first division), liability for damage (the second division) and finally liability for unjust enrichment (the third division).

239 ČEŠKA Z., ŠVESTKA J., *Wstęp* [Introduction], in: *Kodeks cywilny. Kodeks gospodarczy. Kodeks handlu mię dzynarodowego Czechosłowackiej Republiki Socjalistycznej* [Civil code, Economic Code, International commercial code of the Czechoslovak Socialist Republic], Wrocław/ Warszawa/ Kraków/ Gdańsk/ Łódź 1981, p. 27.

240 The fourth book (regarding services) contains: general provisions on supplying services (the first division), commercial sales (the second division), lease of a thing (the third division), manufacturing a thing on request (the fourth division), repair and modification of a thing (the fifth division), services in matters of dealing with affairs (the sixth division), accommodation services (the seventh division), transport services (the eighth division), legal assistance from a bar association (the ninth division), monetary services (the tenth division) and finally insurance (the eleventh division).

Some remarks on the composition of the fourth book on services follow. In the first division (general provisions on supplying services) there are the common provisions, applying to all relationships arising from the fourth book. The primary issue is that the socialist organizations provide the citizens with services, fulfilling their material and cultural needs (§ 222 part 1). The socially justified needs of the citizens need to be met properly and on a regular basis (§ 223). The principle is that services are payable (§ 225 part 1). A citizen has a duty of cooperation with a socialist organization in the scope necessary for performing a service (§ 227).

In the first division there are also provisions on price (§§ 229 – 232), responsibility for performing a service and damage (§§ 233 – 238). Those provisions (I mean §§ 229 – 238) could be classified among the general part of obligations, if it was extracted in the civil code.

Commercial sales is put in the second division; settling sales in front of particular contracts is the most common resolution. The adjective "commercial" signals that those provisions do not apply to a sales concluded between the citizens.

Afterwards the commercial sales there is the lease of a thing (the third division). Arranging contracts enabling the use of things after the contracts enabling the transfer of ownership is a typical composition.

An interesting issue concerning the third division is that those provisions do not apply to the lease of housing units or flats. The traditionally perceived contract of lease was eliminated from the second socialist Czechoslovak civil code (1964), because lease gives only a temporary possibility of using a housing unit.

RYBÁRIK K., *Le droit d'usage personnel d'habitations*, Bulletin de Droit Tchécoslovaque 1973 no. 1 – 2, pp. 242 – 245.

The content of the fourth division (manufacturing a thing on request) as well as the fifth division (repair and modification of a thing) enable use of things; for this reason those contracts

the fourth book deals with contracts between socialist organizations and citizens, accordingly the fifth book (rights and duties from other juridical acts) contains the regulation of the contracts concluded between the citizens[241]. The arrangement of agreements settled in the fifth book is outlined in the footnote reference[242].

---

are systematically close to lease.

In the bourgeois civil codes usually after the contracts enabling use of things contracts supplying services come; if we cannot do something on our own, then we may use the services of other people; in the second socialist Czechoslovak civil code (1964) it is possible to ask a socialist organization for assistance. In this case the services services in matters of dealing with affairs from the sixth division would apply.

The next systematic category are accommodation services, set in the seventh division. This division considers only temporary accommodation (hotels, guest rooms, etc.). This is specified in services in the part 1 of § 300.

A citizen may also use transport services (the eighth division) or request for legal assistance from a bar association (the ninth division).

The tenth division includes monetary services. In the first chapter (of the tenth division) there are financial contributions. If the socialist citizens need money, then can take a loan from a socialist organization (part 1 of § 341), a loan needs to have a designated purpose; loans are arranged in the second chapter of the tenth division.

The last eleventh division deals with insurance. In a civil comprising around 500 provisions the regulation of insutance is extensive (§§ 345 – 383).

241 ČEŠKA Z., ŠVESTKA J., *Wstęp* [Introduction], in: *Kodeks cywilny. Kodeks gospodarczy. Kodeks handlu mię dzynarodowego Czechosłowackiej Republiki Socjalistycznej* [Civil code, Economic Code, International commercial code of the Czechoslovak Socialist Republic], Wrocław/ Warszawa/ Kraków/ Gdańsk/ Łódź 1981, p. 28.

242 In the second socialist Czechoslovak civil code (1964), the fifth book contains the rights and duties from other juridical acts. Comparing to the fourth book of services (§§ 222 – 383) there are few provisions in the fifth book on the rights and duties from other juridical acts (§§ 384 – 414).

The catalogue of contracts is very brief; it seems that for the socialist legislator the most important point was not introducing into a civil code the full regulation of the particular contracts concluded between citizens, but designating the principles of the (property and contractual) relationships between the citizens. Particular contracts represent the different possibilities available in our social and economic functioning. The fifth book is a legal instrument for implementing socialist principles, dictating to citizens how should they act.

The first division of the fifth book deals with civic aid, which can also be understood as citizens assisting one another. A new institution aims at fulfilling the needs of citizens, which cannot be met by the state and its subjects – especially in the countryside.

VONDRACEK Th. J., *Commentary on the Czechoslovak civil code*, Dordrecht/ Boston/ Lancaster 1988, pp. 341 – 342.

According to § 384 (part 1) civic aid is provided whenever one citizen, at the request of another citizen, performs some work for him, grants him a loan, or otherwise aids him. Part 2 states that the rendering of civic aid must conform with the rules of socialist community life.

§ 385 is also interesting. According to part 1, a citizen who renders civic aid is entitled to the reimbursement of appropriately incurred expenses. In Part 2, a citizen is entitled to remuneration only insofar as has been agreed upon and insofar as it corresponds to the nature of the aid, especially where the result has been accomplished by his personal effort.

In the first division (of the fifth book) first there are common provisions (§§ 384 – 386); two were already adduced. The regulation of loans follows (§§ 387 – 389). According to part 1 of

The systematization of particular contracts in the second Czechoslovak civil code (1964) is not substantially considered in the section on particular contracts, because its significant variationswould disrupt the clarity of the analysis of this area.

While the second socialist Czechoslovak civil code alters the arrangement of obligations most significantly, the East German civil code (1975) makes the most changes to the systematization of *ius in re*. Interestingly, the deletion of the construct of an obligation from a socialist civil code can be present in a written law that preserves the most typical sequence (general part – *res* – obligations – inheritance law). The new structure of a socialist civil code is always elaborated either at the expense of the law of obligations (Czechoslovakia – 1964) or *ius in re* (East Germany – 1975). The systematization of the general part is also significantly modified in both codifications. Primarily, the socialist arrangement of a civil code is obtained at the cost of family law, which is always removed from a socialist civil code.

4. East Germany (1975)

a) General remarks on the systematization of the East German civil code

The structure of the East German civil code (1975) has features of the Pandect systematization, but its shape is significantly different from all other codifications[243]. A contract determines the arrangement of obligations in the East German civil code. The third book (containing contracts relating to material and cultural life) includes the law of contracts, whereas the fifth book (dealing with the protec-

---

§ 387, with respect to a financial loan, interest may be claimed only where it has been agreed upon. Interest may not exceed the extent established by subsidiary legislation. Agreement on other material advantages is invalid.

Besides the (first) division (of the fifth book) concerning civic aid outlined above, there are the second and third divisions. The third division, referring to the public prize competition (§§ 412 – 414), does not require further analysis. This study concentrates here on the second division, including other contracts.

The first chapter of the second division regards leasing a dwelling unit in a family house. The second chapter involves leasing a part of a dwelling unit. The third chapter deals with leasing real property for temporary use.

The first three chapters (of the second division on other contracts) serve the fulfilment of housing needs by giving citizens the chance to enter into agreements between themselves. The fourth chapter deals with sales, exchange and donation; contracts enabling the transfer of ownership are placed after lease; the same arrangement is also visible in Russia (1922) and East Germany (1975), where lease precedes sales. The final, fifth chapter (of the second division) regulates arranging the affairs of another person.

243 The East German civil code (1975) contains: fundamental principles of socialist private law – socialist ownership and personal ownership – *contracts relating to material and cultural life* – use of real estate and buildings for residential and recreational purposes – *protection of life, health and property from damage* – inheritance law – *specific provisions of the respective relationships of private law.*

tion of life, health and property from damage) contains non-contractual sources of obligations[244]. Some institutions of the law of obligations are arranged in the seventh book (on the specific provisions of the respective relationships of private law). The first chapter (of the final, seventh book) considers the specific features of performing contractual obligations. The second chapter includes the participation of some contractors in a contract. The third chapter deals with securing claims. The East German arrangement of obligations might surprise some readers, but it resembles the systematization of the third and final book of the ABGB (1811). This issue is explained a little further here.

In East Germany, the regulations of the law of obligations are separated by *ius in re* (the fourth book on use of real estate and buildings for residential and recreational purposes). Provisions relating to obligations are also placed at the beginning of the final, seventh book, a systematic equivalent of the general part[245]. In the East German civil code, none of the books containing the regulations of obligations are situated side by side[246].

In the East German civil code, the third book is placed after two books that designate the direction of the entire code – that is, the first book (on the fundamental principles of socialist private law) and the second book (on socialist ownership and personal ownership). The first two books might, in certain aspects, be considered as an equivalent of the abstract general part of the East German civil code. Both are crucial for the entire functioning of the code; the first book contains that which is discrete and *personae*[247]. The first book takes the function of Gaian *per-*

244 The fifth book (containing the protection of life, health and property from damage) of the East German civil code comprises: prevention of damage (the first chapter) – reparation of damage (the second chapter) – duty of returning unjustifiably obtained benefits (the third chapter) – duty of returning found objects (the fourth chapter).

245 The first chapter of the final, seventh book (regarding the specific provisions of the respective relationships of private law) of the East German civil code (1975) considers the special features of performing contractual obligations. The second chapter (of the seventh book) concerns the participation of some contractors in a contract. In the second subdivision of the third chapter, referring to securing claims, guarantee is settled.

246 This arrangement differs from the systematization present in the second socialist Czechoslovak civil code (1964), where the regulations of the law of obligations are set next to each other (the fourth book concerns services, the fifth book: rights and duties from other juridical acts; the sixth book deals with responsibility for damage and unjust enrichment).

In the East German civil code the regulations of the law of obligations are arranged in the third, fifth and seventh books. The third book contains contracts relating to material and cultural life. The fifth book concerns protection of life, health and property from damage. The seventh book addresses specific provisions of the respective relationships of private law.

In this respect, the East German arrangement varies from the German BGB (1896), where all the regulations of the law of obligations are settled next to each other – numerous provisions of obligations are arranged in the general part. The law of obligations is positioned directly after the general part, in the second book.

247 In the first book (on fundamental principles of socialist private law) of the East German civil

sonae in the system of the code. In the socialist civil codes, socialist ownership is glorified; for this reason the second book deals with socialist ownership and personal ownership. That is *res*. The third book (on contracts relating to material and cultural life) adopts the systematization of the German BGB (1896), where the law of obligations (*actiones*) is put directly after the general part. In the East German civil code this arrangement was modified, because the first two books act as *persona*[248].

b) The East German civil code, the ABGB and a contract

The central construct of the East German civil code is a contract instead of obligation, which is most typical. The East German arrangement discloses many similarities to the composition of the ABGB (1811). In the ABGB the law of obligations is separated into two books. The second division (of the second book on *ius rerum*) refers to personal rights. That is the law of obligations, and it is the area of the ABGB which is dedicated to them[249]. In the ABGB the content of the law of obligations in the second book is focused on a contract (the seventeenth chapter regards contracts in general). The second area is in the third book, comprising the provisions common to personal rights and *ius in re*, and almost exclusively includes institutions of the law of obligations, but the construct applied in the third book concerns rights and obligations[250].

In East Germany there is a much stronger focus on contract than in the ABGB. The third book of the East German civil code includes contracts relating to material and cultural life. To assure a greater balance in the law of obligations in the East German civil code, contract is mentioned in the divisions of the seventh book (concerning the specific provisions of the respective relationships of private law):

---

code there are: tasks of private law (the first chapter), the status of citizens in private law (the second chapter), the status of enterprises in private law (the third chapter) and the rules of cooperation between citizens and enterprises (the fourth chapter).

248 Obviously, classifying a book on socialist ownership and personal ownership in the terms of the general part might surprise some. The second book has a rather "decorative" function in the structure of the East German civil code; in the East German civil code the fourth book deals with the use of real estate and buildings for the residential and recreational purposes. It contains the actual volume of *ius in re*; the fourth book comprises everything that concerns the use of immovables. Furthermore, the fourth chapter (of the fourth book) contains the regulation of the personal ownership of immovables and buildings.

Just like in the German BGB, in the East German civil code *ius in re* is also set after the law of obligations. In the German BGB (1896), there are: general part – law of obligations – *ius in re* – family law – inheritance law.

249 In the ABGB (1811), the seventeenth chapter (of the second book) refers to contracts in general. This is the general part of the law of obligations. Then the particular obligations are established (from the eighteenth chapter to the thirtieth).

250 In the ABGB, the first chapter (of the third book) regards the security of rights and obligations. The second chapter: modification of rights and obligations. The third chapter: cancellation of rights and obligations. The fourth chapter: prescription and usucaption.

the first chapter of the seventh book regards the specific features of performing contractual obligations, whereas the second chapter considers the participation of contractors in a contract[251].

c) Systematization of the third book of the East German civil code

The systematization of the third book on contracts relating to material and cultural life is now addressed in this section. Before describing the third book, we must explain its title ("contracts relating to material and cultural life"). East German legal science uses this term to refer to the most important contracts for citizens. Contracts relating to material and cultural life are distinguished in four groups: leases (*die Wohnungsmiete*), sales (*der Kauf*), services (*die Dienstleistungen*) and further contracts, connected with supplying the needs of socialist citizens (*weitere Versorgungsbeziehungen*)[252].

The first chapter (of the third book) concerns the general provisions regarding contracts; that is the general part of obligations. The first subsection of the first chapter considers the fundamental provisions. These are: the tasks of contracts (§ 43), the duty of cooperation (§ 44), as and how to determine the content of a contract (§ 45). Although the final provision mentioned is strongly technical, in its text we may see a reflection of freedom of contract[253]. A general precept on the

---

[251] The seventh book of the East German civil code (on the specific provisions of the respective relationships of private law) is an intersection between the third book of the ABGB, the Pandect general part and the compounds which did not fit with other books of the East German code.

The third chapter (of the seventh book) comprises securing claims. The fourth chapter: incapacitation, death in absentia and cancellation of instruments. The fifth chapter: explanation of the legislative terms. The sixth chapter: prescription.

The institutions on the security of rights are included also in the third book of the ABGB; the first chapter refers to the security of rights and obligations. In the ABGB Prescription is written in the fourth and final chapter of the third book.

In the East German civil code the fifth chapter (comprising a dictionary) of the seventh book is an outcome of the Pandect systematization, always attempting to settle together this what is the most general and common to other books of the code. Besides prescription is also institution which is placed in the general part.

[252] GÖHRING J. (ed.), *Grundfragen des sozialistischen Zivilrechts*, Berlin 1978, pp. 17 – 18.

More about the classification of contracts in East Germany: *Ibidem*, pp. 16 – 18.

About the systematization of the specific contracts in the German BGB (1896): HOFER S., *vor § 433. Die Systematik des Besonderen Schuldrechts*, in: RÜCKERT J., SCHÄFER F. L. (ed.), *Historisch-kritischer Kommentar zum BGB. Band III Schuldrecht: Besonderer Teil §§ 433 – 853*, Tübingen 2013, pp. 26 – 27.

[253] *§ 45. Bestimmung des Vertragsinhalts. (1) Die Rechte und Pflichten beim Abschluß und bei der Erfüllung von Verträgen ergeben sich aus den Bestimmungen dieses Gesetzes.*

(2) Werden von den Partnern besondere Vereinbarungen getroffen, sollen sie ihre gegenseitigen Rechte und Pflichten im Vertrag so festlegen, daß der mit dem Vertrag beabsichtigte Zweck eindeutig bestimmt und Streit über den Vertragsinhalt vermieden wird.

(3) Die Partner können auch Vereinbarungen treffen, die in diesem Gesetz nicht geregelt sind oder die von seinen Bestimmungen abweichen, soweit ihre Anwendung nicht verbindlich vorgeschrieben ist. Die Vereinbarungen dürfen jedoch nicht gegen Inhalt und Zweck dieses Gesetzes

autonomy of citizens is expressed in the second part of § 8, stating that with in the limits of this bill citizens are authorized to enter into any contracts which are supposed to satisfy their material and cultural needs.

The last provision in the first subsection (on fundamental provisions) is § 48. It is crucial from the systematic point of view; according to the first part of § 48 the general provisions apply to all the contractual relationships regulated in this bill. They are also a foundation for establishing those contractual relationships, which in this bill were not separately regulated. The second part of § 45 is much more interesting; the general provisions regarding contracts also apply accordingly to unilateral legal actions, as well as other rights and duties which do not arise from contracts, insofar as the following provisions do not otherwise provide for[254].

§ 48 indicates that the third book is the systematic heart of the East German civil code as regards the validity of provisions:its precepts also apply to other books of the written law. The first book (on the fundamental principles of socialist private law) designates the tasks of the system as well as the theoretical and abstract background necessary in the Pandect systematization and in the socialist civil codes; furthermore, it primarily includes numerous provisions of *personae*[255] and takes the place of the Gaian (and also the Pandect) *persona*. The second book (on socialist ownership and personal ownership) comprises *res*, which is vital in the socialist codifications. The third book (on contracts relating to material and cultural life) contains the most significant volume, from a practical point of view. Interestingly, in the East German civil code the first three books that are the most relevant from a systematic point of view are arranged next to each other (in the first book, fundamental principles of socialist private law (*persona*) are addressed; the second book concerns socialist ownership and personal ownership (*res*); the third book deals with contracts relating to material and cultural life (*actiones*). This composition resembles the most typical Pandect systematization visible in

---

verstoßen.

(4) Die Verantwortlichkeit wegen vorsätzlicher oder grob fahrlässiger Pflichtverletzung kann nicht ausgeschlossen oder eingeschränkt werden; das gleiche gilt für die Verantwortlichkeit für nicht qualitätsgerechte Leistung, soweit dieses Gesetz nicht abweichende Vereinbarungen zuläßt.

254 *§ 48. Geltungsbereich der allgemeinen Bestimmungen über Verträge. (1) Die allgemeinen Bestimmungen über Verträge gelten für alle in diesem Gesetz geregelten vertraglichen Beziehungen: Sie sind auch Grundlage für die Gestaltung solcher Vertragsverhältnisse, die in diesem Gesetz nicht besonders geregelt sind.*

(2) Die allgemeinen Bestimmungen über Verträge gelten entsprechend auch für einseitige Rechtsgeschäfte sowie andere nicht durch Vertrag begründete Rechte und Pflichten, soweit im folgenden nichts anderes bestimmt ist.

255 The first chapter of the first book (on the fundamental principles of socialist private law) considers the tasks of private law. The second chapter: status of citizens in private law. The third chapter: status of enterprises in private law. The fourth chapter: rules of cooperation between citizens and enterprises.

the socialist civil codes, where the general part (*persona*), *res* and obligations (*actiones*) are positioned alongside each other.

The ensuing subsections of the first chapter (of the third book) require closer examination. The second subdivision deals with legal capacity, representation and power of attorney. This is a natural arrangement, which can also be found in other codifications; if we consider the system of private law in the category of contracts – and a contract is the fundamental systematic category in a civil code – then the perspective and the structure of a civil code is adapted to a contract. We perceive private law in the terms of when a contract may occur; for this reason, the legal capacity is the first necessary criterion. We also consider what can be included in a contract: representation and power of attorney fit perfectly here.

The third subsection (of the first chapter) refers to the conclusion and form of contracts. The fourth subsection regards the performance of contracts, whereas the fifth subsection deals with the modification and the termination of a contract. The sixth and final subsection considers liability for the breach of contractual obligations. The East German legislator clearly introduced the chronology of a contract. First, the general provisions are stated, then a contract is concluded and performed as well as modified and terminated.

Some provisions of the law of obligations (which in the East German civil code are transformed into the law of contracts) are transposed to the seventh and final book on the specific provisions of the respective relationships of private law. Among others, the seventh book contains thespecific features related to performing contractual obligations (the first chapter) and the participation of contractors in a contract (the second chapter). The third chapter of the seventh book deals with securing claims. The fourth chapter regulates incapacitation, death in absentia and cancellation of instruments. The fifth chapter explains the legislative terms, and the sixth and final chapter involves prescription. In the East German civil code, the seventh book resembles a store room, including the systematic elements which did not fit in the other books.

Having analyzed the arrangement of the general part of obligations in the East German civil code, it is now possible to proceed to the particular obligations. Non-contractual sources of obligations are put in the fifth book regarding the protection of life, health and property from damage. The particular contracts are put in the third book (on contracts relating to cultural and material life). The second chapter of the third book refers to the lease of flats. Lease is accented in the composition of the East German civil code and it is placed before sales (the third chapter). This systematization arises from the socialist approach, whereby supplying citizens with housing units is the most fundamental issue.

The arrangement of particular contracts in the East German civil code was primarily inspired by the composition of the second socialist Czechoslovak civil code (1964), where the fourth book includes services and the fifth book contains the rights and duties from other juridical acts. The Czechoslovak arrangement is determined by two distinct contexts in the immediate living environment; either a contract is concluded between a citizen and a unit of the nationalized economy (in which case, it is a service and it is payable), or a contract is concluded between citizens (and it is gratuitous);in the case of the second category the regulations of the fifth book should apply. Such a composition resulted in doubling the provisions on sales[256]. Already having access to Czechoslovak legal works, East German lawyers perfected the arrangement.

In the East German civil code the division of particular contracts is not exclusive and dualistic; as in the Czechoslovak codification, the fourth chapter deals with services. Among the general provisions (the first subdivision of the fourth chapter on services) it is stated that the fourth chapter includes contracts between socialist enterprises and citizens[257]. In the fourth chapter there are general provisions (the first subdivision) – services and repairs regarding the household (the second subdivision) – construction services (the third subdivision) – personal services (the fourth subdivision) – travel and leisure (the fifth subdivision) – hire (the sixth subdivision) – storage of things (the seventh subdivision) – services concerning communications and telecommunications (the eighth subdivision).

The fifth chapter (of the third book) deals with agreements for savings accounts, credit and loans. The sixth chapter involves insurance. The final, seventh chapter (of the third book) refers to communities of citizens, mutual assistance and gifts. This area of the East German civil code strongly resembles the fifth book of the second socialist Czechoslovak civil code (1964), containing rights and duties from other juridical acts.

This concludes the analysis of the systematization of the law of obligations in the East German civil code. Much more could be written about the second

---

[256] In the second socialist Czechoslovak civil code (1964), the second division of the fourth book on services regards the commercial sales. Then the second division (of the fifth book on rights and duties from other juridical acts) refers to other contracts. The fourth chapter (of the second division) comprises sales, exchange and donation.

[257] *§ 162. Aufgaben und Ziele. (1) Die Dienstleistungsbetriebe und wirtschaftsleitenden Organe sind in Verwirklichung der staatlichen Versorgungspolitik verpflichtet, die Bevölkerung planmäßig mit solchen Dienstleistungen zu versorgen, die den Bedürfnissen der Bürger, insbesondere nach Verminderung und Erleichterung der Hausarbeit, nach Verbesserung der Wohnverhältnisse und nach sinnvoller Nutzung der Freizeit und Erholung entsprechen.*

(2) Die Bestimmungen über Dienstleistungen regeln die Beziehungen zwischen Bürgern und Betrieben über hauswirtschaftliche Dienstleistungen und Reparaturen, Bauleistungen, persönliche Dienstleistungen, Leistungen für Reise und Erholung sowie die Ausleihe und Aufbewahrung von Sachen. Sie dienen der Sicherung der Rechte der Bürger und der Erhöhung der Verantwortung der Betriebe für eine termin- und qualitätsgerechte Durchführung der ihnen übertragenen Aufgaben entsprechend den Bedürfnissen der Bürger.

(3) Für Dienstleistungen, die in den folgenden Bestimmungen nicht geregelt sind, gelten die Bestimmungen über diejenige Dienstleistungsart, die ähnliche Beziehungen zum Gegenstand hat.

socialist Czechoslovak civil code and the East German civil code, especially when it comes to the arrangement of particular contracts. However, each study has its limits and there are already publications that deal more thoroughly with those codifications[258].

VIII. Arrangement of the drafts of a European civil code

The systematization of the drafts of a European civil code is considered here. The analyzed drafts are the result of an academic discussion and are not binding legal texts. Not all material researched can be discussed to the same extent; this study's main focus is the systematization of the civil codes in Central and Eastern Europe. For this reason, the drafts of a European civil code are not analyzed in the subsequent sections of the chapter on the law of obligations. First, the composition of the French-Italian draft of 1927 is presented, followed by the Principles of European Contract Law, and finally the Draft Common Frame of Reference.

1. The French-Italian draft of 1927

a) The systematization of the French-Italian draft of 1927

The French-Italian draft of 1927 has a broader context, connected with many years of work undertaken by French and Italian lawyers on the possibility of unifying European private law[259]. This involved legal scholars mainly operating with in Romanic legal systems. In the table of contents of the French-Italian draft we can observe a division into a general part and a particular part (*partie spéciale*). Its first title – general provisions – includes the entire content of the general part of obligations.

The particular contracts subsequently follow. They are: sales (the second title), exchange (the third title), lease (the fourth title), employment (*du contrat de travail*, the fifth title), work contracts *(du contrat d'enterprise*, the sixth title), partnerships (the seventh title), mandates (the eighth title), settlement (the ninth title), life annuity contracts *(du contrat de rente pérpetuelle*, the tenth title), annuity contracts *(du contrat de renteviagère*, the eleventh title), gaming and betting (the twelfth title), gratuitous loans for use *(du prêt à usage ou commodat*, the

---

[258] E.g. VONDRACEK Th. J., *Commentary on the Czechoslovak civil code*, Dordrecht/ Boston/ Lancaster 1988. EMINESCU Y., POPESCU T., *Les codes civils des pays socialistes. Étude comparative*, Bucarest/ Paris 1980.
LUBY Š. (ed.), *Le droit civil tchécoslovaque*, Bratislava 1969.
PETEV V., *Sozialistisches Zivilrecht. Eine rechtsvergleichende Einführung unter Berücksichtigung der Rechte der Volksrepublik Bulgarien, der ČSSR, der DDR, der Volksrepublik Polen, der Rumänischen Sozialistischen Republik, der Ungarischen Volksrepublik und der UdSSR*, Berlin/ New York 1975.

[259] The text of the French-Italian draft from 1927 for the analysis was taken from here:
DOCAN G. P., *Code comparé des obligations. Le projet franco-italien des obligations et contrats comparé avec les codes civils français, roumain, suisse et polonais des obligations. Avec notes et renvois aux codes civils allemand et italien*, Bucuresti 1937.

thirteenth title), consumer loans *(du prêt de consommation*, the fourteenth title), deposits (the fifteenth title), sequestration (the sixteenth title), special provisions on transport and hotel agreements (the seventeenth title), security (the eighteenth title), antichresis (the nineteenth title), and finally guarantees (the twentieth title).

The composition of the first title, containing the general provisions, is now discussed. The first chapter (of the first title) includes the sources of obligations. They are: contracts (the first section), unilateral promises (the second section), *negotiorum gestio* (the third section), payment of a debt non due (the fourth section), unjust enrichment (the fifth section) and lastly unlawful acts (the sixth section). The second chapter (of the first title) considers the effects of obligations. The third chapter concerns special kinds of obligations. The fourth chapter handles extinction of obligations. The fifth chapter addresses transfer of claims. The final, sixth chapter deals with the proof of obligations and payment.

b) Roman Longchamps de Berier on the systematization of the French-Italian draft

Before proceeding to the further drafts (the PECL and the DCFR), it is worth citing some remarks of Roman Longchamps de Berier, the author of the Polish Code of obligations (1933), concerning the systematization of the French-Italian draft. His opinions enhance the debate on the structure of the civil codes. First, Longchamps de Berier states that the structure of the draft is very similar to the arrangement of the *Code civil* (the third and fourth titles of the third book), apart from the fact that there is a chapter on the sources of obligations; in addition, the provisions on the transfer of claims were transferred from the title on sales (particular contracts) with in the general part of the law of obligations[260]. Furthermore, the opening should not include provisions on the formation of obligations. According to Longchamps de Berier, an obligation and its types should be settled first; the sources of obligations can be tackled afterwards. This composition can be found in the German BGB (1896), the Japanese civil code, the Brazilian civil code, the Soviet Russian civil code and the Polish draft of obligations. Longchamps de Berier claims that beginning the code of obligations with the definition of a contract could seem strange for readers not accustomed to the French *Code*

[260] LONGCHAMPS DE BERIER R., *Quelques observations sur le projet franco-italien de code des obligations (Partie générale)*, Varsovie 1931, p. 9.

civil – this arrangement can be found both in the French *Code civil*[261] (1804) and in the French-Italian draft[262].

The systematization of a European civil code and the national codification should vary; the national version may account for our habits and preferences. In the civil codes the systematic patterns can be just as we like, and as we are used to. Simultaneously, what is supranational must be universal, and national arrangements should be eliminated if they vary from the usual tendencies. The composition of a draft of a European civil code must be as universal and objective as possible. Longchamps de Berier goes on to criticize the systematic pattern of "*des effets des obligations*"[263]. The third particularity of the CC, preserved in the French-Italian draft, is the introduction of the chapter on proof into the general part of obligations – this problem rather pertains to the civil procedure[264]. Besides, Longchamps de Berier mentions that identifying cause as a condition of the validity of a contract – as is the case in the CC – should be deleted from the draft[265]. Finally, I add a short remark, or rather a supposition. I suggest that the

---

261 In the French *Code civil* the first provision of the the third title considering contracts and conventional obligations in general (the third title is placed is placed in the third book comprising different ways of acquiring ownership) includes the definition of a contract.

Article 1101 Le contrat est un accord de volontés entre deux ou plusieurs personnes destiné à créer, modifier, transmettre ou éteindre des obligations.

262 LONGCHAMPS DE BERIER R., *Quelques observations sur le projet franco-italien de code des obligations (Partie générale)*, Varsovie 1931, p. 10.

263 *«La seconde particularité du code Napoléon avec laquelle il est difficile de se rallier pour des motifs de la logique, est le chapitre: « les effets des obligations ». Dans la conception moderne du droit civil et, avant tout, du droit des obligations, nous discernons les causes et les effets juridiques de ces causes. Les causes sont des faits, éventuellement des états de faits, plus ou moins compliqués; les effets – sont les conséquences juridiques qui en découlent. Or, l'obligation n'est point un fait ou une cause entraînant des effets juridiques, mais elle est précisement l'effet juridique d'un état de fait quelconque (contrat, lésion, délit, gestion d'affaires, etc.) Par conséquent, l'obligation ne provoque aucun effet juridique, elle n'a que son contenu et notamment – du côté pass if elle comporte différents engagements du débiteur et du côté actif – différents droits du créancier. Puisque le genre de ces engagements, éventuellement de ces droits, dépend non seulement de la source de l'obligation donnée, mais aussi des états de fait variés, qui se sont produits pendant l'existence du rapport d'obligation, tout le droit des obligations traite en réalité de ces engagements et de ces droits, en dépendance avec la phase donnée du développement du rapport d'obligation, et il est donc impossible de renfermer toutes ces questions dans un seul chapitre. En effet, ni le code Napoléon, ni le projet franco-italien n'ont réussi ày arriver, et ce que nous trouvons dans le chapitre sur « les effets des obligations » n'est en réalité qu'une juxtaposition des effets principaus de la non exécution des obligations, car la non exécution est un fait, qui provoque un effet, consistant en la configuration adéquate des engagements du débiteur, éventuellement des droits du créancier. Toutefois, avant de parler des effets de la non exécution, il faut parler de l'exécution, ainsi que les font le code suisse, le code brésilien et le projet polonais ».*

Ibidem, pp. 10 – 11.

264 *Ibidem*, p. 11.

265 *Ibidem*, pp. 30 – 31.

term "*des effets des obligations*" sounds unfamiliar. Just as Longchamps de Berier stated, Polish lawyers do not consider the effects arising from obligations, but instead think of the performance or execution of obligations. This is reminiscent of what Cornu wrote: while considering the arrangement of the law of obligations, he mentioned that some areas in the law of obligations are the most crucial and their distribution mostly determines the systematization of obligations. They are common to all kinds of obligations and constitute the general theory of obligations. These include the effect of obligations (*effet des obligations*), special relationships relating to obligations (*modalités des obligations*), transfer of obligations and the extinction of obligations[266]. Cornu's monograph is invaluable and his perspective is comparative, but the term "*modalités des obligations*" does not have a clear equivalent in German or Polish. The German text of the Swiss Code of obligations (1911), where this systematic category can be found (the fourth title) considers *besondere Verhältnisse bei Obligationen*. The systematic categories originating from the national languages are one of the factors impacting the arrangement of the civil codes. We are not likely to adopt a national codification with concepts that do not fit our thinking patterns. I comment briefly on the arrangement of the special relationships relating to obligations in the researched material in the footnote reference[267] (*modalités des obligations*).

---

[266] CORNU G., *Regards sur le titre III du livre III du Code civil « contrats ou des obligations conventionnelles en général » (Essai de lecture d'un titre du Code)*, Paris1976, p. 178.

[267] Following the reform of the CC in 2016 the fourth title (of the third book on different ways of acquiring ownership) considers the general regime of obligations (the third title regards the sources of obligations). The first chapter of the fourth title concerns the modalities of obligations. In the first chapter there are conditional obligations (the first section), time-delayed obligations (the second section) and plural obligations (the third section).

In the Swiss Code of obligations (1911), the fourth title deals with the special relationships relating to obligations. In the fourth title there are joint and several obligations (the first chapter) and conditional obligations (the second chapter), as well as earnest money, forfeit money, salary deductions and contractual penalties.

The systematic category of "*modalités des obligations*" does not match the set of legal concepts elaborated in this monograph. The systematic perception it adopts is based on whether an institution can be transposed to a general part or not. In both codifications the institutions arranged among "*modalités des obligations*" are multi-party obligations and conditional obligations. Condition can be transferred to the general part because it applies to different branches of private law. Multi-party obligations cannot be placed in the general part because this systematic compound is an element of the law of obligations only.

From the perspective of the German systematization, those institutions are, at least partially, contradictory. The Pandect model isolates condition and multi-party obligations between two books of the civil code.

The systematic nature of "*modalités des obligations*" needs to be considered. Condition is a weaker element, and multi-party obligations prevail among "*modalités des obligations*". From the systematic perspective, multi-party obligations are a neutral systematic compound – they can be isolated and arranged in different areas of the general part of obligations. As multi-party obligations dominate "*modalités des obligations*" then (here a weaker element) condition

2. The Principles of European Contract Law

The Principles of European Contract Law, as its title indicates, refer solely to contracts. Consequently, this is the central construct visible in the arrangement of the PECL. The general provisions are in the first of its seventeen chapters. The first chapter includes three sections. The first section comprises the scope of the Principles. Freedom of contract is expressed in the first part of Article 1:102: parties are free to enter into a contract and determine its contents, subject to the requirements of good faith and fair dealing, and the mandatory rules established by these Principles. The general clauses introduced in Article 1:102 (good faith and fair dealing) enable courts and legal practice to reinterpret this precept and its creative development.

The second section of the first chapter (general provisions) contains the general duties (of parties), and the third section deals with the terminology and other provisions. Here we can see the inspiration drawn from the Pandect systematization and its general part; treating the meaning of terms (Article 1:301) and the computation of time (Article 1:304) as part of the general provisions, and seeking a common factor in private law (even though the PECL applies only to contracts), are features of the Pandect model.

follows the multi-party obligations.

The second chapter regulates the formation (of contracts). The chronological sequence is visible in the PECL, which places the general provisions first and follows a clear and logical arrangement after the formation (of contracts). The third chapter establishes the authority of agents. Situating representation at the opening of the written law is based on a rationale regarding to whom the actions related to a contract may be connected. The next stage of the deliberations on a contract concerns its validity (the fourth chapter): what requirements must be met to conclude a valid agreement? The fifth chapter deals with the interpretation (of a contract). Once a contract is already in force, it may be interpreted. The sixth chapter presents the contents and effects (of a contract). In turn, the contract can be performed, the subject of the seventh chapter.

If this does not occur then we proceed to the eighth chapter, dealing with the non-performance (of a contract) and resolutions in general. The ninth chapter (specific solutions for non-performance) is an extension of the content established in the eighth chapter. The accessible resolutions if a contract is not performed are: right to performance (the first section of the ninth chapter), with holding performance (the second section), termination of the contract (the third section), price reduction (the fourth section) and finally damages and interest (the fifth section). These are the available solutions from among which the parties of the contract may choose.

In the tenth chapter, the plurality of parties is established. This is a neutral element in the chronology of a contract, and for this reason it can appear almost anywhere among the general provisions of obligations. The eleventh chapter contains the assignment of claims, and the twelfth chapter remarks on the substitution of a new debtor: transfer of contract. Positioning transfer after the termination of a contract is a logical resolution. The thirteenth chapter mentions set-off and the fourteenth chapter prescription. Prescription is the last systematic segment in the life of a contract. Chapters fifteen, sixteen and seventeen are the final systematic divisions in the PECL. The fifteenth chapter concerns illegality. In the sixteenth chapter conditions are stipulated, whereas the seventeenth and final chapter regulates the capitalization of interest.

3. The Draft Common Frame of Reference

The first issue that comes to the fore when examining the DCFR is that its scope of application, compared to the PECL, is much wider: the second book refers to contracts and other juridical acts. Furthermore, apart from obligations, it also addresses the acquisition and loss of ownership of goods (book VIII), proprietary security rights in movable assets (book IX) and trusts (book X). The present analysis concentrates solely on the systematization of the law of obligations. Contrary to the PECL, definitions are included in an annex, at the end of the DCFR.

DCFR book I includes the general provisions. Book II comprises contracts and other juridical acts. In the first chapter (of book II) there are the general provisions, containing what is most general; in II. – 1:101 a contract and a juridical act are defined, whereas II. – 1:102 looks at party autonomy, which it understands in similar terms to the PECL (according to the first part of the provision, the parties are free to make a contract or other juridical act and to determine its contents, subject to any applicable mandatory rules). The second chapter (of book II) expresses non-discrimination, crucial in private law. Subsequently, book II addresses problems that are significant both for contracts and for juridical acts, presented in chronological sequence: marketing and pre-contractual duties (the third chapter), formation (the fourth chapter), rights of with drawal (the fifth chapter), representation (the sixth chapter), grounds for invalidity (the seventh chapter), interpretation (the eighth chapter) and finally the contents and effects of contracts (the ninth chapter).

Book III deals with obligations and corresponding rights. The title of the first chapter (of book III) is "general"; this area contains the most general content of book III. In Article III. – 1:101 the scope of book III is determined: this book applies, unless otherwise stated, to all obligations with in the scope of these rules, whether they are contractual or not, and to corresponding rights to performance. Immediately following this, in III. – 1:102, are definitions, and, among others, the definition of an obligation (part 1 of III. – 1:102). The second chapter of book III considers performance, and the third chapter outlines solutions for non-performance. The fourth chapter includes the plurality of debtors and creditors. The fifth chapter concerns change of parties. The sixth chapter, set-off and merger. The seventh chapter deals with prescription.

The sequence is very similar to that of the PECL, but in the DCFR the general part of obligations is divided between two books: II and III. In the case of the PECL it is only possible to recall the general provisions regarding contracts. Furthermore, in the DCFR, the particular obligations follow the general provisions on obligations. Book IV comprises the specific contracts and the rights and obligations arising from them. After the particular contracts the non-contractual sources of obligations follow, isolated between three books (book V: benevolent intervention into another person's affairs; book VI: non-contractual liability arising from damage caused to another; book VII: unjust enrichment).

The final issue which is mentioned in connection with the DCFR is the systematization of the particular contracts therein. Part A of book IV (on the specific contracts and the rights and obligations arising from them) concerns sales. Part B deals with the lease of goods, and part C looks at services. Among the services the mentioned, the systematic categories are: general provisions (the first chapter), rules applying to service contracts in general (the second chapter), construction (the third chapter), processing (the fourth chapter), storage (the fifth chapter), design (the sixth chapter), information and advice (the seventh chapter) and finally treatment (the eighth chapter). Part D regulates mandate contracts, part E concerns commercial agency, franchise and distributorship, part F covers loan contracts, part G deals with personal security and finally part H with donation.

IX. General considerations on the position of obligations in the system of books of the code

In the Pandect codes researched for this study, only in the German BGB do obligations come directly after the general part[268]. In the most current codes in Central and Eastern Europe[269] obligations come after *ius in re*. The systematization introduced by Gaius in *Institutes* has also inspired legislators in the 21st century. The shift in significance between *ius in re* (*res*) and obligations (*actiones*) did not result in the automatic precedence of obligations before *ius in re* in the structure of the civil codes. In most of the codes, *ius in re* is situated directly after the general part. That is a clear reference to the Gaius scheme, which favours *res* in its composition.

The preference for the Gaius model in the researched material (Czechia – 2012, Hungary – 2013) is possibly related to the experience of socialist private law; feeling the need to stabilize their civil codes, the legislators saw the necessity of the Gaius scheme, sensing that is provided the firmest foundation on which to build material for their civil codes. There are two main bases for structuring civil codes: the Pandect systematization and the Gaius model. Each implementation of socialism is connected with the Pandect structure (or at least some of its features), because socialism in private law is based on introducing the general rules in private law, in this case informed by the legislative ideology. Having experience o fsocialism and of the Pandect model (both issues strongly interact with each other), the Gaius scheme might be considered as the most accessible foundation of civil codes.

Furthermore, the systematization of the law of obligations in the socialist civil codes is almost identical to that of the bourgeois civil codes (Russia – 1922, 1964; Czechoslovakia – 1950; Hungary – 1959; Poland – 1964). The attempts to establish a socialist arrangement of private law in civil codes (Czechoslovakia – 1964, East Germany – 1974) involved modifying prior systematic patterns. The East German arrangement resulted from altering most of the composition of *ius in*

268 Outside the researched jurisdictions obligations are placed immediately after the general part in other legal systems (e.g. Greece – 1940, Portugal – 1966).

Apart from this, in the event of the adoption of a new civil code in Poland, the order of books should be reversed; obligations should be positioned immediately after the general part, in front of *ius in re*. The current shape is inconvenient, because the general part and obligations are divided by *ius in re*, a less frequently used branch of private law.

269 The Russian civil code (1994 – 2006), the Czech civil code (2012), the Hungarian civil code (2013).

re, while the Czechoslovak systematization was connected with negating the law of obligations in its divisions.

C) Composition of the legal concepts in the analyzed codifications

This section discusses the possibilities of arranging the fundamental concepts of obligations in the civil codes. Obligation is at the top of the hierarchy of legal constructs. Contracts are in a subcategory of obligation. What is their relation to the structure of the researched codes? This problem varies between different codifications. This section considers the issue in terms of five divisions. The first involves obligations distinguished in the system of books of a civil code. The second concerns the hierarchy of the legal concepts in codes based on the Gaius model. The third division presents the hierarchy of the legal concepts in the later codifications, containing the law of obligations in a single book. The fourth deals with the Pandect systematization. The fifth and final division refers to the hierarchy of the legal constructs in the socialist civil codes.

I. Obligations identified in the system of the books of a civil code

In most of the researched codifications, obligations is the term applied in exterior divisions[270]. A different hierarchy of concepts is visible in civil codes prior to the typical arrangement, or they result from an attempt to elaborate a new socialist arrangement. Before the most typicalclassification was implemented in the German BGB (1896), the construct of claims was introduced in the Saxon civil code (1863). The third book of the Saxon civil code (including the law of obligations) involves the law of claims. The Saxon arrangement involves a transition between the composition based on the Gaius scheme and the Pandect systematization. In the Saxon codification, the Pandect model is already visible in the code,

[270] In the German BGB (1896), the second book regards the law of obligations.

That is also the construct used in the Swiss Code of obligations (1911), acting as the fifth book of the Swiss civil code (1907).

The fifth book of the Russian draft (1905) considers the law of obligations.

In the first and the second socialist Russian civil code (1922, 1964) the third book deals with the law of obligations.

In the current Russian civil code (1994 – 2006), the third book concerns the general part of obligations and the fourth book comprises the particular kinds of obligations.

In the Hungarian draft (1928), the third book refers to the law of obligations.

In the socialist Hungarian civil code (1959), the fourth book contains the law of obligations.

In the current Hungarian civil code (2013), the sixth book includes the law of obligations.

In the Polish Code of obligations (1933), the term obligation is visible in its title.

In the Polish civil code (1964), the third book considers obligations.

In the first socialist Czechoslovak civil code (1950), the fourth book comprises the law of obligations.

In the current Czech civil code (2012), the fourth book applies to the relative property rights. Those are obligations.

but the third book considers the law of claims instead of the law of obligations. In the general part of the Saxon civil code an equivalent of *actiones* is (legal) actions (*Handlundgen*) instead of juridical acts. The third component of the Gaius scheme in the Saxon civil code (*Handlungen*) considers only the substantive private law, but for readers this term is associated with all actions that an individual can take in private law, which obviously results in court proceedings. For this reason, a new construct needed to be applied. As a result, in the German BGB (1896) juridical acts (concerning only substantive private law) constitute the third element (*actiones*) in the systematization of the general part.

The analysis in this section concentrates on the Pandect model and the codes isolating the law of obligations in their divisions. The centre of gravity of the deliberations belongs to the differences in the systematization of the civil codes. First, in the context of the earlier codifications that enabled the most typical arrangement to be elaborated, and second, in reference to the civil codes that modified the most typicalcomposition. In the area of the law of obligations socialist legislators prefer to keep the traditional arrangement. The new systematic patterns adopted for the law of obligations in the socialist codifications were primarily connected with national preferences, and sometimes with local socialist "inventions".

II. Hierarchy of the legal concepts in the codes based on the Gaius model

This section begins by analyzing the hierarchy of the legal concepts is in the codes that follow the Gaius model: the CMBC (1756), the CC (1804) and the ABGB (1811). Their common feature is that they dedicate considerable attention to the law of contracts[271]. In the CMBC and the CC, obligations are placed in one book[272], whereas in the ABGB (1811) they are in two books[273]. In the CMBC (1756) a central construct is an obligation[274]. In the ABGB (1811), personal rights occupy a key position, but this term is evidently associated with obligations[275]. Both the CMBC (1756) and the ABGB (1811) directly contributed later standards, in which an obligation is the primary component in the system of the civil codes. The CC (1804) was also an indirect inspiration – it was a legal experiment that attempted to insert the agreement (*convention*) of the parties in the system of the law of obligations.

---

[271] In the systematization of the CMBC (1756) contracts prevail; among eighteen chapters of the fourth book (concerning obligations) the first twelve chapters refer to contracts.

In the fourth book on obligations there are contracts, therefrom arising duties in general (the first chapter); nominate contracts *(benannten Vertragen)* and contracts which come by means of actual delivery of a thing (the second chapter); consensual contracts, in particular sale (the third chapter); particular (kinds of) sales (the fourth chapter); entry (the fifth chapter); lease and tenancy (the sixth chapter); emphytheusis and superficies (the seventh chapter); partnership (the eighth chapter); mandate and power of attorney (the ninth chapter); guarantee (the tenth chapter); literal contracts (*von Literal-Verträgen*; the eleventh chapter); innominate contracts (*von unbenannten Verträgen*; the twelfth chapter).

The thirteenth chapter involves the claims similar to contracts *(Quasi-Verträge)*. The fourteenth and fifteenth chapters refer to obligations (the fourteenth chapter: performance of obligations, particularly payment; the fifteenth chapter: other kinds of cancellation of obligations).

Afterwards there are non-contractual sources of obligations – the sixteenth chapter mentions the claims arising from offenses and seventeenth chapter defamation.

The systematization of the CC (1804) becomes clear after reading on the composition of the legal concepts in the CC.

In the ABGB (1811), regulations of the general part of obligations are included in the seventeenth chapter (the second book on *ius rerum*, the second division regarding personal rights) considering contracts in general (§§ 859 – 937). The first four provisions of the seventeenth chapter (§§ 859 – 862) refer to the sources of personal rights (obligations). Subsequently, provisions (§§ 863 – 937) contain general precepts relevant to agreements. The next chapters (from eighteenth to twenty-ninth; §§ 938 – 1292) include different kinds of contracts. After them in the thirty-first chapter regulation of law of damages is contained (§§ 1293 – 1341).

[272] In the CMBC (1756) that is the last fourth book concerning the law of obligations *(Obligationen-Recht)*.

In the CC (1804), this is the third book comprising different ways of acquiring ownership.

[273] In the ABGB obligations are arranged in the second division (regarding personal rights/ *von den persönlichen Sachenrechten)* of the second book on *ius rerum*. Besides some provisions of obligations are put in the last third book, including the provisions common to personal rights and *ius in re*; this systematic choice does not affect the arrangement of the legal concepts in the ABGB – that is an additional issue.

In the ABGB the first chapter (of the third book) concerns the security of rights and obligations. The second chapter: modification of rights and obligations. The third chapter: cancellation of rights and obligations. The fourth chapter: prescription and usucaption.

[274] In the CMBC (1756) the fourth book includes the law of obligations.

[275] In the ABGB (1811), the second division (of the second book on *ius rerum*) comprises the personal rights.

The most interesting rule in the composition of the codes established according to the Gaius scheme is that even though an obligation is visible in their divisions[276], contracts prevail in their systems. For the lawyers, as for us, it was clear that an obligation is the highest construct in the hierarchy of legal concepts, but contracts constitute the majority of obligations. In later codes an obligation is most likely to be a main construct, and a contract is usually a systematic subset of an obligation. Before we proceed to further discussion, this section outlines the composition in the CC (1804) and then in the ABGB (1811). The CMBC (1756) does not require a distinct division; all that significant to note here regarding the composition of its legal concepts is included in the references.

1. French *Code civil* (1804)

The CC content relevant to obligations begins with the third title of the third book (of contracts and of conventional obligations in general[277]). Contracts and obligations in which the common agreement (*convention*) of the parties is required come first. In the third title, constituting the heart of the French law of obligations, the term "obligation" is applied consistently[278]. The fourth title of the third book considers commitments formed without an agreement (*des engagements qui se forment sans convention*). The third title of the third book includes more than 250 provisions (Articles 1101 – 1369). The fourth title of the third book contains two chapters. In the first chapter quasi-contracts are established (Articles 1371 – 1381), with unlawful acts appearing in the second[279] (Articles 1382 – 1386). The fourth title is very short in comparison to the third title.

As a result, an obligation referred to in the French structure differs significantly from an obligation in the sense belonging to the neutral Pandect systematization[280]. The French system is based on duality: is an obligation based on the agreement of the parties (*convention*) or not? This perspective was crucial, because it intersected with the ideals of the French Revolution, where the freedom of

---

[276] In the CMBC (1756) the fourth book considers the law of obligations and in the ABGB (1811) there are personal rights (title of the second division of the second book on *ius rerum*).

In the CC (1804), the third title (of the third book on different ways of acquiring ownership) comprises contracts and conventional obligations in general, whereas the fourth title contains the commitments formed without an agreement.

[277] *Des contrats ou des obligations conventionnelles en général.*

[278] In the CC (1804), the first chapter (of the third title of the third book) includes the preliminary provisions. The second chapter: essential requirements for the validity of agreements. The third chapter: effect of obligations. The fourth chapter: various kinds of obligations. The fifth chapter: extinction of obligations. The sixth chapter: proof of obligations and payment.

[279] *Des délits et des quasi-délits.*

[280] About the French systematization also here:

De Vincelles C. A., *France: Position of the Law of Obligations in National and Supra national Law*, in: Schulze R., Zoll F. (ed.), *The Law of Obligations in Europe. A New Wave of Codifications*, Munich 2013, p. 322 and p. 324.

an individual (for both ownership and contracts) was the foundation of the new concepts introduced in the CC. Even though an obligation is visible in the original structure of the CC, it is an obligation based on the agreement of the parties: *une obligation conventionnelle*. The first provision of the third title (on contracts and conventional obligations in general) comprises the notion of a contract[281]. As a result, the French law of obligations is concentrated on a contract, but perceived differently from other codifications[282].

The hierarchy of the legal constructs in the CC is just as the titles imply: contracts and conventional obligations in general come first (the third title of the third book, on different ways of acquiring ownership). French legislative ideology enforced the necessity to seek agreement, because freedom of contract is the issue of the utmost importance. The French classification is not founded on the question of whether an obligation arises from a contract or not. The main problem is: "Is there an agreement of the parties?". If yes, then it is a contract or a conventional obligation. If not, then there is the fourth title (of the third book on different ways of acquiring ownership), regarding commitments formed without an agreement.

The most accurate question might be: "Couldn't the French hierarchy of the legal constructs be different?" No, it could not. Although being an excellent legislative accomplishment, the CC is impacted by state ideology. In this aspect it resembles the socialist civil codes. Written laws ruled by a state ideology cannot be fully objective and neutral, because the system needs to favour the rights of a particular subject. In the CC, this is an individual, whereas in the socialist civil codes it is the state. The French arrangement of the law of contracts was amended in the 2016reform. Now, contracts prevail among the sources of obligations, and they are followed by provisions relating to obligations[283].

2. ABGB (1811)

The term personal rights (obligations) is applied in the exterior divisions of the ABGB. This is the title of the second division of the second book on *ius rerum*. In the ABGB, the concept of an agreement is clearly favoured; the seventeenth chapter, referring to contracts in general, uses the construct of a contract. The

---

[281] The impact of the definition of a contract elaborated by the French pre-revolutionary scholar Robert-Joseph Pothier is worth mentioning.

KÖTZ H., *Europäisches Vertragsrecht. Band I: Abschluß, Gültigkeit und Inhalt des Vertrages. Die Beteiligung Dritter am Vertrag*, Tübingen 1996, p. 3 and the following pages.

[282] *Article 1101 Le contrat est un accord de volontés entre deux ou plusieurs personnes destiné à créer, modifier, transmettre ou éteindre des obligations.*

[283] In the CC after the reform of 2016 the third title (of the third book on different ways of acquiring ownership) deals with the sources of obligations. The sources of obligations include contracts (the first sub-title), extra-contractual liability (the second sub-title) and other sources of obligations (the third sub-title).

The fourth title considers the general regime of obligations.

particular contracts follow, and then the non-contractual sources of obligations[284]. Furthermore, the third book comprising the provisions on common personal rights and *ius in re* applies a very wide construct: rights and obligations[285].

After over 200 years of its existence, the ABGB requires reform, but legal scholars have already adapted the arrangement of the code to the legal concepts applied by legal science. For this reason, currently the seventeenth chapter (the second book on *ius rerum*, the second division on personal rights) concerns contracts and juridical acts in general; the original version of the code contained no reference to juridical acts[286]. Atthe time of the ABGB's adoption, the construct of juridical acts was not sufficiently elaborated to be implemented in the legislation[287]. Contrary to the CC, the hierarchy of the legal constructs in the ABGB following its adoption was objective and neutral. There are obligations (personal rights), which are mentioned in the divisions of the second book on *ius rerum*. The second division of the second book considers personal rights. The idea of a contract is clearly visible in the original Austrian structure. The seventeenth chapter concerns contracts in general, followed by the particular contracts and then non-contractual sources of obligations.

III. Hierarchy of the legal concepts in the later codes containing obligations in a single area

This section explores the arrangement of the legal concepts in the later codes in which obligations are located in a single area. Contrary to the codes that include a general part, here the entire "action" takes place in one area. The systematic options are considered from four angles in this section. First, the arrangement in which an obligation is a central construct and a contract is a systematic subset of obligations. Second, the systematization in which both obligations and contracts are extracted in the civil codes is analyzed. Further systematic possibilities are subsequently mentioned, with reference to the Hungarian systematization. Finally, I draw conclusions from the examination.

284 Chapters 18 – 29 include the particular contracts. Chapter 20 deals with the right to damages and compensation.

285 In the ABGB (1811), the first chapter (of the third book) considers the security for rights and obligations *(Rechte und Verbindlichkeiten)*. The second chapter: modification of rights and obligations. The third chapter: cancellation of rights and obligations. The fourth chapter: prescription and usucaption.

286 More in: Stagl F.J., *Die Rezeption der Lehre vom Rechtsgeschäft in Österreich durch Joseph Unger*, Zeitschrift für Europäisches Privatrecht 2007, pp. 37 – 55.

287 *Conf.* Posch W., *Grundzüge fremder Privatrechtssysteme*, Wien/ Köln/ Graz 1995, p. 34.

1. Obligation as a central construct, contract as a systematic subcategory of obligations

In the first systematization, an obligation is a central concept and the main construct visible in the table of contents[288]. Contract is a systematic subset of the law of obligations[289]. This composition can be found in, for instance, the Polish Code of obligations (1933).

2. Isolating both obligations and contracts

The second opportunity is to extract two systematic areas: obligations and contracts. This structure is a compromise between the most neutral composition (in which an obligation dominates and a contract is a subset of the law of obligations) and the arrangement deriving from the codes based on the Gaius model (where a contract is the most significant factor in the structure of the law of obligations). If a legislator focuses more attention on obligations, then they are placed before contracts. This systematization is visible in the current Hungarian civil code[290] (2013). In the Hungarian arrangement both obligations and contracts are crucial, but an obligation precedes a contract. A general part was never introduced in Hungary.

In the CC, following the reform of 2016, agreements are arranged first (being the first possible source of obligations) and then obligations[291]. In the French structure two tendencies are present. The first is the attachment to a contract, the foundation of the CC. The second inclination is the need to objectivize the system of the CC[292]. Even though an obligation prevails in the titles of the code, the constructs are established in such a way that a contract potentially receives the most attention. This shows the impact of the original French arrangement, where the third title (of the third book, on different ways of acquiring ownership) conside-

---

[288] In the Polish Code of obligations (1933), the first title considers the sources, the substance and the kinds of obligations. The second title deals with the formation of obligations. The third title regulates the transfer of rights and duties (*obowiązków*), arising from obligations. The fourth title concerns the expiration of obligations.

[289] In the Polish Code of obligations, the second title concerns the formation of obligations. The first division of the second title contains the declaration of will. The fourth chapter (of the first division) deals with contracts in general.

[290] The first systematic division of the sixth book (referring to the law of obligations) of the current Hungarian civil code (2013) regards the common provisions relating to obligations and the second division concerns the general provisions on contracts.

[291] In the CC after the reform in 2016 the third title (of the third book on different ways of acquiring ownership) contains the sources of obligations. Among the sources of obligations there are contract (the first sub-title), extra-contractual liability (the second sub-title) and other sources of obligations (the third sub-title).

The fourth title regulates the general regime of obligations.

[292] The CC (1804) is founded on subjective criteria. These are ownership (the second book: goods and different ways of modifying ownership, the third book: different ways of acquiring ownership) and agreement of the parties *(convention)*, the main determinant of the law of obligations in France.

red contracts and conventional obligations in general. Following the reform, the first provision of the third title now contains the definition of a contract[293]. The system of the CC is still based on a contract.

3. Subsequent systematic possibilities with reference to the Hungarian systematization and to contract in Soviet Russian legal science

The Hungarian development needs to be mentioned separately, because in Hungary a general part was never introduced. This section considers the Hungarian draft (1928), the socialist Hungarian civil code (1959) and the current Hungarian civil code (2013).

a) Contract in the Hungarian systematization

The socialist Hungarian civil code (1959) is centred on contract. In the divisions of the socialist Hungarian civil code (1959) and the East German civil code (1975) the contract prevails. In Hungary an obligation is a term visible in the exterior divisions of the codes[294], but the Hungarian system always places preference on contract[295]. Both in the Hungarian draft (1928) and in the socialist Hungarian civil code (1959) agreements are the most visible systematic factors in the structure of the law of obligations[296].

---

[293] *Article 1101 Le contrat est un accord de volontés entre deux ou plusieurs personnes destiné à créer, modifier, transmettre ou éteindre des obligations.*

[294] In the Hungarian draft (1928), the third book regards the law of obligations.
In the socialist Hungarian civil code (1959), the fourth book includes the law of obligations.
In the current Hungarian civil code (2013), the sixth book considers the law of obligations.

[295] In the Hungarian draft (1928), the third book concerns obligations.
The first title of the third book, containing a significant amount of the general part of obligations, refers to agreements. Subsequently, two titles of the third book refer to a wider construct – an obligation. The second title (of the third book) deals with the content of obligations, whereas the third title includes multi-party obligations. The fourth title contains the transition of claims and obligations, whereas the fifth and final title of the general part of obligations considers expiration and prescription of claims.
In the socialist Hungarian civil code (1959) the fourth book comprises the law of obligations. The first title of the fourth book considers agreements – that is the general part of the law of obligations. The second title of the fourth book includes responsibility for damage caused out of contract and for unjust enrichment. The last third title of the fourth book comprises various contracts.
In the current Hungarian civil code (2013), in the sixth book on obligations the first division refers to common provisions relating to obligations. The second division of the sixth book includes general provisions on contracts. The first two divisions constitute the general part of obligations.
The third division of the sixth book contains particular contracts (designated as express contracts).

[296] There is a difference in the arrangement of both Hungarian codes.
In the socialist Hungarian civil code (1959), the fourth book refers to obligations, but in the divisions of the general part of obligations the concept of a contract is applied – the first title (of the fourth book on obligations) regulates agreements. Here the whole content of the general part

In the Hungarian draft (1928), the gradation of the legal constructs is applied. The first visible legal construct are agreements, followed by obligations, and finally by claims and obligations[297]. This resolution is a neat compromise between the composition based on the Gaius model and the Pandect systematization. In the socialist Hungarian civil code (1959), a contract is the only concept applied in the table of contents of the general part of obligations[298]. According to the Hungarian lawyers, "a contract is an extensive and flexible legal form, able to regulate various legal relationships, differing from each other by their content" (*Der Vertrag ist eine umfassende und elastische Rechtsform, die sich zur Regelung inhaltlich verschiedenster Verhältnisse eignet*)[299]. In Hungary the unity of a civil code was chosen. A civil code (and a contract) was used as a legal instrument for implementing the socialist economy[300]. As the units of the nationalized economy conclude agreements, as an outcome of the socialist plan, then a contract gains new relevance and justification in the structure of the socialist Hungarian civil code. A contract and ownership are particularly traditional concepts, which appeal to people and are consistent with their thinking habits. The natural constructs can also perform their function successfuly in the system of a socialist civil code[301]. This shows the adaptability of ownership and contract to the different conditions and times.

The fourth book of the socialist Hungarian civil code (1959) refers to the law of obligations. The fourth book includes three titles. The first title is contract. The second title, responsibility for damage caused out of contract and for unjust enrichment. The third title concerns various contracts. This structure is grounded

---

of obligations is settled.

In the Hungarian draft (1928) an agreement is preferred [the first title (of the third book on obligations) considers agreements], but further in the table of contents an obligation is visible [the second title (of the third book on obligations) deals with the content of obligations, whereas the third title refers to multi-party obligations].

[297] In the Hungarian draft (1928), the first title (of the third book on obligations) considers agreements. The second title: content of obligations. The third title: multi-party obligations. The fourth title: transition of claims and obligations. The fifth title: expiration and prescription of claims.

[298] In the socialist Hungarian civil code (1959), the first title (of the fourth book on obligations) considers contracts. In this title there is the entire volume of the general part of obligations. Chapter 17: general rules. Chapter 18: the making of a contract. Chapter 19: representation. Chapter 20: contents and objects of the contract. Chapter 21: voidness and voidableness. Chapter 22: modification of contract and acknowledgement of debt. Chapter 23: collateral obligations securing the contract. Chapter 24: performance and set-off. Chapter 25: breach of contract. Chapter 26: particular cases of termination of contract and prescription. Chapter 27: assignment and assumption of debt. Chapter 28: several obligees or several obligors in the contract.

[299] KEMENES B., *Die prinzipiellen Grundlagen des Vertragsystems im Ungarischen Zivilgesetzbuch*, in: EÖRSI G., *Das ungarische Zivilgesetzbuch in fünf Studien*, Budapest 1963, p. 188.

[300] *Ibidem*, p. 188.

[301] *Ibidem*, p. 188.

in Hungarian legal science, which states that contract and responsibility (*Verantwortlichkeit*) are the most significant segments of the law of obligations. A contract settles the exchange of goods in a socialist society, whereas responsibility regulates what does not arise from contract[302]. The third title (of the fourth book on obligations) contains various contracts.

Those are the most relevant elements of the structure of the socialist Hungarian civil code (1959). We should also consider the grounds for such an arrangement. First, a contract is the most important systematic segment in the law of obligations in codes based on the Gaius model, and the Hungarians are strongly inspired by the ABGB (1811). Second, such a viewpoint was already present in the systematization of the Hungarian draft (1928), where the first title (of the third book on obligations) contains the most significant volume of the law of obligations. The Hungarians needed to simplify the previous structure. By this point the gradation of legal concepts (contracts, obligations, claims) was no longer relevant. The Soviet impact must have enforced the full separation of substantive private law from civil procedure. It is more effevtive to use more basic legal forms when implementing socialism. A contract is the best fit here, acting as a compromise between the Hungarian tradition and the new legislative philosophy. Furthermore, Soviet Russian legal science did not contradict the concept of a contract, and has appreciated its utility for the socialist economy[303]. Eliminating *ius in re* from the civil code is possible by replacing it with *ius in re*, but I cannot recall any successful (!) attempts to reformulate a contract. Simultaneously, the Russians themselves were primarily inspired by German legal science, because even before the October Revolution they had adopted the Pandect model in the structure of the pre-revolutionary Russian draft of a civil code (1905).

In the socialist Hungarian civil code (1959), there are: introductory provisions – persons – right of ownership – law of obligations – inheritance law – final provisions. After the elimination of additional books we have: persons – right of ownership – law of obligations – inheritance law. As there is no family law, the Gaius scheme visible in the Hungarian code is weakened. This can be discerned in the categories of: persons (*personae*) – right of ownership (*res*) – law of obligations/contracts (*actiones*). In the Hungarian systematization, law of succession is classified among *actiones*.

The next problem to consider is the arrangement of the first title (regarding contracts) of the fourth book (obligations) of the socialist Hungarian civil code (1959). Chapter 17 opens the first title, and includes the general rules. In the first provision of the title (§ 198) there is no mention of an obligation; instead, it refers to a contract. The eighteenth chapter involves the formation of a contract. If we

[302] *Ibidem*, p. 217.

[303] More in: CHAŁFINA R. O., *Znaczenie i istota umowy w radzieckim prawie cywilnym* [Significance and substance of contract in Soviet private law], Warszawa 1956.

consider the system of private law based on the idea of a contract, then the conception of an agreement comes first. Chapter 19 deals with representation – that is, an institution enabling another person to take actions on our behalf. Subsequently, the "details" follow – chapter 20 considers the contents and object of a contract. Chapter 21:voidness and voidableness. Chapter 22: modification of contract and acknowledgement of debt. Chapter 23 includes the collateral obligations securing the contract. Such a systematic categorization is typical of socialist civil codes. Gradually we approach the end of the life of a contract. A contract can be terminated by its performance or set-off. That is the title of the twenty-fourth chapter. Chapter 25 concerns breach of contract. Chapter 26, particular cases of termination of contract and prescription. Chapter 27 addresses assignment and assumption of debt. Chapter 28 deals with several obligees or several obligors in the contract. What is clear after looking at the divisions of the title on contracts of the socialist Hungarian civil code (1959) is that chronology is a crucial systematic factor, and a natural way of arranging a civil code. Furthermore, a contract appears repeatedly in the table of contents of the written law.

Having examined the socialist Hungarian civil code (1959), we move to analyzing the relation of an obligation and contract in the current Hungarian civil code (2013); obligations come first and then agreements[304]. Both systematic patterns vary from the arrangement in the Hungarian draft (1928). In the socialist Hungarian code, contracts dominate the entire arrangement of the general part of obligations, almost displacing obligations. In the current Hungarian civil code, the composition is different – evidently, the construction of an obligation comes before a contract.

b) Soviet Russian literature on contracts

The role of contracts in Hungary can be further understood with reference to the position of Soviet Russian legal science regarding contracts. Soviet legal literature was distributed to socialist jurisdictions in Central and Eastern Europe. In the socialist economy there are multiple relationships between the units of the nationalized economy. They include the immense enterprises and the legal persons that serve the purposes of the state. State enterprises execute the socialist plan. Socialist planning forms the basis of the socialist economy and of the operation of the entire society. People were also impacted by the goals of the state in their work. The relationships between the units of the nationalized economy required a legal form appropriate to their demands, for which purpose a contract was chosen. "Achieving this purpose – implementing the national economic plan – is connected in the Soviet state with the principle of economic balance, as the me-

304 The first systematic division of the sixth book (referring to the law of obligations) of the current Hungarian civil code (2013) regards the common provisions relating to obligations and the second division concerns the general provisions on contracts.

thod of the operation of the state enterprises, and the measure of conjoining the planning principle with the principle of the economic balance, is obviously a contract"[305]. Furthermore, "a contract is a fundamental legal form, by means of which the relationships in terms of production and the exchange of goods and services are performed in the USSR"[306]. "In this way a contract constitutes a fundamental legal form of the relationships between socialist organizations"[307].

Arguments were even put forward that a contract is a measure of the realization of a scheduled task, that a contract assists in controlling planning or that it forms a very flexible and comprehensive system of the mutual control of socialist organizations[308]. In the socialist reality a contract was indispensable, just as in any other society and economy. The significant agreements from the economic point of view were concluded between the units of the nationalized economy (state-owned enterprises)[309]. The deliberations included here are crucial to comprehending fully our discussion on the socialist civil codes (the section concerning freedom of contract in the structure of the civil codes). As a result, the socialist civil codes (Hungary – 1959, East Germany – 1975) could be founded on a contract.

c) Some considerations on the Hungarian systematization

In the current Hungarian code, an inspiration with the general part can be discerned; the institutions placed at the beginning of the book on obligations are the elements usually transferred to the general part[310]. The contracts are situated after it. In the first division (including the common provisions relating to obligations) the systematic compounds applying to all obligations are placed. An obligation consequently dominates the systematization of the general part of obligations. Although the most significant volume of the law of obligations is established in the second division (of the sixth book, on obligations), containing the general provi-

---

305 NOWICKI I. B., ŁUNC Ł. A., *Ogólna nauka o zobowiązaniach* [The general science of the law of obligations], Warszawa 1954, p. 104.

306 CHAŁFINA R. O., *Znaczenie i istota umowy w radzieckim prawie cywilnym* [Significance and substance of contract in Soviet private law], Warszawa 1956, p. 6.

307 *Ibidem*, p. 18.

308 *Ibidem*, pp. 18 – 22.

309 In socialist legal systems citizens were not allowed to own the means of production (e.g. land). Their right of ownership was restricted to the means of consumption. That automatically reduces the scope of contracts that citizens in socialist legal systems concluded.

310 In the current Hungarian civil code (2013), the first division (of the sixth book on obligations) contains the common provisions relating to obligations. The first title (including the general provisions) includes: obligation (the first chapter), legal statements (the second chapter), representation (the third chapter), statute of limitations (the fourth chapter) and acknowledgement of debt as well as the composition (the fifth chapter).

The volume in the second, third and fourth chapters constitute the systematic compounds classified usually into the general part.

The second title (of the first division) regards the multi-party obligations. The third title: settlement of an obligation.

sions on contracts, an obligation is so tightly interwoven that a contract is unable to displace it. After all, the first chapter of the sixth book concerns an obligation.

In the Hungarian composition, contracts never act as a subset of obligations. They are at least an equal element. Furthermore, in the current Hungarian civil code the size of the volume arranged in the division on contracts asserts contracts asa factor even in relevance to an obligation. Even though obligations are settled before contracts, the hierarchy is introduced in a very harmonious way, reconciling the tendencies deriving from the systematization based on the Gaius scheme and the German Pandect model. The structure of the current Hungarian civil code (2013) is much more neutral than in the socialist Hungarian civil code (1959) or the Hungarian draft (1928). If the system is based on a contract, then the legal science attributes the features of contracts to other institutions of the law of obligations[311]. That could be one of the reasons why, over the course of time, the most predominant resolution became found ing the system of a civil code on an obligation.

The final issue which must be mentioned regarding the Hungarian systematization is that the arrangement of the legal constructs in the socialist Hungarian code (1959) resembles the Austrian structure, where obligations (personal rights) are the central construct, but where contracts dominate the arrangement of the general part of obligations.

IV. Conclusions drawn from the study of the arrangement of the legal constructs in codifications that include the entire volume of the law of obligations in a single book

In a civil code with the book on obligations (and which is outside the general part) there are more opportunities for arranging the legal concepts. They can be used by legislators who seek a balance between the traditional arrangement in which a contract prevails and the neutral Pandect systematization, which introduced an obligation. That is evident in France and Hungary. If a legislator preserves the typical systematization of a civil code, then there is a space for some creativity. Such an arrangement suits both a bourgeois and a socialist civil code, but an abstract general part incorporates socialist ideas into the system of private law more efficiently.

V. Pandect systematization

The next area discussed is the Pandect systematization. The issues examined in this part of the analysis result from arranging the content of the law of obligations from the most general to the most specific. Contrary to the Austrian composition, the arrangement of the legal constructs in the Pandect model is not horizontal, but

[311] BETTI E., *Système du code civil allemand*, Milano 1965, p. 63.

vertical. Evidently in Austria "personal rights" are higher in the hierarchy of the legal concepts than contracts, but the Austrian composition has only two levels. This strict priority became a feature of the Pandect systematization. The Pandect arrangement has more levels of generality. They are: juridical acts – contracts – general part of obligations – particular obligations. That is the arrangement in the German BGB (1896), but the number of levels may be reduced if there are no provisions on contracts in the code (e.g. in the current Russian civil code 1994–2006). In the German BGB, the provisions on contracts in the general part are a systematic subset of juridical acts[312].

Why do I identify four levels of generality? In applying the provisions of the law of obligations in the German BGB, we must search for the relevant provisions in four places. For instance, if we conclude a sales contract, then we primarily apply the provisions referring to sales, found among the particular obligations. If the problem we must deal with is not addressed there, then we need to move onto the more general provisions. Those are the provisions of the general part of obligations. In the same way we can proceed to two more areas: provisions on contract settled in the general part and then the provisions on juridical acts.

After this short introduction, it is necessary to list the issues examined in the division concerning the Pandect systematization. First, the study addresses the composition of the legal constructs in the Prussian *Landrecht* (1794). The first subdivision shows that the Pandect systematization derives from Prussia; the arrangement of the legal concepts in the Prussian *Landrecht* is discussed. The analysis subsequently considers the hierarchy of the legal concepts in codes that include a general part and their impact on other codifications; the general constructs related to the law of obligations and integrated into the general part constitute the legal rules of the greatest systematic significance from the point of view of the law of obligations. The second subdivision examines the arrangement of the legal concepts in the general part. The third subdivision deals with the significance of juridical acts in the Pandect systematization. Furthermore, is a juridical act exclusive to civil codes that include a general part (the fourth subdivision)? A juridical act is an expression of the declarations of will of individuals; for this reason, the composition of the declaration of will in the codifications analyzed is verified (the fifth subdivision). Finally, the analysis concludes with the systematization of the legal concepts in a book containing the law of obligations (the sixth subdivision).

1. Prussian *Landrecht* (1794)

In the Prussian *Landrecht* all actions that an individual can take are settled first, followed by declarations of will and agreements[313]. The constructs are graded from

---

[312] In the German BGB (1896), the third chapter of the general part deals with juridical acts. The third title (of the third chapter) concerns contract.

[313] In the Prussian *Landrecht* (1794) the third title (of the first part) considers all legal actions that

the most general to the most specific. An obligation is not visible in the Prussian structure, being displaced by *res* and ownership, which appear multiple times in its divisions[314]. The Prussian *Landrecht* provides a model for later codifications in arranging a general part, particularly in terms of settling the legal constructs. As regards the composition of the concepts in the general part of obligations, it seems that the ABGB provided the most significant formula.

2. Arrangement of the legal concepts in the general part

In codes including a general part, the Gaius scheme is introduced at the beginning of the general part. The third element of the scheme are *actiones*, representing the dynamic element in private law. The arrangement of the legal constructs in the general part was inspired by the Prussian *Landrecht* (1794). In the Prussian *Landrecht* and in the Saxon civil code (1863), which was the first codification to include a general part, an equivalent of *actiones* in the Gaius scheme (introduced in the opening of the code) are actions that an individual might take in private law (*Handlungen*); concurrently, in Saxony juridical acts are a systematic subset of actions[315].

Evidently juridical acts are a systematic subset of actions, because the actions of individuals in the substantive private law (juridical acts) can be contained among the actions (applying also to the civil procedure). The problem that arises is how to differentiate the substantive private law from the civil procedure. If such a distinction is included with in the civil codes, then accordingly the idea of the actions of individuals must be excluded from the civil codes, because the civil codes consider only the substantive private law. The juridical act dominates the arrangement of the general part and the Pandect systematization – in the general part of BGB juridical acts are equivalent to *actiones*[316]. The juridical act became a hallmark of German systematization and was later implemented in other codes that included a general part[317].

---

can be taken by an individual *(von Handlungen und den daraus enstehenden Rechten)*. The fourth title considers declarations of will and the fifth title agreements.

[314] This issue becomes clear after reading the description of the Prussian systematization in the chapter on *ius in re*.

[315] In the Saxon civil code (1863), both actions and juridical acts are present in the structure of the general part. The fourth division of the general part includes actions. The third subsection (of the fourth division) concerns juridical acts.

[316] In the German BGB (1896), the third chapter (of the general part) considers juridical acts.

[317] This systematization was transposed to Czechia (1950, 1964, 2012), Poland (1964) and Russia (1905, 1922, 1964, 1994 – 2006).

In the Russian draft (1905), the third division (of the general part) considers acquisition and loss of rights. The second division includes things. Juridical acts are mentioned in the third division.

VON SEELER W., *Der Entwurf des Russischen Zivilgesetzbuches*, Berlin 1911, p. 22.

Before moving on to the composition of the legal concepts in the book on obligations (in the codifications comprising a general part), the analysis addresses the arrangement of juridical acts and the declaration of will in the researched codifications, regardless of whether they contain a general part or not. A juridical act functions like a bridge between the general part and the law of obligations. This is a concept around which obligations are arranged in the general part. The provisions on contracts can be arranged among the provisions on juridical acts[318], but in many codifications there are no provisions on agreements in the general part[319].

3. The significance of juridical acts in the Pandect systematization (the German BGB – 1896)

This section discusses the significance of juridical acts in civil codes including a general part. A juridical act is an expression of the legislative consequences of the declarations of will (*Willenserklärung*). Juridical acts gather all results of declarations of will in a single place. That is the framework around which the general part and the Pandect scheme are arranged. A juridical act encompasses both unilateral legal actions and contracts; a juridical act is an equivalent of Gaian *actiones* in the general part. Thanks to this, it is possible to enclose provisions on contracts in the general part, because they act as a systematic subdivision of juridical acts. A juridical act enables a hierarchy of concepts to be established in a civil code. A construct wider than an obligation can hold a significant amount of private law in the general part. Juridical acts provide a grounding for the further institutions of the law of obligations in the general part. A condition might be introduced into a contract; it is also possible to appoint a proxy representing our

---

In the first socialist Russian civil code (1922), the fourth chapter of the general part refers to juridical acts.

In the second socialist Russian civil code (1964), the third chapter of the general part concerns juridical acts.

In the current Russian civil code (1994 – 2006), the fourth subsection of the general part regards deals [juridical acts] and representation.

In the first socialist Czechoslovak civil code (1950), the third chapter of the general part includes juridical acts.

In the second socialist Czechoslovak civil code (1964), the fourth division of the general part considers juridical acts.

In the current Czech civil code (2012), the fifth title of the general part deals with legal facts. The first chapter of the fifth title contains juridical acts.

In the (socialist) Polish civil code (1964) the fourth title of the general part comprises juridical acts.

318 In the German BGB (1896), the third chapter of the general part concerns juridical acts. The third title (of the third chapter) considers contract.

In the Polish civil code (1964), the fourth title of the general part regards juridical acts. The second division (of the fourth title) approaches the conclusion of contract.

319 E.g. this arrangement is typical for the Russian civil codes (1922, 1964, 1994 – 2006).

interests. Those institutions act as an extension of obligations in the general part. They also apply simultaneously to other branches of private law.

There are three fundamental constructs in the general part: *personae – res – actiones* (persons – things – juridical acts). This sequence replicates the order elaborated by Gaius in *Institutes*, where *actiones* (now termed juridical acts, their equivalent) are the last systematic factor among *personae – res – actiones*. Contrary to a person and a thing, a juridical act is an artificial construct[320]. Nonetheless, from the point of view of arranging a civil code, a juridical act is the most important among the components of the Gaius scheme, because it maintains the Pandect model and assures the connection of the general part with the law of obligations. A juridical act constitutes a junction between the lawful acts and the consequences resulting from them. Juridical acts are a concept useful not only for the general part and obligations, but also all other branches of private law – they can also be found in the area of *ius in re*, family law and inheritance law[321].

The law of obligations may be arranged directly after the general part (e.g. Germany – 1896), after the general part and the book on *ius in re* (e.g. Poland – 1964), or in the last book of the code (e.g. Czechia – 2012), but that does not significantly impact the arrangement of the written law. Placing the law of obligations immediately after the general part results in the strongest relation between the general part and the law of obligations. Nonetheless, the Pandect systematization provides such a strong building material for a civil code that without any great detriment to the system of a civil code the law of obligations can be settled in different areas of the civil code. The juridical act supports the entire structure of a civil code, holding the whole system of the written law and the law of obligations. In the codes that do not include a general part and which extract the law of obligations in their divisions (Switzerland, Hungary) the only possibility is to put the law of obligations at the end of the civil code or near its end[322]. The superstructure of the Pandect model results in opportunities to modify the law of obligations, such as those evident in the last socialist civil codes that address the needs of citizens in their structure (Czechoslovakia – 1964, East Germany – 1975).

4. Is a juridical act exclusive to civil codes that include a general part?

Juridical acts have also proved to be useful for jurisdictions where there is no general part. This study is restricted to a few examples. Due to the impact of German

---

[320] SCHERMAIER M.J., *vor §§ 104. Das Rechtsgeschäft*, in: SCHMOECKEL M. (ed.), *Historisch-kritischer Kommentar zum BGB. Band I Allgemeiner Teil §§ 1 – 240*, Tübingen 2003, p. 355.

[321] MEDICUS D., *Schuldrecht I. Allgemeiner Teil*, München 2006, p. 24.

[322] The arrangement in both jurisdictions is thoroughly portrayed among the obligations in the external divisions of the researched civil codes. In a code that does not contain a general part, the Gaius model is applied in its structure. The sequence of elements is *personae – res – actiones*; as *actiones* are associated with the law of obligations, then obligations are settled at the end of a written law.

legal science, juridical acts were implemented in the ABGB[323] (1811). A reference to unilateral legal actions is visible in the CC (1804), after its reform of the law of contracts and obligations in 2016[324]. In the current Hungarian civil code (2013), a juridical act is mentioned in the first division of the sixth book on obligations, including the common provisions relating to obligations[325]. In Hungary the juridical acts provide the basis for the new structure of the general part of obligations; the sequence of institutions is: juridical acts – representation – prescription.

These cases indicate that the construction of juridical acts is universal, and is also useful in codifications that do not necessarily contain a general part. Even though originally the idea was to establish the arrangement for the codes with a general part, this classification also impacted the civil codes with a different structure[326]. For an abstract and artificial legal construct, it has been highly successful. It needs to be stated that there is no such thing as bilateral juridical acts; they are simply contracts[327]. This demonstrates how wide a juridical act is: for the precision of applied terms, in Germany the most basic construct of a contract was widened in order to cover all an individual's declarations of will. In this way a juridical act was established.

---

323 In the ABGB (1811) currently the seventeenth chapter (the second book on *ius rerum*, the second division referring to the personal rights) considers contracts and juridical acts in general. When the code was adopted, the title of the seventeenth chapter was: on contracts in general.

The same systematization is present in the Czechoslovak draft (1937), often replicating the Austrian systematization.

The twenty-fifth section (the second book concerning property law, the second division including claims) regards contracts and juridical acts.

324 Article 1100 Obligations arise from juridical acts, juridically significant facts or from the sole authority of legislation. (…)

Article 1100-1 includes a definition of juridical acts: Juridical acts are manifestations of will intended to produce legal effects. They may be based on agreement or unilateral. As far as appropriate, they are subject, both as to their validity and as to their effects, to the rules governing contracts.

325 In the current Hungarian civil code (2013), the sequence of content is: obligation (the first chapter), legal statements (the second chapter), representation (the third chapter), statute of limitations (the fourth chapter) and finally acknowledgement of debt and composition (the fifth chapter).

Those institutions are settled in the sixth book on obligations, the first division: common provisions relating to obligations, the first title: general provisions. Even though in this area there are also institutions not belonging to the general part and specific for the law of obligations (obligation, acknowledgement of debt and composition), the arrangement of the compounds as well as the designation of the first title (general provisions) recall the typical Pandect arrangement.

326 *Conf*. SCHERMAIER M.J., *vor §§ 104. Das Rechtsgeschäft*, in: SCHMOECKEL M. (ed.), *Historisch-kritischer Kommentar zum BGB. Band I Allgemeiner Teil §§ 1 – 240*, Tübingen 2003, p. 364.

327 EISENHARDT U., *Allgemeiner Teil des BGB*, Heidelberg 1989, p. 52.

5. Declaration of will

Declaration of will in codes that include a general part is settled in the general part[328]. In the general part, declaration of will may be arranged in a separate systematic unit[329]. This idea is strongly connected with juridical acts and the further content of the law of obligations in the general part[330]. The Pandect systematization with a general part also impacted later codes that do not contain a general part, where the declaration of will is settled among the law of obligations; it might beplaced in a distinct systematic unit on the declaration of will[331] or it can be mentioned solely in the text of the code[332].

In the Polish Code of obligations (1933), that which is associated with juridical acts (declaration of will) receives considerable attention in its divisions. If we underline the declaration of will, then this construct is perceived equally in connection to juridical acts and contracts; accordingly, if juridical acts prevail then the arrangement is concentrated on the unilateral legal actions. In the Polish Code of obligations (1933), declaration of will is placed in the general part of obligations, but without any detriment to the system of a civil code; those provisions could be transferred to the general part, if such a composition were to be chosen for the Polish civil code[333].

---

328 The first codifications mentioning the declaration of will are the Prussian *Landrecht* (1794) and the ABGB (1811).

RANIERI F., *Europäisches Obligationenrecht. Ein Handbuch mit Texten und Materialien*, Wien 2003, pp. 46 – 47.

329 That is the case in the German BGB (1896), where in the general part the second title (of the third chapter on juridical acts) deals with the declaration of will.

330 SCHERMAIER M.J., *vor §§ 116 – 124. Willensmängel*, in: SCHMOECKEL M. (ed.), *Historisch-kritischer Kommentar zum BGB. Band I Allgemeiner Teil §§ 1 – 240*, Tübingen 2003, p. 403 and the following pages.

331 In the Polish Code of obligations (1933), the second title refers to the formation of obligations. The first division of the second title considers the declaration of will.

In the socialist Hungarian civil code (1959), contractual intention and its expression is placed in Articles 205 – 207 (the fourth book on obligations, the first title regarding contract, the eighteenth chapter containing the making of a contract). That is the first subdivision in the eighteenth chapter.

In the current Hungarian civil code (2013), legal statements are situated in Sections 6:4 – 6:10 (the sixth book on obligations, the first division comprising the common provisions relating to obligations, the first title on general provisions, the second chapter regarding the legal statements).

332 In the Hungarian draft (1928), the declaration of will is mentioned in its divisions. The fifth chapter (of the first title regarding contracts, in the third book on obligations) refers to the interpretation of contracts and the lack of the contractual will *(Auslegung von Verträgen. Mängel des Vertragswillens)*.

333 DOMAŃSKI L., *System Kodeksu zobowiązań* [The system of the Code of obligations], Warszawa 1934, pp. 11 – 12.

6. Arrangement of the legal concepts in the book on obligations

In the codifications containing a general part and a book on obligations the most typical solution is to construct the book based on the concept of an obligation[334]. In the Saxon civil code (1863), the first codification containing a general part, the third book refers to the law of obligations (*das Recht der Forderungen*). A full separation of the substantive private law from the civil procedure was not introduced in the Saxon civil code; in the general part, actions are an equivalent of *actiones*, not juridical acts. After examining the first code with the Pandect systematization, it is necessary to focus on the later codifications following the Pandect model. In the current Czech civil code (2012), the final, fourth book (including the law of obligations) deals with relative property rights. The book includes only the law of obligations[335].

Here the examination is restricted to the opportunities of settling the contract law in the book on obligations, to the extent necessary to present the hierarchy of the legal concepts. In codes including a general part, the law of contracts is the subset of the law of obligations in the book on obligations[336]. A contract might be given more or less attention in the table of contents; it may be put in a separate

---

334 In the German BGB (1896), the second book refers to the law of obligations.

In the Russian draft (1905), the fifth book concerns the law of obligations.

In the first socialist Russian civil code (1922), the third book contains the law of obligations.

In the second socialist Russian civil code (1964), the third book considers the law of obligations.

In the current Russian civil code (1994 – 2006), the third book comprises the general part of the law of obligations and the fourth book the particular kinds of obligations.

In the Polish civil code (1964), the third book regards the law of obligations.

In the first socialist Czechoslovak civil code (1950), the fourth book deals with the law of obligations.

In the current Czech civil code (2012), the fourth book includes the relative property rights. Concurrently the first title (of the fourth book) contains the general provisions on obligations.

335 The systematization in the current Czech civil code (2012) resembles the composition in the ABGB (1811), where the second book concerning *ius rerum* includes two divisions. Those are: *ius in re* (the first division) and personal rights (the second division).

336 In the German BGB (1896), the second chapter (of the second book on obligations) includes contractual obligations.

In the Polish civil code (1964), the third title (of the third book on obligations) comprises the general provisions on contractual obligations.

In the first socialist Russian civil code (1922), the second chapter (of the third book on obligations) deals with contractual obligations.

In the current Russian civil code (1994 – 2006), the second division (of the third book concerning the general part of obligations) regards the general provisions on the contract.

section[337] or be set in a section on obligations[338], but the hierarchy of the legal concepts remains undisturbed.

In bourgeois codifications that follow the Pandect systematization, a juridical act is always a central construct in the general part and an obligation is the main concept of the law of obligations. In the current Russian civil code (1994 – 2006), the third book includes the general part of obligations, whereas the fourth book contains the particular kinds of obligations; nonetheless, distinguishing the law of obligations in two books does not in any way affect the arrangement of the legal constructs, because the concepts are arranged in the same way, no matter the formal divisions into books. It should be mentioned that the usual Pandect classifications may be modified in the socialist codifications.

VI. Arrangement of the legal constructs in the socialist civil codes

Here the systematization of the legal concepts in the socialist civil codes is analyzed. The codifications retaining the traditional arrangement are first examined, followed by the systematic alterations in the structure of the Czechoslovak (1964) and East German (1975) civil codes.

1. Systematization not different from the traditionalmodel

The systematization of codes that follow the unity of private law (Czechoslovakia – 1950; Hungary – 1959; Poland – 1964; Russia – 1922 and 1964) does not differ significantly from the traditional model. In codes that comprise a general part (Russia – 1922, 1964; Czechoslovakia – 1950; Poland – 1964), there is a juridical

---

337 In the German BGB (1896), the second chapter (of the second book on obligations) encompasses contractual obligations.

In the Polish civil code (1964), the third title (of the third book on obligations) regards the general provisions on contractual obligations.

In the first socialist Russian civil code (1922), the second chapter (of the third book on obligations) includes contractual obligations.

In the current Russian civil code (1994 – 2006), the second division (of the third book concerning the general part of obligations) contains the general provisions on the contract.

338 In the first socialist Czechoslovak civil code (1950), the eleventh chapter (the first chapter in the fourth book on obligations) deals with the formation and content of obligations. It contains Articles from 211 to 250. Contractual obligations are settled in Articles 213 – 217.

In the second socialist Russian civil code (1964), the fifteenth chapter (the first chapter in the third book on obligations) deals with the formation of obligations. It includes Articles 158 – 167; Articles 160 – 167 concern contracts.

act in the general part[339], whereas an obligation is visible in the system of the books[340].

The fourth book of the socialist Hungarian civil code concerns obligations, but the fundamental element of this part is a contract. The socialist composition strongly resembles that which can be found in the Hungarian draft (1928). Systematization as applied in the socialist Hungarian civil code is much simpler and less refined than the arrangement in the Hungarian draft, but the arrangement visible in the socialist Hungarian civil code (1959) could also potentially be implemented in a bourgeois codification.

The specific feature of settling the legal constructs in the socialist civil codes may cling to the construct of an obligation[341] (Czechoslovakia – 1950, Russia – 1964), but the same arrangement could be introduced in a capitalist civil code. That is only a slight alteration, with in the usual opportunities for arranging private law. This arrangement may be a reaction to the alterations implemented in the systems of both codes; in both codifications there is no family law, and the system of the second socialist Russian civil code (1964) is settled on ownership instead of *ius in re*. The apprehensions of the lawyers working on both codes could result in strengthening an obligation, which should solidify their structure.

---

339 In the first socialist Russian civil code (1922), the fourth chapter of the general part considers juridical acts.

In the second socialist Russian civil code (1964), the third chapter of the general part deals with juridical acts.

In the Polish civil code (1964), the fourth title of the general part comprises juridical acts.

In the first socialist Czechoslovak civil code (1950), the third chapter of the general part includes juridical acts.

340 In the first socialist Russian civil code (1922), the third book regards the law of obligations.

In the second socialist Russian civil code (1964), the third book concerns the law of obligations.

In the first socialist Czechoslovak civil code (1950), the fourth book includes the law of obligations.

In the Polish civil code (1964), the third book considers the law of obligations.

341 In the first socialist Czechoslovak civil code (1950), only an obligation can be noticed in the table of contents.

In the general part of obligations, settled in the fourth book on obligations, there are: formation and content of obligations (the eleventh chapter), modifications of the content of obligations (the twelfth chapter), change of a creditor or a debtor (the thirteenth chapter), securing obligations (the fourteenth chapter) and extinction of obligations (the fifteenth chapter).

In the second socialist Russian civil code (1964), an obligation is the only construct visible in the table of contents.

The fifteenth chapter (the first chapter in the third book on obligations) deals with the formation of obligations. The sixteenth chapter: performance of obligations. The seventeenth chapter: securing of the performance of obligations. The eighteenth chapter: transfer of a claim and change of a creditor. The nineteenth chapter: liability for the breach of obligations. The twentieth chapter: extinction of obligations.

The Russian (1964) and Czechoslovak (1964) civil codes begin the provisions on juridical acts with a definition of a juridical act. This arrangement is considered a typical feature of the legislative technique of the socialist civil codes, but the reasons behind such a claim are not explained[342]. This statement indicates one of the possibilities of arranging a socialist codification. A contract may be marginalized in the structure of a socialist civil code, because it can be associated with the autonomy of an individual and natural law. A juridical act is neutral, and more substantial. Concurrently, a contract is an indispensable legal construct, and lies at the centre of the systems of the socialist Hungarian civil code (1959) and of the East German civil code (1975).

2. Systematic alterations in the structure of Czechoslovak (1964) and East German civil codes (1975)

The final issue to discuss is the systematic alterations visible in the structure of the second socialist Czechoslovak civil code (1964) and the East German civil code (1975). Attempts at finding a new socialist arrangement were convergent with implementing systematic patterns different from other codifications. The research is considered in two aspects here. First, the analysis presents the attempts made to replace an obligation with other ideas, which may be a contract. The discussion then considers whether a juridical act is appropriate for a socialist codification that addresses the needs of citizens; the answer to this question is different in both jurisdictions.

In Czechoslovakia (1964) and East Germany (1975) the term "obligation" is not applied in the divisions of the codes[343]. This issue is common to both codifications, but the analysis principally focuses on the system of the East German civil code. Instead of an obligation, a contract appears in the code; the third book in-

---

342 EMINESCU Y., POPESCU T., *Les codes civils des pays socialistes. Étude comparative*, Bucarest/ Paris 1980, pp. 89 – 90.

In the second socialist Russian civil code (1964), a definition of a juridical act is mentioned in Article 41, whereas in the second socialist Czechoslovak civil code (1964) that is § 34.

343 The Czechoslovak civil code (1964) includes: general provisions – socialist collective ownership and personal ownership – personal use of dwelling units, other living space, and tracts of land – services – rights and duties from other juridical acts – responsibility for damage and unjust enrichment – inheritance of property constituting personal ownership – final provisions.

An obligation is not mentioned in the table of contents of the general part (including the general part of obligations), but it is elaborated among the subdivisions of the general part. The seventh division of the general part concerns the extinction of rights and duties. The first subdivision in the seventh division (visible only in the text of the code and not in the table of contents) regards the performance of an obligation.

In the East German civil code (1975) there are: fundamental principles of socialist private law – socialist ownership and personal ownership – contracts relating to material and cultural life – use of real estate and buildings for residential and recreational purposes – protection of life, health and property from damage – inheritance law – specific provisions of the respective relationships of private law.

cludes contracts relating to material and cultural life. In East Germany, a contract displaces obligations, in a way that is not present even in codes based on the Gaius model. The account of the Hungarian systematization and the composition of the socialist Hungarian civil code (1959), addressed the adequacy of contracts for the socialist codifications. Those claims also partially suit the East German civil code; the socialist Hungarian civil code follows the unity of a civil code, whereas the East German codification is concentrated on the needs of the socialist citizens. Problems that are not relevant to these citizens (e.g. the functioning of socialist enterprises) are regulated in other written laws.

In the second socialist Czechoslovak civil code (1964), a contract seems to be replaced with a "service" – the fourth book is about services. The juridical act is placed before the institutions of the law of obligations arranged in the general part[344], and a contract is solely a systematic subset of juridical acts[345]. In the Czechoslovak code the most significant hint is provided by the title of the fifth book, which includes the rights and duties from other juridical acts. Probably the Czechoslovak codification is based on the union between *personae* and *actiones*. The general part at the beginning of the code has two functions in its structure:both *persona* and *actiones*. In the Pandect systematization, the general part always acts as *persona*, but here, due to the amount of the multiple institutions of the general part of obligations, it can also be perceived also as *actiones*. The second and third books (the second book on socialist collective ownership and personal ownership, the third book on personal use of dwelling units, other living spaces, and tracts of land) perform the function of *res*.

Despite the marginalization of contract in the composition of the Czechoslovak code, contracts are at the centre of its structure. The books in this systematization that accord with *actiones* (the fourth book on services, the fifth book on rights and duties from other juridical acts, the sixth book on responsibility for damage and unjust enrichment), include content mentioning contracts. Services, in the fourth book on services, are contracts concluded between citizens and state enterprises. The fifth book (on rights and duties from other juridical acts) regulates contracts concluded between citizens. The differentiation that depends on a subject (person) is visible in the divisions of the code. The entire codification is concentrated on the needs of *persona* (a socialist citizen). The sixth book (responsibility for damage and unjust enrichment) contains the non-contractual sources of

[344] In the second socialist Czechoslovak civil code (1964), the fourth division (of the general part) considers juridical acts. The fifth division: giving security to rights and duties. The sixth division: transition of rights and duties. The seventh division: extinction of rights and duties. The eighth division: prescription.

[345] In the Czechoslovak code, the fourth division of the general part contains juridical acts (§§ 34 – 51). In the text of the division there is a subdivision regarding contracts, not visible in the table of contents; contracts are settled in §§ 43 – 51.

obligations[346]. By simplifying it, we can reduce the Czechoslovak arrangement of the law of obligations: general provisions on obligations are tackled in the general part, followed by particular obligations in the fourth and fifth books, whilen on-contractual sources of obligations appear in the sixth book. A contract manages the composition of particular obligations.

Following these remarks on the Czechoslovak civil code, we now consider the system of the East German civil code, in which a contract is a central construct: the third book comprises contracts relating to material and cultural life. Elaborating a peculiar systematization of private law[347] could disrupt the functioning of the system. The main reason for arranging private law in the East German civil code was to elaborate an arrangement different from the German BGB[348] (1896). In East Germany, basing the system of the code on contracts provided a perfect solution. It varies from the BGB, and at the same time it is a very natural arrangement, present in codes that follow the Gaius model. A contract is flexible and can encompass the entire structure of a civil code. Natural and clear contract enforced the structure of the East German civil code.

Finally, this section considers whether juridical acts fit a definitive socialist civil code that addresses the needs of socialist citizens. The Czechoslovak civil code includes the general part with a juridical act, and content relevant to the law of obligations is situated after juridical acts in the general part[349]. Such a composition results from adapting the general part of obligations to the general part – the content written in the general part should apply to all books of the code. The juridical act receives fresh attention in the civil code as being central to all actions of a socialist citizen, regardless of whether they concern the law of obligations, *ius in re* or inheritance law. The East German civil code, constituting the negation

346 This results from concentrating on the particular obligations in the exterior divisions of the Czechoslovak code. We divide the particular obligations into particular contracts and non-contractual sources of obligations. The same approach is visible in the Czechoslovak systematization, but additionally there is a systematic differentiation depending on the subject with whom a citizen enters into an agreement.

347 The books of the East German civil code (1975) comprise: fundamental principles of socialist private law – socialist ownership and personal ownership – contracts relating to material and cultural life – use of real estate and buildings for residential and recreational purposes – protection of life, health and property from damage – inheritance law – specific provisions of the respective relationships of private law.

348 SOŚNIAK M., *Zasady kodeksu cywilnego Niemieckiej Republiki Demokratycznej* [Principles of the civil code of the German Democratic Republic], in: *Kodeks cywilny Niemieckiej Republiki Demokratycznej* [Civil code of the German Democratic Republic], Wrocław/ Warszawa/ Kraków/Gdańsk 1979, p. 16.

349 In the second socialist Czechoslovak civil code (1964), the fourth division (of the general part) comprises juridical acts. The fifth division: giving security to rights and duties. The sixth division: transition of rights and duties. The seventh division: extinction of rights and duties. The eighth division: prescription.

of the German BGB, does not apply the construct of a juridical act, and only a contract is visible in its divisions.

VII. Conclusions

Implementing the general part in the structure of a civil code reduces the possibilities for arranging the legal concepts. In the studied codifications including a general part, a juridical act and an obligation are the basic constructs. The majority of the accessible solutions is found in codifications where the entire content of the law of obligations is written in one book. According to the legislative choices available, either an obligation or a contract can prevail in the table of contents. Furthermore, there are no general rules that apply exclusively to the codes based on the Gaius scheme. They favour contracts in their arrangement, but at this point the arrangement of the law of obligations was not yet fully elaborated; preferring *res* (*ius in re*) in the structure of the civil codes resulted in neglecting obligations – the time for development in this area was yet to come. Among the socialist civil codes the state ideology does not have a significant impact on the composition of the legal concepts, but most often there is a juridical act in the general part and in the book on obligations. It is also possible to elaborate a new socialist arrangement of the law of obligations (Czechoslovakia – 1964, East Germany – 1975).

D) Arrangement of the general part of obligations

In the civil codes the general part of obligations is arranged at the beginning of the book on obligations, before the particular obligations[350]. That ordering is natural,

[350] In the CC (1804), the third title (of the third book on different ways of acquiring ownership) regards contracts and conventional obligations in general. The fourth title: commitments formed without an agreement. The fifth title contains the matrimonial property law. The sixth title: sales. That is already the content corresponding with the particular obligations.

Since the reform in 2016, the third title (of the third book) considers the sources of obligations, whereas the fourth title deals with the general regime of obligations.

In the ABGB (1811), the seventeenth chapter (the second book on *ius rerum*, the second division on the personal rights) deals with contracts in general. The further provisions of the general part of obligations are established in the last third book of the ABGB, comprising the provisions common to personal rights and *ius in re*. The first chapter (of the third book) includes the security for rights and obligations. The second chapter: modification of rights and obligations. The third chapter: cancellation of rights and obligations. The fourth chapter: prescription and usucaption.

In the Saxon civil code (1863), the third book regarding the law of claims is isolated in two divisions: claims in general and particular kinds of claims.

In the German BGB (1896), the first six chapters of the second book on obligations constitute the general part of obligations. The first chapter: content of obligations. The second chapter: contractual obligations. The third chapter: extinction of obligations. The fourth chapter: assignment of claims. The fifth chapter: assumption of debt. The sixth chapter: plurality of debtors and creditors. The seventh chapter of the second book includes the particular obligations.

In the Swiss Code of obligations (1911), the first division comprises the general provisions.

In the Polish Code of obligations (1933), the first five titles contain the general part of obligations. The first title: the sources, the substance and the kinds of obligations. The second title: formation of obligations. The third title: the transfer or rights and duties, arising from obligations. The fourth title: expiration of obligations. The fifth title: suing the actions of a debtor with the detriment of creditors. The further titles include particular contracts.

In the Polish civil code (1964), the first title (of the third book on obligations) deals with the general provisions. The second title: plurality of debtors or creditors. The third title: general provisions on contractual obligations. [In the original version of the code there was also the fourth title, regulating an obligation of concluding agreements between the units of the nationalized economy; it was deleted from the code after the fall of socialism]. The fifth title: unjust enrichment. The sixth title: delicts. The seventh title: performance of obligations and effects of their non-performance. The eighth title: set-off, novation and release from debt. The ninth title: change of creditor or debtor. The tenth title: protection of creditor in case of debtor's insolvency. The further titles (of the third book on obligations) include the particular contracts.

In the first socialist Czechoslovak civil code (1950), in the fourth book on obligations firstly the general part of obligations is situated (the eleventh chapter: formation and content of obligations, the twelfth chapter: modifications of the content of obligations, the thirteenth chapter: change of a creditor or a debtor, the fourteenth chapter: securing obligations, the fifteenth chapter: extinction of obligations). Then the law of damages (the sixteenth chapter) and unjust enrichment (the seventeenth chapter) and the particular contracts are placed (chapters from eighteenth to thirty-third).

In the current Czech civil code (2012), the first title (of the fourth book on the relative property rights) regards the general provisions on obligations.

In the Hungarian draft (1928), the first five titles (of the third book on obligations) contain the general part of obligations. The first title: contracts. The second title: content of obligations. The third title: multi-party obligations. The fourth title: transition of claims and obligations. The fifth title: expiration and prescription of claims. The further titles (from sixth to sixteenth) include the particular obligations.

In the socialist Hungarian civil code (1959), the first title (of the fourth book on obligations) regards contracts.

In the current Hungarian civil code (2013), the first two divisions (of the sixth book on obligations) include the general part of obligations. The first division: common provisions relating to obligations. The second division: general provisions on contracts.

In the Russian draft (1905), the first division (of the fifth book on obligations) considers an obligation in general.

In the first socialist Russian civil code (1922) the first two chapters of the third book on obligations comprise the general part of obligations. The first chapter: general provisions. The second chapter: contractual obligations.

In the second socialist Russian civil code (1964), the fifteenth chapter (the first chapter in the third book on obligations) refers to the formation of obligations. Further there are: performance of obligations (the sixteenth chapter), securing of the performance of obligations (the seventeenth chapter), transfer of a claim and change of a creditor (the eighteenth chapter), liability for the breach of obligations (the nineteenth chapter) and the extinction of obligations (the twentieth chapter). The twenty-first chapter: sales.

In the current Russian civil code (1994 – 2006), the third book encompasses the general part of obligations. The fourth book: particular kinds of obligations.

The books in the code are: general provisions – right of ownership and other rights to estate – general part of obligations – particular kinds of obligations – inheritance law – international private law – rights to results of intellectual activities and means of individualisation.

because the more general should come before the more specific; isolating the general part of obligations partly resembles the separation of the general part in the systematization of a civil code[351]. Nonetheless a general part of obligations can be observed in all currently binding civil codes, whereas a general part may, but does not have to, be included in a civil code. A general part of obligations is a necessary requirement for a clearly structured civil code, and many modern codifications do not contain a general part (e.g. the Hungarian civil code of 2013). From the perspective of German legal science the general part of obligations constitutes a further degree of legal abstraction while also applying the provisions of the law of obligations[352]. The general part of obligations is supposed to include provisions that could be applied to all, or at least to the majority of obligations[353].

It is worth making some remarks here regarding a possible systematization of the general part of obligations. In the Pandect model multiple institutions of the law of obligations are transposed to the general part. The division on the general and particular obligations is a feature of the Pandect codes. This classification later became standard for all codifications, regardless of whether they contain a general part or not.

The formal divisions of the general part of obligations should also be briefly mentioned. The first possibility is to adopt a clear systematization, presented in the table of contents. An area that includes the general part of obligations may encompass one section[354] or two sections[355] in the book on obligations. The general part of obligations may be also be situated in a separate book[356]. It is, additionally, possible not to create a formal division between the general and particular obligations; instead, the systematic units located at the beginning of the book on obligations constitute the general part of obligations, whereas subsequent units include the particular obligations[357].

---

[351] MICHAELS R., *vor § 241. Systemfragen des Schuldrechts*, in: ZIMMERMANN R. (ed.), *Historisch-kritischer Kommentar zum BGB. Band II Schuldrecht: Allgemeiner Teil §§ 241–432*, Tübingen 2007, pp. 4–5.

[352] *Ibidem*, pp. 4–5.

[353] MEDICUS D., LORENZ S., *Schuldrecht II. Besonderer Teil. Ein Studienbuch*, München 2010, p. 1.

[354] This arrangement can be found e.g. in the Saxon civil code (1863); the third book regarding the law of claims is isolated in two systematic divisions: of claims in general and of particular kinds of claims.

[355] The discussed systematization is present e.g. in the current Hungarian civil code (2013), where the first two systematic divisions of the sixth book on obligations comprise the general part of obligations. The first division: common provisions relating to obligations. The second division: general provisions on contracts.

[356] In the current Russian civil code (1994–2006), the third book includes the general part of obligations. The fourth book comprises the particular obligations. That is solely a technical distinction of the law of obligations between two books.

[357] This arrangement can be found in the Hungarian draft (1928), in the Polish Code of obligations

This summary provides an essential foundation for the ensuing analysis of the composition of the general part of obligations in the codifications examined. The discussion concerns several aspects of the arrangement of the general part of obligations. First, the systematization of the general part of obligations in the books of the civil codes is investigated. That is a primary problem, from which all subsequent considerations arise. Second, the shape of the general part of obligations, resulting from the legal concepts applied in the codes, is analyzed. Those two questions can be formulated concisely. The third issue requires multiple observations concerning the methods of arranging the general part of obligations. The analysis subsequently deals with the distribution of the general provisions of the law of contracts in the civil codes. Further areas of discussion include: the main systematic segments of the general part of obligations and their arrangement in the civil codes; the institutions of the general part of obligations classified in the general part; exemplary additional sections which can be found in the general part of obligations; and, finally, the impact of socialist ideology on the arrangement of the general part of obligations.

I. The general part of obligations and its arrangement in the books of the civil codes

This section discusses the arrangement of the general part of obligations in the civil codes. The content of the general part of obligations may be systematized differently in the various books of the code. This section introduces further aspects of organizing the general part of obligations discussed in due course. As with the Pandect model, in which private law is arranged from the most general to the most specific, this volume determines the further aspects that I discuss in the section on the arrangement of the general part of obligations.

The first possibility is to arrange the entire content of the general part of obligations in a single area of the code. This solution is common in the codes, where obligations are arranged in one book[358]. It is present also in the CC (1804). In the civil codes that comprise a general part, a significant volume of the general part of obligations is transferred to the general part. This systematization may be modified; attempts to find a socialist arrangement in Czechoslovakia (1964) resulted in transposing the majority of provisions belonging to the general part of obligations into the general part.

(1933), in the first socialist Russian civil code (1922), in the second socialist Russian civil code (1964), in the first socialist Czechoslovak civil code (1950) and in the Polish civil code (1964). All codifications are presented in the first reference of the section on the arrangement of the general part of obligations.

358 That is in the Swiss Code of obligations (1911), the Polish Code of obligations (1933), the Hungarian draft (1928) and in the Hungarian codes (1959, 2013).

Austria (1811) and East Germany (1975) offer a typical compositions. The general provisions on contracts are settled among the provisions of obligations, whereas the subsequent volume of the general part of obligations is perceived as containing that which is more specific, and it is arranged in the last book of the code.

Before moving on to the further analysis, it is necessary to mention that the general provisions on contracts can be systematized differently. They may either be placed among the contractual agreements, in the general part of obligations, or in the general part. That is related to the fact that contracts are particularly important to the daily life of individuals. Different systematic patterns are the result of the legislative visions that legislators implement in the civil codes.

II. The shape of the general part of obligations, resulting from the legal concepts applied in the civil codes

The next issue to be analyzed is the exemplary presentation of the shape of the general part of obligations, resulting from the legal concepts introduced in the codes. As has already been demonstrated, there are codifications where only an obligation is visible in the divisions of the codes[359] (e.g. Russia – 1964). In the socialist Hungarian civil code (1959), contracts are the only concept in the general part of obligations[360], but that is a fairly uncommon composition. Another option is to divide the general part of obligations into two systematic segments: obligations and contracts[361]. This systematic pattern can be included in civil codes that comprise a general part and those that do not[362].

---

[359] In the second socialist Russian civil code (1964), there are: the formation of obligations (the fifteenth chapter of the third book on obligations), the performance of obligations (the sixteenth chapter), securing of the performance of obligations (the seventeenth chapter), the transfer of a claim and change of a creditor (the eighteenth chapter), the liability for the breach of obligations (the nineteenth chapter) and the extinction of obligations (the twentieth chapter).

[360] In the socialist Hungarian civil code (1959), the first title (of the fourth book on obligations) regards contracts. In this title there is an entire volume dedicated to the general part of obligations.

[361] In the current Russian civil code (1994 – 2006) the first subsection (of the third book on the general part of the law of obligations) includes the general provisions on obligations, whereas the second subsection contains the general provisions on contract.

In the current Hungarian civil code (2013), the first division (of the sixth book on obligations) regards the common provisions relating to obligations, whereas the second division the general provisions on contracts.

[362] In the current Russian civil code (1994 – 2006), the books are: general provisions – right of ownership and other rights to estate – general part of obligations – particular kinds of obligations – inheritance law – international private law – rights to results of intellectual activities and means of individualisation.

The current Hungarian civil code (2013) includes: introductory provisions – individual as subject of law – legal entity – family law – *ius in re* – law of obligations – succession law.

III. Methods of arranging the general part of obligations

The next issue to consider are the methods of arranging the general part of obligations. We could also speak of the factors determining the systematization of the general part of obligations; this set is not exclusive. By exclusive is meant that if factor A is present in the code, then factor B cannot appear in the civil code. Different systematic patterns may coincide in the composition of the general part of obligations, without clashing. This analysis is an attempt to track the ways of arranging the general part of obligations and presenting them to readers. The examination is focused on showing the most significant tendencies visible in the civil codes. This research could be compared to a pencil sketch.

Five factors have been isolated: dividing the content of the general part of obligations between the general part and the book on obligations (the first division); erasing the general part of obligations and transposing the volume of the general part of obligations into the general part (the second division);devising an arrangement according to the sources of obligations (the third division) and chronological order (the fourth division). In the final (fifth) division the discussion considers the systematization in which the general provisions on contracts are isolated, whereas the further content of the general part of obligations is placed in the last book of the code.

1. Dividing the content of the general part of obligations between the general part and the book on obligations

The first systematic pattern is the best known. The content of the general part of obligations can be divided between the general part and the book on obligations. The general part contains the rules which are of the utmost importance for the law of obligations. The legal precepts placed in the general part are also necessary for other branches of private law. Nonetheless, some regulations crucial for other branches of private law can also be found in the book on obligations of the German BGB (1896). The distinction of the branches of private law into the books of the code in the BGB is not complete[363].

[363] E.g. since the reform of the BGB (come into force 2002) in § 305 (in the second book on obligations) there are the general conditions of trading, which should be put into the general part.

§ 305 Einbeziehung Allgemeiner Geschäftsbedingungen in den Vertrag

(1) Allgemeine Geschäftsbedingungen sind alle für eine Vielzahl von Verträgen vorformulierten Vertragsbedingungen, die eine Vertragspartei (Verwender) der anderen Vertragspartei bei Abschluss eines Vertrags stellt. Gleichgültig ist, ob die Bestimmungen einen äußerlich gesonderten Bestandteil des Vertrags bilden oder in die Vertragsurkunde selbst aufgenommen werden, welchen Umfang sie haben, in welcher Schriftart sie verfasst sind und welche Form der Vertrag hat. Allgemeine Geschäftsbedingungen liegen nicht vor, soweit die Vertragsbedingungen zwischen den Vertragsparteien im Einzelnen ausgehandelt sind.

(2) Allgemeine Geschäftsbedingungen werden nur dann Bestandteil eines Vertrags, wenn der Verwender bei Vertragsschluss

The composition discussed here is a feature of the Pandect model, currently present in Germany, Russia, Czechia and Poland. The general institutions of private law of obligations (also strongly connected with the law of obligations) can be found in the general part. They are: juridical acts (declaration of will), condition, representation and prescription. There may also be the general provisions of contract law. This composition is cited in connection with the German BGB[364] (1896).

2. Erasing the general part of obligations and transposing the volume of the general part of obligations into the general part (Czechoslovakia – 1964)

The next option for arranging the general part of obligations is to transfer the volume of the general part of obligations into the general part. When they elaborated the socialist systematization of a civil code, the Czechoslovak lawyers modified a typical Pandect model with a general part. In the general part of the second socialist Czechoslovak civil code (1964) there are more institutions of the general part of obligations than in other codifications[365].

3. Arrangement according to the sources of obligations

Another composition is an arrangement according to the sources (of the formation) of obligations. That is a clear and neutral systematic pattern. It was first applied to the Swiss Code of obligations (1911). The sources of obligations are at the centre of the arrangement of the French-Italian draft (1927) and the Polish Code of obligations (1933), and in the French *Code civil* they are placed after the

---

1. die andere Vertragspartei ausdrücklich oder, wenn ein ausdrücklicher Hinweis wegen der Art des Vertragsschlusses nur unter unverhältnismäßigen Schwierigkeiten möglich ist, durch deutlich sichtbaren Aushang am Ort des Vertragsschlusses auf sie hinweist und

2. der anderen Vertragspartei die Möglichkeit verschafft, in zumutbarer Weise, die auch eine für den Verwender erkennbare körperliche Behinderung der anderen Vertragspartei angemessen berücksichtigt, von ihrem Inhalt Kenntnis zu nehmen, und wenn die andere Vertragspartei mit ihrer Geltung einverstanden ist.

(3) Die Vertragsparteien können für eine bestimmte Art von Rechtsgeschäften die Geltung bestimmter Allgemeiner Geschäftsbedingungen unter Beachtung der in Absatz 2 bezeichneten Erfordernisse im Voraus vereinbaren.

[364] In the German BGB (1896), the third chapter of the general part considers juridical acts. In the third chapter there are: capacity to contract (the first title), declaration of will (the second title), contract (the third title), conditions and specification of time (the fourth title), agency and power of attorney (the fifth title) and consent and ratification (the sixth title). The fourth chapter of the general part refers to periods of time and fixed dates. The fifth chapter: prescription.

[365] In the second socialist Czechoslovak civil code (1964), the general part contains: private law relationships and their protection (the first division) – participants of the private law relationships (the second division) – representation (the third division) – juridical acts (the fourth division) – giving security to rights and duties (the fifth division) – transition of rights and duties (the sixth division) – extinction of rights and duties (the seventh division) – prescription (the eighth division) – explanation of certain (legal) terms (the ninth division).

reform of the law of contracts and obligations (2016). This systematization fits both the civil codes established for an obligation and a contract.

In the Swiss Code of obligations (1911), the first title considers the formation of obligations. In the first title there are three chapters. In sequence: obligations arising by contract (the first chapter), obligations in tort (the second chapter) and finally obligations arising from unjust enrichment (the third chapter). An obligation prevails in the composition of the general part of obligations[366], but the central construct in Switzerland is a contract instead of an obligation[367].

In the Polish Code of obligations (1933), the system is based on an obligation – the first title of the Code considers the sources, the substance and the kinds of obligations. The second title deals with the formation of obligations, and it contains two divisions. The first division (of the second title) includes declaration of will, whereas the second division comprises the formation of obligations from other sources. Contrary to Switzerland, in Poland the declaration of will prevails in the systematization of the general part of obligations. That is a visible sign of the impact of the German Pandect model.

In the French *Code civil*, following the 2016 reform the third title (of the third book on different ways of acquiring ownership) regards the sources of obligations. The third title consists of three sub-titles. They are: contract (the first sub-title), extra-contractual liability (the second sub-title) and other sources of obligations (the third sub-title).

The last civil code discussed here is the Polish civil code (1964). After the Second World War, Polish lawyers needed to simplify the arrangement of the Polish Code of obligations (1933) and adapt it to a new reality. After the first two titles of the third book on obligations (the first title on general provisions, the second title on plurality of debtors or creditors) come the sources of obligations. They are: general provisions on contractual obligations (the third title); the obligation of concluding agreements between the units of the nationalized economy (the fourth title); unjust enrichment (the fifth title); and delicts (the sixth title). In the Polish civil code the sources of obligations include an additional systematic segment (the

---

[366] In the Swiss Code of obligations (1911), the first division considers the general provisions. In the first division there are: the formation of obligations (the first title), the effect of obligations (the second title), the extinction of obligations (the third title), the special relationships relating to obligations (the fourth title) and finally assignment of claims and assumption of debt (the fifth title).

About the Swiss systematization also here:

BUCHER E., *Schweizerisches Obligationenrecht. Allgemeiner Teil ohne Deliktsrecht*, Zürich 1988, p. 5.

[367] Article 1 *1 Le contrat est parfait lorsque les parties ont, réciproquement et d'une manière concordante, manifesté leur volonté.*

2 Cette manifestation peutêtre expresse ou tacite.

fourth title), aimed at managing the sector of the planned economy. After the fall of socialism it was removed from the Polish civil code.

This examination on the arrangement of the civil codes has showed that there are more possibilities to combine sources of obligations. Contracts tend to go first (Switzerland – 1911, France – 2016), but if there is a preference towards for the German concepts, then contracts can be replaced by a declaration of will. Furthermore, in a socialist civil code that is systemized according to the sources of obligation a systematic unit considering the socialist planning might be included.

4. Chronological order

This section outlines the chronology in the arrangement of the general part of obligations. It can be found, for instance, in Hungary[368] (1928, 2013), Poland[369] (1933), Russia[370] (1964) and the French *Code civil* following the reform of 2016[371]. Such a systematization might be included with in the entire general part of obli-

---

368 In the Hungarian draft (1928), the first title (of the third book on obligations) considers contracts. The second title: the content of obligations. The third title: multi-party obligations. The fourth title: transmission of claims and obligations. The fifth title: extinction and expiration of claims.

In the current Hungarian civil code (2013), the chronological order is visible in the second division of the sixth book on obligations, including the general provisions on contracts.

In the second division firstly the fourth title (considering the contracts and the fundamental principles of contracts) is situated. The fifth title: conclusion and interpretation of contracts. The sixth title: invalidity. The seventh title: the scope of contracts and ineffectiveness. The eighth title lists the claims that cannot be enforced by judicial process. The ninth title: the contract performance. The tenth title: non-performance. The eleventh title: the confirmation and amendment of contracts. The twelfth title: assignment, subrogation, assumption of debt and transfer of contract. The last thirteenth title establishes the termination of a contract by mutual consent or unilaterally.

369 In the Polish Code of obligations (1933), the first title includes the sources, the substance and the kinds of obligations. The second title: formation of obligations. The third title: transfer of rights and duties, arising from obligations. The fourth title: expiration of obligations. The fifth title: suing the actions of a debtor with the detriment for creditors.

370 In the second socialist Russian civil code (1964), in the third book on obligations the fifteenth chapter refers to the formation of obligations. The sixteenth chapter: the performance of obligations. The seventeenth chapter: securing of the performance of obligations. The eighteenth chapter: transfer of a claim and change of a creditor. The nineteenth chapter: the liability for the breach of obligations. The twentieth chapter: extinction of obligations.

371 In the French *Code civil,* the third title (of the third book on different ways of acquiring ownership) deals with the sources of obligations. The chronology is visible in the first sub-title (of the third title) regarding contract. In the first sub-title there are: introductory provisions (the first chapter), formation of contracts (the second chapter), contractual interpretation (the third chapter) and the effects of contracts (the fourth chapter).

After the first sub-title on contract there are the extra-contractual liability (the second sub-title) and other sources of obligations (the third sub-title).

The further systematic segments are visible in the fourth title containing the general regime of obligations. The fourth title includes: modalities of obligations (the first chapter), transactions relating to obligations (the second chapter), actions available to creditors (the third chapter), extinction of obligations (the fourth chapter) and finally restitution (the fifth chapter).

gations (Hungary – 1928, Poland – 1933) or only in part of it (Hungary – 2013). This composition may be applied to codes that also comprise a general part (Russia – 1964), but the arrangement discussed here is more typical of the codes that include obligationsin a single book. Furthermore, a chronology can easily be conjoined with the classification that accords with the sources of obligations.

The sequence of a contract (or an obligation), from its formation until its "death", is reflected in the systematization of the civil codes. Applying the chronology in the general part of obligations is one of the most natural and logical patterns. Arranging the formation of obligations at the beginning of obligations and removing obligations from the end of the general part of obligations is one such example[372]. This applies to all codifications; among the first codifications chronology is visible, for instance, in the CMBC[373] (1756). Nonetheless, legislators might also break with the sequence of obligations – e.g. in the Saxon civil code (1863) the provisions on the performance (of obligations) are situated before their formation[374].

5. Isolation of the general provisions regarding contracts; the remaining provisions of the general part of obligations are placed in the last book of the code (Austria – 1811, East Germany – 1975)

Another possibility is to include everything concerning contracts in one area of the code; concurrently, the remaining provisions of the general part of obligations would feature in the final book of the code. In the ABGB, the second division (of the second book, on *ius rerum*) includes personal rights. The general provisions

---

372 This systematic principle is visible also in the East German civil code (1975); its structure varies significantly from the bourgeois civil codes, but the written law follows the chronological order in the general part of obligations.

In the third book of East German civil code (including contracts relating to material and cultural life) the first chapter contains the general provisions concerning contracts. The first subdivision (of the first chapter) refers to the fundamental principles. The second subdivision: legal capacity, representation and power of attorney. The third subdivision: conclusion and form of contracts. The fourth subdivision: performance of contracts. The fifth subdivision: the modification and the termination of a contract. The last sixth subdivision: liability for the breach of the contractual obligations.

Here the chronology of a contract is also present – there are: the conclusion and the form of the contracts (the third subdivision), then the performance of contracts (the fourth subdivision) and the modification and the termination of a contract (the fifth subdivision).

373 In the CMBC (1756), in the fourth book on obligations the first chapter considers contracts and therefrom arising duties in general. Further there is the content corresponding with the particular contracts (chapters from the second to the thirteenth). The fourteenth chapter refers to the performance of obligations, particularly payment. The fifteenth chapter contains other kinds of cancellation of obligations. Putting the performance and extinction of obligations at the back of the book is a clear sign of chronology of obligations, applied in the CMBC.

374 In the Saxon civil code (1863), the second chapter (the third book on the law of claims, the first division on the claims in general) considers the performance of obligations. The third chapter: formation of claims.

on contracts are situated first, followed by the particular obligations[375]. In the final, third book (which includes the provisions common to personal rights and *ius in re*) are: security of rights and obligations (the first chapter), modification of rights and obligations (the second chapter), cancellation of rights and obligations (the third chapter), and finally prescription and usucaption (the fourth chapter).

The East German civil code (1975) contains a third book on contracts relating to material and cultural life. The third book comprises the general provisions regarding contracts (the first chapter) and the particular contracts (chapters from the second to the eighth). As with the ABGB, the final seventh book (on the specific provisions of the respective relationships of private law) concerns some institutions regarding the general part of obligations. They are: specific features of performing contractual obligations (the first chapter), participation of some contractors in a contract (the second chapter) and securing claims (the third chapter). Additionally, the final, sixth chapter of the seventh book deals with prescription. The grounds for adopting this arrangement in East Germany are listed in the first section of the chapter, among the obligations in the external divisions of the civil codes.

IV. Distribution of the general provisions of the law of contracts in the civil codes

Having outlined the most relevant aspects of the arrangement of the general part of obligations, this section deals with the systematization of the general provisions on contracts in the civil codes. In observing the place of contracts, we may determine their significance in the systems of the civil codes. There is no codification that does not refer to a contract. The analysis here is limited to the general part of obligations. The examination considers the composition of contracts in four aspects. First, the arrangement of contracts in the codes based on the Gaius scheme. Second, the systematization of contracts in the codes that include a general part. Third, the composition of contracts in the codifications that isolate obligations in a single book, and which do not comprise a general part. Finally, this section considers the arrangement of contracts in the socialist civil codes.

1. Arrangement of contract law in the civil codes structured according to the Gaius model

In the codes based on the Gaius scheme, provisions on contracts constitute a dominant factor in the arrangement of the general part of obligations[376]. More infor-

[375] In the ABGB (1811), the seventeenth chapter (the first chapter in the second division on personal rights, the second book on *ius rerum*) encompasses contracts in general. Then the particular obligations are located (from chapters eighteen to thirty).

[376] In the CC (1804), provisions on agreements are placed in the third title of the third book (on different ways of acquiring ownership), regarding contracts and conventional obligations in general.

mation can be found in the section on the composition of the legal concepts in the civil codes.

2. Arrangement of contract law in the codes containing a general part

In the codes that include a general part, the provisions on contracts can be split between the general part and the book on obligations; this arrangement can be found in the German BGB[377] (1896). One reason for the adoption of such a systematization in the BGB was the fact that a contract is considered to be one of the most general concepts of private law, applying to the law of obligations, *ius in re*, family law and inheritance law[378]. In such an arrangement, a contract is an institution of the general part[379], even though the first, most natural association is with the law of obligations. In the general part of the BGB more attention is given to juridical acts than to contracts[380].

In the civil codes with a general part it is also possible to include all provisions of contract law in the general part of obligations[381]; at the same time, the general part only has provisions on juridical acts. In the general part of obligations, the provisions on contracts may constitute a separate systematic unit[382]. The general provisions of contracts might also be situated among the formation of obligations[383].

In the ABGB (1811), provisions on contracts are included in the second division (on personal rights) of the second book on *ius rerum*, in the seventeenth chapter, concerning the contracts in general.

377 In the German BGB (1896), in the general part the third title (of the third chapter on juridical acts) concerns contract.
The second chapter (of the second book on obligations) includes the contractual obligations.

378 HOFER S., *vor § 145 Vertrag*, in: SCHMOECKEL M. (ed.), *Historisch-kritischer Kommentar zum BGB. Band I Allgemeiner Teil §§ 1 – 240*, Tübingen 2003, p. 819.
More about the discussion on the German arrangement: *Ibidem*, pp. 818 – 820.

379 MEDICUS D., *Schuldrecht I. Allgemeiner Teil*, München 2006, p. 28.

380 LEHMANN H., HÜBNER H., *Allgemeiner Teil des Bürgerlichen Gesetzbuches*, Berlin 1966, p. 233.

381 In the current Russian civil code (1994 – 2006), the second subsection (of the third book including the general part of obligations) comprises the general provisions on the contract.

382 In the German BGB (1896), the second chapter (of the second book on obligations) deals with the contractual obligations.
In the Polish civil code (1964), the third title (of the third book on obligations) contains the general provisions on contractual obligations.

383 In the second socialist Russian civil code (1964), the general provisions of the contract law are arranged in the third book on obligations, in the fifteenth chapter (the first chapter in the third book) regarding the formation of obligations. The fifteenth chapter contains Articles 158 – 167 and Articles 160 – 167 consider contracts.

3. Arrangement of contract law in the civil codes separating the book on obligations (and not including a general part)

This section considers the systematization of contract law in the civil codes where the entire volume of the general part of obligations is situated in one book. In such an arrangement, the general provisions of contracts are situated in the general part of obligations, in one area of the code (Switzerland – 1911; Hungary – 1928, 1959, 2013; Poland – 1933).

In the Swiss Code of obligations, contracts are perceived as the primary source of obligations[384]. It is very likely that the Swiss systematization was inspired by the ABGB (1811), where contract is also the central construct[385]. Both codifications share this arrangement, and it is the result of their attachment to the Gaius scheme. Contrary to the CC (1804), the Swiss composition is clearly concentrated on a contract, without any reference to the agreement of the parties. In the Polish Code of obligations a contract is the result of the declaration of the will of an individual[386]. The arrangement discussed here varies significantly from the Swiss composition described above. In Poland, the declaration of will is a dominant factor. This reasoning is the outcome of the German Pandect model, in which a juridical act and declaration of will precede contract.

Turning now to the Hungarian arrangement, the lack of the general part and the favouring of a contract is a feature of the Hungarian systematization. Both in the Hungarian draft (1928) and in the socialist Hungarian civil code (1959), a contract is the principal construct in the general part of obligations[387], but in the Hungarian draft, apart from contracts in the divisions of the general part of obligations, there is also are ference to obligations and claims[388]. The current Hungarian civil code (2013) features a different arrangement. The general part of obligations contains

---

384 In the Swiss Code of obligations contract law is put at the beginning of the code (the first title: formation of obligations, the first chapter: obligations arising by contract).

385 LIPP M., *Die Bedeutung des Naturrechts für die Ausbildung der Allgemeinen Lehren des deutschen Privatrechts*, Berlin 1980, p. 28.

386 In the Polish Code of obligations (1933), the second title considers the formation of obligations. The first division of the second title includes the declaration of will. The fourth chapter (of the first division) refers to contracts in general.

387 In the Hungarian draft (1928), the first title of the third book on obligations refers to contracts. It is one of the five titles of the third book constituting the general part of obligations. The second title: the content of obligations. The third title: multi-party obligations. The fourth title: transmission of claims and obligations. The fifth title: extinction and expiration of claims.

In the socialist Hungarian civil code (1959), the first title of the fourth book on obligations considers contracts. In the socialist Hungarian code the entire content of the general part of obligations is put in the first title of the fourth book.

388 In the Hungarian draft (1928), the first title of the third book on obligations deals with contracts. The second title: content of obligations. The third title: multi-party obligations. The fourth title: transmission of claims and obligations. The fifth title: extinction and expiration of claims.

two divisions. These are, in sequence, common provisions relating to obligations and general provisions on contracts.

4. Systematization of contract law in the socialist civil codes

The question next addressed in this chapter is whether socialism affects the arrangement of contract law in the socialist civil codes. In Hungary, a general part was never introduced; in the socialist Hungarian civil code (1959) the content of the general part of obligations is assembled around the concept of a contract[389]. In the East German civil code (1975), contract is also the main construct: the third book considers contracts relating to material and cultural life. Contracts may be arranged in the book on obligations, in the chapter on the formation of obligations (Czechoslovakia – 1950, Russia – 1964), constituting a systematic subset of the formation of obligations[390]. In the second socialist Czechoslovak civil code contracts are solely a subcategory of juridical acts[391] (1964). In the socialist civil codes attempts to establish the socialist systematization of the law of obligations may have resulted in putting contracts at the centre of the system, or in reducing their significance.

V. Main systematic segments of the general part of obligations and their arrangement in the civil codes

Having outlined the possibilities of settling the provisions of contract law, this section indicates the systematization of the systematic components in the civil codes. The first among them is an obligation. The second issue discussed here is the formation of obligations. The third division involves multi-party obligations. The fourth division considers the execution of obligations. The fifth division concentrates on the transition of obligations. The extinction of obligations is examined in the final sixth division. That is the final component, which terminates the chronology of an obligation. The systematization of the institutions of the law of obligations that are classified in the general part is subsequently described, although it belongs to the next area discussed, the further systematic subdivisions. The purpose of this analysis is to trace the most significant systematic patterns

---

[389] In the socialist Hungarian civil code (1959), the first title (of the fourth book on obligations) refers to contracts.

[390] In the first socialist Czechoslovak civil code (1950), the eleventh chapter (the fourth book on obligations) concerns the formation and content of obligations. The contractual obligations are mentioned in Articles 213 – 217. The eleventh chapter comprises Articles 211 – 250.

In the second socialist Russian civil code (1964), the fifteenth chapter (the third book on obligations) encompasses the formation of obligations. The fifteenth chapter contains Articles 158 – 167. Contract is recalled in Articles 160 – 167.

[391] In the second socialist Czechoslovak civil code (1964), the fourth division of the general part considers juridical acts (§§ 34 – 51). In the fourth division on juridical acts there is a systematic unit referring to contracts (§§ 43 – 51), not visible in the table of contents.

in the civil codes as well as the possibilities for arranging the main systematic segments in the general part of obligations.

1. An obligation

An obligation is usually placed at the beginning of the book on obligations[392]; in a civil code there might be a separate systematic unit concerning an obligation[393]. The most logical location for an obligation is among the provisions referring to obligations. Yet, if the general part of the law of obligations is assembled around the idea of a contract, then instead of an obligation, a codification may include a definition of an agreement in its place. The systematization mentioned here can be found in, for instance, the French *Code civil* (1804); according to Article 1101, a contract is an agreement by which one or several persons bind themselves, towards one or several other persons, to transfer, to do or not to do something[394].

This study establishes that an obligation is a concept that is often defined in the civil codes. Including a definition in a civil code makes it binding for all books of the code and for the entire private law. In the German BGB (1896) the definition of an obligation can be found in§ 241[395]. That information is important from the perspective of constructing a civil code; not all basic constructs are defined in the text of a written law – the German BGB does not comprise the definition of a juridical act. Considering a juridical act as an obvious legal category, the German lawyers did not find it necessary to place such a definition in the code[396].

---

[392] In the German BGB (1896), § 241, the first provision of the second book on obligations (the first chapter referring to the content of obligations), indicates the content of an obligation.

In the Polish civil code (1964), an obligation is defined in the first provision of the third book on obligations (Article 353), in the first title including the general provisions.

[393] In the current Hungarian civil code (2013), the first chapter (the sixth book on obligations, the first division comprising the common provisions relating to obligations, the first title on the general provisions) regards an obligation.

[394] The text of Article 1101 was changed in 2016: *Le contrat est un accord de volontés entre deux ou plusieurs personnes destiné à créer, modifier, transmettre ou éteindre des obligations.*

In the socialist Hungarian civil code (1959), in the first provision of the fourth book on obligations a contract is indicated. That is Section 198. According to the first part of Section 198: a contract creates an obligation to discharge a performance and a title to claim the performance.

[395] *§ 241 Pflichten aus dem Schuldverhältnis*

(1) Kraft des Schuldverhältnisses ist der Gläubiger berechtigt, von dem Schuldner eine Leistung zu fordern. Die Leistung kann auch in einem Unterlassen bestehen.

(2) Das Schuldverhältnis kann nach seinem Inhalt jeden Teil zur Rücksicht auf die Rechte, Rechtsgüter und Interessen des anderen Teils verpflichten.

[396] RANIERI F., *Europäisches Obligationenrecht. Ein Handbuch mit Texten und Materialien*, Wien 2003, p. 47.

2. Formation of obligations and the provisions on entering into agreements

The most accurate location for the formation of obligations is at the beginning of the book on obligations[397]. In codifications that include a general part, provisions on the formation of agreements might be transposed to the general part[398]; if that is the case, then they apply also to all other contracts, for instance, in the German BGB the provisions on the formation of agreements settled in the general part are applied to contracts for gaming and betting[399]. If a contract prevails in the arrangement of the general part of obligations, then the precepts on the formation of obligations are placed in the section concerning contract law[400].

3. Multi-party relationships

The next problem is the arrangement of multi-party relations in the civil codes researched for this study. Multi-party relations are a firmly neutral element in the structure of the general part of obligations. They can be located at the beginning of the general part of obligations[401], its middle[402] or its end[403]. Due to its neutrality

---

[397] In the Swiss Code of obligations (1911), the first title (of the first division containing the general provisions) regards the formation of obligations.

In the Polish Code of obligations (1933), the second title deals with the formation of obligations.

In the first socialist Czechoslovak civil code (1950), the eleventh chapter (constituting the first chapter of the fourth book on obligations) encompasses the formation and content of obligations.

In the second socialist Russian civil code (1964), the fifteenth chapter (the first chapter in the third book on obligations) concerns the formation of obligations.

[398] In the German BGB (1896), the third title (of the third chapter on juridical acts, set in the general part) considers contract. Here there are provisions on entering into contracts.

In the Polish civil code (1964), the second division (of the fourth title on juridical acts, situated in the general part) refers to the conclusion of contract.

[399] WERTENBRUCH J., *BGB. Allgemeiner Teil*, München 2021, p. 122.

[400] In the socialist Hungarian civil code (1959), the eighteenth chapter (the fourth book on obligations, the first title on contract) considers the making of a contract.

In the current Hungarian civil code (2013), the fifth title in the sixth book on obligations (the second division including the general provisions on contracts) concerns the conclusion and interpretation of contracts.

[401] That is the arrangement in the Polish Code of obligations (1933), where the second division of the first title (referring to the sources, substance and the kinds of obligations) includes joint liability.

In the current Hungarian civil code (2013), the second title of the sixth book on obligations (set in the first division of the sixth book, considering the common provisions relating to obligations) deals with multi-party obligations.

[402] The mentioned systematization is visible in the Hungarian draft (1928), where the third title (among the five titles constituting the general part of obligations, in the third book on obligations) refers to obligations with more creditors or debtors.

[403] In the Saxon civil code (1863), the sixth chapter (of the third book regarding the law of claims, the first division comprising the claims in general) deals with multi-party obligations *(Gesammtschuldverhältnisse)*. The fifth chapter considers the extinction of obligations and the seventh chapter looks at bearer instruments. The seventh chapter constitutes the last chapter of the ge-

in the civil codes, there might be a preference for situating multi-party obligations at the end of the general part of obligations, following the provisions on the extinction of obligations[404]. This systematization does not affect the chronology of obligations. Multi-party obligations can also be arranged among the provisions relevant to the performance of obligations[405]. In such a composition they are perceived as one of the aspects of the execution of obligations.

4. Execution of obligations

Having considered this neutral systematic component (multi-party obligations) we pass to the execution of obligations. From this point onward we approach the end of the general part of obligations. This section first deals with the execution of obligations, then the transition of obligations and finally the extinction of obligations. Provisions on the execution of obligations might be placed in a separate systematic unit[406]. As the performance of obligations results in their extinction, the provisions on the execution of obligations can be placed in the section regarding the extinction of obligations[407].

The execution of obligations might be viewed in the codes in two ways. It may be a way in which obligations may expire, and for this reason it functions as a subtype of obligation expiry[408]. Another perspective is also possible; as perfor-

---

neral part of obligations.

In the German BGB (1896), the last sixth chapter of the general part of obligations (set in the second book on obligations) concerns the plurality of debtors and creditors.

In the socialist Hungarian civil code (1959), the last chapter of the general part of obligations [the twenty-eighth chapter, placed at the end of the first title (referring to contracts) of the fourth book on obligations] regards several obligees or several obligors in the contract.

404 In the Saxon civil code (1863), the sixth chapter (of the third book concerning the law of claims, the first division dealing with the claims in general) refers to multi-party obligations *(Gesammtschuldverhältnisse)*. The fifth chapter considers the extinction of obligations and the seventh chapter (the last chapter of the general part of obligations) deals with bearer instruments.

In the German BGB (1896), the last sixth chapter of the general part of obligations (put in the second book on obligations) mentions the plurality of debtors and creditors.

405 In the second socialist Russian civil code (1964), the regulation of the multi-party obligations can be found in the sixteenth chapter (of the third book on obligations) concerning the performance of obligations (Articles 168 – 185). Articles 179 – 185 contain the content relevant to multi-party obligations.

406 This arrangement can be found e.g. in the Polish civil code (1964), where the seventh title of the third book on obligations considers the performance of obligations and effects of nonperformance.

407 In the Polish Code of obligations (1933), the fourth title considers the extinction of obligations. The first division of the fourth title deals with the execution of obligations.

408 In the first socialist Czechoslovak civil code (1950), provisions on the execution of obligations are a systematic subset of the extinction of obligations. The fifteenth chapter (the fourth book containing the law of obligations) deals with the extinction of obligations (Articles 298 – 336). Provisions concerning the execution of obligations are arranged in the fifteenth chapter, in Article 299 and the subsequent provisions.

In the second socialist Czechoslovak civil code (1964), the seventh division of the general

ming an obligation by a debtor may last even for many years, then that is sufficient to constitute an independent segment of the system[409]. The performance of an obligation and the extinction of an obligation may be arranged in two distinct systematic units. In such a composition, performance is placed first, followed by the extinction of obligations[410], because the execution of an obligation occurs before its extinction. Giving more attention to the performance of obligations in the structure of the law of obligations is a natural consequence of the development in arranging the civil codes.

5. Transition of obligations

The systematic segment next discussed is the transition of obligations. The provisions on the transition of obligations might be settled before a section regarding

---

part considers the extinction of rights and duties (§§ 71 – 99). In the beginning of the seventh division performance of an obligation is settled (§§ 71 – 89).

In the Hungarian draft (1928), the fifth title (of the third book on the law of obligations) deals with the extinction and prescription of claims. The first chapter of the fifth title contains the performance (of obligations).

In the Polish Code of obligations (1933) the fourth title comprises the extinction of obligations. The first division of the fourth title concerns the execution of obligations.

409 VON SEELER W., *Der Entwurf des russischen Zivilgesetzbuches*, Berlin 1911, pp. 193 – 194.

This systematization can be found e.g. in the Polish civil code (1964); the seventh title (of the third book on obligations) comprises the performance of obligations and the effects of their non-performance.

In the second socialist Russian civil code (1964), the sixteenth chapter (the third book on obligations) contains the performance of obligations.

410 In the Russian draft (1905), the fourth subdivision (the fifth book on the law of obligations, the first division regarding an obligation in general) encompasses the performance of an obligation and the sixth subdivision extinction of an obligation.

Between them in the fifth subdivision the transfer of a claim and assumption of debt is arranged.

In the second socialist Russian civil code (1964), the sixteenth chapter (the third book including the law of obligations) comprises the execution of obligations, whereas the twentieth chapter the extinction of obligations.

Between them there are: securing of the performance of obligations (the seventeenth chapter), transfer of a claim and change of a creditor (the eighteenth chapter) and the liability for the breach of obligations (the nineteenth chapter).

In the socialist Hungarian civil code (1959), the twenty-fourth chapter (the fourth book on the law of obligations, the first title regarding contract) considers the performance and set-off, whereas the twenty-sixth chapter comprises the particular cases of termination of contract and prescription. Between them, in the twenty-fifth chapter, breach of contract is settled. The institutions mentioned in those chapters result in the extinction of obligations.

the extinction of obligations[411] or after it[412]. Here, it should be indicated that the transfer of obligations between living partners belongs to the law of obligations, whereas the transfer of obligations related to the death of a creditor or a debtor falls with in the law of succession[413]. Inheritance law itself regulates the transmission of goods belonging to an individual after his death. The distinction discussed here is the logical result of implementing universal legal classifications in legal science and civil codes.

6. Extinction of obligations

In codes that comprise obligations in a single book, all precepts on the extinction of obligations are contained in a book on obligations. In the codes comprising a general part prescription is situated in the general part. The composition of prescription in civil codes that include a general part is presented below, among the institutions of the law of obligations classified in the general part. Prescription is associated primarily with the general part (in the jurisdictions where that is a typical arrangement), but it has a strong link with the law of obligations; prescription is connected with the cessation of actions that we might successfully bring to a court. Despite the fact that prescription also applies to other branches of private law, the law of obligations involves other institutions of private law that are also valid for other areas of private law (e.g. condition). This issue, as well as the relevance of obligations from the systematic and economic point of view, contributes to the importance of obligations.

This area of the study concentrates on the systematization of the extinction of obligations. Precepts regarding the extinction of obligations may be placed in

---

411 In the Hungarian draft (1928), the fourth title (of the third book on obligations) deals with the transition of claims and obligations. The fifth title: expiration and prescription of claims.

In the Polish Code of obligations (1933) the third title concerns the transition of rights and duties, arising from obligations. The fourth title: extinction of obligations.

In the socialist Hungarian civil code (1959), the twenty-sixth chapter (of the fourth book on obligations, the first title referring to contracts) considers the particular cases of termination of contract and prescription. The twenty-seventh chapter: assignment and assumption of debt.

In the second socialist Russian civil code (1964), in the eighteenth chapter (in the third book on obligations) the assignment of claim and the change of a debtor are situated. The nineteenth chapter: liability for the breach of obligations. The twentieth chapter: extinction of obligations.

412 In the German BGB (1896), the third chapter (of the second book on obligations) concerns the extinction of obligations. The fourth chapter: assignment of claims. The fifth chapter: assumption of debt.

In the Swiss Code of obligations (1911), the third title (of the first division including the general provisions) considers the extinction of obligations. The fourth title: special relationships relating to obligations *(des modalités des obligations)*. The last fifth title of the first division refers to the assignment of claims and assumption of debt.

413 LONGCHAMPS DE BERIER R., *Zobowiązania* [Obligations], Lwów 1939, p. 297.

the middle[414], at the end[415] or close to the end of the general part of obligations[416]. They cannot be found at the beginning of the general part of obligations, because such an arrangement would be incompatible with the chronology of obligations. All legislators seek harmony in the systematization of the law of obligations; complying with the sequence of obligations is one of the most significant rules they follow.

If the general part of obligations is separated into two systematic compounds (in order, obligations and contracts), then the provisions on the removal of obligations can be arranged at the end of the provisions relating to obligations[417]. This systematization is the result of a natural chronology applied in the written laws – the same viewpoint influences placing prescription at the conclusion of the general part and inheritance law at the end of a civil code. If the general part of obligations is erased from the systematization of the code, and if at the same time

---

[414] In the German BGB (1896), the third chapter of the second book on obligations considers the extinction of obligations. The fourth chapter: assignment of claims. The fifth chapter: assumption of debt. The sixth chapter: plurality of debtors and creditors. The seventh chapter: particular obligations.

In the Swiss Code of obligations (1911), the third title (in the first division on the general provisions) refers to the extinction of obligations. The first division includes five titles.

[415] In the first socialist Czechoslovak civil code (1950), the fifteenth chapter (the fourth book including the law of obligations) regards the extinction of obligations. They are arranged after the non-contractual sources of obligations (the law of damages in the sixteenth chapter and the unjustified enrichment in the seventeenth chapter) and the particular contracts (the eighteenth chapter includes sales and exchange).

In the Hungarian draft (1928), the fifth title (of the third book on the law of obligations) regards the expiration and prescription of claims. That is the last title of the general part of obligations – the sixth title considers loans, gratuitous loans for use, deposits and the liability of innkeeper.

In the second socialist Russian civil code (1964), the twentieth chapter (of the third book on obligations) concerns the extinction of obligations. The twentieth chapter closes the general part of obligations. The twenty-first chapter: sales and barter.

[416] In the Saxon civil code (1863), the fifth chapter (the third book on the law of claims, the first division comprising claims in general) considers the extinction of claims. Following the extinction of claims there are multi-party obligations (the sixth chapter) and bearer instruments (the seventh chapter).

In the Russian draft (1905), the sixth subdivision (the fifth book containing the law of obligations, the first division considering an obligation in general) deals with the termination of obligations. The seventh subdivision (the last subdivision of the general part of obligations) refers to joint claims and joint debts.

In the Polish Code of obligations (1933), the fourth title encompasses the expiration of obligations. Afterwards there is the fifth title, concerning suing the actions of a debtor, causing damage to creditors. The sixth title: sales and exchange.

[417] In the current Russian civil code (1994 – 2006), the third book includes the general part of obligations. The first subsection of the third book contains the general provisions on obligations. At the end of the first subsection the twenty-sixth chapter considers the termination of obligations. The second subsection of the third book comprises the general provisions on the contract.

the general part is present in the code, then the provisions on prescription and extinction on rights and duties might be placed next to each other, at the end of the general part[418]. To understand more fully the systematization of the extinction of obligations, we must investigate the arrangement of prescription.

VI. Institutions of the law of obligations, classified in the general part

The next problem to consider concerns the composition of institutions belonging to the law of obligations that are transposed to the general part. These are prescription (the first point), condition (the second point) and the power of attorney and representation (the third point). Depending on the arrangement applied in the code, they can be found among the law of obligations or in the general part. Mixed systematization is also possible; a code may not comprise a general part, but it can be inspired by the arrangement of codes containing a general part, as occurs in the current Hungarian civil code (2013).

1. Prescription

The arrangement of prescription is considered in four aspects. First, the composition of prescription in the codes established according to the Gaius model. Next, the systematization of prescription in the codes containing a general part, followed by the location of prescription in the codes not including a general part. Finally, the arrangement of prescription in the current Hungarian civil code (2013).

a) Arrangement of prescription in the codes based on the Gaius scheme

In the codes that follow the Gaius model, the passage of time was perceived as a definite entity, regardless of whether its consequences concerned *ius in re* or the law of obligations. As a result, usucaption and prescription were systematized in tandem. In the CMBC (1756), prescription is situated among *ius in re*, following different ways of acquiring ownership[419], whereas in the CC[420] (1804) and the ABGB[421] (1811) it is arranged at the end of the code. The written law where ownership and its acquisition are crucial could not choose any other systematization. This factor is visible in France (1804); in the CC (1804), the final, third book (containing prescription) comprises different ways of acquiring ownership.

---

418 In the second socialist Czechoslovak civil code (1964), the seventh division (of the general part) concerns the extinction of rights and duties. The eighth division: prescription. The last ninth division includes a glossary (explanation of certain concepts).

419 In the CMBC (1756) the fourth chapter (of the second book on *ius in re*) regards prescription. The third chapter includes different ways of acquiring ownership and the fifth chapter contains possession.

420 In the CC (1804), the last twentieth title (of the third book on different ways of acquiring ownership) considers prescription.

421 In the ABGB (1811), the last fourth chapter (of the third book containing provisions common to personal rights and *ius in re*) deals with prescription and usucaption. That is the last chapter in the code.

In the French composition, prescription is strongly connected both with *res* and *actiones*; it is settled at the end of the third book on different ways of acquiring ownership (*actiones*), but concurrently it is placed next to the institutions of *ius in re*[422]; this provides a reference to *res*. In the CC, prescription is an expiration of *actiones*, bringing an end to legal obligations by converting them into natural ones. Perceiving prescription in the context of the acquisition of ownership (the third book of the CC) resembles the Bavarian systematization (1756).

In the ABGB (1811), prescription is, above all, one one way of removing *actiones* (obligations). The composition of the code gives it a wide application (a concept visible in the table of contents of the third book of the ABGB, which concerns rights and obligations[423]), but the systematization of the third book of the ABGB, which almost exclusively comprises institutions of the law of obligations (except for usucaption, as part of *ius in re*), gives it a stronger connection with obligations (*actiones*). In the later codifications, *actiones* are associated primarily with the law of obligations. In this aspect the ABGB acts as a bridge between the previous arrangement and later systematic patterns.

b) Arrangement in the codes including a general part

Arranging prescription was a problem in the first codifications. Following the first extraction of the general part (Saxony – 1863), prescription and usucaption were isolated from each other. Usucaption is placed among *ius in re*, with prescription at the end of the general part[424]. In codes that include a general part prescription is not likely to be a systematic subset of juridical acts, the concept that holds the institutions of the law of obligations (condition, representation and power of attorney) in the general part. Prescription primarily constitutes a separate systematic segment in the general part[425]. The Pandect systematization was inspired by the

---

422 In the CC (1804), the seventeenth title (of the third book on different ways of acquiring ownership) regards pledges. The eighteenth title: privileges and mortgages. The nineteenth title: forced expropriation and orders between creditors. The twentieth title: prescription.

423 In the ABGB (1811), the first chapter (of the third book) concerns the security for rights and obligations. The second chapter: modification of rights and obligations. The third chapter: cancellation of rights and obligations. The fourth chapter: prescription and usucaption.

424 The regulation of prescription arranged in the general part of the German BGB (1896) is central for the code, but in the further books of the code there are more particular provisions considering special cases of prescription for another institutions of private law. WERTENBRUCH J., *BGB. Allgemeiner Teil*, München 2021, p. 317.

According to the German legal science, prescription results in the loss of a claim. HERMANN H.-G., *§§ 194 – 225. Verjährung*, in: SCHMOECKEL M. (ed.), *Historisch-kritischer Kommentar zum BGB. Band I Allgemeiner Teil §§ 1 – 240*, Tübingen 2003, p. 993 and the following page.

425 In the Saxon civil code (1863), prescription is settled in the general part, in § 150 and the subsequent provisions.

In the German BGB (1896), the fifth chapter of the general part regards prescription.

In the first socialist Russian civil code (1922) the last fifth chapter of the general part deals with the prescription of actions.

Austrian arrangement (1811), where prescription was first treated as an element common to personal rights and *ius in re*.

c) Arranging prescription among obligations

Prescription is an institution that results in the extinction of obligations, which systematically belong to this area. In codes that do not include a general part, this connection is visible in the composition of the codes: prescription is most likely to be settled in the section concerning the extinction of obligations[426]. In considering the systematization of obligations, prescription should be viewed as a subcategory of the extinction of obligations.

d) Hungary (2013)

A different arrangement was applied in the current Hungarian civil code (2013), where prescription is arranged at the beginning of the general part of obligations. This composition resembles the German BGB (1896). Even though the current Hungarian civil code does not include a general part, the most general provisions of obligations are located at the beginning of the book on obligations, usually

---

In the second socialist Russian civil code (1964), the last sixth chapter of the general part concerns the prescription of claims.

In the current Russian civil code (1994 – 2006), the last fifth subsection of the general part considers the term and the limitation of actions.

In the first socialist Czechoslovak civil code (1950), the last sixth chapter of the general part refers to prescription.

In the second socialist Czechoslovak civil code (1964), the eighth division of the general part contains prescription.

In the current Czech civil code (2012), the third chapter (the first book including the general provisions, the fifth title considering the legal facts) refers to the statute of limitations and prescription.

In the Polish civil code (1964) the last sixth title of the general part includes the prescription of claims.

In the East German civil code (1975) the last sixth chapter of the last seventh book (comprising the specific provisions of the respective relationships of private law) considers prescription. In the East German civil code prescription is located at the end of the last seventh book, acting as a systematic equivalent of the general part.

[426] In the Swiss Code of obligations (1911), prescription is located in the third title (Articles 114 – 142) of the general part of obligations, concerning the extinction of obligations. Prescription is set in Articles 127 – 142.

In the Hungarian draft (1928), prescription is placed at the end of the general part of obligations. That is in the fifth title of the third book on obligations, regarding expiration and prescription of claims. It is placed between the fourth title of the third book (considering transition of claims and obligations) and the sixth title containing loans, gratuitous loans for use, deposit and liability of innkeeper.

In the socialist Hungarian civil code (1959), the twenty-sixth chapter (the fourth book on obligations, the first title regarding contract) considers the particular cases of termination of contract and prescription.

In the Polish Code of obligations (1933), the fourth title considers the extinction of obligations. The last seventh division (of the fourth title) deals with prescription.

classified in the general part[427]. At the same time, regulations on the termination of a contract are arranged at the end of the provisions of contract law[428].

2. Condition

The next institution to consider is condition. If a condition is introduced into a juridical act, then its legal effect becomes dependent from an event that may occur in the future. It is a collateral clause that may be introduced in a juridical act[429]. In the codes that contain a general part condition is classified in the general part. Such a classification indicates that it applies to all branches of private law, because a condition may also be adopted in a contract or a will. Concurrently, the relation between condition and the law of obligations is preserved, because condition is usually placed in the section concerning juridical acts[430]. As a result, the systematization of condition in the general part is compatible with its function in the system of private law[431]; additional elements receive less attention than the main constructs, such as contracts or juridical acts.

Following this outline of the composition of the codifications comprising a general part, it is necessary to refer to the first codifications. The ABGB (1811) treats conditions as collateral provisions, which may be introduced into the decrees of the last will (§§ 695 – 708) or contracts (§§ 897 – 901)[432]. In the French

---

[427] In the current Hungarian civil code (2013), prescription is put in the fourth chapter dealing with the statute of limitations, of the first title (the general provisions), the first division of the sixth book on obligations, including the common provisions relating to obligations.

The first title concerning the general provisions comprises the content relevant to the general part – the second chapter refers to legal statements, the third chapter considers representation and the fourth chapter refers to statute of limitations.

The first and the fifth chapters of the first title include the institutions relevant only to the law of obligations – the first chapter deals with an obligation, whereas the fifth chapter (closing the first title) concerns acknowledgement of debt and composition.

[428] In the current Hungarian civil code (2013), the last thirteenth title of the second division considering the general provisions on contracts (of the sixth book on obligations) deals with termination of a contract by mutual consent or unilaterally.

[429] WERTENBRUCH J., *BGB. Allgemeiner Teil*, München 2021, p. 317.

[430] In the German BGB (1896), condition is placed in the fourth title of the third chapter regarding juridical acts, in the general part.

In the first socialist Czechoslovak civil code (1950), condition is located at the end of the third chapter (of the general part) concerning juridical acts (Articles 53 – 55).

In the Polish civil code (1964), the fourth title of the general part contains the juridical acts. The fifth subdivision of the fourth title comprises condition.

In the second socialist Russian civil code (1964), Article 61 refers to juridical acts performed under a condition. Article 61 is the last provision of the third chapter on juridical acts in the general part.

[431] *Conf.* EISENHARDT U., *Allgemeiner Teil des BGB*, Heidelberg 1989, p. 286.

[432] DOMAŃSKI L., *Instytucje Kodeksu zobowiązań. Komentarz teoretyczno-praktyczny. Część ogólna* [Institutions of the Code of obligations. Theoretical and practical commentary. General part], Warszawa 1936, p. 296.

Code civil (1804) condition is settled among different kinds of obligations[433]. In the codifications that extract the law of obligations (and which do not include a general part), condition is located among the law of obligations[434].

3. Power of attorney and representation

Fromthe establishment of a general part onward, power of attorney has been a separate institution from mandate. Power of attorney is now placed in the general part, most typically after the juridical acts. It can either be positioned among the provisions on juridical acts[435] or it can be a separate systematic segment, set after the juridical acts[436]. Representation may also be placed before juridical acts, but this is not a common composition[437]. If a code does not contain a general part, then the provisions on power of attorney are written among the law of obligations[438].

VII. Exemplary additional sections that can be found in the general part of obligations of the examined codes

The next issue to consider involves other systematic divisions that may be found in the general part of obligations. A section regarding the violation of an obligation

---

433 In the CC (1804), the third title (of the third book on different ways of acquiring ownership) considers contracts and conventional obligations in general). The fourth chapter (of the third title) includes various kinds of obligations. The first section (of the fourth chapter) regards the conditional obligations.

434 In the Swiss Code of obligations (1911), condition is placed in the second chapter (on the conditional obligations) of the fourth title (special relationships relating to obligations), in the first part of the Code of obligations comprising the general provisions.

In the Hungarian draft (1928), condition is arranged in the fourth chapter of the first title (regarding contracts) of the third book considering the law of obligations. The fourth chapter includes condition and time designation.

In the socialist Hungarian civil code (1959), condition is positioned in the first title (contract), the twentieth chapter (contents and the object of the contract) of the fourth book on obligations. In the twentieth chapter there is a subsection regarding conditions and periods (§§ 228 – 229).

In the current Hungarian civil code (2013), condition is settled in the seventh title (scope of contracts. ineffectiveness), in the second division (the general provisions on contracts) of the sixth book on obligations (Section 6:116).

In the Polish Code of obligations (1933), the second title deals with the formation of obligations). Condition is arranged in the third chapter of the first division (declaration of will) of the second title.

435 E.g. in the German BGB (1896) the third chapter of the general part considers the juridical acts. The fifth title of the third chapter regards agency and power of attorney.

436 E.g. in the second socialist Russian civil code (1964) the third chapter of the general part includes the juridical acts and the fourth chapter representation and power of attorney.

437 In the second socialist Czechoslovak civil code (1964), the third division (of the general part) conceens representation and the fourth division juridical acts.

438 E.g. in the current Hungarian civil code (2013) at the beginning of the book on obligations there is a regulation of representation; the third chapter deals with representation (the sixth book comprising the law of obligations, the first division including the common provisions relating to obligations, the first title concerning the general provisions).

can be extracted in the general part of obligations[439]. Among some of the socialist civil codes researched here, a section referring to securing of obligations is placed in the general part of the law of obligations[440]. In socialist codifications systematized according to the needs of citizens of the socialist state, securing obligations is arranged in the general part[441].

In Poland, *actio pauliana* is differentiated and settled at the end of the general part of obligations. The composition discussed here is visible both in the Polish Code of obligations (1933) and in the Polish civil code[442]. It does not seem to me that a specific explanation was given as to why this area should be situated at the back of the general part of obligations; lawyers believed it to bea logical arrangement and introduced it in the written law. The Polish civil code (1964) replicated the systematization of the Code of obligations.

---

[439] In the East German civil code (1975), the sixth subsection (the third book on contracts relating to material and cultural life, the first chapter on the general provisions regarding contracts) refers to the liability for the infringement of the contractual duties.

In the second socialist Russian civil code (1964), the nineteenth chapter (the third book on obligations) comprises the liability for the breach of obligations.

In the current Russian civil code (1994 – 2006), the twenty-fifth chapter (the third book on the general part of obligations, the first subdivision on the general provisions on obligations) applies to the responsibility for the violation of obligations.

[440] In the first socialist Czechoslovak civil code (1950), the fourteenth chapter (of the fourth book on obligations) refers to securing obligations.

In the socialist Hungarian civil code (1959), the twenty-third chapter (of the fourth book on obligations, the first title comprising contracts) considers the collateral obligations securing the contract.

In the second socialist Russian civil code (1964), the seventeenth chapter (the third book on obligations) deals with securing the performance of obligations.

In the current Russian civil code (1994– 2006), the twenty-third chapter (the third book on the general part of obligations, the first subdivision on the general provisions on obligations) concerns provisions for the discharge of obligations.

[441] In the second socialist Czechoslovak civil code (1964), the fifth division of the general part encompasses the securing of rights and duties.

In the East German civil code (1975) the third chapter of the seventh book (containing the particular provisions of respective relationships of private law) considers securing claims.

In the East German civil code both the first book (referring to the fundamental principles of the socialist private law) and the seventh book share the function of the Pandect general part.

[442] In the Polish Code of obligations (1933), the fifth title deals with suing the actions of debtor, causing damage to creditors. The fourth title considers the extinction of obligations, whereas the sixth title includes sales and barter.

In the Polish civil code (1964), the tenth title (of the third book on obligations) concerns protection of the creditor in the case of debtor insolvency. The ninth title considers change of creditor or debtor, whereas the eleventh title refers to sales.

VIII. Impact of socialist ideology on the arrangement of the general part of obligations

Here we consider the influence of socialism on the general part of obligations. First, we address the (bourgeois) arrangement visible in the Polish civil code (1964). Second, this section discusses the socialist codifications that retain the traditional composition of the general part of obligations (Czechoslovakia – 1950, Russia – 1964). Next, we pursue a profound analysis of the socialist East German civil code (1975). Finally, we draw some conclusions. The study of the socialist Hungarian civil code (1959) can be found in the section concerning the composition of the legal concepts in the examined codifications, in the area depicting the Hungarian systematization. The impact of socialism on the law of obligations is much more limited than its effect on *ius in re*.

The first socialist Russian civil code (1922) is not examined; being prepared in a short time, its systematization was not sufficiently elaborated. The socialist Hungarian civil code (1959) is structured differently from other socialist codifications, because it does not contain a general part. The second socialist Czechoslovak civil code (1964) does not distinguish a general part of obligations; the provisions of the general part of obligations are transposed to the general part. For this reason, it cannot be juxtaposed with those codifications that include a general part of obligations.

1. As little socialism as possible (Poland – 1964)

The analysis begin with the Polish civil code (1964), because it is the least influenced by socialism among the studied codifications. The examination in this area is based on a gradation: first, we examine the almost entirely bourgeois Polish civil code (1964), then the comparatively more socialist Czechoslovak civil code (1950) and Russian civil code (1964), and finally the most socialist code, the East German civil code (1975).

In the Polish civil code (1964), the fourth title (of the third book on obligations) regulated the obligation to conclude agreements between units of the nationalized economy. This title cannot be found in the current version of the Polish civil code; as with other socialist expressions, which are unnecessary in capitalism, it was removed from the code after the system had changed. Furthermore, in the third title (which includes the general provisions on contractual obligations) there were three provisions (Articles 384 – 386), which specifically settle contracts in the area of the nationalized economy.

According to Article 354 § 1, a debtor should perform an obligation according to its content and in a manner corresponding to its social and economic purpose and to the principles of community coexistence. Here, the legislative method typical of the Polish civil code is discernible; it combines both socialist and bourgeois codifications. The principles of community coexistence are present in the Polish civil code to this day, taking the place of good faith and public policy. The general clause mentioned here does not include a reference to socialism.

Reading the general part of obligations of the Polish civil code indicates that it is sufficient to implement some provisions regarding the operation of the socialist economy (Articles 384 – 386 in the third title and Articles 397 – 404, constituting the volume of the fourth title previously mentioned, and Article 489). This demonstrates that the difference between the general part of obligations in a socialist and in a bourgeois codification can be almost minimal. The final issue concerning the arrangement of the Polish civil code is that it anticipates the liability for damage inflicted by a public officer (Article 417). Such an institution is not typical of socialist civil codes, because socialism favours the state and its public officers.

2. Socialist codifications with a traditional arrangement of the general part of obligations (Czechoslovakia – 1950, Russia – 1964)

In this section, we discuss some features of the general part of obligations in the socialist codifications that retain a traditional systematization (Czechoslovakia – 1950, Russia – 1964). In the systems of both codes little attention is given to contracts[443]. It seems that this legislative choice was related to the focus placed on an obligation in the structure of the general part of obligations[444]. This composition could be dictated by the preference for arranging the system on something very stable. An obligation cements the system of a code that does not contain family law, and which experiments with the systematization of *ius in re*. Furthermore, both codifications include a chapter on securing obligations[445]. In the beginning of the general part of obligations there are provisions that identify the economic

---

[443] In the first socialist Czechoslovak civil code (1950), the eleventh chapter (the first chapter in the fourth book on obligations) deals with the formation and content of obligations. It contains Articles 211 to 250. Contractual obligations are settled in Articles 213 – 217.

In the second socialist Russian civil code (1964), the fifteenth chapter (the first chapter in the third book on obligations) considers the formation of obligations. It includes Articles 158 – 167; Articles 160 – 167 concern contracts.

[444] In both codifications, only an obligation is visible in the table of contents of the general part of obligations.

In the first socialist Czechoslovak civil code (1950), in the fourth book on obligations in the general part of obligations there are: formation and content of obligations (the eleventh chapter), modifications of the content of obligations (the twelfth chapter), change of a creditor or a debtor (the thirteenth chapter), securing obligations (the fourteenth chapter) and extinction of obligations (the fifteenth chapter).

In the second socialist Russian civil code (1964), the general part of obligations (the third book on obligations) includes the formation of obligations (the fifteenth chapter), performance of obligations (the sixteenth chapter), securing of the performance of obligations (the seventeenth chapter), transfer of a claim and change of a creditor (the eighteenth chapter), liability for the breach of obligations (the nineteenth chapter) and extinction of obligations (the twentieth chapter).

[445] In the first socialist Czechoslovak civil code (1950), the fourteenth chapter (the fourth book on obligations) comprises securing obligations.

plan as a valid source of obligations[446]. Contract preserved a strong position in the socialist Hungarian civil code (1959) and in the East German civil code (1975); in the East German codification the third book contains contracts relating to material and cultural life.

3. A last socialist codification with moralizing inclinations (East Germany – 1975)

The discussion in this section concludes with considerations on the East German civil code. As the arrangement of the general part of obligations in the code has already been mentioned in precise detail, only some remarks are added here. The East German civil code is the best example of using the principle of *lex imperat et docet*. Traditionally, the codifications regulate the lives of individuals and do not teach them (*lex imperat, sed non docet*). The East German lawyers introduced multiple provisions, instructing the socialist citizens how they should act[447]. The

---

In the second socialist Russian civil code (1964), the seventeenth chapter (the third book on obligations) deals with securing of the performance of obligations.

The same composition is also present in the socialist Hungarian civil code (1959), where the twenty-third chapter (the fourth book on obligations, the first title on contract) encompasses the collateral obligations securing the contract.

[446] In the first socialist Czechoslovak civil code (1950), the first two provisions of the fourth book on obligations indicate the impact of socialism.

Article 211 Les obligations naissent de l'exécution du plan économique unitaire, des actes juridiques, notamment des contrats, ensuite des dommages causés à autrui, de l'enrichissement indû et des autres faits prévus par les lois.

Article 212 1) L'exécution du plan économique unitaire est assurée par des contrats spécialement adaptés aux besoins de la planification économique (par des contrats économiques). Selon les besoins de la planification économique, les organes compétents peuvent imposer une certaine obligation.

2) Les rapports de droit qui naissent ainsi sont réglés par cette loi, s'il n'en est pas disposé autrement.

In the second socialist Russian civil code (1964), Article 159, the second provision in the third book on obligations, states that the content of obligations arising from the planning acts of the national economy is determined by this act. Furthermore, the content of an agreement concluded on the grounds of a scheduled task should conform to this task.

[447] Among the law of obligations the most interesting are two provisions, established at the beginning of the general part of obligations. They illustrate well the character of the East German civil code (1975); there are many similar provisions in the written law, and the ones chosen are just examples.

§ 43. Aufgabe der Verträge. (1) Die zivilrechtlichen Beziehungen zwischen Bürgern und Betrieben sowie Bürgern untereinander werden insbesondere durch Verträge gestaltet. In den Verträgen sind ausgehend von den Bestimmungen- dieses Gesetzes die gegenseitigen Rechte und Pflichten beim Erwerb von Leistungen zur Befriedigung der materiellen und kulturellen Bedürfnisse der Bürger im beiderseitigen Einverständnis festzulegen.

(2) Die Betriebe haben Verträge mit den Bürgern so abzuschließen und zu erfüllen, daß sie ihre Aufgaben zur Versorgung der Bevölkerung entsprechend der ihnen übertragenen staatlichen Verantwortung planmäßig und allseitig verwirklichen: Die Verträge tragen dazu bei, die individuellen Interessen der Bürger mit den gesellschaftlichen Interessen in Übereinstimmung

East German civil code includes many more precepts that are similar than do other socialist civil codes.

4. Conclusions

The examination provided here offers a sample of the material researched for this study, indicating the impact of socialism on the systematization of the law of obligations. It is not as significant as it might be assumed to be when compared with *ius in re*. There is obviously a certain influence, but there are no rules that simultaneously apply to all socialist civil codes. What shaped the socialist civil codes most profoundly is the refusal to implement the unity of private law or to introduce the duality of private law, connected with the desire to establish codifications that addressed the needs of citizens (Czechoslovakia – 1964, East Germany – 1975).

E) Freedom of contract in the structure of the civil codes

The next issue to be considered is freedom of contract. This lies at the centre of the code, a heart beating slowly and shaping its spirit, determining the direction of the system of private law. Freedom of contract is a distinctive feature of the law of obligations. Expressions of freedom of contract in the provisions of the civil codes are the foundation of this study. Since the codification movement, different solutions were established and then applied in legal practice. Some legislators suppress freedom of contract[448].

Freedom of contract may be solved in the civil codes in different ways[449]. It is a legal problem that cannot be found in the table of contents of the codifications examined in this study. From the systematic point of view it is a detail that neednot imperatively appear in a civil code. Some systematic compounds are always present in a civil code (e.g. ownership or an obligation), but freedom of contract is not among them. The purpose of this analysis is to determine its significance in the civil codes researched. It also addresses the solutions implemented in the civil codes.

---

zu bringen.

§ 44. Pflicht zur Zusammenarbeit. Bei der Vorbereitung, dem Abschluß, der inhaltlichen Ausgestaltung und der Erfüllung von Verträgen haben die Bürger und Betriebe als Vertragspartner vertrauensvoll zusammenzuwirken und sich von den Grundsätzen, der sozialistischen Moral leiten zu lassen.

[448] E.g. the CMBC – 1756, the Prussian *Landrecht* – 1794, the socialist Russian civil codes (1922, 1964), the second socialist Czechoslovak civil code (1964).

[449] The methods of formulating the freedom of contract in the civil codes are described also here: MACHNIKOWSKI P., *Zasada swobody umów jako problem kodyfikacyjny* (The principle of freedom of contract as a codification problem), in: SAWCZUK M. (ed.), *Czterdzieści lat kodeksu cywilnego: materiały z Ogólnopolskiego Zjazdu Cywilistów w Rzeszowie (8 – 10 października 2004 r.)* [Forty years of the civil code: Materials from the National Congress of Civilists in Rzeszów (8th – 10th October 2004)], Kraków/ Warszawa 2006, pp. 211 – 234.

The analysis concentrates on the main perspectives on freedom of contract found in the researched codes. The French CC is well-known for introducing an expression concerning the freedom of an individual into legislation[450]. It is found in Article 1134, but which, since the reform of the French law of contracts and obligations in 2016, has been replaced by a different precept[451]. The CC is the first codification in which freedom of contract is mentioned[452]. In the German BGB (1896) freedom of contract can be deduced from its provisions[453]. According to Ludwik Domański, the system of the CC is directed at the freedom of an individual (legal subject), whereas the system of the German BGB is oriented towardsexecuting the rights of an individual in accordance with the legal object (statutes)[454]. Polish interwar lawyers developed a system positioned exactly in between the French and German codes, in which freedom of contract is a central rule of the system. That is the Polish Code of obligations (1933). The study of the bourgeois civil codes here focuses on the connection between the system and

---

450 Article 1134: Legally formed agreements have the force of the law for individuals who have entered into them. They may be revoked only by mutual consent or for reasons authorized by law. They must be performed in good faith.

451 According to Article 1102, everyone is free to contract or not to contract, to choose the person with whom to contract, and to determine the content and form of the contract, with in the limits imposed by legislation. The second sentence of Article 1102 states that contractual freedom does not allow derogation from rules which are an expression of public policy.

452 More about freedom of contract in the CC:
PLANIOL M., *Traité élémentaire de droit civil conforme au programme officiel des facultés de droit. Tome deuxième*, Paris 1931, p. 437 and the following pages.

453 *§ 134 Gesetzliches Verbot*
Ein Rechtsgeschäft, das gegen ein gesetzliches Verbot verstößt, ist nichtig, wenn sich nicht aus dem Gesetz ein anderes ergibt.
§ 138 Sittenwidriges Rechtsgeschäft; Wucher
(1) Ein Rechtsgeschäft, das gegen die guten Sitten verstößt, ist nichtig.
(2) Nichtig ist insbesondere ein Rechtsgeschäft, durch das jemand unter Ausbeutung der Zwangslage, der Unerfahrenheit, des Mangels an Urteilsvermögen oder der erheblichen Willensschwäche eines anderen sich oder einem Dritten für eine Leistung Vermögensvorteile versprechen oder gewähren lässt, die in einem auffälligen Missverhältnis zu der Leistung stehen.
A provision which was later implemented into the German BGB (1896), from which freedom of contract can also be deduced, is § 305 part 1:
§ 305 Einbeziehung Allgemeiner Geschäftsbedingungen in den Vertrag
(1) Allgemeine Geschäftsbedingungen sind alle für eine Vielzahl von Verträgen vorformulierten Vertragsbedingungen, die eine Vertragspartei (Verwender) der anderen Vertragspartei bei Abschluss eines Vertrags stellt. Gleichgültig ist, ob die Bestimmungen einen äußerlich gesonderten Bestandteil des Vertrags bilden oder in die Vertragsurkunde selbst aufgenommen werden, welchen Umfang sie haben, in welcher Schriftart sie verfasst sind und welche Form der Vertrag hat. Allgemeine Geschäftsbedingungen liegen nicht vor, soweit die Vertragsbedingungen zwischen den Vertragsparteien im Einzelnen ausgehandelt sind.

454 DOMAŃSKI L., *System Kodeksu zobowiązań* [The system of the Code of obligations], Warszawa 1934, pp. 3 – 7.

philosophy of the codes (subjective rights[455], objective rights[456] or subjective and objective rights[457]) and the formulations of freedom of contract.

First, we consider freedom of contract in natural law codifications (the first division). The Pandect systematization and the systems of the objective rights are subsequently discussed (the second division). The Polish Code of obligations (1933) is analyzed in the third division. The Polish lawyers elaborated a mixed systematization – one of objective and subjective rights[458]. The fourth division examines whether the philosophy of a civil code has a connection with its exterior divisions. Do the natural rights of individuals alter the exterior shape of the written laws? The fifth and final division deals with the problem of freedom of contract in the socialist codifications. Does it apply in the socialist reality? The issue of the autonomy of a socialist citizen is also considered.

I. Freedom of contract in natural law codifications – systems of subjective rights

First, this section examines freedom of contract in natural law codifications. It can be found in the CC (1804) and the ABGB (1811); the CMBC (1756) and the Prussian *Landrecht* (1794) do not mention it. The CC and the ABGB are the systems of subjective rights. Positioning freedom of contract at the centre of the system relates it to the site of *personae* in the system of the codes, included in the first book[459]. The analysis is determined by the significance of freedom of contract

---

455 *Ibidem*, pp. 3 – 4.

Domański defines the system of subjective rights and the French *Code civil* (1804) as the most remarkable codification with the system of subjective rights.

456 *Ibidem*, pp. 6 – 7.

On the further pages Domański describes the features of the system of objective rights and the German BGB (1896), the most notable codification with the system of objective rights.

457 *Ibidem*, p. 8.

On this page Domański notes that the Polish Code of obligations (1933) is the codification both of subjective rights and objective rights.

The entire monograph is concentrated on presenting the system of the Code of obligations.

458 The development of legal thought is due to comparative legal science. In the interwar period in the Republic of Poland there were scholars working on Austrian, French, German and pre-revolutionary Russian law. At this time in Poland there was a will to establish something new. Furthermore, having regained independence after 123 years, Polish lawyers doubted into the force of the state and positive law. For this reason, they established that the system would have to contain a reference to natural law, trusting that it is a better determinant. A system with flexibility and based partially on natural law can last much longer, without the need to reform the system of the code entirely.

459 The CC (1804) comprises: persons – goods and different modifications of ownership – different ways of acquiring ownership.

The ABGB (1811) includes: law of persons – *ius rerum* – provisions common to personal rights and *ius in re*.

in the system of the code; for this reason, this section of analysis does not discuss the ABGB in any detail (1811). Second, this issue is portrayed in the CC (1804).

Before we proceed to further deliberations, it needs to be stated that the CMBC (1756) and the Prussian *Landrecht* (1794) should both be classified as systems of subjective and objective rights; even though they are marked by the new trends and philosophy of natural law, they are still feudal codifications, conserving the social system functioning in both jurisdictions – in that respect the binding positive law prevails. The CC (1804) is entirely a written law determined by revolutionary principles, and which opposes feudalism. The ABGB (1811) contains some feudal features, but it is primarily a system of subjective rights, in which an individual can act as an independent legal subject with equal rights. The so-called natural law codifications were inspired by the search of the natural law, which was supposed to be a secular law, common to people of all times and areas; the main purpose of the natural law was serving the welfare of the people[460].

1. Freedom of contract in the ABGB (1811)

In the ABGB freedom of contract is one of the natural rights of an individual. It does not have a particular relevance in the system of the code[461]. The original Austrian lacked regulation of freedom of contract – it listed just four cases of contract invalidity[462]. The missing general precept was introduced into § 879 in 1916, from which point onward a contract that affronts good morals (or which is against a statutory interdiction) would be invalid[463]. The provision is almost identical to Article 20 of the Swiss Code of obligations (1911) and § 138 of the German BGB (1896), both of which state that an agreement that runs counter to good morals is void[464]. Furthermore, freedom of contract is also present in § 861, which defines a

---

460 WESENBERG G., WESENER G., *Neuere deutsche Privatrechtsgeschichte im Rahmen der europäischen Rechtsentwicklung*, Lahr/Schwarzwald 1976, p. 131.

461 In the ABGB (1811), there is no a general precept expressing freedom of contract (§ 861). In § 879 four cases of invalidity of obligations are listed. Freedom of contract is one of the natural rights mentioned in the text of the code.

462 § 879 *Insbesondere sind, außer den am gehörigen Orte angeführten, folgende Verträge ungültig:*
Wenn etwas für die Unterhandlung eines Ehevertrages bedungen wird;
Wenn ein Wundarzt oder was immer für ein Arzt sich von dem Kranken für die Uebernehmung der Cur; oder
Wenn ein Rechtsfreund sich für die Uebernehmung eines Processes eine bestimmte Belohnung bedingt; oder eine ihm anvertraute Streitsache an sich löset;
Wenn eine Erbschaft oder ein Vermächtniß, die man von einer dritten Person hofft, noch bey Lebzeiten derselben veräußert wird.

463 § 879 *Ein Vertrag, der gegen ein gesetzliches Verbot oder gegen die guten Sitten verstößt, ist nichtig.*
LEWY M., *Swoboda umów i jej ograniczenia we francuskim kodeksie cywilnym z punktu widzenia społecznego* [Freedom of contract and its limitations in French civil code from a social point of view], Warszawa 1924, p. 7.

464 *Ibidem*, p. 7.

contract[465]. Even if the codification does not directly contain a precept on freedom of contract, this issue can be reinterpreted from the provisions on contracts; the problem of the limitations When entering into agreements is a primary issue in every system of private law.

2. Freedom of contract in the French *Code civil* (1804)

The complexity of freedom of contract in the French CC can be approached in this section of the analysis most effectively by separating the French systematization into three points. The first point considers the original French systematization. The second point addresses Ludwik Domański's comments on the systems of subjective rights, in connection to the CC. His remarks help us to understand the amendments introduced in the CC, after the reform of the law of contracts and obligations in 2016 (the third point).

a) Original French arrangement

Freedom of contract can be a primary rule of the system – that is the case in the French *Code civil*, expressing the absolute freedom of an individual. A person is identified as one who should have as much self-determination as possible. Article 1134 states that: "Legally formed agreements have the force of the law for those who have entered into them. They may be revoked only by mutual consent or for the reasons authorized by law. Furthermore, they must be performed in good faith"[466]. According to Article 6 of the CC: "Statutes relating to public policy and good morals may not be derogated by private agreements"[467]. Good morals and public policy are the sole limitations of freedom of contract. Everything that is not expressly prohibited by the statutes is allowed. Freedom of contract penetrates the entire system of the CC. The French legislator introduced the smallest number of limitations possible to the parties of a contract.

b) Ludwik Domański on the system of French *Code civil*, as the systematization based on subjective rights

This section includes some remarks regarding the systematization of the CC taken from Ludwik Domański's monograph entitled *System Kodeksu zobowiązań* (The

---

465 § 861 Whoever declares that he will transfer his rights to another, that is, that he will permit him to do something, will give him something, will do something for him, or will omit to do something on his account, makes a promise. If the other accepts the promise validly, a contract is created by the mutual consent of both parties.

HAUSMANINGER H., *The Austrian Legal System*, Wien 2000, p. 254.

466 *Article 1134 Les conventions légalement formées tiennent lieu de loi à ceux qui les ont faites.*

Elles ne peuvent être révoquées que de leur consentement, ou pour les causes que la loi autorise.

Elles doivent être exécutées de bonne foi.

467 *Article 6 On ne peut déroger, par des conventions particulières, aux lois qui intéressent l'ordre public et les bonnes mœurs.*

system of the Code of obligations). The structure of the CC is based on the planned and consequent execution of individual freedom; the authority is obliged not to determine or designate the rights of individuals, but solely to protect them. The code guarantees their integrity[468]. According to the system of subjective rights, any conduct which was not forbidden or mandated by a bill is allowed. An individual may realise his actions just as he wishes, provided that the provisions of the code are obeyed[469].

Among all areas of the French CC, the law of obligations includes the smallest number of provisions limiting the personal freedom and equality of parties in private law relationships[470]. Furthermore, the provisions of the CC are general; lawyers working on the code avoided regulating specific relationships[471]. The code designated the general rules, which were supposed to serve as instructions for the judges who were to settle cases, in harmony with the ethos of the code[472]. It must also be noted that the French *Code civil* acted as a model for the codifications adopted in the Romanic countries[473].

c) After the reform in 2016

The French reform of the CC (the law of contracts and obligations) reshaped the systematization of the CC as well as its assumptions. According to Article 1102, everyone is free to contract or not to contract, to choose the person with whom to contract, and to determine the content and form of the contract, with in the limits imposed by legislation. The second sentence of Article 1102 states that contractual freedom does not allow derogation from rules that are an expression of public policy. The reference to public policy is the result of the impact of Article 6 of the *Code civil*; currently, there is no reference to good morals, because societal evolution has caused this construct to lose its significance[474].

Article 1102 is detailed and descriptive. It lists extensively the prerogatives of a legal subject. It demonstrates the new direction of the French system of private law. The main restrictions on freedom of contract are limits imposed by the legislation. Here we can observe an inspiration drawn from the systematization of objective rights, discussed below. Lawyers attached to the heritage of the CC also included Article 1103: contracts which are lawfully formed have the binding force

---

[468] DOMAŃSKI L., *System Kodeksu zobowiązań* [The system of the Code of obligations], Warszawa 1934, pp. 3 – 4.

[469] *Ibidem*, p. 4.

[470] *Ibidem* , p. 4.

[471] *Ibidem* , p. 5.

[472] *Conf.* Domański, *ibidem*, p. 5.

[473] *Ibidem*, p. 3.

[474] SEUBE J.-B., ATTIAS B., DUMONT-LEFRAND M.-P., GOUT O., LANDEL J., LOIR R., MAFFRE-BAUGÉ A., MARLANGE A., ROUSSILLE M., SOUSTELLE P., TERRIER V., ZATTARA-GROS A. F., *Droit des contrats. Bilan de réforme et loi de ratification*, Montrouge 2018, pp. 20 – 21.

of legislation for those who have made them. This provision is almost identical to the first sentence of the earlier Article 1134[475]. The new French systematization is an attempt to find balance between the original concepts of the *Code civil* and the systems of objective rights, but at the same time arranging the freedom of contract at the opening of the law of obligations demonstrates its relevance[476]. A significant shift in the French perception on the freedom of contract should not be surprising, because it is difficult to consider the autonomy of individuals without referring to the limitations of their rights[477].

3. Conclusions

This section has revealed that in both codifications of subjective rights, freedom of contract needed to be amended. The CC (1804) was based on systematic assumptions, which had to be modified with the passage of time, whereas the more neutrally orientated ABGB (1811) lacked a general precept comprising freedom of contract. The French law of contracts and obligations was reformed in 2016, whereas the ABGB still awaits reform. Our deliberations now move from the systems of subjective rights to the systematization of objective rights.

II. Pandect systematization: a system of objective rights

The Pandect systematization (a system of objective rights) is considered from two angles in this section. First, the features of the systems of objective rights. Second, expressions of freedom of contract in the chosen bourgeois codifications. The deliberations in the fourth division (regarding freedom of contract in the socialist civil codes) constitute a variant of the systems of objective rights.

1. What are the systems of objective rights?

The defects of the systems of subjective rights resulted in the formation of systems founded on contrary principles. In the system of objective rights, the autonomy of an individual is no longer a matter of natural law but of a legislative decision. A person has the freedom to act with in the limits determined by statutes. In the Pandect model, private law is neatly arranged in five books (general part – law of obligations – *ius in re* – family law – inheritance law). The transparency of the systems of objective rights resulted in their circulation. Just as the French *Code civil* (1804) is the most representative codification comprising the system of subjective rights, sois the German BGB[478] (1896) the most encompassing model of objective

---

475 *Article 1134 Les conventions légalement formées tiennent lieu de loi à ceux qui les ont faites.*

476 *Conf.* DESHAYES O., GENICON T., LAITHIER Y.-M., *Réforme du droit des contrats, du régime général et de la prevue des obligations. Commentaire article par article*, Paris 2018, p. 59.

477 *Conf.* GRAHAM-SIEGENTHALER B., *Privatautonomie im Privatrecht – Entwicklungen und Tendenzen*, in: Zeitschrift für Schweizerisches Recht, Band 137 (2018), p. 160.

478 Due to convergence in the legislative philosophy, the German BGB (1896) became a predominant model in the Far East (China, Japan and Korea).

systematization. In the BGB, the courts should follow the rules adopted by the legislation. There is no place for a creative jurisprudence such as that found in the CC. The most crucial concepts of the system are defined in the general part, established in the opening of the code. The written laws are the source of the rights of individuals. One of the greatest accomplishments connected with the system of objective rights is that it achieves a high level of security for the legal transactions in the system of private law.

2. Expressions of freedom of contract in the bourgeois civil codes

In the German BGB (1896), freedom of contract is presumed: what is not prohibited is permitted. Freedom of contract is not expressly mentioned in the text of the German BGB, but it can be deduced from its provisions[479]. For the German legislator freedom of contract has always been evident[480]; this may lead to the conclusion that what is evident does not have to be openly expressed. As a result, keeping silent about freedom of contract in the text of the code does not have to equate to giving little attention to it. In the BGB juridical acts and contracts are the legal instruments accessible to individuals, enabling them to perform their freedom and autonomy in the area of private law[481]; however, in the German systematization juridical acts dominate over contracts[482]. For this reason the general autonomy of an individual (juridical acts) appears more often than the freedom of contract.

The systematization of objective rights became typical for the majority of later codifications[483]. The system of objective rights is evident in the first Pandect code, the Saxon civil code (1863). According to § 664, the determination of the subject cannot be left to mere arbitration by the obliged party[484]. This formulation is contrary to the CC (1804). According to Article 1134 of the CC, legally formed agreements have the force of the law for those who have entered into them (...). In the Saxon codification the wish of one party of a contract cannot be the central

479 *"Die Regelungsgefüge des Bürgerlichen Gesetzbuches wird durch einige wesentliche Grundentscheidungen geprägt. Die wichtigste ist das Bekenntnis zur Privatautonomie. Darunter versteht man die Befugnis der Rechtssubjekte, ihre privatrechtlichen Angelegenheiten selbständig und eigenverantwortlich nach ihrem eigenen Willen zu gestalten".*
BORK R., *Allgemeiner Teil des Bürgerlichen Gesetzbuchs*, Tübingen 2016, p. 41.

480 *Ibidem*, p. 42.

481 LEHMANN H., HÜBNER H., *Allgemeiner Teil des Bürgerlichen Gesetzbuches*, Berlin 1966, p. 140.

482 *Ibidem*, p. 232.

483 The Saxon civil code (1863), the German BGB (1896), the Swiss Code of obligations (1911), the Russian draft (1905), the Russian socialist civil codes (1922, 1964), the current Russian civil code (1994 – 2006), the socialist Czechoslovak civil codes (1950, 1964), the current Czech civil code (2012), the Hungarian draft (1928), the socialist Hungarian civil code (1959), the current Hungarian civil code (2013), the Polish civil code deriving from the socialist times (1964).

484 More about§ 664 in: SIEBENHAAR E., SIEGMANN G., PÖSCHMANN K. M., *Commentar zu dem bürgerlichen Gesetzbuche für das Königreich Sachsen. Zweiter Band. Das Recht der Forderungen*, Leipzig 1869, pp. 8 – 9.

principle of the system. The contractors are bound by the legal regulations, designated by the legislator. A lawmaker designates the limits with in which they are free to perform their actions.

In the German BGB (1896), freedom of contract is not expressly formulated. It is presumed and deduced *a contrario* from the provisions regulating the juridical acts. A legal transaction that violates a statutory prohibition is void, unless a contrary intention appears from the statute (§ 134). This restriction concerns all the binding legal precepts in the German legal system, evenly including private law, criminal law or economic law[485]. The reference to good morals in § 138 of the BGB should be perceived in the context of the moral rules belonging to a society[486]; in other words, the reinterpretation of this precept may evolve with time, in accordance with changing social views. The provisions of the BGB reflect the individualistic liberalism of the Bismarck era, where economic freedom seemed to provide an appropriate path to social wealth[487].

Further expressions of freedom of contract in the bourgeois codifications of objective rights are presented below, in the reference[488]. That is only an exemplary listing, but the analysis here has made it clear that the systematization of objective rights is the most widespread solution in the legal systems researched here. The reason for the frequency of this solution is its simplicty. The final decline in the systematization of subjective rights (and simultaneously the victory of the systematization of objective rights) is visible in the formulations implemented in the French *Code civil* following the reform of the law of contracts and obligations – Article 1102 refers to "the limit imposed by legislation"[489].

---

[485] KÖHLER H., *BGB. Allgemeiner Teil. Ein Studienbuch*, München 2005, p. 176.

[486] *§ 138 (1) Ein Rechtsgeschäft, das gegen die guten Sitten verstößt, ist nichtig.*
LEHMANN H., HÜBNER H., *Allgemeiner Teil des Bürgerlichen Gesetzbuches*, Berlin 1966, p. 32.

[487] POSCH W., *Grundzüge fremder Privatrechtssysteme*, Wien/ Köln/ Graz 1995, p. 30.

[488] According to Article 19 of the Swiss Code of obligations (1911), the terms of contract may be freely determined, with in the limits of the written law.
In the current Russian civil code (1994 – 2006), Article 421 states that the citizens and the legal entities shall be free to conclude contracts. Compulsion to conclude contracts shall be inadmissible, with the exception of the cases, when the duty to conclude the contract has been stipulated by the present Code, by the law or by a voluntarily assumed obligation.
Freedom of contract in the current Hungarian civil code (2013) is included in Section 6:59. According to the first paragraph of the provision, the parties are free to conclude a contract and to choose the other party. The second paragraph: the parties are free to determine the contents of the contract. The parties may depart from the provisions relating to their rights and obligations with mutual consent, unless prohibited by this Act.

[489] Article 1102 Everyone is free to contract or not to contract, to choose the person with whom to contract, and to determine the content and form of the contract, with in the limits imposed by legislation.

III. Polish Code of obligations – mixed system of subjective – objective rights

In Poland a model situated exactly between the French CC (1804) and the German BGB (1896) was established. It was the work of lawyers who applied Austrian, French, German and (pre-revolutionary) Russian law and who were inspired by the concise and clear form of the Swiss Code of obligations (1911). That culminated in the Polish Code of obligations[490] (1933), which aimed to combine the most successful achievements of the earlier codifications.

After sketching a brief background, it is necessary to address the assumptions of the system. A codification can be considered in terms of its spirit and the basic assumptions that impact its solutions. The research here focusses on two provisions of the Code of obligations: Articles 55 and 269. As a system of subjective and objective rights, the Code of obligations gave the central position to freedom of contract. Freedom of contract is expressed in Article 55 of the Code of obligations: parties forming a contract can arrange its relationship according to their own recognition (*Gutdünken, gré*), only if the content and the purpose (*Ziel*) of the contract are not contrary to public policy, statutes or good morals[491]. This provision includes a general rule that persons are free to enter into contracts. Limitations to this principle might emerge from public policy, statutes and good morals. Restrictions are the result of legislative interference and fairness deriving from natural law. The general clauses included in the precept give a judge the possibility of making the best decision in an individual case. Those are the main determinants of the system. The balance of these factors was supposed to ensure succesfully cooperation and interaction between the general and the more specific rules. Interestingly, Article 55 was a faithful representation of the binding legislation in Poland in the interwar period; Austrian, French, German and (pre-revolutionary) Russian regulations were taken into account[492].

---

[490] This text is the result of reading and multiple considerations of some books, portraying the subjective – objective systematization. Those are:

KOSCHEMBAHR-ŁYSKOWSKI I., *W sprawie kodyfikacji naszego prawa cywilnego*, Warszawa 1925.[In the subject of codification of our private law]

DE KOSCHEMBAHR-LYSKOWSKI I., *Quelques dispositions générales d'un projet de Code civil polonais*, Revue trimestrielle de droit civil, n° 3 juillet – septembre 1928, Paris 1928.

DE KOSCHEMBAHR-LYSKOWSKI I., *Les règles de la loi et le droit en droit civil. É tude de droit comparé*, Varsovie 1933.

Assumptions of the system and the functioning of the Code of obligations are mentioned also here:

DOMAŃSKI L., *System Kodeksu zobowiązań* [The system of the Code of obligations], Warszawa 1934.

[491] *Article 55 Les parties contractantes peuvent, à leur gré, créer entre elles tous liens juridiques, pourvu que le contenu et le but du contrat ne soient contraires ni à l'ordre public, ni à la loi ni aux bonnes moeurs.*

[492] *Uzasadnienie projektu Kodeksu zobowiązań z uwzględnieniem ostatecznego tekstu kodeksu w opracowaniu głównego referenta projekta Prof. Romana Longchamps de Berier. Tom I Art.*

A person is the most important element in the assumptions of the system. However, he or she has both rights and obligations (duties), which as a member of a society they need to execute properly. An individual is not alone on a desert island; his or her legal situation is connected with that of other members of society. The focus on rights derives from the systems of subjective rights (the CC), whereas duties come from the systems of objective rights (BGB). The actions of individuals are limited by the legal provisions. There is no place for arbitrariness for the parties to a contract, which results in exploitation. The system is aimed at protecting a weaker party. Here we may observe something contrary to the BGB (1896). The BGB is a liberal codification, related to liberal nineteenth-century philosophy.

The Polish Code of obligations (1933), drafted after the Great War and new changes, could take new experiences into account. After the Great War, people suffered from an economic crisis and inflation, making it difficult to execute binding agreements. The concluded contracts could not be performed without being detrimental to the parties. There was one legal institution, not originally admitted to the CC (1804), the ABGB (1811) or the BGB (1896), which was able to provide a remedy for similar future situations: the clause *rebus sic stantibus*. It was "rediscovered" in the interwar period. Polish lawyers included it in the Code of obligations (1933).

The Code of obligations contains two provisions, constituting its spirit and determining the direction of the entire system. They are Article 55, as previously mentioned, and Article 269. Article 269 regulates the clause *rebus sic stantibus*: "If owing to extraordinary circumstances, such as wars, plagues, total crop failures or other natural disasters, the performance of an obligation would entail excessive difficulties or would threaten one of the parties with a glaring loss, which the parties did not predict at the moment of the conclusion of the contract, a court of law may, if it deems necessary in line with the principles of good faith, having weighed the parties' interests, determine the manner of the obligation's performance, the extent of the obligation or it may even rule on termination of the contract". This provision acts as a brake on the system of the code; if something is going in the wrong direction, a judge may even terminate a contract entirely[493]. The sys-

---

1 – 167 [Justification of the draft of the Polish Code of obligations including the final text of the code elaborated by the main reporter of the draft Prof. Roman LONGCHAMPS DE BERIER. Volume I Articles 1 – 167], Komisja Kodyfikacyjna. Podkomisja Prawa o Zobowiązaniach. Zeszyt 4 – 6 [Codification Committee. Subcommittee on the Law of Obligations. Volume 4 – 6], Warszawa 1936, pp. 71 – 72.

More about Article 55: *Ibidem*, pp. 71 – 77.

[493] On the moral aspects in private law, see also:

BECKER C., *Dekalog. Podwaliny wolności* [Decalogue. The foundations of freedom], Kraków 2006.

BECKER C., *Die Zehn Gebote. Verfassung der Freiheit*, Augsburg 2004.

tem of the code should not be rigidly conserved, but it should be flexible enough to deal with new problems which could not be anticipated. The clause *rebus sic stantibus* does not overrule freedom of contract, but makes it reasonably limited[494].

IV. Is the philosophy of a civil code have a connected with its exterior divisions? Natural rights of an individual versus the systematization of a civil code

Having presented the basic assumptions of the subjective, we now turn to examine objective systematization, the connection between the philosophy of a civil code and its exterior divisions. This is linked to the fact that *personae* are mentioned at the beginning of the Gaius scheme. In the first codifications, *persona* was at the heart of the civil codes. This is the case in the CMBC (1756), the French *Code civil* (1804) and the ABGB (1811). Such an arrangement resulted from implementing the Gaius scheme in the exterior divisions of the first codifications, while those codes simultaneously favoured the natural rights of individuals[495].

We now turn to the contribution of the Prussian *Landrecht* (1794). It consists of two parts. The first part mostly comprises the substantive private law related to the property of persons, whereas the second part contains the regulations on persons. In the *Landrecht,* most of the provisions on property (*res*) are established before *personae*. This impacted the perception of the system of private law and resulted in the formation of a systematization in which the object (content) of private law is a primary issue. Positive law dominates the systems of the civil codes. In the German BGB (1896) the general part, an abstract legal creation, deplaced *persona* as a first book in the system of the code and took its place. The German BGB includes: the general part – law of obligations – *ius in re* – family law – law of succession. The BGB is the written law based on the system of objective rights.

Since the adoption of the German BGB, the systematization of objective rights became the most widespread solution. From that point onward a shift in the systems of the codes may be observed; the new codifications that do not have a general part and which follow divisions based on the Gaius scheme[496] do not adopt

494 LONGCHAMPS DE BERIER R., *Zobowiązania* [Obligations], Lwów 1939, p. 407.

495 The natural rights are defined here: COING H., *Europäisches Privatrecht. Band I. Älteres Gemeines Recht (1500 bis 1800)*, München 1985, p. 72 and the following pages.

496 That is the case in the Swiss civil code (1907), which contains, in sequence: law of persons – family law – inheritance law – *ius in re*. Law of obligations is arranged in the separate Code of obligations, acting as the last and fifth book of the Swiss civil code.

The same systematic pattern is visible in Hungary (1928, 1959, 2013).

In the Hungarian draft (1928) there are: law of persons and family law – *ius in re* – law of obligations – inheritance law.

The socialist Hungarian civil code (1959) comprises: introductory provisions – persons – right of ownership – law of obligations – law of succession.

The current Hungarian civil code (2013) includes: introductory provisions – individual as subject of law – legal persons – family law – *ius in re* – law of obligations – succession law.

the systematization of subjective rights. They implemented a system based on objective rights. One example is provided by the Swiss codification. The Swiss civil code (1907) comprises four books (law of persons – family law – inheritance law – *ius in re*), and the Swiss Code of obligations (1911) acts as the fifth and final book of the civil code. Despite the arrangement replicating the Gaius model, its spirit is much closer to that of the BGB; the Swiss codification is a system of objective rights. The Swiss example indicates that there does not have to be a direct relationship between the exterior divisions of a civil code and its internal systematization.

Among the civil codes researched for this study, the final incarnation of *personae* in the systems of civil codes are the socialist civil codes addressing the needs of socialist citizens (Czechoslovakia – 1964, East Germany – 1975). The needs of citizens as determined by the state are at the centre of the structure of the codes[497]. This arrangement is an intersection between positive law, which in this case can be associated with legislative philosophy, and the Pandect model. After the fall of socialism those codifications became a part of legal history.

V. Freedom of contract in the socialist civil codes – deliberations with in the system of objective rights

The next issue is the application of freedom of contract in the socialist civil codes. As the state enters all areas of the lives of citizens, there is a partial contradiction between freedom of contract and socialism. Consequently, it is not surprising that some socialist lawmakers preferred not to mention it. The system of objective rights is a sole accessible model for the socialist civil codes. As the autonomy of an individual is strongly limited, there is no place for natural law. Statutes, motivated by socialism (and the socialist plan), are the sole source of a person's rights.

This sections discusses four points. The first three points directly consider freedom of contract. In the first point the Russian and Czechoslovak codifications, which do not openly articulate freedom of contract, are assessed. The second point deals with the Hungarian (1959) and East German (1975) civil codes; both explicitly express freedom of contract. In the third point the analysis refers to the

[497] In the second socialist Czechoslovak civil code (1964) there are: general provisions – socialist collective ownership and personal ownership – personal use of dwelling units, other living space, and tracts of land – services – rights and obligations from other juridical acts – responsibility for damage and unjust enrichment – inheritance of property constituting personal ownership.

The East German civil code (1975) contains: fundamental principles of the socialist private law – socialist ownership and personal ownership – contracts relating to material and cultural life – use of real estate and buildings for residential and recreational purposes – protection of life, health and property from damage – inheritance law – specific provisions of the respective relationships of private law.

Polish civil code (1964). The final, fourth point examines the problem of the abuse of rights in the socialist reality.

1. Absence of freedom of contract in the socialist Russian (1922, 1964) and Czechoslovak civil codes (1950, 1964)

This section initially analyzes the Russian solutions, followed by the Czechoslovak codification. In the socialist Russian codes (1922, 1964), freedom of contract is not mentioned. In the first socialist Russian civil code (1922) the reasons for annulling contracts are listed (e.g. conflict with the rules of the socialist state – Article 30). Soviet Russian legal science was not as opposed to the concept of freedom of contract as may appear at first glance[498]. Freedom of contract is primarily restricted by compulsory precepts[499]. As a result, legality is the most crucial issue, and must be deliberated first when concluding an agreement[500]. It is possible to enter into contracts that are not included in the civil code[501]. The first socialist Russian civil code (1922) does not include deposit or gratuitous loans for use. The catalogue of particular contracts in the code is constituted solely by the most common agreements[502]. Having examined the doctrine of the first socialist Russian civil code (1922), we shall turn to the provisions limiting freedom of contract in the second socialist Russian civil code (1964). The most interesting are Articles 49[503] (considering the invalidity of a juridical act concluded for a purpose contrary to the interests of the state and society) and Article 50[504] (regarding the invalidity of a juridical act of a legal person that contradicts its purpose), both settled among the provisions on juridical acts.

After this brief overview of the Russian legal doctrine and provisions, we now move to the Czechoslovak legal system. The second socialist Czechoslovak civil

---

[498] SOŚNIAK M., *Zasada swobody umów w prawie obligacyjnym z perspektywy schyłku XX wieku* [The principle of freedom of contract in the law of obligations from the perspective of the end of the twentieth century], Studia Iuridica Silesiana, Katowice 1985, p. 12.

[499] GIENKIN D. M., *Radzieckie prawo cywilne. Tom I* [Soviet private law. Volume I], Warszawa 1955, p. 322.

[500] *Ibidem*, p. 326.

[501] *Ibidem*, p. 322.

[502] *Ibidem*, p. 322.

[503] Article 49 If a juridical act is concluded for a purpose deliberately contrary to the interests of the socialist state and society, and if there is intent on the part of both parties, then, in the event at both parties have performed, all that has been received by both parties under the juridical act is recovered for the state, or, in the event that only one party has performed the juridical act, all that has been received by the other party is recovered for the state as well as all that is due the first party as compensation for that which has been received; if there is intent on the part of only one of the parties, all that has been received under the juridical act must be returned to the other party, while all that has been received by the latter or is owing to him as compensation for his performance is recovered for the state.

[504] Article 50 A juridical act concluded by a legal person which contradicts the purposes indicated in its charter, in its by-laws, or the general by laws for organizations of that type, is invalid. (...)

code (1964) contains § 51, stating that the parties may also conclude an agreement that was not expressly anticipated in the provisions; such an agreement cannot be contrary to the content or purpose of this written law. In Czechoslovakia (1964) there is no direct statement formulating the autonomy of citizens, but the Czechoslovak legislators saw a need to include a precept in the civil code indicating that the catalogue of particular contracts present in the code is not definitive[505].

The first socialist Czechoslovak civil code (1950), like its successor of 1964, does not include a general precept on freedom of contract. According to the first section of Article 36 of the Czechoslovak code of 1950, a juridical act contrary to the (written) law and public interest is void. In the Russian and Czechoslovak socialist civil codes freedom of contract is reduced to its practical application, ensuring the possibility of entering into agreements which are not anticipated by a civil code.

2. Formulating freedom of contract in the socialist legal systems (Hungary – 1959, East Germany – 1975)

Following this analysis of the Russian and Czechoslovak jurisdictions, which do not mention freedom of contract, we proceed to codifications where it is expressly mentioned (Hungary – 1959, East Germany – 1975). According to the first part of section 200 of the socialist Hungarian civil code (1959), the parties are free to determine the contents of the contract. Furthermore, they may, by common agreement, depart from the provisions relating to the contract unless such a departure is forbidden by statute[506]. Accordingly, in the East German civil code (1975) the second part of § 8 states that with in the limits of this bill citizens are authorized to enter into any contracts that are supposed to satisfy their material and cultural needs[507]. This provision constitutes the foundation of the system of the East German code and determines its spirit; the autonomy of a citizen must be performed with in the limits determined by statutes. This systematization shares similarities with the legislative philosophy of the German BGB (1896), but in East Germany the actions of natural persons need to be performed in accordance with socialism.

---

505 VONDRACEK Th. J., *Commentary on the Czechoslovak civil code*, Dordrecht/ Boston/ Lancaster 1988, pp. 73– 74.

506 About freedom of contract in the socialist Hungarian civil code (1959) here:VÉKÁS L., *Zivilrecht*, in: GROTHUSEN K.-D., *Südosteuropa-Handbuch. Band V. Ungarn*, Göttingen 1984, p. 258.

507 *§ 8. Gestaltung der zivilrechtlichen Beziehungen durch die Bürger. (1) Die Bürger gestalten auf der Grundlage dieses Gesetzes ihre. zivilrechtlichen Beziehungen zu den Betrieben und zu anderen Bürgern.*

(2) Die Bürger sind berechtigt, im Rahmen dieses Gesetzes Verträge aller Art zu schließen, die darauf gerichtet sind, ihre materiellen und kulturellen Bedürfnisse zu befriedigen.

The linguistic formulations used in East German civil code (in this case *berechtigen*) underline the source of the rights of a citizen; this right is given by a legislator, who included it into the written law.

For practical reasons the East German lawyers included a more extensive § 45 in the code [508]. This provision refers to freedom of contract[509].

The autonomy of an individual enters fields not governed by the plan. Where there is no plan, a natural person might do what he or she likes provided that there is no contradiction with the statutes. Furthermore, it seems that the arrangement of both codifications enforces such a systematization. In Hungary and East Germany a contract is a predominant construct[510]. A system based on a contract should include freedom of contract – otherwise it would lack a fundamental element. In East Germany a contract is a concept that binds the entire codification. For this reason freedom of contract is visible in its opening, in § 8. In East Germany, a contract acts like glue, joining all elements of the civil code and encompassing them.

In the East German civil code freedom of contract is given a different justification than that provided in the bourgeois codifications. Instead of perceiving it in connection to the rights of an individual, in East Germany the most crucial issue pertains to the duties of citizens, as designated by the socialist authority. In East Germany freedom of contract is perceived as a very extensive right, which should be used responsibly by a citizen[511]. Furthermore, the East German doctrine underlines the unity of the rights and duties of a citizen[512]. Contrary to the German BGB (1896), the primary perception of freedom of contract in East Germany is

---

508 *§ 45. Bestimmung des Vertragsinhalts. (1) Die Rechte und Pflichten beim Abschluß und bei der Erfüllung von Verträgen ergeben sich aus den Bestimmungen dieses Gesetzes.*

(2) Werden von den Partnern besondere Vereinbarungen getroffen, sollen sie ihre gegenseitigen Rechte und Pflichten im Vertrag so festlegen, daß der mit dem Vertrag beabsichtigte Zweck eindeutig bestimmt und Streit über den Vertragsinhalt vermieden wird.

(3) Die Partner können auch Vereinbarungen treffen, die in diesem Gesetz nicht geregelt sind oder die von seinen Bestimmungen abweichen, soweit ihre Anwendung nicht verbindlich vorgeschrieben ist. Die Vereinbarungen dürfen jedoch nicht gegen Inhalt und Zweck dieses Gesetzes verstoßen.

(4) Die Verantwortlichkeit wegen vorsätzlicher oder grob fahrlässiger Pflichtverletzung kann nicht ausgeschlossen oder eingeschränkt werden; das gleiche gilt für die Verantwortlichkeit für nicht qualitätsgerechte Leistung, soweit dieses Gesetz nicht abweichende Vereinbarungen zuläßt.

509 SOŚNIAK M., *Zasady kodeksu cywilnego Niemieckiej Republiki Demokratycznej* [Principles of the civil code of the German Democratic Republic], in: *Kodeks cywilny Niemieckiej Republiki Demokratycznej* [Civil code of the German Democratic Republic], Wrocław/ Warszawa/ Kraków/ Gdańsk 1979, p. 26.

510 In the socialist Hungarian civil code (1959), the system of the code is settled on a contract; the first title (of the fourth book on the law of obligations) considers contract.

The system of the East German civil code (1975) is also based on a contract; the third book deals with contracts relating to material and cultural life.

511 GÖHRING J. (ed.), *Grundfragen des sozialistischen Zivilrechts*, Berlin 1978, pp. 114 – 115.

A similar concept can be found in reference to the BGB: BORK R., *Allgemeiner Teil des Bürgerlichen Gesetzbuchs*, Tübingen 2016, p. 45.

512 GÖHRING J. (ed.), *Grundfragen des sozialistischen Zivilrechts*, Berlin 1978, p. 114.

considered in accordance with the principles of socialism and not in the context of the freedom of an individual[513].

There is an interesting difference between freedom of contract in the East German civil code (1975) and in other socialist codifications. Most of the socialist civil codes analyzed here (Russia – 1922, 1964; Hungary – 1959; Poland – 1964) follow the unity of private law. That means that their provisions apply not only to individuals, but also to the units of the socialist economy[514]. Addressing solely the needs of the socialist citizens, the East German civil code solely considers a citizen's freedom of contract.

3. Freedom of contract in the Polish civil code (1964)

The Polish civil code is now examined. Polish lawyers established a code in which freedom of contract was not formulated explicitly, but was still present[515]; it could be deduced from the provisions introduced in the code[516]. Removing the symbolic provisions from the Polish civil code (Article 55 on freedom of contract and Article 269 on the clause *rebus sic stantibus*, derived from the Polish Code of obligations of 1933) was an act of the socialist authority aimed at distressing the

---

513 WESTEN K., SCHLEIDER J., *Zivilrecht im Systemvergleich. Das Zivilrecht der Deutschen Demokratischen Republik und der Bundesrepublik Deutschland*, Berlin 1984, pp. 227 – 228.

514 Freedom of contract can be of the utmost importance in the socialist planned economy. In socialist states, agreements are often concluded, because that was a plan; but what about a situation when there is an agreement that was not anticipated in the plan, but which would be beneficial to maintain? Without even a limited application of freedom of contract such a contract should theoretically be invalid.

STELMACHOWSKI A., *Ewolucja autonomii woli* [Evolution of the autonomy of will], in: ŁĘTOWSKA E. (ed.), *Tendencje rozwoju prawa cywilnego* [Tendencies of the development of private law], Wrocław/ Warszawa/ Kraków/Gdańsk/Łódź 1983, pp. 184 – 187.

About freedom of contract in the socialist codifications also here: BRUNNER-KALMAN V., *Vertragsrecht und Vertragsfreiheit in der Volksrepublik Ungarn*, Zürich 1971, pp. 66 – 67.

515 Due to adoption of socialism and discarding achievements of Polish interwar constructs explicit mentioning freedom of contract was not possible – that would be referring to Article 55 of the Polish Code of obligations.

Nonetheless, not in every model bourgeois codification freedom of contract is expressed **positively** – the best example of such a structuring is the German BGB (1896).

SOŚNIAK M., *Zasada swobody umów w prawie obligacyjnym z perspektywy schyłku XX wieku* [The principle of freedom of contract in the law of obligations from the perspective of the end of the twentieth century], Studia Iuridica Silesiana 1985, p. 30.

516 According to Article 56 of the Polish civil code (1964), a juridical act shall have not only the effects expressed in it, but also those which follow from the statutory law, the principles of community coexistence and the established customs.

Article 58 § 1 A juridical act which is inconsistent with statutory law or is designed to circumvent statutory law shall be null and void, unless the appropriate provision envisages a different effect, in particular that those provisions of the statutes which are null and void are replaced by the appropriate provisions of the statutory law.

lawyers. Slightly modified, both were reintroduced into the Polish civil code after the fall of socialism – currently they are Article 353¹[517] and Article 357¹[518].

4. The abuse of rights in a socialist reality

The final issue analyzed in connection to freedom of contract is the abuse of rights in the socialist reality[519]. Before discussing the socialist background, it is necessary to refer to the German BGB (1896). Although the abuse of rights is placed first among most general principles, in the German BGB (1896) abuse of right appears only as an example, in§ 226[520].§ 226 must be applied and interpreted in accordance with with § 242[521]. This short study deals with the abuse of rights and its potential from the socialist point of view. The regulation of abuse of rights can be found in Article 1 of the first socialist Russian civil code (1922), which states that private rights cannot be protected if they have a purpose contrary to their social and economic purpose[522]. The concept of abuse of rights has been very convenient in socialist civil codes. If any legal transaction was not in accordance with the socialist principles, then it could be classified among legal actions contrary to their social and economic purpose.

---

517 Article 353¹ Parties entering into a contract may determine the legal relation at their own discretion, provided that its content or purpose do not prejudice the nature of the relation, a statute or the principles of community coexistence.

518 Article 357¹ § 1. If owing to an extraordinary change of circumstances, the performance of an obligation would entail excessive difficulties or would threaten one of the parties with a glaring loss, which the parties did not predict at the moment of the conclusion of the contract, a court of law may, having weighed the parties' interests, according to the principles of community coexistence, determine the manner of the obligation's performance, the amount of the obligation or it may even rule on termination of the contract. When terminating the contract, a court of law may, where necessary, rule on the settlements between the parties, bearing the principles set out in the preceding sentence in mind.

519 Abuse of rights in France and in the comparative context in the older literature is mentioned here: Lewy M., *Nadużycie prawa według orzecznictwa francuskiego i prawa polskiego* [Abuse of rights according to the French jurisprudence and the Polish law], Warszawa 1938.

More about the abuse of rights in the newer literature:

Eichenhofer P., *Rechtsmissbrauch. Zu Geschichte und Theorie einer Figur des Europäischen Privatrechts*, Tübingen 2019.

520 *§ 226 Schikaneverbot*

Die Ausübung eines Rechts ist unzulässig, wenn sie nur den Zweck haben kann, einem anderen Schaden zuzufügen.

521 *§ 242 Leistung nach Treu und Glauben*

Der Schuldner ist verpflichtet, die Leistung so zu bewirken, wie Treu und Glauben mit Rücksicht auf die Verkehrssitte es erfordern.

More about the abuse of rights in Germany here:

Boemke B., Ulrici B., *BGB Allgemeiner Teil*, Heidelberg/ Dordrecht/ London/ New York 2014, p. 440 and the following pages.

522 Article 1 *Les droits civils sont protégés par la loi, sauf dans les cas où ils sont exercés dans un sens contraire à leur destination économique et sociale.*

Les codes de la Russie Soviétique. Tome 1 Code de la famille Code civil, Paris 1925, p. 124.

A very wide general clause may function as a filter imposed on the entire system of private law. In Soviet Russia the rights of society prevailed over the rights of an individual. A judge had an opportunity to break with the formal provisions of the legislation and to examine the social and economic purpose of a legal transaction in each case. In reading the provisions, we should concentrate not what is expressed, but on the overall limitations included in the precepts. The words and the legal forms do not really matter; it is necessary to delve deeper beneath the formulations and to attempt to find the reality behind them[523]. A single provision introduced in a civil code can enable the control of all relationships of private law[524]. For a socialist legislator who implements a few similar provisions, blocking the key areas in the system of private law is sufficient.

VI. Conclusions from the analysis of freedom of contract

From the perspective of the external systematization of the civil codes, freedom of contract is not essential, although its inclusion obviously enables the content of the civil codes to be categorized neatly. Even if freedom of contract is not expressly mentioned in the texts of the civil codes, it can be interpreted by the legal science from the text of a written law; the core of a civil code can be elaborated and adjusted to apply to many conditions and circumstances. The formulation on freedom of contract can be placed in the book on obligations or in the general part.

Freedom of contract is one of multiple elements of the system, and does not have to be situated in a civil code. In each civil code freedom of contract has its own place and its own systematization; it is necessary for it to remain connected with other compounds of the system. The formulation of freedom of contract is up to a legislator; for instance, the system of the Polish Code of obligations (1933) was formulated in such a way that freedom of contract remains at the centre of its system. The Polish Code of obligations served as the basis for the establishment of the Polish civil code (1964), which contains a general part; when the Polish civil code was adopted into legislation, it did not include the expression on freedom of contract, but it was implemented in the book on obligations after the fall of socialism.

The listing of codifications primarily serves a cognitive value. Nonetheless, the research presented here has demonstrated that, from the systematic point of view, despite its significance freedom of contract holds less value than perhaps it should, resulting in a negative conclusion to the analysis. It must, finally, must

[523] ELIACHEVITCH B., *Le droit contractual dans le système du droit soviétique*, Paris 1938, p. 1.
(extract from *Revue trimestrielle du droit civil*, n° 38 from 1938)

[524] TYLBOR S., *Wstęp* [Introduction], in: *Kodeks cywilny R.S. F.S.R. wraz z kodeksem ustaw o małż eństwie, rodzinieiopiece* [Civil code of RSFSR with the code of bills on marriage, family and guardianship], Warszawa 1930, pp. 13 – 14.

be recalled that despite a plethora of possible solutions the systematization of objective rights, visible in the German BGB, is the most widespread and the safest legislative solution.

F) Cause in the researched civil codes

This section it addresses how cause is treated differently in the systems of the civil codes[525]. Even though cause is primarily related to *ius in re*, this analysis is included in the chapter on the law of obligations, because in the first codifications obligations and *ius in re* are strongly connected to each other and the law of contractsis systematized with *ius in re*[526]. Currently the association of the law of obligations with *ius in re* is visible in the fact that the disposal of a thing is at all times caused by a contract, which secures the entire transaction[527]. Transfer of ownership is the most significant transmission of assets in the system of private law. A cause is one area in which the systematic division on the law of obligations and *ius in re* is visible. The analysis here demonstrates what is required to transfer ownership of a thing in the civil codes effectively. Cause is related to the way legal transactions are settled in the system of the code. *Ius in re* and obligations are the systematic divisions applied by legislators. The systematic decisions of lawmakers also apply to legal transactions.

In German legal thinking a transfer is divided into two theoretical acts. One contract sets the outcome of the law of obligations; the seller is obliged to transfer an object or good and the emptor to pay for it. The seller then transfers ownership to the emptor in a separate transaction. The second contract includes transfer of ownership from the seller to the emptor. This solution is applied in the German BGB (1896). The BGB classifies *ius in re* and law of obligations in the domain of legal transactions.

The lawmaker can decide that a cause is a necessary requirement for the transfer of ownership. In the ABGB (1811), it is a just title. According to § 380, a title and a legal method of acquisition are necessary. The legal grounds of the transaction must be proved to enable the transfer of ownership. Things which already have an owner are passed indirectly, when in a legal way they are relayed from

---

[525] More about cause can be found here:

BECKER C., *Verkauf und Übereignung der Ware bei Anton Friedrich Justus Thibaut. Kausalität oder Abstraktion des Eigentumswechsels in Römischem Recht, Kodifikationen und Pandektenlehre*, in: HATTENHAUER C., SCHROEDER K.-P., BALDUS C. (ed.), *Anton Friedrich Justus Thibaut (1772–1840). Bürger und Gelehrter*, Tübingen 2017, pp. 189–224 (together with a revised note).

RULAND Y. M., *Die Causa der Obligation. Rechtshistorische und rechtsvergleichende Perspektive nach Einführung des Nieuw Burgerlijk Wetboek in den Niederlanden*, Köln 2004.

[526] BUCHER E., *Schweizerisches Obligationenrecht. Allgemeiner Teil ohne Deliktsrecht*, Zürich 1988, p. 5.

[527] *Ibidem*, p. 5.

one owner to another (§ 423). The title of an indirect acquisition arises from a contract, from a dispositon of last will, from a court verdict, or from the regulation of a statute (§ 424). In the ABGB, one legal transaction is necessary for the transfer of ownership, and it is the contract that results in the transmission of a right; at the same time, a valid just title constituting the legal basis of the transfer is also necessary. Furthermore, delivery of a (movable) object is performed by the conveyance of possession of the thing. In a transaction regarding an immovable object, the inscription of a new owner into the real estate register is essential (§ 431). The Austrian resolution derives from Roman law. Due to additional conditions attached to the transmission of a thing, a systematic distinction in *ius in re* and the law of obligations is preserved. Transfer of ownership is not connected exclusively to a contract itself.

I. One transaction necessary for the transfer of ownership (France)

According to Article 1138 of the *Code civil*, an obligation to deliver a thing is completed by the sole consent of the contracting parties[528]. The will of the parties expressed in an agreement gives effects both in the law of obligations and *ius in re*. Article 1582 states that a sale is an agreement by which one person binds himself or herself to deliver a thing, and another to pay for it. There is no mention of any other conditions necessary for transferring the ownership of a thing. The sole contract for transferring ownership is an alteration introduced into the French *Code civil*. According to pre-revolutionary French legal science (*ancienne jurisprudence*) and the Roman law, a contract itself was unable to transfer the ownership of a thing; the delivery of a thing (*traditio*) or another method of transmission (*un autre mode de transfert*) was necessary[529]. The French solution coheres with a Revolutionary civil code, because it indicates the force of a contract. Simultaneously, the systematic division into the law of obligations and *ius in re* became blurred.

The French solution was also appropriate in Soviet Russia[530], because the Revolutionary codifications aim to underline ownership and its force – placing emphasis on ownership comes at the expense of *ius in re*. Diminishing *ius in re* in the structure of a civil code and in legal science may result in the obliteration of the systematic division between *ius in re* and the law of obligations[531]. As a contract

528 *Article 1138 l'obligation de livrer la chose est parfaite par le seul consentement des parties contractantes.*

529 CORNU G., *Regards sur le titre III du livre III du Code civil « contrats ou des obligations conventionnelles en général » (Essai de lecture d'un titre du Code)*, Paris 1976, p. 36.

530 In the first socialist Russian civil code (1922) one legal transaction is enough in order to transfer the ownership of an object. *(Article 6 6: Le droit de propriétésur une chose se transfère par contrat conclu entre "aliénateur et "acquéreur).*

In the second socialist Russian civil code (1964), one legal transaction is necessary for the transfer of ownership (Article 135).

531 MENYHÁRD A., *Property Law in the New Hungarian Civil Code: Key Issues*, in: *New Civil*

gives results both among the law of obligations and *ius in re*, then *ius in re* are reduced in the system of the written law. As with the Revolutionary codifications, where ownership (*res*) enhances the position of *res* at the expense of *ius in re*, a contract connected with *actiones* prevails in the system of a civil code[532].

II. German BGB (1896)

The German lawyers included juridical acts in the BGB while also classifying them in categories unknown in France. The CC was one of the binding codifications in Germany before the BGB was adopted. The German systematization was formulated in opposition to the CC. The aim of the German lawyers was to devise a system that would be divided clearly and exclusively. Juridical acts, as a source of economic benefit for one of the parties (*Zuwendungsrechtsgeschäfte*), cause the property of one of the parties of a contract to increase. They are divided into obliging (those generating an obligation) and disposing juridical acts. The latter regard either transferring, charging, modification or suppression of a right concerning assets. This kind of legal transaction yields results in the domain of *ius in re*.

According to § 433 (the first part) of the BGB, the seller of a thing is bound by the contract of sale to deliver the thing to the purchaser and to transfer ownership of the thing. The seller of a right is bound to transfer the right to the purchaser, and if the right entitles a person to the possession of a thing, the seller must deliver the thing. The second part (of § 433) states that the purchaser is bound to pay the seller the purchase price agreed upon and to take delivery of the thing purchased[533].

The German systematization includes a division in juridical acts with effect in the domain of obligations and *ius in re*. In Germany, a transfer concluded in practice is divided into two separate acts, one of which yields a result in the law of obligations and the second in *ius in re*. For this reason, one legal transaction cannot regulate both fields; the system of the code is settled in such a way that an effect concerning *ius in re* and obligations is set separately. Two distinct legal transactions are necessary for a single agreement. An obliging juridical act is effective

---

Codes in Hungary and Romania, MENYHÁRD A. and VERESS E. (ed.), Budapest/ Cluj Napoca 2017, p. 51.

532 More about cause in France the mentioned monographs:

CAPITANT H., *De la cause des obligations (contrats, engagements unilatéraux, legs)*, Paris 1923.

RULAND Y. M., *Die Causa der Obligation. Rechtshistorische und rechtsvergleichende Perspektive nach Einführung des Nieuw Burgerlijk Wetboek in den Niederlanden*, Köln 2004.

533 More about the transfer of ownership in the German BGB: BECKER C., *Verkauf und Übereignung der Ware bei Anton Friedrich Justus Thibaut. Kausalität oder Abstraktion des Eigentumswechsels in Römischem Recht, Kodifikationen und Pandektenlehre*, in: HATTENHAUER C., SCHROEDER K.-P., BALDUS C. (ed.), *Anton Friedrich Justus Thibaut (1772 – 1840). Bürger und Gelehrter*, Tübingen 2017, pp. 207 – 209 (together with a revised note).

in the domain of obligations, whereas a disposing juridical act results in *ius in re*. In the German BGB (1896) an additional condition for the transfer of ownership (not present in France) is the transmission of possession. A supplementary condition enhances the protection of an acquirer. In the German systematization the division on the law of obligations and *ius in re* is emphasised. The classification into *res* and *actiones* is visible not only in the structure of the BGB, but also in terms of legal transactions in the borderland between the branches of private law. The distinction in *ius in re* and the law of obligations in the German BGB is so strong that even if a contract with results in the law of obligations is ineffective, a contract regarding *ius in re* efficiently transfers ownership. The German solution derives from the Prussian *Landrecht* (1794).

III. Polish civil code (1964)

In Poland, the concept of a juridical act as well as its further classifications, derived from German private law, were implemented in Polish private law after the Second World War. With the adoption of the Pandect systematization, the concept of a contract giving double effect (disposing and obliging) has prevailed. The system of the Polish civil code sits somewhere between the French and German civil codes.

In Poland, one legal transaction is necessary to transfer the ownership of a thing effectively. According to Article 155 (§ 1), a contract of sale, exchange, donation, property transfer or any other contract obliging the transfer of ownership of the thing specified as to its identity will transfer the ownership to the acquiring party, unless a specific provision stipulates otherwise, or the parties decide otherwise. § 2 states that where things specified only as to their kind are the objects of a contract obliging the transfer of ownership, a transfer of ownership shall require a transfer of possession of the things. In the Polish civil code, an additional condition regarding the transfer of possession of a thing is anticipated in the case of things specified only as to their kind. In the Polish civil code, the provisions on cause are arranged in the second book on ownership and other *ius in re*. This systematization is typical, because a cause is primarily connected with the transfer of ownership.

IV. Conclusions

This section has demonstrated that a cause may serve to underline the division between *ius in re* and the law of obligations (e.g. the German BGB – 1896) or to reduce it (the CC – 1804). The transfer of ownership is an area in the centre of the system of the written laws that may be solved differently, depending on the preferences of the legislator. In the codifications impacted by state ideology, more power may be attributed to a contract.

G) Particular obligations

This section considers the arrangement of the particular obligations in the codes researched for this study. In the analyzed codifications, the law of obligations is separated into two areas: the general part of obligations and particular obligations[534]. The separation of the general part of obligations from the particular obligations in the civil codes did not occur at once; the lawyers needed time to introduce such a classification into the written laws. The development in the first codifications is discussed in the footnote reference[535]. In later codifications a distribution among both systematic areas became the rule[536].

---

534 This division might be visible in the table of contents of the codes. As examples the Saxon civil code (1863) and the German BGB (1896) are adduced.

In the Saxon civil code (1863), the third book concerning the law of claims is extracted into two systematic compounds: claims in general and particular kinds of claims. That is the first codification with the Pandect systematization.

In the German BGB (1896), the second book on obligations consists of seven chapters. The last seventh chapter of the second book deals with particular obligations.

535 In the CMBC (1756) there are few general provisions of obligations. The arrangement of the CMBC is mentioned at the beginning of the chapter, among the obligations in the external divisions of the researched civil codes.

The CC (1804) and the ABGB (1811) attempted to separate the general part of obligations, but the isolation was not yet full.

In the CC the third title (of the third book on different ways of acquiring ownership) includes contracts and conventional obligations in general, whereas the fourth title commitments formed without an agreement (those are the non-contractual sources of obligations). The fifth title comprises the matrimonial property law, whereas the sixth title deals with sales. Afterwards there are particular contracts. In France the third title of the third book constitutes the general part of obligations.

In the ABGB (1811), the seventeenth chapter (the second book on *ius rerum*, the second division including the personal rights) regards contracts in general. Afterwards there are particular obligations, in the chapters from the eighteenth to thirtieth; chapters 18 – 29 include the particular contracts, and matrimonial property law is also in this area (chapter 28). Chapter 13 deals with the law of damages and compensation.

536 In the Saxon civil code (1863), the second division (of the third book on the law of claims) deals with the particular kinds of claims.

In the German BGB (1896), the seventh chapter (of the second book on obligations) refers to the particular kinds of obligations.

In the Swiss Code of obligations (1911), the second division comprises various kinds of contracts and the third division commercial companies and cooperatives.

In the Russian draft (1905), the second division (of the fifth book on obligations) includes obligations arising from contracts. The third division encompasses obligations which do not arise from contracts.

In the first socialist Russian civil code (1922) the particular obligations are placed in the third book on obligations, in the chapters from the third to thirteenth.

In the second socialist Russian civil code (1964), the particular obligations are settled in the third book on obligations, from the twenty-first to the forty-second chapter.

In the current Russian civil code (1994 – 2006), the fourth book contains the particular kinds of obligations.

This section of the chapter on the law of obligations includes two systematic segments. First, the composition of the particular contracts. This is the most significant area. Second, this section examines the systematization of non-contractual sources of obligations in the analyzed codifications. The examination does not consider in any detail the systematization of particular contracts in the second socialist Czechoslovak civil code (1964) and the East German civil code (1975), because their composition varies too greatly from the traditional systematization. More extensive discussion of the arrangement of particular contracts in both codifications can be found at the beginning of this chapter, in the section that addresses obligations in the external divisions of the researched civil codes.

I. Arrangement of particular contracts

In the part on particular obligations, the most prominent position is taken by contracts, which prevail both in number and significance over other types of obligations. These contracts more numerous than the cases of unjust enrichment or delicts. The most important agreements are contained in a civil code. There are no rigid rules that would designate the arrangement of particular contracts (and the particular obligations in general). Some principles are applied by legislators who seek a logical arrangement. The systematization of particular contracts differs significantly from the composition of *ius in re* in the analyzed codes. The agreements are loosely arranged, but this area of private law is very flexible, and

---

In the Polish Code of obligations (1933), the particular contracts are put from the sixth to the seventeenth titles.

In the Polish civil code (1964), the particular contracts are set in the titles from 11 to 37, in the third book on obligations.

In the first socialist Czechoslovak civil code (1950), particular contracts can be found in the fourth book on obligations, from the eighteenth to thirty-third chapters. Before there are the non-contractual sources of obligations; those are law of damages (the sixteenth chapter) and unjust enrichment (the seventeenth chapter).

In the current Czech civil code (2012), the second title (of the fourth book on the relative property rights) encompasses obligations arising from juridical acts. In this place the particular contracts are settled. The third title: obligations arising from torts. The fourth title: obligations arising from other legal causes.

In the Hungarian draft (1928), the particular obligations are put in the third book on obligations, from the sixth to sixteenth titles.

In the socialist Hungarian civil code (1959), the third title (of the fourth book on obligations) considers various contracts. The second title: responsibility for damage caused out of contract and for unjust enrichment. The first title: contract.

In the current Hungarian civil code (2013), the third division (of the sixth book on obligations) deals with express contracts. The fourth division: non-contractual liability for damages. The fifth division: securities. The sixth division: other facts establishing obligations.

is not governed by a set of strict rules. There are also several publications that address the arrangement of particular contracts[537].

For this reason, the discussion here is limited to the most important systematic patterns. Furthermore, contrary to the arrangement of *ius in re*, in the law of obligations (and among particular contracts) there are no significant differences in the systematization between the bourgeois and socialist civil codes. The composition of contracts is presented in groups, reflecting the systematization that can be found in the codifications. The most effective order is aligned with the economic purpose of the contracts[538]. Such an arrangement is present in the German BGB[539] (1896) and the Swiss Code of obligations (1911). Both codifications served as a model for the Polish Code of obligations[540] (1933). The systematization of particular contracts in these three codifications serves asa point of reference for all other codes and their systematic patterns. Each comparative scholar concentrates on his or her national jurisdiction, as it sets the standard for our scientific perspective. In Poland's case, only the Polish Code of obligations (1933) can play this role in the domain of particular contracts: the composition of the Polish civil code (1964) is too irregular and strongly impacted by socialism. Later codifications (e.g. the current Hungarian civil code of 2013) had already been partly determined by the multiplication of contracts, and consequently the most universal classifications were already adjusted to changing social needs. Systematization according to the economic purpose of contracts (Germany – 1896, Switzerland – 1911, Poland – 1933)

---

537 SOŚNIAK M., *Zagadnienia typologii i systematyki umów obligacyjnych* [The problems of the typology and the systematization of the contrats], Katowice 1990.

PISULIŃSKI J., *W sprawie systematyki szczegółowej prawa zobowiązań (głos w dyskusji)* [On the systematics of the specific part of law of obligations (a voice in the discussion)], TPP 2012 no. 1, pp. 15 – 23.

ŻABIŃSKI Z., *Systematyka umownych stosunków prawnych pod względem treści* [Systematization of the contractual legal relationships in terms of content], Studia Cywilistyczne [Studies in Private Law] 1972 vol. XIX, pp. 97 – 130.

PECYNA M., ZOLL F., *Założenia projektu struktury części szczegółowej prawa zobowiązań. W poszukiwaniu nowego modelu* [The principles of the draft of the specific part of the law of obligations. In the process of searching for the new model], TPP 2012 no. 1, pp. 25 – 60.

RADWAŃSKI Z., *Wstępny projekt systematyzacji tak zwanej części szczegółowej prawa zobowiązań* [The initial draft of the systematization of the so-called specific part of the law of obligations], TPP 2012 no. 1, pp. 5 – 14.

KOCOT W., *Systematyka prawa zobowiązań umownych w przyszłym kodeksie cywilnym* [Systematics of the law on contractual obligations in the future Civil Code], Państwo i Prawo [State and Law] 2018 no. 3, pp. 82 – 110.

538 LONGCHAMPS DE BERIER R., *Zobowiązania* [Obligations], Lwów 1939, p. 443.

539 About the systematization of the specific contracts in the German BGB (1896): HOFER S., *vor § 433. Die Systematik des Besonderen Schuldrechts*, in: RÜCKERT J., SCHÄFER F. L. (ed.), *Historisch-kritischer Kommentar zum BGB. Band III Schuldrecht: Besonderer Teil §§ 433 – 853*, Tübingen 2013, pp. 3 – 4.

540 LONGCHAMPS DE BERIER R., *Zobowiązania* [Obligations], Lwów 1939, p. 443.

falls between the first codifications and the subsequently written laws, which were supposed to transform the system of contracts.

The typical arrangement provides the basis for the analysis here; it covers the earlier positioning, which is present in the first codifications, as well as transformations of the most usual sequence. Implementing socialist ideology may result in altering the structure of particular contracts. Moreover, a crucial issue concerns the attempt to find the new arrangement of particular contracts, which is connected with the multiplication of contracts in the most current civil codes. This study first concentrates on contracts that enable the transfer of ownership (the first division). Subsequently, contracts deriving from *locatio conductio* are analyzed. These are contracts that enable the use of things (the second division) and contracts for supplying services (the third division). These are followed by deposit contracts (the fourth division), partnership contracts (the fifth division) and aleatory contracts (the sixth division). Finally, the opportunities for systematizing the commercial law are analyzed (the seventh division). The systematization of non-contractual sources of obligations is discussed after particular contracts.

1. Contracts enabling the transfer of ownership

This section first considers agreements that enable the transfer of ownership. This classification includes sales, exchange and donation. Their common feature is that they result in the transmission of ownership. In most codes they are arranged next to each other[541], at the start of particular obligations. They may also constitute a group of contracts in a civil code[542]. The most typical sequence is: sales, exchange

---

541 The sequence of agreements in the German BGB (1896) is: sales, exchange and donation. Sales and exchange are settled together in the first title [seventh chapter (on the particular obligations) of the second book on obligations]. Donation: second title.

The German systematization became the most frequent among the researched codifications.

In the Swiss Code of obligations (1911), sales and barter are set in the sixth title (the second division of the Code of obligations, regarding various types of contracts). Donation: seventh title.

The discussed composition became frequent also in Russia (1905, 1964, 1994–2006).

In the Russian draft (1905), the second division (of the fifth book on obligations) concerns obligations arising from contracts. Sales is arranged as the first agreement. Exchange is the second in the sequence and gift comes third.

In the second socialist Russian civil code (1964), the twenty-first chapter (of the third book on obligations) considers sales. Barter: the twenty-second chapter. Donation: twenty-third chapter.

In the current Russian civil code (1994–2006), sales is put in the beginning of the fourth book comprising particular kinds of obligations, in the thirtieth chapter. Barter: thirty-first chapter. Gift: thirty-second chapter.

In the Polish Code of obligations (1933), the sixth title includes sales and exchange. Donation: seventh title.

In the first socialist Czechoslovak civil code (1950), the eighteenth chapter (of the fourth book on obligations) contains sales and barter. Donation: nineteenth chapter.

542 In the current Czech civil code (2012), the first group of contracts (the fourth book on the relative property rights, second title on the obligations arising from juridical acts, the first chapter in the

and donation. The composition of the sales contract is discussed first, followed by delivery contracts, then exchange, and finally donation.

a) Sales contract

A sales contract is the most frequent type of contract: it is the foundation of the economic functioning of each society. For this reason, in civil codes it requires more provisions than other contracts. Sales is usually the first agreement in the sequence of particular contracts[543]. That is the most common and logical arrangement.

Another composition may be introduced in socialist civil codes; sales can be placed after lease, becoming the second agreement in the sequence of particular

---

second title) concerns "transfer of a thing into the ownership of another".

In the current Hungarian civil code (2013), the fourteenth title (the sixth book on obligations, the third systematic division regarding express contracts) contains the title-transfer contracts.

543 In the CMBC (1756) the third and fourth chapters of the fourth book on obligations include sales. The third chapter refers to consensual agreements, especially sales *(von Consensual-Verträgen, besonders vor dem Kaufe)* and the fourth chapter regards the particular kinds of sales *(von besonderen Käufen)*.

In the French CC (1804) the sixth title of the third book on different ways of acquiring ownership considers sales.

This arrangement is typical, but additionally it corresponds also with the systematic vision of the French revolution. Sales, as the main way of acquiring ownership, had to be the first among the particular contracts in the CC.

In the German BGB (1896), the first title (of the seventh chapter on the particular obligations of the second book on obligations) contains sales and exchange. Sales is the first contract among particular contracts.

In the Polish Code of obligations (1933), the sixth title refers to sales and exchange. The first subdivision of the sixth title comprises sales.

In the Polish civil code (1964), the eleventh title of the third book on obligations deals with sales.

In the Swiss Code of obligations (1911), the sixth title (of the second division regarding various kinds of contracts) concerns sales and exchange. Provisions on sales come first, before exchange.

In the Russian draft (1905), sales is arranged in the first subdivision (the fifth book on obligations, the second division including the obligations arising from contracts).

In the second socialist Russian civil code (1964), the twenty-first chapter (set in third book on obligations) concerns sales.

In the current Russian civil code (1994 – 2006), sales is placed in the opening of the fourth book (on the particular kinds of obligations), in the thirtieth chapter.

In the socialist Hungarian civil code (1959), the thirty-third chapter (the fourth book on obligations, the third title comprising various contracts) considers sales and exchange.

In the current Hungarian civil code (2013), sales is the first agreement in sequence. The fourteenth title (the sixth book on obligations, the third division on express contracts) refers to the title-transfer contracts.

In the fourteenth title first the thirty-second chapter (general provisions relating to sales contracts) is settled. The thirty-third chapter concerns special modes of sale, whereas the thirty-fourth chapter types of sales contracts. The thirty-fifth chapter encompasses exchange contracts and the thirty-sixth contracts of gift.

contracts[544]. Such a positioning is only a slight modification, connected with the need to emphasise lease that is crucial to socialist codes[545]. Systematization that varies from the most usual arrangement is also evident in the ABGB (1811). In the ABGB sales is set after exchange[546], because historically sales derives from barter[547]. Furthermore, in the ABGB gratuitous contracts prevail in the composition of particular contracts, being settled before payable agreements[548]. The Austrian systematization also exerted an impact on other codifications; as a result, sales is placed at a later point among the particular contracts[549].

---

544 In the first socialist Russian civil code (1922) the fourth chapter (of the third book on obligations) refers to sales.

The first chapter: general provisions. The second chapter: contractual obligations. The third chapter: lease of things. The fourth chapter: sales.

This arrangement was later abandoned in the second socialist Russian code (1964) where sales is the first contract in order.

In the East German civil code (1975) sales is settled in the third chapter of the third book (including contracts relating to material and cultural life).

The first chapter (of the third book): general provisions regarding agreements. The second chapter: lease of flats. The third chapter: sales.

545 SOŚNIAK M., *Z zagadnień systematyki prawa obligacyjnego* [From the questions of the systematization of the law of obligations], in: RADWAŃSKI Z., *Studia z prawa zobowiązań* [Studies from the law of obligations], Warszawa/Poznań1979, p. 270.

In his paper Sośniak states that in the East German civil code (1975) the contracts were classified according to their social tasks and not according to the structure of concepts.

As a result in the East German civil code putting lease in front of sales was for emphasis. The East German systematization the most likely was inspired by the composition of the first socialist Russian civil code (1922).

546 In the ABGB (1811), the twenty-third chapter (of the second division on personal rights, of the second book on *ius rerum)* includes barter and the twenty-fourth chapter deals with sales.

547 TILL E., *Wykład nauki o stosunkach obowiązkowych. II. (Część szczegółowa)* [Study on the law of obligations. II. (Particular part)], Lwów 1897, p. 115.

548 In the ABGB (1811), the seventeenth chapter (the second book on *ius rerum*, the second division on the personal rights) comprises contracts in general. The eighteenth chapter: donation. The nineteenth chapter: deposit. The twentieth chapter: gratuitous loans for use. The twenty-first chapter: loans. The twenty-second chapter: power of attorney and other kinds of agency. The twenty-third chapter: exchange. The twenty-fourth chapter: sales.

549 In the Saxon civil code, donation comes first [the first section (of the third book on the law of claims, the second division on the particular kinds of claims, the first chapter regarding claims arising from contracts and contractual obligations)], then loans (the second section), sales (the third section) and exchange (the fourth section).

In the current Czech civil code (2012), donation comes first and after that sales; donation is arranged in the first division (the fourth book comprising relative property rights, the second title including obligations arising from juridical acts, the first chapter regarding transfer of a thing into the ownership of another). The second section of the first chapter considers sales.

In the Hungarian draft (1928), the sixth title (of the third book on obligations) regards loans, gratuitous loans for use, deposit and liability of innkeeper. The seventh title: sales and barter. The eighth title: donation.

b) Delivery contract

One of the systematic dilemmas for socialist civil codes was the composition of delivery. Delivery is a term used only to differentiate terminologicallytheelement of sales contracts that is concluded in practice[550]. In socialist civil codes that follow unity of private law, delivery is settled in a separate section after sales and exchange[551]. Such a location is connected to the fact that delivery is a legal instrument, used to regulate the functioning of the socialist economy. Delivery may be also arranged among provisions relevant to sales[552]. This composition is visible either in bourgeois civil codes (Russia 1994 – 2006, Hungary – 2013) or in socialist codifications that address the needs of citizens (East Germany – 1975). The East German civil code includes only those aspects that are useful for citizens – in the table of contents, only the delivery of electricity and water is mentioned.

c) Exchange

In pre-monetary eras of human society, barter was the foundation of the economy. Sales evolved from exchange. The connection between sales and barter is evident in the arrangement of the codes researched for this study. In the most common arrangement, exchange comes after sales[553]. These contracts are very similar to

---

[550] GRZYBOWSKI S., *Sprzedaż a dostawa w nowym kodeksie cywilnym* [Sales and delivery contracts in the new civil code], Państwo i Prawo [State and Law] 1965 vol. 10, pp. 465 – 466.

[551] In the Polish civil code (1964), delivery is arranged in the thirteenth title (of the third book on obligations) and delivery of agricultural goods is placed in the fourteenth title.

The eleventh title: sales. The twelfth title: exchange.

In the socialist Hungarian civil code (1959), sales and barter are placed in the thirty-third chapter (of the third title on various contracts, of the fourth book on obligations). The thirty-fourth chapter: contract of delivery and of public utility services. The thirty-fifth chapter: enterprise (work contract). The thirty-sixth chapter: contract of delivery of agricultural produce.

In the second socialist Russian civil code (1964), the twenty-first chapter (of the third book on obligations) considers sales, the twenty-second chapter barter and the twenty-third chapter gifts. The twenty-fourth chapter: delivery. The twenty-fifth chapter: delivery of agricultural goods.

[552] In the East German civil code (1975), sales is positioned in the third chapter (of the third book regarding contracts relating to material and cultural life). The last fourth subdivision of the third chapter deals with the delivery of electricity and water.

In the current Russian civil code (1994 – 2006), the thirtieth chapter (of the fourth book on the particular kinds of obligations) involves purchase and sale (Articles 454 – 566). § 3 includes delivery of goods (Articles 506 – 524). § 4 contains delivery of goods for state or municipal needs (Articles 525 – 534). § 5 deals with the sale of agricultural produce (Articles 535 – 538), whereas § 6 looks at power supply (Articles 539 – 548).

In the current Hungarian civil code (2013), provisions on delivery contracts of personally produced agricultural goods are included into the code (Sections 6:232 – 6:233).

The discussed regulations are placed in the thirty-fourth chapter referring to the types of sales contracts (the sixth book on obligations, the third division on express contracts, the fourteenth title comprising the title-transfer contracts).

[553] In the CC (1804), the sixth title (of the third book regarding different ways of acquiring ownership) considers sales. The seventh title: exchange.

In the Saxon civil code (1863), the third section (the third book regarding the law of claims,

each other, as they enable the transfer of ownership of an object. The main difference between them is that sales is connected with remuneration, whereas barter is linked with exchange of ownership. Exchange might be placed in a separate section following sales. Sales and barter can also be situated in one section; in the arrangement discussed here, exchange acts as a systematic subset of sales. In the ABGB sales is located after barter[554]. In all other civil codes, exchange is a subset of sales, whereas in Austria sales acts as a systematic subset of barter.

d) Donation

Donation is an agreement that enables the acquisition of ownership of an object without charge. In most cases it is arranged after sales and exchange. In the oldest

---

the first division on the particular kinds of claims, the first chapter comprising claims from contracts and contractual obligations) considers sales. The fourth section: barter.

In the German BGB (1896), the first title (the second book on obligations, the seventh chapter including the particular obligations) deals with sales and exchange.

In the Swiss Code of obligations (1911), the sixth title (opening the second division of the code, comprising various kinds of contracts) refers to sales and exchange.

In the Russian draft (1905), the first section (of the fifth book on obligations, the second division containing obligations arising from contracts) encompasses sales. The second section: exchange.

In the first socialist Russian civil code (1922) in the fourth chapter (of the third book on obligations) sales is situated. The fifth chapter: barter.

In the second socialist Russian civil code (1964), the twenty-first chapter (in the third book on obligations) considers sales. The twenty-second chapter: exchange.

In the current Russian civil code (1994 – 2006), the thirtieth chapter (in the fourth book on the particular kinds of obligations) considers sales. The thirty-first chapter: barter.

In the Polish Code of obligations (1933), the sixth title concerns sales and exchange.

In the Polish civil code (1964), the eleventh title (of the third book on obligations) refers to sales. The twelfth title: barter.

In the Hungarian draft (1928), the seventh title (of the third book on obligations) includes sales and exchange.

In the socialist Hungarian civil code (1959), the thirty-third chapter (the fourth book on obligations, the third title comprising various contracts) contains sales and exchange.

In the current Hungarian civil code (2013), the fourteenth title (the sixth book on obligations, the third division referring to express contracts). Sales is placed first (chapters from the thirty-second to thirty-fourth). Exchange is situated in the thirty-fifth chapter.

In the first socialist Czechoslovak civil code (1950), the eighteenth chapter (in the fourth book on obligations) contains sales and barter.

In the current Czech civil code (2012), donation is placed first, in the first division (the fourth book concerning relative property rights, the second title on the obligations arising from juridical acts, the first chapter considering transfer of a thing into the ownership of another). The second division: sales. The third division: barter.

554 This arrangement is visible in the ABGB (1811); the twenty-third chapter (the second book on *ius rerum*, the second division on the personal rights) comprises barter. The twenty-fourth chapter: sales.

TILL E., *Wykład nauki o stosunkach obowiązkowych. II. (Część szczegółowa)* [Study on the law of obligations. II. (Particular part)], Lwów 1897, p. 115.

codes (the CMBC – 1756, the CC – 1804) it was classified with inheritance law[555]. This arrangement was connected with the fact that donation is also an institution of succession law (*donatio mortis causa*). The ABGB (1811) also reveals another tendency, where donation is placed first among particular contracts. In Austria gratuitous contracts are situated before payable contracts; for this reason gifting, the most significant among gratuitous agreements, is the first agreement in the sequence[556]. The Austrian impact can be discerned in the systematic organization of donation as the first contract in the Saxon civil code (1863)[557] and the current Czech civil code[558] (2012).

Donation was classified for the first time after sales and exchange in the German BGB (1896); the German arrangement was later adopted in other codifications[559]. That is the most common systematization. It must nevertheless also be

---

555 In the CMBC (1756) the eighth chapter (of the third book on inheritance law) considers the donations between the living ones and in the case of death *(von Schenkungen unter Lebenden und von Todeswegen)*.

In the CC (1804), the first title (of the third book on different ways of acquiring ownership) encompasses successions. The second title: donations *inter vivos* and wills.

556 In the ABGB (1811), the seventeenth chapter mentions contracts in general (the second book on *ius rerum*, the second division on the personal rights). The eighteenth chapter: donation. The nineteenth chapter: deposit. The twentieth chapter: gratuitous loans for use. The twenty-first chapter: loans. The twenty-second chapter: power of attorney and other kinds of agency. The twenty-third chapter: barter. The twenty-fourth chapter: sales. The twenty-fifth chapter: tenancy (, emphyteusis agreements and rent charge) agreements. The twenty-sixth chapter: contracts relating to services. The twenty-seventh chapter: contract with respect to a co-ownership of property (partnership).

557 In the Saxon civil code (1863), donation is set in the first section (of the third book on the law of claims, the second division on the particular kinds of claims, the first chapter regarding claims arising from contracts and contractual obligations).

558 In the current Czech civil code (2012), donation is placed in the first division of (the fourth book comprising the relative property rights, the second title on the obligations arising from juridical acts, the first chapter regarding transfer of a thing into the ownership of another). The second division (of the first chapter): sales.

559 In the German BGB (1896), the first title (the second book on obligations, the seventh chapter containing the particular obligations) includes sales and exchange. The second title: donation.

In the Swiss Code of obligations (1911), the sixth title (the second division on different kinds of contracts) encompasses sales and exchange. The seventh title: donation.

In the Russian draft (1905), the first section (the fifth book on obligations, the second division on the obligations arising from contracts). The second section: barter. The third section: donation.

In the second socialist socialist Russian civil code (1964) the twenty-first chapter (of the third book on obligations) comprises sales. The twenty-second chapter: barter. The twenty-third chapter: gift.

In the current Russian civil code (1994 – 2006), the thirtieth chapter (the first contract in the fourth book on the particular kinds of obligations) encompasses sales. The thirty-first chapter: barter. The thirty-second chapter: donation.

In the Polish Code of obligations (1933), the sixth title considers sales and exchange. The seventh title: gift.

underlined that donation is a rather specific form of contract, impacting different areas of private law. In the BGB, donation is situated with in the law of obligations, separated from family law and inheritance law, but provisions that refer to gifting may be also found among family law and inheritance law; one example is the promise of donation upon death[560] (§ 2301).

The gratuitous nature of donation is a feature that might influence the systematization of socialist civil codes the most demonstrably. As a result, donation is often located next to life annuity and pension, not far from the conclusion of particular contracts[561]. This arrangement is related to the alimentary function of donation;for instance, it was used at atime when there was as yet no social security system for farmers, and donation was perceived to bea way of securing their interests. Life estate agreement was often concluded in conjunction with a donation[562]. It is a form of exchange: the lifetime care of property. The systematization discussed here is only anticipated in socialist civil codes that permit the ownership of land by individual farmers (Hungary – 1959, Poland – 1964).

2. Contracts enabling the use of things

In ancient Rome, *locatio conductio* was an agreement for settling the lease of work (*locatio conductio operarum*), a thing (*locatio conductio rei*) or a particular piece of work (*locatio conductio operis*). All contracts enabling the use of objects and relating to the right to another's work evolved from *locatio conductio*. Here, we analyze the systematization of contracts enabling the use of things. Agreements supplying services are presented in the next division.

The first question to be answered is whether contacts enabling the use of things are systematized together in the civil codes. If they are arranged next to each other, then they are usually placed after contracts enabling the transfer of ownership[563].

In the first Czechoslovak civil code (1950), the eighteenth chapter (of the fourth book on obligations) regards sales and exchange. The nineteenth chapter: donation.

In the current Hungarian civil code (2013), the fourteenth title (the sixth book on obligations, the third division on express contracts) includes sales, exchange and gift. Sales is placed first (from the thirty-second to thirty-fourth chapters), then exchange (the thirty-fifth chapter) and at the end gift (the thirty-sixth chapter).

560 DOMAŃSKI L., *Instytucje Kodeksu zobowiązań. Komentarz teoretyczno – praktyczny. Część szczególna* [Institutions of the Code of obligations. Theoretical and practical commentary. Particular part], Warszawa 1938, p. 137.

561 In the socialist Hungarian civil code (1959) the forty-seventh chapter (of the fourth book on obligations, the third title on various contracts) considers gift, the forty-eighth chapter gratuitous loan for use, the forty-ninth chapter contracts for maintenance and life annuity and the fiftieth chapter offer of prize and assumption of obligation for purposes of public interest.

In the Polish civil code (1964) the thirty-third title (of the third book on obligations) includes donation. The thirty-fourth title: annuity and life annuity. The thirty-fifth title: settlement.

562 OHANOWICZ A., GÓRSKI J., *Zobowiązania. Część szczegółowa* [Obligations. Specific part], Warszawa/ Poznań 1964, p. 327.

563 In the German BGB (1896), first come sales and exchange (the second book on obligations, the

Contracts enabling the use of things may constitute a group of contracts in the civil codes[564]. If contracts enabling the use of things are situated next to each other, then the most typical order is: lease – gratuitous loans for use – loan[565]. The sequence may also be: loan – lease – gratuitous loans for use[566] or gratuitous loans

seventh chapter on the particular obligations, the first title), then donation (the second title). The third title: lease and usufructuary lease. The fourth title: gratuitous loans for use. The fifth title: loans.

In the Russian draft (1905), sales is placed in the first section (the fifth book on obligations, the second division concerning obligations arising from contracts). The second section: barter. The third section: gift. The fourth section: lease. The fifth section: gratuitous loans for use. The sixth section: loans.

In the second socialist Russian civil code (1964), the twenty-first chapter (in the third book on obligations) comprises sales. The twenty-second chapter: exchange. The twenty-third chapter: gift. The twenty-fourth chapter: delivery. The twenty-fifth chapter: agricultural procurement contract. The twenty-sixth chapter: loans. The twenty-seventh chapter: lease of goods. The twenty-eighth chapter: lease of a housing unit. The twenty-ninth chapter: gratuitous loans for use.

In the Polish Code of obligations (1933), the sixth title: sales and exchange. The seventh title: gift. The eighth title: lease and tenancy. The ninth title: gratuitous loans for use. The tenth title: loans.

In the first socialist Czechoslovak civil code (1950), the eighteenth chapter (in the fourth book on obligations) refers to sales and exchange. The nineteenth chapter: gift. The twentieth chapter: lease. The twenty-first chapter: gratuitous loans for use. The twenty-second chapter: loans.

564 In the current Czech civil code (2012), the second chapter (the fourth book on the relative property rights, the second title on obligations arising from juridical acts) regards relinquishing a thing to be used by another.

In the current Hungarian civil code (2013), the seventeenth title (the sixth book on obligations, the third division including express contracts) comprises licensing contracts (contracts enabling use of things). Such a systematization does not exclude placing loans among the credit and account agreements (the twentieth title). Loan agreements are located in the fifty-third chapter (in the twentieth title).

565 In the German BGB (1896), lease and usufructuary lease (tenancy) are arranged together in the third title (the second book on obligations, the seventh chapter on the particular obligations). The fourth title: gratuitous loans for use. The fifth title: loans.

In the first socialist Czechoslovak civil code (1950), the twentieth chapter (of the fourth book on obligations) regards lease. The twenty-first chapter: gratuitous loans for use. The twenty-second chapter: loans.

In the Polish Code of obligations (1933), the eighth title contains lease and usufructuary lease. The ninth title: gratuitous loans for use. The tenth title: loans.

In the Polish civil code (1964), the seventeenth title (of the third book on obligations) refers to lease and usufructuary lease. The eighteenth title: gratuitous loans for use. The nineteenth title: loans.

In the Russian draft (1905), lease is arranged in the fourth section (of the fifth book on obligations, in the second division regarding obligations arising from contracts). The fifth section: gratuitous loans for use. The sixth section: loans.

566 In the second socialist Russian civil code (1964), the twenty-sixth chapter (in the third book on obligations) concerns loans. The twenty-seventh chapter: lease of goods. The twenty-eighth chapter: lease of a housing unit. The twenty-ninth chapter: gratuitous loans for use.

for use – lease – loan[567], but neither order is common. With the development of an economy based on credit, credit agreements were included in the civil codes. As a result contracts enabling use of things may be arranged together, whereas loans can be placed among credit agreements[568]. This composition is visible in the newer codifications. The German arrangement, in which contracts enabling use are placed together, is the most typical. The systematization was different in codes that preceded the German BGB (1896)[569].

The systematization in socialist civil codes arranged according to the needs of citizens is worth mentioning (Czechoslovakia – 1964, East Germany – 1975). In both codifications, lease is placed at the beginning of particular contracts[570], whereas loans are included among credit relationships[571].

---

567 In the current Czech civil code (2012), the second chapter (the fifth book comprising relative property rights, the second title including obligations arising from juridical acts) concerns relinquishing a thing to be used by another. The first division (of the second chapter): precarious loans. The second division: loans for use. The third division: lease. The fourth division: usufructuary lease. The fifth division: licences. The sixth division: loans for consumption. The seventh division: credit.

568 In the current Russian civil code (1994 – 2006), the thirty-fourth chapter (in the fourth book, including the particular kinds of obligations) encompasses lease. The thirty-fifth chapter: renting of living accommodation. The thirty-sixth chapter: gratuitous loans for use.

The forty-second chapter considers loans and credits.

In the current Hungarian civil code (2013), the seventeenth title (of the sixth book on obligations, the third division on express contracts) regards licensing contracts (contracts enabling the use of things). In the seventeenth title there are: lease, residential lease, leasehold (tenancy) and lending arrangements (gratuitous loans for use).

The twentieth title (of the sixth book) considers credit and account agreements. The fifty-second chapter (the first chapter set in the twentieth title) includes credit agreements. The fifty-third chapter: loan agreements.

569 In the CC (1804), the eighth title (of the third book considering different kinds of acquiring ownership) includes lease. The ninth title: partnership contracts. The tenth title: loans.

In the ABGB (1811), gratuitous loans for use can be found in the twentieth chapter (the second book on *ius rerum*, the second division referring to personal rights). The twenty-first chapter: loans. In the twenty-fifth chapter tenancy [, emphyteusis agreements and rent charge] agreements are positioned.

In the Saxon civil code (1863), loan is the second agreement (the second section) in the sequence among the particular contracts (of the third book on the law of claims, the second division on the particular kinds of claims, the first chapter regarding claims arising from contracts and contractual obligations). The eighth section: gratuitous loans for use *(Gebrauchsleihe)*. The ninth section: lease and tenancy.

570 In the East German civil code (1975), lease of flats is arranged in the second chapter of the third book (on contracts relating to material and cultural life).

In the second socialist Czechoslovak civil code (1964), the third division (of the fourth book on services) deals with lease of a thing.

571 In the East German civil code (1975), the fifth chapter (of the third book on contracts relating to material and cultural life) considers bank account agreements, savings accounts agreements, credit agreements and loan agreements.

In the second socialist Czechoslovak civil code (1964), the tenth division (of the fourth book

Before proceeding to an analysis of these contracts, we must first establish the sequence of the depicted agreements. First, the systematization of lease is described, followed by gratuitous loans for use, loans and finally other contracts with in contracts enabling the use of things.

a) Lease

Among the systematization of lease two problems are considered: the systematic differentiations of lease and the positioning of lease in particular contracts. Tenancy is the most significant component of lease. Lease and tenancy regulate the use of a thing belonging to another. Both a lessee and a tenant can use an object, but a tenant may also collect the benefits (fruits) from a thing[572]. Tenancy is an agreement for regulating the cultivation of land. Lease and tenancy may be arranged together in one section[573] or they can be settled next to each other[574]. Furthermore, in the civil codes lease of housing units may be distinguished[575].

After verifying the systematic subcategories of lease, this section moves to the composition of lease among particular contracts. If the contracts that enable the use of things are placed next to each other, then lease is most likely to be located at the beginning[576]. This is partly because lease is the strongest agreement of all the contracts enabling the use of things. Furthermore, in socialist civil codes lease

---

on services) comprises monetary services. The first chapter of the tenth division: financial contribution. The second chapter: loans.

572 In this aspect fruits are an important systematic detail, because they serve as a basis for the distinction between lease and tenancy.

The systematic relations of both contracts is visible in § 581 of the German BGB (1896):

§ 581 Vertragstypische Pflichten beim Pachtvertrag

(1) Durch den Pachtvertrag wird der Verpächter verpflichtet, dem Pächter den Gebrauch des verpachteten Gegenstands und den Genuss der Früchte, soweit sie nach den Regeln einer ordnungsmäßigen Wirtschaft als Ertrag anzusehen sind, während der Pachtzeit zu gewähren. Der Pächter ist verpflichtet, dem Verpächter die vereinbarte Pacht zu entrichten.

(2) Auf den Pachtvertrag mit Ausnahme des Landpachtvertrags sind, soweit sich nicht aus den §§ 582 bis 584b etwas anderes ergibt, die Vorschriften über den Mietvertrag entsprechend anzuwenden.

573 In the German BGB (1896), the third title (the second book on obligations, the seventh chapter on the particular obligations) considers lease and usufructuary lease (tenancy).

In the Hungarian draft (1928), the tenth title (of the third book on obligations) includes lease and tenancy.

574 In the socialist Hungarian civil code (1959), the thirty-seventh chapter (the fourth book on obligations, third title comprising various contracts) refers to lease. The thirty-eighth chapter: tenancy.

575 In the current Russian civil code (1994 – 2006), the thirty-fourth chapter (of the fourth book on the particular kinds of obligations) regards lease. The thirty-fifth chapter: renting of living accommodation.

576 This arrangement can be found e.g. in the German BGB (1896); lease and usufructuary lease are set in the third title (the second book on obligations, the seventh chapter on the particular obligations). The fourth title: gratuitous loans for use. The fifth title: loans.

may be identifiedand situated before sales[577]. Such an arrangement is related to the fact that socialist ideology favours the needs of citizens and, in consequence, lease. In the traditional arrangement, sales is the most important agreement, positioned at the beginning of particular contracts.

b) Gratis loan for use

Gratuitous loan for use is a contract that enables the use of an object that is the property of another person free of charge. Because it derives from the Latin phrase *locatio conductio*, it is usually arranged next to lease. In most codifications gratis loans for use form part of a separate agreement[578]. Gratuitous loans for use might be found among the provisions on loan[579]. In civil codes that situate contracts enabling the use of things next to each other the most typical order is: lease – gratuitous loans for use – loan[580]. If only loan is isolated among the contracts enabling use of things, then the order of agreements is: lease – gratuitous loans for use[581]. Gratuitous contracts (and, among other components, gratuitous loans for use) may be positioned at the beginning of particular contracts[582].

---

577 The discussed arrangement is visible in the first socialist Russian civil code (1922) and the East German civil code (1975).

In the first socialist Russian civil code (1922) lease is arranged in the opening of particular contracts. Lease is put in the third chapter (of the third book on obligations). The second chapter: contractual obligations. The fourth chapter: sales.

In the East German civil code (1975) the first chapter (of the third book on contracts relating to material and cultural life) comprises the general provisions regarding contracts. The second chapter: lease of flats. The third chapter: sales.

578 E.g. in the German BGB, where the fourth title (the second book on obligations, the seventh chapter on the particular obligations) concerns gratuitous loans for use.

579 This systematization is visible e.g. in the CC (1804). The tenth title (of the third book on different ways of acquiring ownership) deals with loan. The first chapter (of the tenth title) considers gratuitous loans for use *(commodatum)*, the second chapter (gratuitous) loan, whereas the third chapter loan at interest.

580 This composition is visible e.g. in the Polish civil code (1964); the seventeenth title (of the third book on obligations) comprises lease and tenancy. The eighteenth title: gratuitous loans for use. The nineteenth title: loans.

581 In the current Russian civil code (1994 – 2006), the thirty-fourth chapter (of the fourth book on the particular kinds of obligations) regards lease. The thirty-fifth chapter: the renting of living accommodation. The thirty-sixth chapter: gratuitous loans for use.

In the current Hungarian civil code (2013), the seventeenth title (the sixth book on obligations, the third division on express contracts) refers to licensing contracts (contracts enabling use of things). The forty-fourth chapter (the first chapter set in the seventeenth chapter) concerns lease agreements. The forty-fifth chapter: leasehold contracts (tenancy). The forty-sixth chapter: lending arrangements (gratuitous loans for use).

582 In the ABGB (1811), gratuitous loans for use is the third contract in the sequence of the particular contracts (the second book on *ius rerum*, the second division including the personal rights).

The eighteenth chapter: donation. The nineteenth chapter: deposit. The twentieth chapter: gratuitous loans for use. The twenty-first chapter: loans.

In the Hungarian draft (1928), loan and gratuitous loans for use are located in the sixth title

Distinguishing gratuitous and payable agreements could be of utmost importance in a socialist civil code. In the socialist Hungarian civil code (1959), gratuitous contracts (and consequently gratuitous loans for use) are set close to the end of particular contracts[583]. The character of agreements (are they payable or gratuitous?) was the fundamental criterion of the systematization of contracts in the second socialist Czechoslovak civil code (1964) and the East German civil code (1975); this issue is discussed in greater detail in the description of both codifications found in the beginning of this chapter, among the obligations in the external divisions of the researched civil codes.

c) Loan

Loan can be settled near to the beginning of particular contracts; this arrangement can be found in the ABGB (1811) and in the codifications impacted by the ABGB[584]. This positioning is connected with the emphasis placed on gratuitous contracts, made by placing them at the beginning of particular contracts. In civil codes where agreements enabling the use of things are arranged in one area, the most typical sequence is: lease – gratuitous loan for use – loan. In this sequencing loan, as the weakest right, is systematized as the final contract[585]. In later codes

---

(of the third book on obligations). The sixth title of the third book is the first title of the particular obligations, including (in order): loan, gratuitous loans for use, deposit and liability of innkeepers.

[583] In the socialist Hungarian civil code (1959), the chapter 47 (the fourth book on obligations, the third title on various contracts) comprises donation, the chapter 48 gratuitous loans for use, the chapter 49 contracts for maintenance and for life annuity and the last chapter 50 offer of prize and assumption of obligation for purposes of public interest.

In the Polish civil code (1964), the reasoning is similar like in Hungary; gratuitous contracts are systematized at back of particular contracts, but gratuitous loans for use is settled among the contracts enabling use of things. Title 33 title (of the third book on obligations): donation. Title 34 pension and life annuity. Title 35: settlement. Title 36: public promise).

Title 17: lease and tenancy. Title 18: gratuitous loans for use. Title 19: loans.

[584] In the ABGB (1811), loan is the fourth agreement in order. It is settled in the twenty-first chapter, the second division considering the personal rights, the second book on *ius rerum*.

The eighteenth chapter: donation. The nineteenth chapter: deposit. The twentieth chapter: gratuitous loans for use. The twenty-first chapter: loans.

In the Saxon civil code loan is the second agreement in the sequence among the particular contracts. It is placed in the second section (the third book on claims, the second division on the particular kinds of claims, the first chapter including claims from contacts and contractual obligations). The first section considers gift, the second section loan and the third section sales.

In the Hungarian draft (1928), agreements are classified into groups. The sixth title of the third book on obligations is the title opens the particular obligations. The sixth title includes, in sequence: loans, gratuitous loans for use, deposit and liability of innkeeper.

[585] This composition is visible e.g. in the Polish Code of obligations (1933); the ninth title comprises lease and usufructuary lease. The tenth title: gratuitous loans for use. The eleventh title: loans.

loan can be placed among the contracts relating to credit instead of the contracts enabling the use of things[586].

d) Arrangement of other contracts belonging to contracts enabling the use of things

Here the systematization of other agreements, which were later set apart among contracts enabling the use of things, is considered. The relationship between credit agreement and loan, as well as the systematization of licence and leasing agreement, is analyzed. Credit (account) agreements can be a subset of loan[587] or loans and credits are arranged together[588]. Licence can be situated among the contracts enabling the use of things[589], after deposit[590] or before a credit agreement[591]. If in the civil code there is a book that includes intellectual property law, then licence is arranged in it[592]. Leasing agreements can be arranged after lease and before gra-

---

586 In the current Russian civil code (1994 – 2006), the thirty-fourth chapter (in the fourth book including the particular kinds of obligations) regards lease. The thirty-fifth chapter concerns the renting of living accommodation and the thirty-sixth chapter gratuitous (loan for) use.

The forty-second chapter refers to loans and credits.

In the current Hungarian civil code (2013), the seventeenth title (of the sixth book on obligations, the third division on express contracts) considers licensing contracts (contracts enabling use of things).

The twentieth title deals with credit and account agreements. In the twentieth title there are the credit agreements (the fifty-second chapter) and loan agreements (the fifty-third chapter).

587 In the Polish civil code (1964), the nineteenth title (of the third book on obligations) deals with loan. The twentieth title: bank account agreement.

588 In the current Russian civil code (1994 – 2006), the forty-second chapter (of the fourth book on the particular kinds of obligations) considers loans and credits.

589 In the current Czech civil code (2012), the second chapter (the fourth book on the relative property rights, the second title containing obligations arising from juridical acts) deals with relinquishing a thing to be used by another. The first division (of the second chapter) considers precarious loans. The second division: loans for use. The third division: lease. The fourth division: usufructuary lease. The fifth division: licences.

590 In the current Hungarian civil code (2013), the eighteenth title (the sixth book on obligations, the third division on express contracts) refers to deposit arrangements. The nineteenth title: distribution contract and license (franchise) agreement.

591 In the current Czech civil code (2012), the fifth division (the fourth book on the relative property rights, the second title concerning obligations arising from juridical acts, the second chapter regarding relinquishing a thing to be used by another) considers licence. The seventh division: credit.

In the current Hungarian civil code (2013), the nineteenth title (the sixth book on obligations, the third division on express contracts) deals with distribution contract and license (franchise) agreement. The twentieth title: credit and account agreements.

592 In the current Russian civil code (1994 – 2006), the seventh book contains the rights to the results of intellectual activities and means of individualisation. In the beginning of the seventh book there is the sixty-ninth chapter (Articles 1225 – 1254), including the general provisions. The licence contract is mentioned in Articles 1235 – 1239. The seventieth chapter deals with copyright law (Articles 1255 – 1302). Article 1286 mentions a licence contract granting the right of using a work, whereas Article 1287 establishes the special terms of a publisher's licence

tuitous loans for use[593]. Financial leasing might be positioned among credit and account agreements[594] or it may constitute a subtype of lease[595].

3. Contracts for supplying services

This section discusses the systematization of contracts for supplying services. As a work contract derives from *locatio conductio*, then this genealogy can be discerned in the systematization of particular contracts, and contracts for supplying services can be placed immediately after contracts enabling the use of things[596]. Contracts for supplying services include the actions that an individual might undertake on behalf of others. The system of contracts deriving from Roman law had to be adapted to modern times. Roman law considers contracts entered into by Roman citizens. Gainful employment was perceived as an offence to the dignity of a Roman citizen, who could only work free of charge. Now, in most cases we cannot imagine doing multiple tasks and being unpaid for them. That explains why unpaid mandate was either transformed or marginalized.

After this short historical introduction, we may now proceed to the civil codes. In the first codifications there were few systematic categories regarding services[597]. In the German BGB (1896), more contracts referring to services were included[598].

---

contract.

593 In the Polish civil code (1964), the original sequence of agreements was: lease and tenancy (the seventeenth title of the third book on obligations), gratuitous loans for use (the eighteenth title) and loan (the nineteenth title). Leasing was introduced into the code in the title 17.1. As a result the order of contracts is: lease and tenancy – contract of leasing – gratuitous loans for use – loans.

594 In the current Hungarian civil code (2013), financial leasing contract is arranged in the twentieth title concerning credit and account agreements (the sixth book on obligations, the third division on express contracts). The title contains regulation of numerous contracts; the fifty-ninth chapter regards the financial leasing agreements.

595 In the current Russian civil code (1994 – 2006), the thirty-fourth chapter (of the fourth book on the particular kinds of obligations) regards lease (Articles 606 – 670). § 6 includes financial lease (Articles 665 – 670).

596 This composition is visible e.g. in the Polish Code of obligations (1933). The eighth title considers lease and tenancy. The ninth title: gratuitous loans for use. The tenth title: loans. The eleventh title: contracts supplying services. The second division of the eleventh title deals with work contract.

597 In the CMBC (1756) the ninth chapter (of the fourth book on obligations) encompasses mandate and power of attorney.

In the CC (1804), work contract is not isolated among the particular contracts; yet the third chapter of the eighth title regarding lease (of the third book on different ways of acquiring ownership) deals with the lease of work and industry *(du louage d'ouvrage et d'industrie)*. Besides the thirteenth title of the third book refers to mandate.

In the ABGB (1811), the twenty-second chapter (the second book on *ius rerum*, the second division comprising the personal rights) concerns the power of attorney and other kinds of agency. The twenty-sixth chapter includes contracts relating to services. That is the regulation of work contract.

598 In the German BGB (1896), the sixth title (the second book on obligations, the seventh chapter

Adopted later, the Swiss Code of obligations (1911) follows the unity of private law. As a result the volume that was later regulated in the commercial code or in separate legislation was included in the Code of obligations; that affected the systematization of contracts for supplying services[599]. Currently all codifications in Central and Eastern Europe apply the unity of private law; contracts for supplying services featre among the contracts in the codes mentioned here [600]. We now proceed to analyze, first, the relation between work contract and mandate in the civil codes is considered, then the composition of a work contract, and finally mandates.

a) Work contracts and mandates

Among the provision of services, two basic agreements should be mentioned. A work contract is based on achieving a certain result, whereas a mandate requires appropriate diligence from a contractor. In Roman law, a work contract was

---

comprising the particular obligations) regards contract of service. The seventh title: work contract. The eighth title: brokerage agreement. The ninth title: reward. The tenth title: mandate. The eleventh title: management without mandate.

599 In the Swiss Code of obligations (1911), the tenth title (of the second division including different kinds of contracts) considers employment contract. The eleventh title: work contract. The twelfth title: publishing contract. The thirteenth title: mandate. The fourteenth title: management without mandate. The fifteenth title: commission contract. The sixteenth title: contract of carriage. The seventeenth title: registered power of attorney and other forms of commercial agency.

600 The Polish civil code (1964), the Russian civil code (1994 – 2006), the Czech civil code (2012) and the Hungarian civil code (2013).

Next the arrangement of contracts supplying services in those codifications is presented.

In the Polish civil code (1964), title 15 (of the third book on obligations) concerns work contract. Title 16: construction works contract. Title 21: mandate. Title 22: management without mandate. Title 23: agency contract. Title 24: commission (consignment) contract. Title 25: contract of carriage. Title 26: forwarding contract.

In the current Russian civil code (1994 – 2006), chapter 37 (of the fourth book on the particular kinds of obligations) regards contract of hiring work. Chapter 38: performance of research and development of technological works. Chapter 39: the repayable rendering of services. Chapter 40: carriage. Chapter 41: transport forwarding. Chapter 49: agency. Chapter 50: actions in the interest of other people without commission. Chapter 51: commission (mandate). Chapter 52: agency service.

In the current Czech civil code (2012), the fifth chapter (the fourth book on the relative property rights, the second title referring to obligations arising from juridical acts) regards obligations arising from mandate-type contracts. The sixth chapter: package tour. The seventh chapter: obligations arising from contracts of carriage. The eighth chapter: work contract.

In the current Hungarian civil code (2013), the fifteenth title (the sixth book on obligation, the third division on express contracts) contains contracts for professional services. In the opening of the title in the thirty-seventh chapter works contracts are situated. The thirty-eighth chapter: contracts of carriage. The sixteenth title concerns engagement-type contracts – those are agreements related to mandate. The thirty-ninth chapter: personal service contracts. The fortieth chapter: consignment contracts. The forty-first chapter: agency contracts. The forty-second chapter: shipping contracts. The forty-third chapter: fiduciary asset management contracts.

classified with in *locatio conductio*, whereas a mandate – together with power of attorney – was perceived as a single institution. In the civil codes mandate and work contract can be situated next to each other, in neighbouring sections[601] or at least in close proximity[602].

b) Work contract

The most important feature of a work contract is the achievement of a certain result: producing work that was negotiated as the objective of the contract. Just as in Roman law, where a work contract is arranged with in *locatio conductio*, so in the CC (1804) a work contract is not a separate systematic unit, and it is placed together with lease[603]. A work contract is often situated after contracts enabling the use of things[604]. The sequence may also be: contracts enabling the transfer

---

[601] In the Russian draft (1905), mandate is situated in the eighth section (the fifth book on obligations, the second division including obligations arising from contracts) and work contract in the ninth section.

In the Hungarian draft (1928), the eleventh title (of the third book on obligations) comprises legal relationships resulting from work. The first chapter of the eleventh title: mandate. The second chapter: work contract.

In the current Hungarian civil code (2013), the fifteenth title (the sixth book on obligations, the third division on express contracts) deals with contracts for professional services (work contract). The sixteenth title encompasses engagement-type contracts (mandate).

[602] In the German BGB (1896), the seventh title (the second book on obligations, the seventh chapter on the particular obligations) concerns work contract. The tenth title: mandate.

In the Swiss Code of obligations (1911), the eleventh title considers work contract. The thirteenth title: mandate.

In the socialist Hungarian civil code (1959), the thirty-fifth chapter (the fourth book on obligations, the third title including various contracts) deals with work contract. Mandate is placed in the fortieth chapter.

In the current Czech civil code (2012), the fifth chapter (the fourth book considering the relative property rights, the second title referring to obligations arising from juridical acts) regards obligations arising from mandate-type contracts. The eighth chapter: work contract.

[603] In the CC (1804), the eighth title (of the third book on different ways of acquiring ownership) encompasses lease (Articles 1708 – 1831).

In Article 1708 two kinds of lease are mentioned: lease of things and lease of work *(ouvrage)*.

The first chapter (of the eighth title) includes the general provisions (Articles 1708 – 1712). The second chapter concerns lease of things (Articles 1713 – 1778). The third chapter considers the lease of work and industry (Articles 1779 – 1799). The last fourth chapter comprises the lease of livestock (Articles 1800 – 1831).

[604] In the German BGB (1896), the third title (the second book on obligations, the seventh chapter on the particular obligations) contains lease and usufructuary lease. The fourth title: gratuitous loans for use. The fifth title: loans. The sixth title: contract of service. The seventh title: contract for work.

In the Swiss Code of obligations (1911), work contract is arranged in the eleventh title. The eighth title considers lease. The ninth title: loans. The tenth title: labour contract *(Arbeitsvertrag)*. The eleventh title: work contract.

In the second socialist Russian civil code (1964), the twenty-sixth chapter (the third book on obligations) concerns loans. The twenty-seventh chapter: lease of goods. The twenty-eighth

of ownership – work contract – contracts enabling the use of things[605]. If contracts supplying services are set apart in the arrangement of the code, then the work contracts are placed in this group[606]. A legislator might also distinguish legal relationships resulting from work and situate work contract in this area[607]. In socialist civil codes a construction works contract, a subset of work contract, can be isolated[608]. Locating the construction works contract as a subset of the work contract enables the provisions of the work contract to be applied to the construction works contract. Arranging similar agreements next to each improves their functioning in legal practice and the accurate use of legal provisions by lawyers.

c) Mandate

Traditionally, a mandate is a gratuitous contract; if there is no stipulation to the contrary then it is free of charge[609]. The innovation implemented in the Polish Code of obligations (1933) was the rule that mandate is payable[610]. In the first

---

chapter: lease of a housing unit. The twenty-ninth chapter: gratuitous loans for use. The thirtieth chapter: work contract.

In the current Russian civil code (1994 – 2006), lease is situated in the thirty-fourth chapter (the fourth book on the particular kinds of obligations). In the thirty-fifth chapter renting of living accommodation is set. The thirty-sixth chapter includes gratuitous (loan for) use and the thirty-seventh chapter contract of hiring work.

605 In the Polish civil code (1964), the eleventh title (of the third book on obligations) encompasses sales. The twelfth title: exchange. The thirteenth title: delivery. The fourteenth title: precontracted deliveries of agricultural production. The fifteenth title: work contract. The sixteenth title: construction works contract. The seventeenth title: lease and tenancy. The eighteenth title: gratuitous loans for use. The nineteenth title: loans.

The composition in the current Hungarian civil code (2013) is similar: first there are title-transfer contracts (the fourteenth title of the sixth book on obligations), then work contracts (the fifteenth title regards contracts for professional services), mandate (the sixteenth title concerns engagement-type contracts) and contracts enabling use of things [the seventeenth title considers licensing contracts; in the opening of the seventeenth title the forty-fourth chapter deals with lease agreements, the forty-fifth chapter leasehold contracts (tenancy) and the forty-sixth chapter lending arrangements (gratuitous loans for use)].

606 In the Polish Code of obligations (1933), the eleventh title considers contracts supplying services. The second division (of the eleventh title) refers to work contract.

607 In the Hungarian draft (1928), the eleventh title (of the third book on obligations) encompasses legal relationships resulting from work. The second chapter (of the eleventh title) comprises work contract.

608 In the Polish civil code (1964), the fifteenth title (of the third book on obligations) regards work contract. The sixteenth title: construction works contract.

In the second socialist Russian civil code (1964), the thirtieth chapter (the third book on obligations) concerns work contract. The thirty-first chapter: construction works contract.

609 The discussed solution is visible e.g. in the German BGB (1896) – according to § 662, by the acceptance of a mandate the mandatary binds himself gratuitously to take care of some matter for the mandator entrusted to him by the latter.

610 According to Article 500 § 1 of the Polish Code of obligations (1933), if it does not result from the contract or the circumstances that the mandatee has undertaken to perform the contract gratuitously, it is assumed that the contract shall be performed against remuneration.

of the codifications researched for this study power of attorney and mandate are arranged together; in the CC (1804) and the ABGB (1811) they are merged into a single institution[611]. Later they are set separately; their systematic seclusion was connected with their dissociation in practice[612]. In codes that contain a general part representation and power of attorney are set in the general part[613].

It is now necessary briefly to mention a possible systematization of mandate in the civil codes. Mandate may be set next to contracts enabling the use of things[614],

---

The same rule is present in the Polish civil code (1964) – Article 735 § 1 of the Polish civil code corresponds to the Article 500 § 1 of the Polish Code of obligations.

611 In the CMBC (1756) both institutions are arranged together in the ninth chapter of the fourth book on obligations *(Von der Vollmacht (Mandato) und anderen ähnlichen Verträgen)*.

The CMBC was innovative in considering mandate and power of attorney as separate institutions. Adopted later the CC (1804) and the ABGB (1811) perceived mandate and power of attorney as one institution. The legal discovery was that mandate and power of attorney can function separately happened much later.

In the CC (1804), the thirteenth title (of the third book regarding different ways of acquiring ownership) concerns mandate.

In the ABGB (1811), the twenty-second chapter (the second book on *ius rerum*, the second division on the personal rights) regards the power of attorney and other types of agency.

Despite using different names in the French *Code civil* (mandate – *mandat*) and in the ABGB (power of attorney *Bevollmächtigungsvertrag*) the content of the institutions in both codifications is similar.

LUDWICZAK W., *Umowa zlecenia* [Mandate contract], Poznań 1955, p. 15.

Merging mandate and power of attorney into one institution does not work well from the systematic point of view, because it results in the thinking that both institutions cannot function independently.

The French jurisprudence admitted solutions enabling distinct operation of mandate and power of attorney *(convention de prête-nom)*.

Ibidem, p. 17.

The Austrian lawyers experienced similar dilemmas to their French counterparts; the solutions adopted in Austria strongly resemble the French ones – in Austria mandate without power of attorney and power of attorney without mandate was introduced.

Ibidem, pp. 18 – 19.

612 The mentioned composition is visible e.g. in the German BGB (1896). The fifth title (put in the third chapter on juridical acts) includes agency and power of attorney.

Mandate is placed in situated in the tenth title (the second book on obligations, the seventh chapter on the particular obligations).

613 E.g. in the German BGB (1896) agency and power of attorney are put in the fifth title (of the third chapter on juridical acts), in the general part.

614 In the Polish civil code (1964), the seventeenth title (of the third book on obligations) regards lease and tenancy. The eighteenth title: gratuitous loans for use. The nineteenth title: loans. The twentieth title: credit account agreement. The twenty-first title: mandate.

In the current Hungarian civil code (2013), the sixteenth title (the sixth book on obligations, the third division on express contracts) concerns engagement-type contracts (mandate). The seventeenth title: licensing contracts (contracts enabling use of things).

next to deposit[615], after work contract[616] or before brokerage agreement[617]. In many codifications management without mandate (*negotiorum gestio*) is situated after mandate[618]. Before moving onto deposit, we should recapitulate the systematization of brokerage agreements and carriage contracts. Brokerage agreements can

---

[615] In the German BGB (1896), the tenth title (the second book on obligations, the seventh chapter comprising the particular obligations) considers mandate. The eleventh title: management without mandate. The twelfth title: deposit.

In the first socialist Czechoslovak civil code (1950), the twenty-third chapter (the fourth book on obligations) deals with deposit. The twenty-fourth chapter: mandate.

In the socialist Hungarian civil code (1959), the thirty-ninth chapter (the fourth book on obligations, the third title on various contracts) includes deposit. The fortieth chapter: mandate.

In the second socialist Russian civil code (1964), the thirty-fifth chapter (the fourth book on obligations) encompasses mandate. The thirty-sixth chapter: commission. The thirty-seventh chapter: deposit.

In the current Czech civil code (2012), the fourth chapter (the fourth book on the relative property rights, the second title referring to obligations arising from juridical acts) includes obligations arising from safekeeping contracts. The fifth chapter: obligations arising from mandate-type contracts.

[616] In the Polish Code of obligations (1933), the third division (of the eleventh title referring to contracts supplying services) refers to mandate. The fourth division: brokerage agreement. The fifth division: deposit.

In the Russian draft (1905), the ninth section (the fifth book on obligations, the second division containing obligations arising from contracts) regards work contract. The tenth section: carriage. The eleventh section: mandate and power of attorney *(Vollmacht und Kommission)*.

In the Polish Code of obligations (1933), the second division (of the eleventh title considering contracts supplying services) deals with work contract. The third division: mandate.

In the current Hungarian civil code (2013), the fifteenth title (the sixth book on obligations, the third division on express contracts) encompasses contracts for professional services. In the opening of the fifteenth title there is the thirty-seventh chapter concerning work contracts. The sixteenth title refers to engagement-type contracts (mandate).

[617] In the Polish Code of obligations (1933), the third division (of the eleventh title on contracts supplying services) concerns mandate. The fourth division: brokerage agreement.

[618] The discussed composition is visible e.g. in the German BGB (1896), where the tenth title (the second book on obligations, the seventh chapter comprising the particular obligations) deals with mandate. The eleventh title: management without mandate.

Among the analyzed codifications always mandate *(Auftrag)* is placed next to management without mandate (not contract for services – *Dienstvertrag*).

be arranged among contracts for supplying services[619] or after work contract[620]. Carriage contracts can be a subset either of work contract[621] or mandate[622].

4. Deposit contract

A deposit might be systematized at the beginning of particular contracts[623]. This classification is connected with gratuitous contracts being arranged first. A deposit can be arranged after contracts enabling the use of things[624]. A depositary is obliged to keep in his custody a movable delivered to him by a depositor. Due to the insurance factor in his work, deposit can be placed next to insurance con-

---

619 In the Polish Code of obligations (1933), the eleventh title refers to contracts supplying services. The fourth division (of the eleventh title) encompasses brokerage agreement.

620 In the German BGB (1896), the seventh title (the second book on obligations, the seventh chapter on the particular obligations) considers work contract. In the eighth title broker's contract is situated.

621 In the Russian draft (1905), work contract is set in the ninth section (the fifth book on obligations, the second division containing obligations arising from contracts). The tenth section: carriage contract.

In the second socialist Russian civil code (1964), the thirtieth chapter (the third book on obligations) considers work contract. The thirty-first chapter: specific construction works contract. The thirty-second chapter: carriage.

In the current Hungarian civil code (2013), the fifteenth title (the sixth book on obligations, the third division on express contracts) deals with contracts for professional services. In the beginning of the title the thirty-seventh chapter regards works contract. The thirty-eighth chapter: carriage contracts.

622 In the Polish civil code (1964), carriage together with a number of other contracts is treated as a subtype of mandate. The twenty-first title (of the third book on obligations) considers mandate. The twenty-second title: management without mandate. The twenty-third title: agency contract. The twenty-fourth title: consignment contract. The twenty-fifth title: carriage contract.

623 In the ABGB (1811), deposit is positioned in the nineteenth chapter (the second book on *ius rerum*, the second division considering the personal rights). Deposit is set after donation, the first among the particular contracts, systematized in the eighteenth chapter. The twentieth chapter: gratuitous loans for use.

In the Hungarian draft (1928), deposit and liability of innkeepers are settled together in the sixth title of the third book on obligations. The sixth title opens the particular obligations and contains: loan, gratuitous loans for use, deposit and liability of innkeepers.

624 In the first socialist Czechoslovak civil code (1950), the twentieth chapter (in the fourth book on obligations) considers lease. The twenty-first chapter: gratuitous loans for use. The twenty-second chapter: loans. The twenty-third chapter: deposit.

In the current Hungarian civil code (2013), the eighteenth title (the sixth book on obligations, the third division on express contracts) concerns deposit arrangements. The seventeenth title comprises licensing agreements (contracts enabling use of things).

tract[625]. Similar thinking might result in arranging deposit next to guarantee[626]. Another possible resolution involves systematizing deposit contract close to mandate[627]. Deposit can be arranged among contracts supplying services[628]. In this arrangement deposit is perceived as one of several possible undertakings that an individual might assume in private law. The final issue mentioned here concens the systematic subcategories of the deposit contract, which are the liability of innkeepers[629] and storage[630].

5. Partnership contract

Partnership is a contract in which partners commit to strive to achieve a common economic purpose. A partnership needs to be distinguished from commercial companies with a legal personality. In most of the codes researched in this study, partnership is established close to the end of particular obligations or it is the final contract in the sequence[631]. In the composition of the civil codes, partnership can

---

625 In the Polish civil code (1964), the twenty-seventh title (of the third book on obligations) comprises insurance contract. The twenty-eighth title: deposit.

In the current Russian civil code (1994 – 2006), deposit (storage) is located in the forty-seventh chapter (of the fourth book on the particular kinds of obligations). The forty-eighth chapter: insurance.

626 E.g. in the Swiss Code of obligations (1911) deposit is placed in the nineteenth title (of the second division on different kinds of contracts). The twentieth title: guarantee.

627 In the German BGB (1896), deposit is positioned in the twelfth title (the second book on obligations, the seventh chapter comprising the particular obligations). In front of deposit mandate is placed (in the tenth title) and management without mandate (in the eleventh title)

In the first socialist Czechoslovak civil code (1950), deposit is placed in the twenty-third chapter (the fourth book on obligations). The twenty-fourth chapter: mandate.

In the socialist Hungarian civil code (1959), deposit is arranged in the thirty-ninth chapter (the fourth book on obligations, the third title on various contracts). The fortieth chapter: mandate and management without mandate.

628 In the Polish Code of obligations (1933), the eleventh title contains contracts supplying services. The first division (of the eleventh title) deals with employment contract. The second division: work contract. The third division: mandate. The fourth division: brokerage agreement. The fifth division: deposit contract.

629 In the German BGB (1896), the twelfth title (the second book on obligations, the seventh title including the particular obligations) concerns deposit. The thirteenth title: delivery of things to innkeepers.

In the Polish civil code (1964), the twenty-eighth title (of the third book on obligations) regards deposit. The twenty-ninth title refers to the liability of innkeepers (liability, right of pledge and limitation of claims of persons running hotels and similar establishments).

630 In the Polish civil code (1964), the twenty-eighth title (of the third book on obligations) considers deposit. The twenty-ninth title: liability of innkeepers. The thirtieth title: storage.

631 E.g. in the Swiss Code of obligations (1911) partnership is the last agreement in the second division of the code, referring to different kinds of contracts. It is located in the twenty-third title.

In the current Hungarian civil code (2013) the twenty-fourth title (of the sixth book on obligations, the third division containing express contracts) includes civil law partnership agreement. It is second-to-last among the particular contracts – civil partnership is placed later in the

be viewed in connection to the joint ownership and the common factor in private law[632]. Partnership might also be used as an opening to commercial law in the civil code. This arrangement was applied in the Swiss Code of obligations (1911), where partnership is the final agreement in the second division of the code, referring to different kinds of contracts. The third division of the Code of obligations includes commercial companies and cooperatives.

6. Aleatory contracts

Another category includes contracts in which the main determinant is chance. It is the luck of an individual that influences the final result of a legal transaction. Gaming, betting, life annuity and life maintenance are classified among aleatory contracts. Aleatory contracts may be placed at the end of particular contracts or close to their end[633]. In the codes they might constitute a group of contracts[634] or

---

twenty-fifth title.

In the German BGB (1896) partnership is also situated far from the beginning of the particular contracts; in the BGB partnership is put in the fourteenth title. In the seventh chapter (of the second book on obligations) there are twenty-five titles. In the BGB there are only the general provisions on partnership, without isolating different kinds of partnership.

DOMAŃSKI L., *Instytucje Kodeksu zobowiązań. Komentarz teoretyczno – praktyczny. Część szczególna* [Institutions of the Code of obligations. Theoretical and practical commentary. Particular part], Warszawa 1938, p. 551.

This is only one potential way to arrange the provisions on partnership, because in a civil code there may be systematic subdivisions in the systematic unit including partnership. The discussed systematic pattern is visible e.g. in the socialist Hungarian civil code (1959), where the fifty-sixth chapter (the fourth book on the law of obligations, the third title on various contracts) comprising partnership contains: economic partnership (§§ 568 – 572), civil law company (§§ 573 – 574), building community (§§ 575 – 577) and common relations of persons living in common household (§ 578).

632 E.g. in the German BGB (1896) partnership is located in the fourteenth title (the second book on obligations, the seventh chapter including the particular obligations). Afterwards, in the fifteenth title joint ownership is situated. Both titles constitute a certain systematic whole, referring to a common factor in private law.

633 In the ABGB (1811), the twenty-ninth chapter (the second book on *ius rerum*, the second division comprising the personal rights) encompasses aleatory contracts. This is the end of the particular contracts – the thirtieth chapter includes the right to damages and compensation.

In the Swiss Code of obligations (1911), the twenty-first title (the second division containing different kinds of contracts) considers gambling and betting and the twenty-second life annuity and the lifetime maintenance agreements. Afterwards in the twenty-third title simple partnership is situated, constituting the last among particular contracts.

In the socialist Hungarian civil code (1959) the forty-ninth chapter (the fourth book on obligations, the third title on various contracts) deals with contracts for maintenance and for life annuity. The fiftieth chapter (the last chapter of the third title) contains an offer of prize and the assumption of an obligation for the purposes of public interest.

634 In the CC (1804) the twelfth title (of the third book on different ways of acquiring ownership) refers to aleatory contracts.

In the ABGB (1811), the twenty-ninth chapter (the second division on the personal rights of the second book on *ius rerum*) considers aleatory contracts.

they can be arranged next to each other, in separate systematic sections[635]. Finally, it should be stated that socialism was not in favour of capitalist leisure pursuits like gaming and betting. Consequently, the agreements mentioned here disappeared from the systematization of all socialist civil codes, except the first socialist Czechoslovak civil code of 1950[636]. In the Polish civil code (1964), gaming and betting are mentioned in Article 413.

7. Arrangement of commercial law

The final issue analyzed here regarding the arrangement of particular contracts is the composition of commercial law. In the oldest codifications the most typical solution was to establish a separate commercial code, which is a way of slimming down a civil code. That is the duality of private law, described first in this section, followed by the unity of private law. If unity of private law is introduced to the system, then commercial law is positioned with in a civil code.

a) Duality of private law – arranging commercial law in a commercial code

Private law and commercial law can be arranged in two separate written laws. The French *Code de commerce* (1807) was a correlate to the French *Code civil* (1804). In Germany a different solution was chosen; the German *Handelsgesetzbuch* (1897) is independent from the German BGB (1896). Polish lawyers followed the German model, and for this reason the Polish Commercial Code (1934) was independent from the Polish Code of obligations (1933). Commercial law is related to the concept of a merchant, which can be defined differently. According to Article 1 of the French *Code de commerce*, merchants are those who perform commercial actions, and pursue their usual job[637]. The first part of § 1 of the German *Handelsgesetzbuch* states that in the meaning of this code a merchant is one who runshis (or her) commercial business[638]. According to Article 1 of the Polish Commercial Code, a merchant runs a business in his own name. Furthermore, only the legal transactions of a merchant connected with his enterprise are commercial

---

[635] In the German BGB (1896), the sixteenth title (the second book on obligations, the seventh chapter containing the particular obligations) refers to annuity. The seventeenth title: gaming and betting.

In the Swiss Code of obligations (1911), twenty-first title (of second division on different types of contracts) concerns gaming and betting. The twenty-second title refers to life annuity and lifetime maintenance agreements.

[636] In the first socialist Czechoslovak civil code (1950), gaming and betting were located in the thirty-second chapter of the fourth book on obligations.

[637] *Article 1 Sont commerçans ceux qui exercent des actes de commerce, et en font leur profession habituelle.*

[638] § 1 (1) *Kaufmann im Sinne dieses Gesetzbuchs ist, wer ein Handelsgewerbe betreibt.*

More about a merchant here: JUNG P., *Handelsrecht*, München 2019, p. 18 and the following pages.

transactions[639] (Article 498 § 1). There was a presumption that each legal transaction of a merchant is a commercial transaction[640] (Article 498 § 2).

b) Unity of private law

If commercial law is preserved in a civil code, then that is the unity of a civil code. One of the possible locations for commercial law in a civil code is among particular obligations – e.g. in the Swiss Code of obligations, commercial law is placed after particular contracts[641]. Unity of private law is now a very common systematic pattern (Poland 1964; Czechia 2012; Hungary 2013; Russia 1994 – 2006). It is a feature of all Russian codifications (1905, 1922, 1964, 1994 – 2006), and it was the most typicalsystematization adopted in socialist civil codes (Russia 1922, 1964; Czechoslovakia 1950; Hungary 1959; Poland 1964). Among the socialist codifications only civil codes that address the needs of socialist citizens (Czechoslovakia 1964, East Germany 1975) chose to place content regarding the commercial law in separate statutes.

Here we consider the relevance of the unity of private law in socialist jurisdictions. In socialism, a contract is an instrument for performing the socialist plan. Introducing the mechanisms of the socialist economy to a civil code disrupts the division on *ius privatum* and *ius publicum*. Units of the nationalized economy conclude agreements based on the civil codes, in accordance with the plan, and there is no place left for freedom of contract. In Czechoslovakia (1964) and East Germany (1975) the content of private law was redistributed between more written laws. In both jurisdictions the civil codes only include a volume that considers socialist citizens and their needs[642]. For this reason, the provisions regarding

---

[639] This provision is identical to the provision from the German *Handelsgesetzbuch* (1897):
§ 343 (1) *Handelsgeschäfte sind alle Geschäfte eines Kaufmanns, die zum Betriebe seines Handelsgewerbes gehören.*

[640] More about the Polish Commercial Code (1934) in: SZCZYGIELSKI A. D., *Zasady prawa handlowego Tom I. Podstawy konstrukcyjne polskiego Kodeksu handlowego. Zasady podstawowe – Czynności handlowe – Pojęcie kupca* [The principles of commercial law Volume I. The structural foundations of Polish Commercial Code. Basic principles. Commercial operations. The concept of a merchant], przedmowa J. NAMITKIEWICZ, Warszawa 1936.

[641] The Swiss legislator included the whole content applicable to the law of obligations in one written law. When the Swiss codification entered in force, it was an innovative arrangement, because at this time in most legal systems there was a commercial code. Among the researched jurisdictions that was the case in France, Austria, Germany and Hungary.

Among the divisions of the Swiss Code of obligations (1911) there are: general provisions (the first division) – various kinds of contracts (the second division) – commercial companies and the cooperatives (the third division).

[642] The second socialist Czechoslovak civil code (1964) contains: general provisions – socialist collective ownership and personal ownership – personal use of dwelling units, other living space, and tracts of land – services – rights and duties from other juridical acts – responsibility for damage and unjust enrichment – inheritance of property constituting the personal ownership – final provisions.

agreements that can be found in the East German civil code do not apply to the contracts concluded between socialist state enterprises[643].

The state economy was governed by immense state enterprises and units of the nationalized economy. Those units were legal persons. Due to the differences between the capitalist and socialist legal systems, we apply a term from economic law. The legal literature lists some features of socialist economic law: planning, unity of state ownership, protection of social(ist) ownership, economic settlement and the operative and legal independence of the economic units arising from it, as well as the cooperation of economic units[644].

Socialist engineering did not predominantly affect the composition of those codes that retain the unity of private law[645] (Czechoslovakia – 1950, Hungary – 1959, Russia – 1964, Poland – 1964). Unity of private law was the simplest solution in the socialist jurisdictions. The return to the traditional concepts of private law after the fall of socialism was easier in legal systems with civil codes less affected by state ideology. It needs to be stated that maintaining the unity of private law in socialist codifications enabled the provisions of private law to be more easily applied to the contracts concluded between the units of the state economy. The absence of the division of a civil code (similar to that found in the second socialist Czechoslovak civil code of 1964 and in the East German civil code of 1975) resulted in the core of private law being retained in a single written law. In the Polish civil code (1964) the general provisions on contracts placed in the general part and those placed in the third title (of the third book on obligations), which includes the general provisions on contractual obligations, could be used for the agreements entered into between the immense socialist state enterprises.

II. The systematization of the non-contractual sources of obligations

The final issue analyzed in the chapter on the law of obligations is the arrangement of non-contractual sources of obligations. The foundation for the legal relationships mentioned here is not freedom of contract and the will of the parties or of an

---

In the East German civil code (1975) there are: fundamental principles of the socialist private law – socialist ownership and personal ownership – contracts relating to the material and cultural life – use of real estate for residential and recreational purposes – protection of life, health and property from damage – inheritance law – specific provisions of the respective relationships of private law.

643 WESTEN K., SCHLEIDER J., *Zivilrecht im Systemvergleich. Das Zivilrecht der Deutschen Demokratischen Republik und der Bundesrepublik Deutschland*, Berlin 1984, p. 81.

644 MADEY M., STELMACHOWSKI A., *Zarys prawa gospodarczego* [Introduction to economic law], Warszawa 1980, p. 19.

645 About the development of commercial law in Czechoslovakia, Hungary and Poland: PASHCHENKO T., *Das Recht der Handelsgeschäfte in der Russischen Föderation*, Frankfurt am Main 2003, pp. 29 – 38.

In Russia: *Ibidem*, pp. 77.

individual; that is the main difference between contracts and the non-contractual sources of obligations.

The most popular composition is to position non-contractual sources of obligations at the end of particular obligations[646]. Another option is to place them after the general part of obligations[647]. In civil codes arranged according to the

---

[646] In the CMBC (1756) the sixteenth chapter (of the fourth book on obligations) considers claims from offences *(Forderungen aus Vergehen)*. The seventeenth chapter refers to the law of damages *(von Injurien)*. The last eighteenth chapter of the fourth book includes feudal law *(vom Lehenrecht)*.

In the ABGB (1811), the last thirtieth chapter (of the second book on *ius rerum*, the second division including the personal rights) contains the right to damages and compensation.

In the Saxon civil code (1863), the non-contractual sources of obligations are set at the end of particular obligations. The second division (of the third book on the law of claims) concerning particular kinds of claims includes three chapters. Those are: claims from contracts and contractual obligations (the first chapter), claims from tortious acts (the second chapter) and claims from different grounds (the third chapter).

In the German BGB (1896), in the seventh chapter on particular obligations (of the second book on obligations) the last two titles of the second book contain the non-contractual-sources of obligations. The twenty-fourth title: unjust enrichment. The twenty-fifth title: law of damages.

In the Russian draft (1905), the last third division of the last fifth book on obligations considers obligations which do not originate from contracts.

In the first socialist Russian draft (1922), the last two chapters of the third book on obligations comprise the non-contractual sources of obligations. The twelfth chapter: obligations originating from unjustified enrichment. The thirteenth chapter: obligations originating from damage caused to another.

In the second socialist Russian code (1964), the last three chapters of the third book on obligations comprise the non-contractual sources of obligations. The fortieth chapter: obligations resulting out of inflicting damage with an illicit act. The forty-first chapter: obligations arising from the protection of socialist property. The forty-second chapter: obligations from unjustified acquisition or economizing property.

In the current Russian civil code (1994 – 2006), that is at the end of the fourth book considering the particular kinds of obligations. The fifty-ninth chapter of the fourth book: liabilities for damage. The sixtieth chapter: obligations due to unjust enrichment.

In the current Hungarian civil code (2013), the fourth division of the sixth book on obligations regards the non-contractual liability for damages. The fifth division: securities. The last sixth division contains other facts establishing obligations.

In the current Czech civil code (2012), the third title (of the fourth book on the relative property rights) includes obligations arising from torts. The last fourth title: obligations arising from other legal causes.

[647] In the first Czechoslovak civil code (1950), the sixteenth chapter (of the fourth book on obligations) includes the law of damages and the seventeenth chapter unjust enrichment. The fifteenth chapter: extinction of obligations. The eighteenth chapter: sales and barter.

In the socialist Hungarian civil code (1959), the non-contractual sources of obligations are arranged in the second title (of the fourth book on obligations), including the responsibility for damage caused out of contract and unjust enrichment. The first title of the fourth book: contracts. The third title: various contracts.

In the CC (1804), the non-contractual sources of obligations are situated at the end of the general part of obligations. The third title (of the third book on different ways of acquiring

sources of obligations, non-contractual sources of obligations are situated in the general part of obligations, after the general provisions on contracts[648]. This shows that the issue of the arrangement of non-contractual sources of obligations may be perceived in many ways; even though it is primarily an issue that belongs among particular obligations, non-contractual sources of obligations can be transposed to the general part of obligations. Nonetheless, at the same time management without mandate may be arranged among the particular contracts, next to mandate. Article 1 of the Polish Code of obligations (1933) lists the sources of obligations. They are: declaration of will, actions and other occurrences, with which the written law connects the formation of obligations.

In socialist civil codes settled according to the needs of citizens the non-contractual sources of obligations are extracted in a separate book (Czechoslovakia – 1964, East Germany – 1975). Subsidiary elements are underlined in order to obtain a socialist arrangement of the law of obligations[649].

H) Conclusions on the arrangement of the law of obligations

The research covered in this chapter shows that the division of general and particular obligations is the most significant rule for arranging obligations. Since the classification was established[650] it has been present in all codifications, including the second socialist Czechoslovak civil code (1964) and the East German civil

ownership) considers contracts and conventional obligations in general. The fourth title: commitments formed without an agreement.

648 In the Swiss Code of obligations (1911), the first title refers to the formation of obligations. The first chapter of the first title: obligations arising by contract. The second chapter: obligations from illicit acts (torts). The third chapter: obligations from unjust enrichment.

In the Polish Code of obligations (1933), in the second title (regarding the formation of obligations) the first division concerns the declaration of will. The second division: formation of obligations from other sources. In the second division the first chapter encompasses management without mandate. The second chapter: unjust enrichment. The third chapter: undue benefit *(des prestations indues)*. The last fourth chapter of the second division includes tortious acts.

In the Polish civil code (1964), the third title (of the third book on obligations) comprises the general provisions on contractual obligations. The fourth title: obligation of concluding agreements between the units of the nationalized economy. The fifth title: unjust enrichment. The sixth title: delicts.

In the CC (1804), since the reform in 2016 the third title (of the third book on different ways of acquiring ownership) includes the sources of obligations. The first sub-title (of the third title) considers contract. The second sub-title: extra-contractual liability. The third sub-title: other sources of obligations.

649 In the second socialist Czechoslovak civil code (1964), the fifth book deals with responsibility for damage and for unjust enrichment.

The fifth book of the East German civil code (1975) refers to protection of life, health and property from damage.

650 In the CMBC (1756) and the Prussian *Landrecht* (1794) the distinction on the general and particular obligations is not yet elaborated, but it is visible already in the CC (1804) and the ABGB (1811).

code (1975), both of which modify the traditional systematic patterns the most markedly. The second factor influencing the composition of the law of obligations is the relation between an obligation and a contract. In the first codifications, a contract may be a central construct in the code (CC – 1804). A more common systematization is the arrangement in which an obligation can be found in the exterior divisions, but where a contract prevails in the further sections (the CMBC – 1756, the ABGB – 1811)

In later codifications, an obligation is usually evident in the system of the books. Most typically, a contract constitutes a systematic subset of an obligation. In a civil code that includes a general part, the only opportunity is to assemble the system around an obligation. In the general part there are juridical acts, which concentrate the volume of the law of obligations in the general part. The most popular solution is to establish the entire volume of the general part of obligations in a single book, or to transfer some provisions of obligations to the general part. The final systematic segment in the chapter on obligations are particular obligations; in that area, the possibilities for systematizing particular contracts and the non-contractual sources of obligations are listed, based on examples. Contrary to *ius in re*, the arrangement of the law of obligations is not governed by rigid rules. Furthermore, the impact of socialism on the systematization of the law of obligations in socialist civil codes is rather minimal.

Chapter 3: Ius in re

A) Introduction

The aim of this chapter is to research different ways of arranging *ius in re* in the structure of the civil codes from a historical and comparative perspective. This area of the study provides a foundation for developing familiarity with current legislative schemes and the possible options for settling *ius in re* in the systems of the civil codes. In terms of *ius in re*, the discussion concentrates on listing the differences between the bourgeois and socialist civil codes.

One of the essential problems of *ius in re*, which also affects its systematization, pertains to their catalogue. The catalogue and the definition of a thing together are two main determinants of *ius in re* in a civil code. Alongside these two issues, other factors also exert impact on the arrangement of *ius in re*, which are listed and explained in this chapter. The sequence of chapters in this study follow the pattern of the German BGB (1896), in which rights relating to objects follow obligations. The chapter on *ius in re* is the second longest chapter in this study.

Ius in re is a branch of private law that concerns objects or assets. It regulates legal relationships regarding the property of an individual. They are governed with different rules from those applied in other areas of private law. The primary attribute of *ius in re* is a thing (object) – not a performance, the main characteristic of obligations. *Ius in re* are effective towards everybody (*erga omnes*). Statutes ensure the legal protection of *ius in re* against all those who infringe them. This kind of security is solely an attribute of *ius in re* – the protection of obligations is valid only towards another party of an obligation.

As the security provided to *ius in re* is strong, its catalogue cannot be open. Therefore, individuals cannot establish new *ius in re*, but are free to move with in the limits already functioning in the system (*numerus clausus*). Arrangement of *ius in re* is connected with the list present in each code; composition of the elements is related to the number of available compounds.

B) Definitions of *res* (object) in the structure of the civil codes

I. Introduction

This part of the chapter determines the position of *res* (object, thing) in the structure of the analyzed codes. Here, I describe the solutions adopted in the codes and I present the legislative possibilities in this field. Only a thing can be granted protection that is effective for everybody (*erga omnes*). A thing is a systematic buttress of *ius in re* in the civil codes, because a thing is defined differently in the jurisdictions researched for this study. No *ius in re* can be applied if that which we possess is not a thing. That is why it is described in the opening of this chapter. A thing is granted the broadest security available in the system of private law.

II. Ways of formulating objects (*res*) in the researched codes

Before analyzing the definitions implemented in the civil codes, we must outline the ways in which an object is formulated. The first option is to establish a definition, in which everything that it encompasses is a thing. There are also codes in which an object is not defined. If a legislator does not leave any indications as to how *res* is shaped in the code, then it is first necessary to apply the linguistic meaning of the terms assigned in the text of the code.

III. Content of *res – res corporales* or also *res incorporales*?

One of the most important issues considered by lawmakers is the catalogue of objects granted the protection *erga omnes*. Does this security apply solely to things or also to rights? Do all the belongings of an individual receive the legislative security of *ius in re*, or only material objects (*res corporales*)? Should a legislator also grant the protection of *ius in re* to incorporeal things (*res incorporales*)?

IV. Plan of the section

Before discussing the solutions implemented in the codes, it is necessary to consider how things are presented in the *Institutes* of Gaius. Gaius proposes a wide definition, including both *res corporales* and *res incorporales*. This became the basis for the Prussian *Landrecht* (1794) and for codes with a systematization based on the Gaius model. Gaius's ideas were a primary inspiration for the earliest codes. The Gaian definition is also present in later codes, including those that do not follow Gaius's composition. That is not surprising, given that all later structures of the codes are an elaboration of the Gaius scheme. The definition of a thing has a connection with the exterior shape of the code, but there is no inherent rule in this field.

The definition of an object was narrowed in the German BGB, granting the protection *erga omnes* only to *res corporales*. The first solution that variedfrom the Gaian resolution was related to the will of establishing a new systematic model.

Later codifications were impacted both by these German ideas and by Gaius's concept. The purpose of this section is to approach the main solutions that can be observed in the civil codes. The analysis does not mention all provisions referring to things that can be found in the codes. Instead, the examination concentrates on civil codes in Central and Eastern Europe because they are not widely known.

V. *Res* in *Institutes* of Gaius

In *Institutes*, Gaius stated: "Besides, certain objects are material, others immaterial. Material objects are those which can be touched, such as land, slaves, clothing, gold and silver, as well as countless other things. Immaterial objects are those which cannot be touched, so these are the ones which are a right, such as inheritance, usufruct or obligations committed in any way[651]".

VI. Formulating *res* in the codes directly inspired by the *Institutes* of Gaius

If Gaius's idea is introduced into legislation, then the widest possible definition of an object is adopted. The security *erga omnes* applies both to *res corporales* and *res incorporales*. This approach is visible in the codifications analyzed here, especially those that follow the systematization based on *Institutes*. Even though the structure of the Prussian *Landrecht* (1794) does not replicate the Gaian arrangement, its divisions are also strongly impacted by the *Institutes*.

1. *Res* in the CMBC (1756)

The structure of the CMBC is founded on the *Institutes*[652]. In § 1 of the second book on *ius in re* it is stated that in the code *res* is all that can be of human use[653].

2. *Res* in the Prussian *Landrecht* (1794)

The Prussian *Landrecht* is not entirely based on the Gaius scheme, but it was partly inspired by the *Institutes*. As a result, in Prussia the widest possible meaning of *res* was applied. According to § 1 of the second title (regarding things and their rights in general) of the first part, in law, a thing is anything that can be the object of a right or an obligation.

---

651 " *Quaedam praeterea res sunt, quaedam incorporales. <Corporales> hae<sunt>, quae tangi possunt, veluti fundus homo vestis aurum argentum et denique aliae res innumerabiles. Incorporales sunt quae tangi non possunt, qualia sunt ea qua <in> iuret, sicut hereditas ususfructus obligationes quoquo modo contractae*".

652 The first book of the CMBC (1756) comprises the legal rules in general and the law of persons *(personae)*. The second book contains *ius in re* and the third book includes inheritance law. Those two books constitute *res*. Obligations *(actiones)* are arranged in the last, fourth, book.

653 The title of the first chapter (of the second book on *ius in re*), where *res* is defined, also implies a wide meaning of *res* – it regards the rights and duties generally concerning one's property *(von den Rechten und Pflichten in Ansehen Hab und Guts überhaupt)*.

3. *Res* in the French *Code civil* (1804)

The French *Code civil* is structured according to the Gaius model[654]. Goods are mentioned in the title of the second book regarding goods and different modifications of ownership. The CC is the only code among those researched for this study in which goods (or things) are recalled in the divisions of the code into books. The structuring of *res* in the CC is strongly connected with the linguistic terms used in the code. A thing (*chose*) is distinguished from a good[655] (*bien*). There is a broad list of goods, which are immovables[656] (Articles 517 – 526) or movables (Articles 527 – 536), but the code does not include a definition of an object.

4. *Res* in the ABGB (1811)

The ABGB is the final code of those discussed here that follows the systematization based on *Institutes*. Its first book regards the law of persons (*personae*), the second book *ius rerum* (*res*), and the third book comprises provisions common to personal rights and *ius in re*. The third book is an equivalent of *actiones*. The second book encompasses a human's whole environment, and all that he or she might take possession of. The definition of *res* introduced in the ABGB is the consequence of Gaius's broad interpretation of a thing; furthermore, it is also the result of the ancestry of the natural law[657]. According to § 285 of the ABGB, in legal understanding everything that is different from a person and serves human use is a thing. The entire content of the second book (including *ius in re*, inheritance law, law of obligations and matrimonial property law) is classified among *res*[658].

---

[654] In the CC (1804) the first book deals with *personae*. The second book concerns goods and different modifications of ownership *(res)*. The last, third, book considers different ways of acquiring ownership *(actiones)*.

[655] First, in the CC [in the first title (of the second book on goods and different modifications of ownership) referring to the distinction of goods] the term *goods* is applied consistently. But later (in the second title concerning ownership) in the famous Article 544 things are recalled.

Article 544 La propriété est le droit de jouir et disposer ***des choses*** *de la manière la plus absolue, pourvu qu'on n'en fasse pas un usage prohibé par les lois ou par les réglemens.*

[656] In the CC there are many provisions including the listing of goods. Article 526 classifies as immovables usufruct of immovables, servitudes, land services and actions for the purpose of recovering an immovable by the object to which they apply.

[657] WESENBERG G., WESENER G., *Neuere deutsche Privatrechtsgeschichte im Rahmen der europäischen Rechtsentwicklung*, Lahr/Schwarzwald 1976, p. 136.

[658] In the ABGB (1811) the second book on *ius rerum* includes two divisions. The first of them regards *ius in re*, whereas the second division comprises the personal rights.

The first division contains *ius in re* (chapters from the first to the seventh) and inheritance law (chapters from the eighth to the fifteenth). The sixteenth chapter concerns co-ownership.

The second division (personal rights) encompasses the law of obligations (chapters from the seventeenth to the thirtieth). Matrimonial property law is put among the particular contracts, in the twenty-eighth chapter.

VII. Impact of the Austrian concepts

The Austrian definition of a thing has significantly impacted other codifications. They have adopted different structures. This section first approaches definitions of a thing in Czechia and Hungary, and then in Saxony[659] (1863).

1. Austrian definition in Czechia and Hungary

The definitions in Czechia and Hungary are primarily inspired by the Austrian constructs[660]. A different formulation is visible only in the second socialist Czechoslovak civil code[661] (1964). In the interwar Czechoslovak draft (1937), Czechoslovak lawyers simplified the Austrian provisions and adapted them to their needs[662]. In the first socialist Czechoslovak civil code (1950), "the conception of things was substantially narrowed down since by them it understood not also rights as the so-called movable things, but only controllable physical objects and natural powers serving the needs of a human"[663]. In the current Czech civil code, the Austrian definition was incorporated into Section 489: "A thing in a le-

---

659 While observing the formulations of *res* in the civil codes, it seems that the Austrian concept was the most influential among all definitions of a thing. Apart from the above-mentioned codes, the Polish constructs (the draft on *ius in re* from 1937) were also inspired by the ABGB (1811).

660 The Czechoslovak draft of the civil code from 1937 – § 80 In legal understanding everything that is different from a person and serves human use is a thing.

The first socialist Czechoslovak civil code from 1950 – Article 23 Things in the legal sense are material objects capable of appropriation and natural forces serving the needs of a human.

The current Czech civil code from 2012 – Section 489 A thing in a legal sense (hereinafter "a thing") is everything that is different from a person and serves the needs of people.

The Hungarian draft from 1928 – § 433 The objects of ownership are things. All corporeal objects are things. Forces of nature which may be subject to law can also be regarded as things insofar as the provisions applicable to things are applicable to them.

The formulation "all corporeal objects are things" resembles § 90 of the German BGB (1896).

The socialist Hungarian civil code from 1959 – § 94 (1) Each thing which can be taken into possession can also be an object of ownership.

(2) Unless exception is made by law, the rules governing property shall apply, with the necessary changes, to money and securities as well as to such powers of nature as can be turned to use like corporeal things.

The current Hungarian civil code from 2013 – Section 5:14 (the first subpoint) There may be ownership of all things of a tangible nature which are capable of appropriation.

The second subpoint: The provisions pertaining to things shall apply also to money and securities, including natural resources that can be utilized as capital goods.

661 § 118 The object of civil law relationships can be things and rights, insofar as the nature of a right so admits.

The Austrian definition introduced into the Czechoslovak Code of International Trade from 1963 ("things are corporeals and controllable forces of nature, serving the needs of men") impacted the civil code.

VONDRACEK Th. J., *Commentary on the Czechoslovak civil code*, Dordrecht/ Boston/ Lancaster 1988, p. 127.

662 BAZOVSKÝ J., *La codification du droit civil en Tchéco-Slovaquie*, Paris 1927, pp. 151 – 152.

663 SCHELLE K., TAUCHEN J., *A Brief Introduction to Czech Civil Law*, München 2011, p. 27.

gal sense (hereinafter "a thing") is everything that is different from a person and serves the needs of people"[664].

According to § 433 of the Hungarian draft (1928), "the objects of ownership are things. All corporeal objects are things. Forces of nature which may be subject to law can also be regarded as things insofar as the provisions applicable to things are applicable to them". "The New Hungarian Civil Code [of 2013] provides that things of a tangible nature, being capable of being possessed, are the objects of ownership. The provisions [sic!] pertaining to things also applies to money and securities, including natural resources that can be utilised as things (Section 5:14). Natural resources cannot be defined as things in the traditional sense of the word, as they do not have physical limits, but this extension of the concept of things resulted from court practice and was already accepted in the Civil Code (1959) in order to penalize the illegal use of electricity under the crime of theft"[665].

In the first codifications (the CMBC – 1756, the CC – 1804, the ABGB – 1811) the impact of the Gaius scheme is visible in two fields: exterior divisions that follow the systematization based on *Institutes*, and the designation of a thing. That changed in later codifications, where there was no longer any connection between the definition of a thing and the structure of the code. Codes that introduced the Austrian definition adopted different structures. The interwar Czechoslovak draft (1937) replicated the structure of the ABGB[666]. The first socialist Czechoslovak civil code (1950) follows the Pandect model and includes a general part[667]. The current Czech civil code (2012) similarly includes a general part, but it also replicates the Gaius scheme in the system of the books[668]. In Hungary there is no general part, but its exterior shape was inspired by *Institutes*. At its beginning are law of persons and family law (*personae*), then *ius in re* (*res*), and finally law of

---

[664] More about a thing in the current Czech civil code (2012) can be found here: WABNITZ H.-B., KORBEL F., NOVOTNÝ P., THEISS C. (ed.), *Einführung in das tschechische Recht*, München 2020, p. 169.

[665] MENYHÁRD A., *Property Law in the New Hungarian Civil Code: Key Issues*, in: *New Civil Codes in Hungary and Romania*, MENYHÁRD A. and VERESS E. (ed.), Budapest/ Cluj Napoca 2017, p. 47.

[666] The Czechoslovak draft (1937) contains three books. These are: rights and persons, property law *(des droits patrimoniaux)* and the common provisions of property law *(les dispositions communes des droits patrimoniaux)*.

This arrangement is very similar to the ABGB (1811) but not identical. The first book of ABGB includes persons, the second book *ius rerum*, whereas the last, third, book concerns provisions common to personal rights and *ius in re (les dispositions communes aux droits patrimoniaux)*.

[667] The first socialist Czechoslovak civil code (1950) comprises: introductory provisions – general provisions – *ius in re* – law of obligations – succession law.

[668] The Czech civil code (2012) includes four books: general part – family law – absolute property rights *(res)* – relative property rights *(actiones)*.

The first two books encompass *personae*. The third book is an equivalent of *res* and the fourth book of *actiones*.

obligations and inheritance law, which together constitute *actiones*[669]. The Gaian influence in Hungary is visible both in the exterior divisions of the codes and in the wide definition of a thing.

2. *Res* in the Saxon civil code (1863)

The Saxon civil code is the first Pandect codification, and it includes a general part. The influence of *Institutes* is evident in the definition of a thing. The Saxon legislators established a wide definition of a thing in the code in § 58, comprising both *res corporales* and *res incorporales*[670]. According to § 58, items of any kind can be the subject of a right insofar as they are not out of circulation.

VIII. *Res corporales* – structuring in the German BGB (1896)

In the German BGB the definition of a thing was narrowed for the first time. Only corporeal objects are things in the legal sense (§ 90). Rights that are connected with the ownership of a piece of land are deemed to be component parts of land (§ 96). The structuring of *res* in Germany excludes granting protection that is efficient *erga omnes* to numerous immaterial goods, such as patents, energy or computer programs. The German solution stands opposed to the definitions included in the codifications previously discussed[671], which replicate the Gaian model[672].

---

[669] The Hungarian draft (1928) contains: law of persons and family law – *ius in re* – law of obligations – inheritance law.

The socialist Hungarian civil code (1959) includes: introductory provisions – persons – right of ownership – law of obligations – law of succession.

In the current Hungarian civil code (2013) there are: introductory provisions – individual as subject of law – legal persons – family law – *ius in re* – law of obligations – succession law.

[670] The Saxon civil code (1863) comprises: general provisions – *ius in re* – law of claims (obligations) – family law (including guardianship law) – law of succession.

In the Saxon systematization the impact of the *Institutes* is visible in two aspects. First, the Gaian definition of a thing was adopted in § 58. Second, just like in the *Institutes ius in re (res)* is underlined.

Since the general part was implemented, different books could be settled after the general part. In this case putting *ius in re* directly after the general part invokes the Gaian arrangement, where *res* is accented.

[671] BECKER C., *Die "res" bei Gaius – Vorstufe einer Systembildung in der Kodifikation? Zum Begriff des Gegenstandes im Zivilrecht*, Köln/ Berlin/ Bonn/ München 1999, p. 11.

[672] The German BGB (1896) contains: a general part – law of obligations – *ius in re* – family law – succession law.

In the BGB the law of obligations is an equivalent of *actiones*. *Ius in re* is *res*. Concurrently, the general part takes the systematic position of Gaian *personae*.

The intention of the German lawyers was to break with the Gaian systematization. Instead of placing *ius in re (res)* after the general part *(persona)*, law of obligations *(actiones)* is underlined in the system of the code.

Such a systematic choice is connected with introducing the new definition of a thing, opposing the *Institutes*. In the case of Germany, there is a strong connection between the definition of a thing and the exterior divisions of the code. Their main attribute is opposing the Gaian *res*.

IX. *Res* in the Swiss civil code (1907)

The Swiss civil code does not define *res*, but the term *thing* (*chose, Sache*) is used in the text of the code to designate an object (Article 642). There is no demand that only *res corporales* are things. Apart from land, rights inscribed in the land register (*Grundbuch*) and mines are also objects (Article 655). To a certain extent the forces of nature are also things[673] (Article 713). The Swiss definition was impacted both by the BGB and by the codifications based on the Gaius scheme (the CC – 1804, the ABGB – 1811). This is an interesting resolution, as it occupies the middle ground between German *res corporales* and Gaian *res incorporales*[674]. Among the codes researched here the direct influence of the Swiss idea is discernible in the Russian draft (1905).

X. Poland

1. *Res* in the interwar Polish draft on *ius in re* (1937)

In the Polish draft on *ius in re* (1937) things are only corporeal objects[675] (Article 1), but an additional construct that gained the protection applicable to *ius in re* was introduced. It includes goods that are not things (but which are objects of *ius in re*)[676]. An example of a catalogue is included in Article 17. The constructs implemented in the draft had the same effect as the definitions provided in codes based on the Gaius scheme[677]. The Polish solution is more neutral than the Austrian de-

---

Being first in its systematization, the BGB has designated the standards for the later codifications.

673 ŻABIŃSKI Z., *Wpływ pojęcia rzeczy na kształtowanie się systemu prawa cywilnego* [The influence of the concept of the thing on the formation of the system of private law], Zeszyty Naukowe Uniwersytetu Jagiellońskiego [Jagiellonian University Research Bulletin] Vol. CCCXLVI. Prace z zakresu prawa cywilnego i praw na dobrach niematerialnych [Works on private law and proprietary rights in intangible assets] Vol. 1 (1974), pp. 253 – 254.

Article 713 The ownership of movables aims at the things which can be transported from one place to another, accordingly the natural forces which are susceptible to appropriation and not included in the buildings.

674 The Swiss civil code (1907) comprises four books. Those are: law of persons – family law – inheritance law – *ius in re*. The first two books (law of persons and family law) contain *personae*. The further two books are *res*.

The law of obligations is settled in the separate Code of obligations (1911), serving as the last, fifth, book of the civil code and as *actiones*.

Even though in Switzerland the Gaian systematization was replicated, the Gaian definition of a thing was not adopted.

675 This formulation is identical to § 90 of the German BGB (1896).

676 *Gegenstände den dinglichen Rechten, objets de droits réels.*

677 The widest possible formulation of *res* was also proposed by Ignacy Koschembahr-Łyskowski in the draft of the general part in the interwar Polish civil code – according to Article 129 a thing is what can be an object of a legal relationship.

Komisja Kodyfikacyjna Rzeczypospolitej Polskiej. Podsekcja III Prawa Cywilnego. Tom I. Zeszyt 3 c [Codification Committee of the Republic of Poland. Subsection III of Private Law. Vol. I. Issue 3 c], content: *Kodeks cywilny Rzeczypospolitej Polskiej. Księga pierwsza przepisy*

finition[678] – in Poland there is no reference to a man and his authority towards his surroundings.

2. Adopting the German definition in the Polish civil code (1964)

After the Second World War the Pandect systematization was chosen for the Polish civil code, and Polish expressions were aligned with German terminology as early as 1946[679]. According to Article 45 of the Polish civil code (1964), with in the meaning of this code, only material objects are things.

XI. East Germany (1975)

In the East German civil code (1975), a thing is defined in § 467, which states that according to this law, things are only movable things, immovables and buildings. This provision is almost identical to § 90 of the German BGB, according to which only corporeal objects are things in the legal sense. § 467 is placed in the final, seventh book, which considers the specific provisions of the respective relationships of private law. In the code § 23 also includes objects of personal ownership[680].

XII. Defining an object in Russia

The formulations of an object in Russia are finally mentioned here. In Russia more solutions were applied than in other legal systems. The Pandect model is an inherent feature of the Russian systematization. In the Russian draft (1905) only *res corporales* are things. In the socialist Russian civil codes (1922, 1964) a thing is not defined. In the current Russian civil code (1994 – 2006) both *res corporales* and *res incorporales* receive the protection *erga omnes*. This doubling is not present in any other jurisdictions.

---

ogólne [Civil Code of the Republic of Poland. The first book general provisions], Warszawa 1931, p. 3.

678 According to § 285 of the ABGB (1811), in the legal understanding everything that is different from a person and serves human use is a thing.

679 These systematic choices were already applied in the decree on *ius in re* from 11*th* October 1946. Later, this systematization was adopted in the Polish civil code (1964). Article 45 of the Polish civil code is a copy of § 90 from the German BGB (1896).
According to Article 1 of the decree on *ius in re*, only corporeal objects are things.

680 *§ 23. Gegenstand des persönlichen Eigentums. (1) Zum persönlichen Eigentum gehören insbesondere die Arbeitseinkünfte und Ersparnisse, die Ausstattung der Wohnung und des Haushalts, Gegenstände des persönlichen Bedarfs, die für die Berufsausbildung, Weiterbildung und Freizeitgestaltung erworbenen Sachen sowie Grundstücke und Gebäude zur Befriedigung der Wohn- und Erholungsbedürfnisse des Bürgers und seiner Familie. Zum persönlichen Eigentum gehören auch die dem Wesen des persönlichen Eigentums entsprechenden Rechte, einschließlich vermögensrechtlicher Ansprüche aus Urheber-, Neuerer- und Erfinderrechten.*
(2) Auf das überwiegend auf persönlicher Arbeit beruhende Eigentum der Handwerker und Gewerbetreibenden sind die Bestimmungen über das persönliche Eigentum entsprechend anzuwenden, soweit in Rechtsvorschriften nichts anderes festgelegt ist.

1. Russian draft (1905)

In the Russian draft (1905) the protection, efficient *erga omnes*, applies only to corporeal objects[681]. Concurrently, the catalogue of *ius in re* in the Russian draft is the widest among the researched codes[682] (ranging from the right to mineral extraction to copyright law). This structuring suggests the possibilities of creating a wider formulation of *res* in the draft. Additionally, the regulation of copyright law is included in the fourth book on *ius in re*[683]. This solution most resembles the Swiss systematization, where the definition of a thing is narrow, but can be extended to a certain extent. The external divisions of the Russian draft (1905) also invoke the Swiss civil code[684] (1907). The Swiss draft is older than the Russian draft.

2. Socialist Russian civil codes (1922, 1964)

Neither of the socialist Russian civil codes (1922, 1964) contain a definition of a thing. Highlighting socialist ownership has resulted in neglecting the compounds of the system applicable to the rights of individuals in relation to objects – which included removing a definition of a thing from the codes. The second socialist Russian civil code (1964) does not include the second element of the Gaius scheme

---

681 VON SEELER W., *Der Entwurf des Russischen Zivilgesetzbuches*, Berlin 1911, p. 22.

682 In the Russian draft (1905), apart from the typical limited property rights there are also rights not present in other codes, for instance the right of interests to inheritance or the right of mineral extraction.

Limited property rights are placed in the fourth and fifth divisions (of the fourth book on *ius in re*).

The fourth division comprises the rights on the thing of another *(Rechte an fremden Sachen)*.

The fourth division contains four lines. The first line concerns the general provisions and the second line the rights of interests to inheritance *(Erbzinsrecht)*. The third line includes the right of mineral extraction *(Recht der Mineraliengewinnung)*. The last, fourth, line of the fourth division embraces, in sequence: usufruct, servitudes and realty charges.

The fifth division (of the fourth book) concerns mortgages and pledges.

I have not observed a wider catalogue of *ius in re* implemented than in the Russian draft (1905).

683 The sixth division (of the fourth book on *ius in re*) refers to copyright law *(Autorrecht)*. The seventh division deals with the right to inventions, trademarks and to companies *(Recht auf Erfindungen, auf Warenzeichen und auf eine Firma)*.

684 The Russian draft (1905) includes: a general part – family law – succession law – *ius in re* – law of obligations.

The first two books constitute *personae*, inheritance law and *ius in re* are *res*, whereas the law of obligations is an equivalent of *actiones*.

The books of the Swiss civil code (1907) are: law of persons – family law – law of succession – *ius in re*. The last, fifth, book is the Code of obligations (1911).

The sequence of the systematic compounds in both codifications is identical: *personae*, *res* (inheritance law and *ius in re*) and *actiones* (law of obligations). The main difference is that the Russian draft contains a general part.

In the systematization there seems to be a double inspiration with the Swiss codification: in the external divisions applied in the draft as well as in the formulation of a thing.

(*res*), restricting it only to *personae – actiones*[685]. The first socialist Russian civil code (1922) contains the full Gaius scheme in the general part[686], but instead of the definition of a thing it regulates those things that could only be the property of the state[687] (*res extra commercium*). A remark added under Article 21 notes that the liquidation of the private ownership of land results in repealing the differentiation of movables and immovables[688]. As land could not be traded in Soviet Russia, the distinction between movables and immovables did not have any meaning[689]. After the fall of socialism, in the 1990s, when land could be traded, the traditional classification was restored[690].

3. Current Russian civil code (1994 – 2006)

The current Russian civil code (1994 – 2006) presents the widest possible formulation of a thing[691]. There is no definition in the code, only a sample catalogue of goods that are things. Article 130 lists movables and immovables. This solution is logical if the entire structure of the current Russian civil code is analyzed. In such a systematization the content of the seventh book (concerning rights to the results of intellectual activities and to the means of individualisation) is also awarded the protection applicable to *ius in re*. Inspiration from the Russian draft (1905) is also evident[692], but in the draft a thing was viewed more narrowly.

---

685 In the second socialist Russian civil code (1964) the first chapter (in the general part) comprises the fundamental principles, the second chapter persons, and the third chapter juridical acts.

686 In the first socialist Russian civil code (1922) the precepts relevant to objects are placed in the third chapter of the general part (objects of rights – goods).

The first chapter: subjects of rights (persons). The second chapter: objects of rights (goods). The third chapte r: juridical acts.

687 *Article 20 Une chose qui est exclue du commerce civil ne peutêtre objet des droits civils que dans les limites où cela est expressément indiqué par la loi.*

Article 21 Le sol est propriété de l'Etat et ne peutêtre objet de commerce privé. La possession sur le sol n'est admise que sur la base de droits de jouissance.

Remarque. – Avec la suppression de la propriété privée sur le sol est supprimée la distinction des choses en mobilières et immobilières.

688 The handbook of Gienkin does not mention the division on movables and immovables in the part referring to things.

GIENKIN D. M., *Radzieckie prawo cywilne. Tom I* [Soviet private law. Volume I], Warszawa 1955, pp. 172 – 184.

689 СУХАНОВ Е.А, *Вещное право. Научно-познавательный очерк*, Москва 2017, p. 36.
Sukhanov E.A., *Veshchnoyeo. Naučno-poznavatelnyjočerk*, Moskva 2011, p. 36.
[Sukhanov E.A., Ius in re. *A scientific and instructive study*, Moskva 2011, p. 36.]

690 *Ibidem*, p. 38.

691 Article 128 To the objects of civil rights are referred items, including money and securities, as well as other property, including property rights; works and services; protected results of intellectual activity and the means of individualisation that are equated to them (intellectual property); non-material benefits.

692 In the Russian draft (1905) the sixth division (of the fourth book on *ius in re*) considers copyright law *(Autorrecht)*. The seventh division includes the right to inventions, trademarks and to companies *(Recht auf Erfindungen, auf Warenzeichen und auf eine Firma)*.

XIII. Conclusions from the analysis of the definition of a thing in the researched codes

Here I provide some concluding comments drawn from my analysis. The first problem I address is the influence of the Gaian formulation of *res* on the definitions implemented in the codes. The development of the structure of the codes and possible ways of constructing an object inspire the second question: does a definition of a thing interact with the exterior structure of a civil code? I subsequently discuss the impact of socialism on the definitions of things. Finally, I draw concluding remarks based on the inquiry as a whole.

1. The influence of the Gaian formulation of *res* on the definitions implemented in the codes

Interestingly, in the most recent codifications in Central and Eastern Europe (Russia 1994 – 2006, Czechia – 2012, Hungary – 2013) the widest possible definition of a thing was chosen. In Czechia and Hungary such a systematic choice relates to the Austrian heritage, but a similar solution was also applied in Russia. A comparable resolution can be found in interwar Poland, too. The concepts of Gaius (and the Gaian definition of a thing) still inspire legislators.

2. Does a definition of a thing interact with the exterior structure of a civil code?

The most significant advancement in the field of the systematization of the civil codes is evident in the plethora of solutions adopted. In the first codifications the wide definition of a thing was implemented. The Gaius scheme is also manifest in the divisions of the codes. An examination of the later codes discloses the absence of an obvious relation between the definition of a thing and the exterior divisions of the codes. The systematic model might still exert an effect on the definition of a thing, but that is not the only possible option[693].

The Gaian definition can also be observed in codes that include a general part (Saxony – 1863, Czechia – 2012). The narrower formulation is visible in the Swiss civil code (1907), which does not a general part and which replicates the Gaius

[693] In interwar Poland, when the shape of the code was not yet determined, the widest possible formulation of *res* was applied. But when the Pandect systematization was definitively chosen in Poland after the Second World War, the German definition prevailed. The German model has dominated instead of the ideas of Gaius.

The Polish civil code (1964) contains: a general part – ownership and other *ius in re* – law of obligations – succession law.

At the same time, currently in Czechia the Austrian definition is present in the code with a general part and introducing the Gaius model in its exterior divisions.

In the Czech civil code (2012) the first book regards a general part, the second book family law, the third book absolute property rights, and the last, fourth, book relative property rights.

The first two books are an equivalent of Gaian *personae*. The third book includes *ius in re* and succession law – those are *res*. The last, fourth, book contains the law of obligations *(actiones)*.

model in its exterior divisions. In the newer codifications there is no direct connection between the structure of the code and the definition of a thing. As the first codes followed the Gaius scheme, they also adopted the widest possible interpretation of an object. Although that was the most natural and obvious resolution at the time, it is no longer the case anymore, because there are more systematic models available now. These systematic compounds can be combined by legislators in whatever form they chose. A code based on the Gaius scheme may comprise a narrow definition of a thing, and accordingly the widest formulation of a thing can be adopted in a codification that includes a general part.

3. The reaction of socialist ideology against the definition of a thing in the analyzed codes

In the socialist civil codes (the definition of) a thing may be neglected. In Soviet Russia (1922, 1964) a thing is not defined. The definitions of a thing typical for bourgeois civil codes are visible in socialist codifications that follow a more traditional arrangement (Czechoslovakia – 1950, Hungary – 1959, Poland – 1964). In the first socialist Czechoslovak civil code (1950) the definition is similar to that found in the Czechoslovak draft (1937) and in the current Czech civil code (2012). Narrowing the definition of a thing to *res corporales* in a socialist civil code might be preferable, as was the case in Poland (1964), where the protection applicable to *ius in re* was restricted only to corporeal things; in the interwar Polish draft on *ius in re* (1937) *res incorporales* was also granted the security of *ius in re*. The East German definition produces almost the same effect as the formulation present in the German BGB (1896), but instead of comprising a general principle[694] it lists the objects which are things[695]. In most socialist codifications the definitions are similar to those found in earlier codes (or drafts).

4. Final remarks

The analysis in this section has shown that in most of the inspected jurisdictions the concept of a thing results from legal custom rather than an ideology (whether capitalism or socialism). The definition, once adopted, is often preserved in the legal system. The designation of a thing and the exterior divisions of the code may respond to each other. A code that comprises a general part can include a narrow definition of a thing, and a code that replicates the Gaius scheme (and which does not contain a general part) may admit the protection *erga omnes res* only to *res corporales*.

---

694 In the German BGB (1896) only corporeal objects are things in the legal sense (§ 90).

695 § 467 of the East German civil code (1975): according to this law, things are only movable things, immovables and buildings.

C) Location of the provisions regarding objects *(res)* in the civil codes

Having provided information concerning the definitions of things in the civil codes researched for this study, we now address the location of provisions regarding objects (*res*) in the civil codes. This section is divided into four divisions. First, I discuss the location of *res* in codes structured according to the Gaius model. I then consider where, in the codifications, *ius in re* are fully extracted in the system of books[696]. Subsequently, I analyze the systematization of things in the codifications that include a general part. Finally, I deal with the modifications introduced to the arrangement of objects in the socialist civil codes (that include a general part). The general part is the most common resolution among the socialist civil codes, but it is not the only possible composition.

I. Location of *res* (object) in the codes structured according to the Gaius scheme (Bavaria – 1756, France – 1804, Austria – 1811)

In the codes based on the Gaius model precepts regarding objects are placed at the beginning of the second book[697]. In the first generation of the codes based on the Gaius scheme the second book comprises *res*. In the CMBC (1756) the second book regards *ius in re*, in the ABGB (1811) *ius rerum* and in the CC (1804) goods and different modifications of ownership[698]. Interestingly, the CC is the only code among those researched here in which goods are mentioned in the division of books[699]. The footnote reference discusses the possible grounds for such a systematization[700]. An object may have additional specifics in the codes. This is

[696] This systematic pattern can be observed in Switzerland (1907) and in Hungary. In both legal systems the Gaius scheme was introduced in the system of the books, and there is no general part. As there is no general part, there is no other place where things can be settled other than in the opening of the book on *ius in re*.

For this reason, the arrangement of things in these codes is almost identical to that used in the first generation of codes based on the Gaius model (Bavaria – 1756, France – 1804, Austria – 1811).

[697] In the CMBC (1756) this is in the first chapter (of the second book on *ius in re*) considering rights and duties mainly in the area of property *(von den Rechten und Pflichten in Ansehen Hab und Gut überhaupt)*.

In the CC (1804) precepts relevant to *res* are included in the first title (of the second book comprising goods and different modifications of ownership) concerning the distinction of goods.

In the ABGB (1811) objects are located at the beginning of the second book on *ius rerum*, in the chapter on things and their legal classification (§§ 285 – 306).

[698] Among the later codifications Austrian composition was replicated completely in the Czechoslovak draft (1937).

In the Czechoslovak draft (1937) at the opening of the second book (regarding property law) there is a chapter (the fourth chapter in the table of contents) regarding things.

[699] In the CC (1804) the second book regards goods *(des biens)* and different modifications of ownership.

[700] In the CC ownership is recalled in the titles of two books (the second book – goods and different modifications of ownership, the third book – different ways of acquiring ownership).

visible in the ABGB (1811), where the definition of a thing is a central concept of the second book on *ius rerum* (*res*)[701]. A thing holds together the second book, containing *ius in re*, succession law, law of obligations and matrimonial property law[702].

II. Conclusions from the arrangement of things in the codifications based on the Gaius model

In two of the three codes based on the Gaius model, *res* (a thing or goods) is an essential element of the system of the code. If a code is not arranged according to the branches of private law (as with the CMBC, which includes divisions on *personae, ius in re*, succession law and law of obligations), then it is necessary to combine elements. The structure of the written law needs to be based on something stable. A thing (*res*) proves to be the most obvious resolution.

This reasoning results from deliberations on the Gaius scheme. Gaius emphasizes things (*res*); his thinking impacted the arrangement of the CC (1804) and the ABGB (1811), where things are the primary component integrated into their structure. In the CC, goods solidify the second book, which refers to goods and different modifications of ownership. What other systematization could there be? Persons (the first book) – ownership (the second book) and different ways of acquiring ownership (the third book). Evidently, goods and different modelsof ownership are more noteworthy formulations than sole ownership[703]. In the

In France a stable and immobile construct had to be introduced in order to consolidate the structure of the code. Goods were chosen, resulting in the second book concerning goods and different modifications of ownership.

Ownership is a subjective concept, and it needs to be supported by goods, an incarnation of Gaian *res*.

Goods also fit the vision of revolutionary France, underlining the worldy aspects of the surrounding reality and the opportunity of owning objects.

701 In the ABGB (1811) a thing is placed at the beginning of the second book on *ius rerum*, in the chapter on things and their legal classification.

This content is settled at the beginning of the first division (regarding *ius in re*). The second division concerns personal rights (obligations). A thing is arranged in front of the systematic divisions on *iura in re* and *iura in personam*.

702 In the ABGB the first division (of the second book on *ius rerum*) concerns *ius in re*. *Ius in re* is mentioned firstly (chapters from the first to the seventh) and then inheritance law comes (chapters from the eighth to the fifteenth). The last, sixteenth, chapter (of the first division on *ius in re*) deals with co-ownership.

The second division (of the second book) concerns personal rights (obligations). Those are the chapters from the seventeenth to the thirtieth. Matrimonial property law is arranged among the particular contracts (the twenty-eighth chapter).

703 Subjective concepts (such as ownership) may evolve significantly with in the passage of time; this could negatively impact the structure of the CC. Goods do not "move" and change too much.

Obviously, the CC had to be amended; but it would get old much faster if it were based solely on ownership.

ABGB, a thing, placed at the beginning of the second book on *ius rerum* (*res*), enables non-property regulations (*personae*) to be distinguished from private law regarding property (*res*). As with the *Institutes* of Gaius, the second book (*res*) includes *ius in re*, succession law, the law of obligations and matrimonial property law[704].

The problems associated with arranging things and underlining them in codes that do not extract *ius in re* in a distinct book (the CC, the ABGB) show that this was a blind path in the systematization of the civil codes. In the CMBC (1756), where *ius in re* is settled in a separate book, there was no such necessity. For this reason, in the subsequent codifications founded on the Gaius scheme and that do not contain a general part (Switzerland – 1907, Hungary), things are placed at the beginning of book on *ius in re*, and from the outset they are fully separated in the table of contents.

III. Location of objects in codes with a separate book on *ius in re* (Switzerland – 1907, Hungary)

A code may not include a general part but still follow the Gaius model in its exterior divisions. At the same time, *ius in re* is fully extracted in the system of the books; as there is no general part, regulations on things are placed at the beginning of the book on *ius in re*. That is the case in Switzerland (1907) and in Hungary (1928, 1959, 2013). Object is arranged in the opening of *ius in re*, among the precepts on ownership. In Switzerland there is no specific section regarding objects[705], whereas in Hungary there is always a separate systematic unit referring to the objects of ownership[706].

---

704 In the ABGB (1811) the second book on *ius rerum* comprises two divisions. The first division concerns *ius in re*, whereas the second division regards personal rights.

In the first division the first seven chapters include *ius in re*. The chapters from the eighth to the fifteenth contain the law of succession. The sixteenth chapter at the end of the first division concerns co-ownership.

The second division encompasses the law of obligations (chapters from the seventeenth to the thirtieth). Matrimonial property law is approached among the particular contracts, in the twenty-eighth chapter.

705 The first division of the fourth book on *ius in re* of the Swiss civil code (1907) regards ownership. In the eighteenth title of the civil code, among the general provisions (of ownership), an object is recalled (Article 641 and next provisions).

706 In the Hungarian draft (1928) that is in the opening of the second book on *ius in re*. The first title of the second book considers ownership. In the first chapter of the second book (general provisions) there is a second subsection, titled: objects of ownership – things.

In the socialist Hungarian civil code (1959) that is in the front of the third book on ownership. The first title of the third book includes the general provisions of ownership. The ninth chapter of the code (the second chapter situated in the first title of the third book) deals with the objects of ownership.

In the current Hungarian civil code (2013) that is in the start of the fifth book on *ius in re*. The second division of the fifth book comprises ownership. The third title of the fifth book (and

IV. Location of things (*res*) in codes that include a general part

In the codes that include a general part *res* is isolated from *ius in re* and it is settled at the beginning of the general part. This systematization results from the application of *res* to all books of the code. *Res* is the part of the Gaius scheme (*personae – res – actiones*) placed in the opening of the code. This arrangement was inspired by the Prussian *Landrecht* (1794), where *res* (objects) are located in the second title of the first part[707]. Following the introduction of the general part into the code, objects are now arranged among the general provisions. They can be designated in the codes as things[708], property[709], objects of rights[710] or things and rights[711]. Another option is to retranspose things from the general part to the

---

the first title of the second division) contains the general rules of ownership. The fourth chapter (second chapter) of the third title concerns the objects of ownership.

707 In the Prussian *Landrecht* (1794) the second title (of the first part) contains things and their rights in general *(von Sachen und deren Rechten überhaupt).*

708 For the first time this solution was implemented into the Saxon civil code (1863). The third division of the general part considers things *(von den Sachen).*

In the German BGB (1896) the second chapter of the general part regards things.

In the Russian draft (1905) the second division of the general part concerns things.

In the current Czech civil code (2012) the fourth title of the general part deals with things and their division.

709 In the Polish civil code (1964) the third title of the general part refers to property.

710 In the first socialist Russian civil code (1922) the third chapter of the general part considers the objects of rights (goods).

In the current Russian civil code (1994 – 2006) the third subsection of the general part concerns the objects of civil rights.

711 In the first socialist Czechoslovak civil code (1950) the second chapter of the general part deals with things and rights *(choses et droits).*

opening of the book on *ius in re*[712]. Such a composition can be justified by the inherent relationship between objects and *ius in re*, which requires placing things among *ius in re* instead of in the general part[713].

V. Modifications of arranging objects in the socialist civil codes (that include a general part)

In the socialist civil codes, the systematization of objects might not be affected by socialism[714]. As with the bourgeois codifications, in the first socialist Russian civil code (1922) the second chapter of the general part includes *res*[715], but instead of the definition of a thing *res extra commercium* are mentioned in this area[716]. In so-

[712] *Księga pierwsza kodeksu cywilnego. Projekt z uzasadnieniem* [First book of the civil code. Draft with a justification], Warszawa 2009.

The Polish draft of the general part (elaborated by Zbigniew Radwański) in the table of contents does not comprise any divisions regarding things.

The arrangement suggested by Radwański was also adopted in the later Polish draft of a civil code.

Kodeks cywilny. Księga pierwsza. Część ogólna. Projekt Komisji Kodyfikacyjnej Prawa Cywilnego przyję ty w 2015 r. z komentarzem członków zespołu problemowego KKPC [Civil code. First book. General part. The draft of the Codification Committee of Private Law adopted in 2015, commented on by the members of the Codification Committee of Private Law], Warszawa 2017.

The drafts on *ius in re* have not been published yet.

[713] RADWAŃSKI Z., *Aktualność posłużenia się częścią ogólną kodeksu cywilnego jako instrumentu regulacji prawa prywatnego* [The actuality of using the general part of the civil code as an instrument of the regulation of private law], TPP 2010 no. 4, p. 19.

[714] In the first socialist Russian civil code (1922) the second chapter of the general part refers to the objects of rights (goods).

In the first socialist Czechoslovak civil code (1950) the second chapter of the general part considers things and rights.

In the Polish civil code (1964) the third title of the general part concerns property.

The socialist Hungarian civil code (1959) does not comprise a general part. In Hungary, the systematization of the provisions on objects is not affected by socialism – it is identical to the Hungarian draft (1928).

[715] In the first socialist Russian civil code (1922) the second chapter of the general part regards legal subjects (persons), the third objects of rights (goods), and the fourth juridical acts.

[716] *Article 53 Le sol, le sous-sol, les forêts, les eaux, les chemins de fer d'utilité générale, leur matériel roulant et les appareils volants peuvent être exclusivement propriété de l'Etat.*

Article 54 Peuvent être objet de propriété privée: les bâtiments non municipalisés, les enterprises commerciales, les enterprises industrielles qui occupent des ouvriers salariés dont le nombre n'excède pas les chiffres prévus par les lois spéciales, les instruments et moyens de production, l'argent, les valeurs mobilières et autres objets de valeur y compris les monnaies d'or et d'argent et les devises étrangères, les objets d'utilité domestique ou mènagère ou à usage personnel, les marchandises dont la vente n'est pas interdite par la loi et tous les biens non exclus du commerce privé.

Article 55 Les enterprises où le nombre des ouvriers salariés dépasse celui qui est prévu par la loi, le télégraphe et le radiotélégraphe, et les autres installations qui intéressent l'Etat, ne peuvent être objet de propriété privée que sur la base des concessions obtenues du gouverne-

cialist codifications the second element of the Gaius scheme (*res*) can be removed from the opening of the general part (Russia[717] – 1964, Czechoslovakia[718] – 1964), resulting in *personae – actiones* in lieu of *personae – res – actiones*. Things may be transferred to a glossary, placed at the end of the general part (Czechoslovakia – 1964, East Germany – 1975). A thing is one legislative term that must be located somewhere. Such thinking is deeply rooted in the Pandect model; elaborating a glossary that explains the legislative terms implies that things are just one of the general terms, also common to other areas of private law. In the Czechoslovak code objects are placed in a glossary at the end of the general part[719], whereas in the East German civil code things are situated in a glossary at the end of the seventh book[720] (comprising the specific provisions of the respective relationships of private law). In the East German civil code, the content of the general part is divided between the first book (which includes the fundamental principles of socialist private law) and the seventh book previously mentioned. In the East German code, the arrangement of the Gaius scheme in the seventh book was modified in a way that cannot be found anywhere else[721]. In socialist legal systems pri-

---

ment.

Les codes de la Russie Soviétique. Tome 1 Code de la famille Code civil, Paris 1925, pp. 137 – 138.

717 In the second socialist Russian civil code (1964) there are no precepts on objects and *(res)* in the general part.

The first chapter of the general part concludes the fundamental principles, the second chapter persons, and the third chapter juridical acts.

718 In the second socialist Czechoslovak civil code (1964) the first division of the general part considers private law relationships and their protection, the second division the participants of the private law relationships, the third division representation, and the fourth division juridical acts.

719 In the second socialist Czechoslovak civil code (1964) in the last ninth division (explanation of certain terms) of the general part things and rights are included (§§ 118 – 121).

Provisions on things are present in the code, but they are marginalized in its structure. In the second socialist Czechoslovak civil code (1964) inspiration by the previous Czechoslovak civil code (1950) is visible; in order to address *res* in the dictionary, the legislator refers to things and rights.

720 In the East German civil code (1975) objects are arranged close to the end of the seventh book (on the specific provisions of the respective relationships of private law), in the fifth chapter concluding the explanation of the legal terms (§§ 467 – 468). Afterwards in the sixth chapter prescription is arranged.

721 The East German civil code (1975) is the only codification where *res* in the general part and objects are separated from each other. The first book (on the fundamental principles of socialist private law) comprises only the systematic compounds applicable only to *personae* as well as the abstract elements of the Pandect model, designating the direction of the system of the code.

The first chapter designates the tasks of private law. The second chapter of the first book mentions the status of citizens in private law, whereas the third chapter considers the status of enterprises in private law. The fourth chapter determines the rules of cooperation of citizens and enterprises.

Yet at the same time there is a certain form of the Gaius scheme in the seventh book (contai-

vate law is manifested in the category of what a citizen is allowed to own. This impacts the location of the provisions on things – in the second socialist Czechoslovak civil code (1964) and the East German civil code the provisions on things are distributed between the glossary at the end of the general part and the book on ownership[722].

VI. Conclusions

The composition of things in the civil codes is mostly determined by the systematic model applied in each code. There are two main ways of arranging objects:

---

ning the specific provisions of the respective relationships of private law). It could seem that it is not there.

The first chapter: the specific features of performing contractual obligations. The second chapter: participation of some contractors in a contract. The third chapter: securing claims. The fourth chapter: incapacitation, death in absentia and cancellation of instruments. The fifth chapter: explanation of legislative terms. The sixth chapter: prescription.

That is why it could seem that there is no Gaius model in the seventh book. It is there, but it is reversed: instead of *personae – res – actiones* there is *actiones – res – personae.*

In the first and the second chapters of the seventh book there are institutions related to obligations *(actiones).* Those are the specific features of performing contractual obligations (the first chapter) as well as the participation of some contractors in a contract (the second chapter).

The third chapter pertains to securing claims *(res).* It includes pledges, mortgages, guarantees and provisions relevant to the protection of socialist property *(Eigentum)* in the case of construction works (...). In the fourth chapter (constituting the trace of *personae*) incapacitation, death in absentia and announcements are contained.

Even though this is just a trace of the Gaius model, it can be observed that even in the codification which is the furthest from the bourgeois arrangement, inspirations by the Pandect systematization and the Gaius model are still visible.

A dictionary where things are arranged is placed in the fifth chapter, after the reinterpretation of the Gaius scheme in the seventh book. Prescription is set in the last, sixth, chapter of the seventh book. It is arranged after the legislative reinterpretation of the Gaius model.

722 In the second socialist Czechoslovak civil code (1964) in the second book regarding socialist collective ownership and personal ownership, there is § 127:

§ 127 Personal ownership comprises first and foremost income and savings out of labor and social security. In addition, personal ownership comprises in particular things for domestic and personal use, family houses and recreational cottages.

In the East German civil code (1975), the objects of personal ownership are regulated in § 23, in the second book concerning socialist ownership and personal ownership:

§ 23. Gegenstand des persönlichen Eigentums. (1) Zum persönlichen Eigentum gehören insbesondere die Arbeitseinkünfte und Ersparnisse, die Ausstattung der Wohnung und des Haushalts, Gegenstände des persönlichen Bedarfs, die für die Berufsausbildung, Weiterbildung und Freizeitgestaltung erworbenen Sachen sowie Grundstücke und Gebäude zur Befriedigung der Wohn- und Erholungsbedürfnisse des Bürgers und seiner Familie. Zum persönlichen Eigentum gehören auch die dem Wesen des persönlichen Eigentums entsprechenden Rechte, einschließlich vermögensrechtlicher Ansprüche aus Urheber-, Neuerer- und Erfinderrechten.

(2) Auf das überwiegend auf persönlicher Arbeit beruhende Eigentum der Handwerker und Gewerbetreibenden sind die Bestimmungen über das persönliche Eigentum entsprechend anzuwenden, soweit in Rechtsvorschriften nichts anderes festgelegt ist.

at the beginning of *ius in re/ res* or in the opening of the general part. The first systematization is typical for all codes that follow the Gaius model. The second composition is visible in codes that include a general part, regardless of whether they are capitalist or socialist. Socialist legislators might also remove the provisions on things from the codes or transpose them to a glossary placed at the end of the general part. Such an arrangement results from the marginalization of *ius in re* (and things) in the structure of the socialist civil codes. Following the fall of socialism, the traditional arrangement was applied in the new codifications in Central and Eastern Europe[723].

D) Main framework of *ius in re* in the researched codes

The next problem to consider is the main framework of *ius in re*. In most codes, *ius in re* is arranged around the abstract and neutral category of *ius in re*. In such a code *ius in re* are the main determinants in the system. However, this is not the only option; another solution involves composing the system of the code around ownership. This section first considers codes with the *ius in re* framework. Codes founded on ownership are subsequently analyzed – these are the French *Code civil* (1804) and the socialist civil codes. In addition, a new idea emerged – ownership and other *iura in re*.

I. Codes with the main framework of *ius in re*

The main framework of *ius in re* is the most common and natural solution[724]. It is visible in the CMBC (1756), the Saxon civil code (1863), the German BGB (1896) and the Swiss civil code (1907). *Ius in re* is also present in all drafts in Central and Eastern Europe[725] (Russia – 1905, Hungary – 1928, Czechoslovakia –

[723] The Czech civil code (2012) follows the Pandect model and things are placed in the general part.

In the current Hungarian civil code (2013) just like always in Hungary, provisions on things are arranged at the beginning of the book on *ius in re*.

Also, in the current Russian civil code (1994 – 2006) things were introduced in the general part, even though in both socialist Russian civil codes (1922, 1964) a thing is not defined.

Being a fusion of the bourgeois and socialist concepts, in this aspect in the current Russian code the bourgeois systematization was applied.

[724] In the CMBC (1756) the second book regards *ius in re*.

In the ABGB (1811) the second book concerns *ius rerum*. Also, the first division (of the second book) refers to *ius in re*.

In the Saxon civil code (1863), the first Pandect code, *ius in re* is included in the second book.

In the German BGB (1896) the third book considers *ius in re*.

In the Swiss civil code (1907) the fourth book contains *ius in re*.

[725] In the Russian draft (1905) the fourth book concerns *ius in re*.

The framework of *ius in re* is visible in the Polish draft on *ius in re* (1937).

In the Hungarian draft (1928) the second book considers *ius in re*.

1937, Poland – 1937), as well as in the first socialist civil codes[726] (Russia – 1922, Czechoslovakia – 1950). In later socialist civil codes *ius in re* is displaced by ownership[727]. In the most current codes in Central and Eastern Europe the system is most typically arranged around *ius in re*[728] (Czechia – 2012, Hungary – 2013).

II. Codes settled on ownership (France – 1804 and socialist civil codes)

Another possibility of arranging *ius in re* involves settling it around ownership. Ownership is a subjective and non-autonomous legal concept; we view it in terms of the one to whom a right belongs. That is why the structure of *ius in re* in the code is redrawn to fit its systematic assumptions.

1. French *Code civil*

The first code with this structure is the CC[729] (1804). In France *ius in re* is replaced by the strongest right of an individual: ownership. Consequently, the rights of a natural person should dominate in the system of the code. In the CC all other rights to objects are placed below ownership. They are treated as the fragments of the most powerful right of an owner in relation to his things (*démembrements*)[730]. In this model, ownership becomes an overlord of *ius in re*.

In the Czechoslovak draft (1937) the first division (of the second book on property law) refers to *ius in re*.

726 The second book of the first socialist Russian civil code (1922) encompasses *ius in re*.
The third book of the first socialist Czechoslovak civil code (1950) deals with *ius in re*.

727 In the socialist Hungarian civil code (1959) the third book comprises the right of ownership.
In the Polish civil code (1964) the second book includes ownership and other *ius in re*. In Poland there is a reference both towards capitalist *ius in re* as well as socialist ownership.
In the second socialist Russian civil code (1964) the second book concerns the right of ownership.
In the second socialist Czechoslovak civil code (1964) the second book contains socialist collective ownership and personal ownership.
In the East German civil code (1975) the second book includes socialist ownership and personal ownership.

728 The central construct of *ius in re* has been applied in Czechia (2012) and Hungary (2013).
In the current Czech civil code (2012) the third book concerns absolute property rights. The first title of the third book contains general provisions, the second title *ius in re* and the third title inheritance law.
In the current Hungarian civil code (2013) the fifth book considers *ius in re*.

729 The second book of the CC (1804) regards goods and different modifications of ownership, whereas the third book concerns different ways of acquiring ownership.
Ownership of an individual and the protection of his property are keystones of the French structure. The second book (goods and different modifications of ownership) and the third book (different ways of acquiring ownership) interact with the first book encompassing *personae*, designating the scope of ownership of an individual. Ownership is a natural right of an individual which prevails in the structure of the CC.

730 OVERSTAKE J. F., *Essai de classification des contrats spéciaux*, Paris 1969, p. 57.

2. Socialist civil codes

The framework of ownership is the most typical arrangement of the socialist civil codes[731] (Hungary – 1959, Russia – 1964, Czechoslovakia – 1964, East Germany – 1975). In socialism the favoured right is the ownership of the state. Before ownership became a central construct in socialist civil codes, it was placed first among *ius in re* in the book on *ius in re*[732]. As a result, the system of the code is reformulated to fit socialist ideas: ownership can be the only *ius in re* included in the book on ownership[733] (Russia – 1964, Czechoslovakia – 1964, East Germany – 1975).

III. Codes settled both on ownership and other *ius in in re*

The last possibility forsettling the main framework of *ius in re* involves arranging it between ownership and *ius in re*, resulting in a systematization that places it between both constructs. Its application in the system is linked to an attempt to find a compromise between bourgeois and socialist concepts. Such an arrangement is present in the Polish civil code[734] (1964) and in the current Russian civil code[735] (1994 – 2006).

IV. Conclusions

The discussion in this section demonstrates that the main framework of *ius in re* is the most frequently found. Following the fall of socialism, the construct of *ius in re* was reintroduced in Central and Eastern Europe[736].

---

[731] In the socialist Hungarian civil code (1959) the third book deals with the right of ownership.
In the second socialist Russian civil code (1964) the second book considers the right of ownership.
In the second socialist Czechoslovak civil code (1964) the second book refers to socialist collective ownership and personal ownership.
In the East German civil code (1975) the second book concerns socialist ownership and personal ownership.

[732] In the first socialist Russian civil code (1922) the first chapter (of the second book on *ius in re*) deals with ownership.
In the first socialist Czechoslovak civil code (1950) the seventh chapter includes the right of ownership. That is the first chapter set in the third book on *ius in re*.
The same arrangement is visible in the Polish civil code (1964), based on ownership and other *ius in re*. The first title (of the second book on ownership and other *ius in re*) comprises ownership.

[733] This issue is approached precisely in the area describing the arrangement of ownership.

[734] The second book of the Polish civil code (1964) concerns ownership and other *ius in re*.

[735] The second book of the Russian code (1994 – 2006) considers the right of ownership and the other rights of estate.

[736] The Czech (2012) and Hungarian (2013) arrangements have already been mentioned. Even though in Poland a new civil code is not to be introduced soon, legal science has already adopted bourgeois constructs.
The most notable legal series is the System of Private Law, covering all areas of private law. In the socialist times, when the first series of the System was edited, the title of the volume referred to ownership and other *ius in re*.

In the current Russian civil code (1994 – 2006) there is a different composition, but as the second book comprises ownership and the other rights of estate, then this solution sits between (socialist) ownership and (bourgeois) *ius in re*. The construct of *ius in re* remains the most significant concept, affecting all the codes (even the most socialist codes), because even while attempting to negate it, legislators refer to and react to it[737].

IGNATOWICZ J., *System Prawa Cywilnego. Prawo własności i inne prawa rzeczowe* [System of Private Law. The right of ownership and other *ius in re*], Wrocław/ Warszawa/ Kraków/Gdańsk 1977.

In the second series published more recently, in connection to the recodification works in Poland, the new volume regards *ius in re* instead of ownership and other *ius in re*.

DYBOWSKI T., *System Prawa Prywatnego. Tom 3 Prawo rzeczowe* [System of Private Law. Volume 3 *Ius in re*], Warszawa 2007.

The concept of *ius in re* is used in Poland in reference to the new Polish civil code, not only in the System of Private Law, but it is also recalled in the Green Book, designating the further direction of the works on the shape of a new Polish civil code.

RADWAŃSKI Z. (ed.), *Zielona Księga. Optymalna wizja Kodeksu cywilnego w Rzeczypospolitej Polskiej* [Green Book. The optimal vision of the Civil Code in the Republic of Poland], Warszawa 2006, p. 63.

737 Even those socialist codifications furthest from the typical bourgeois codifications (Czechoslovakia – 1964, East Germany – 1975) the legislators respond to *ius in re* by attempting to erase it from their divisions. Negation is just another form of reaction, different from the majority of the codes.

In the second socialist Czechoslovak civil code (1964) there are: general provisions – socialist collective ownership and personal ownership – personal use of dwelling units, other living space, and tracts of land – services – rights and duties from other juridical acts – responsibility for damage and unjust enrichment – inheritance of property constituting personal ownership – final provisions.

The content relevant to *ius in re* is placed in the second book (on socialist collective ownership and personal ownership) and in the third book (on the personal use of dwelling units, other living spaces and tracts of land).

In Czechoslovakia (1964) an effort to negate *ius in re* is limited solely to distributing it between the second book (on ownership) and the third book (including limited property rights). In the bourgeois civil codes this volume is usually placed in one book; here it is placed in two.

The East German civil code (1975) includes: fundamental principles of socialist private law – socialist ownership and personal ownership – contracts relating to material and cultural life – use of real estate for residential and recreational purposes – protection of life, health and property from damage – inheritance law – specific provisions of the respective relationships of private law.

In the East German civil code (1975) the institutions of *ius in re* are dispersed between numerous books, but at this point only two books matter. They are the second book (on socialist ownership and personal ownership) and the fourth book (on the use of real estate for residential and recreational purposes).

The second book contains ownership – that is the typical systematization for socialist civil codes (Hungary – 1959, Russia – 1964, Czechoslovakia – 1964). Arranging *ius in re* after the law of obligations (the third book, containing contracts relating to material and cultural life) almost entirely replicates the systematization of the German BGB, where *ius in re* (the third book) is placed after the law of obligations (the second book).

An interesting systematic pattern that can be observed in the codes researched here concerns mixed systematization, placing the starting point between ownership and *ius in re*, openly manifested in the current Russian civil code (1994–2006) and in the Polish civil code (1964). This arrangement is typical for the codifications that attempt to find a middle ground between socialist and capitalist concepts. Settling a code on ownership is typical for the codifications that adopt state ideology into private law. That was the case in the CC (1804), influenced by the concepts of the French Revolution, and in socialist legal systems that introduced the ideas of the October Revolution (Hungary – 1959, Russia – 1964, Czechoslovakia – 1964, East Germany – 1975). Once the ideology is rejected, then the legislators in the new codifications usually return to the original construct of *ius in re* (Czechia – 2012, Hungary – 2013).

E) Distribution of *ius in re* in the systems of books of the analyzed codes

The next issue considered here concerns the arrangement of *ius in re*. What are the methods for organising *ius in re* in the systems of the books of the investigated codes? First, I discuss codes founded on the Gaius model. These are the CMBC (1756), the CC (1804) and the ABGB (1811). Subsequently, I analyze the Prussian *Landrecht* (1794). Being one of the first codifications, its arrangement was also influenced by the *Institutes* of Gaius. I then deal with structuring in the codes that adopt the Pandect divisions. This systematization results from work undertaken on the Gaius model by German law professors in the nineteenth century. They divided private law into five books: general part – *ius in re* – law of obligations – family law – inheritance law.

Their ideas could be transposed into the codes in numerous ways. In this study, by the Pandect divisions I mean all codifications that extract the branches of private law (and as a result also *ius in re*) in their exterior divisions. Most later codes include a general part, but that is not the only potential resolution. In referring to the Pandect structure, we usually mean those codes that include a general part, but this term can also potentially be applied to other codifications. Introducing the branches of private law in relevant books of the code (such as *ius in re*, law of obligations and law of succession) is the most typical feature of the Pandect structure.

Codes that do not comprise a general part are first depicted. They follow the sequence of *Institutes* in their structure, in which the division into the branches of private law is discernible (law of persons – family law – *ius in re* – law of obli-

---

As a result, even the most socialist codifications did not manage to establish a completely new arrangement of *ius in re*. The new systematization involves nothing more than the modification of prior systematic patterns.

gations – law of succession). I consider these to be result from Pandect systematization. The discussion then moves to the place of *ius in re* in bourgeois codes that contain a general part. Socialist civil codes that include a general part are discussed in greater detail, in relation to the systematization of *ius in re* in the socialist civil codes.

Finally, the discussion addresses the composition of *ius in re* in socialist civil codes. Socialist lawmakers could either replicate (or slightly modify) the bourgeois arrangement or attempt to find a new socialist systematization of private law (and in consequence also of *ius in re*). Most comprise a general part, but the systematization of *ius in re* varies so significantly between the bourgeois and socialist civil codes that they must be mentioned separately. The composition of the respective institutions of *ius in re* is further described, in terms of their possible arrangement.

I. Codes structured according to the Gaius model

In codes based on the Gaius scheme, *res* is designated to the second place. The way *res* is understood in the structure of the codes has been interpreted differently. *Ius in re* could be either located in a single book or separated between multiple books.

1. *Ius in re* in the structure of the CMBC (1756)

The oldest of the codes, the CMBC, consists of four books: legal rules in general and law of persons, *ius in re*, succession law, and the law of obligations. In the CMBC *res* comprises two books: *ius in re* and inheritance law. Succession law is classified as one of the ways of acquiring ownership[738], a viewpoint that accords with the Gaius scheme. The CMBC is the only code among those based on the Gaius model that follows the divisions compliant with the Pandect systematization. In this respect it has provided the basis for later codifications.

2. *Ius in re* in the system of the French *Code civil* (1804)

The first book of the CC includes persons (*personae*), the second book (*res*) concerns goods and different modifications of ownership and the third book (*actiones*) regards different ways of acquiring ownership. Ownership is mentioned in the titles of two of the three books of the code. Ownership, the right of an individual, is of paramount importance, and it is a main determinant in the system of the code. In the French code, *ius in re* is distributed between two books – the second book (*res*) and the third book (*actiones*).

In the second book, goods, ownership and limited property rights modifying ownership are settled. The first title of the second book regards the distinction

738 PÖPPERL P., *Quellen und System des Codex Maximilianeus Bavaricus Civilis*, Bamberg 1967, p. 88.

of goods. The second title addresses ownership. The third title, usufruct, use and habitation. The final, fourth title of the second book includes servitudes and land services (*services fonciers*). Institutions placed in the second book include, just as its title suggests, goods and different ways of modifying ownership. There is no place for possession in such an approach; it is therefore transferred to the end of the code. The entire content of the second book is subsidiary to ownership, the central construct of the code[739].

Further *iura in re* are settled at the end of the third book (on different ways of acquiring ownership). Those are the institutions that can result in the termination of an individual's ownership. First, pledges are arranged in the seventeenth title of the third book (in the CC a pledge is defined as a contract[740]), and privileges and mortgages are in the eighteenth title. The nineteenth title deals with forced expropriation and orders between creditors. The twentieth title, concerning prescription, includes prescription, usucaption and possession[741]; at this period it was typical to arrange prescription and usucaptionin the same location. In the first codifications possession was arranged separately instead[742].

The area of the CC described here (with *ius in re* at the end) was reformed[743], but in this study, as a matter of principle, the original arrangement adopted in the codes is mostly analyzed. This study researches the systematic patterns that were introduced into the legislation, not how they were later modified. Even if, with

---

739 In the CC ownership encompasses the whole codification and affects its content. It is not pressed into the structure of the code. In the CC ownership designates the standards of the system of the code.

740 *Article 2071 Le nantissement est un contrat par lequel un débiteur remet une chose à son créancier pour sûreté de la dette.*

741 In the CC (1804) the twentieth title (of the third book on different ways of acquiring ownership) considers prescription. As prescription is defined in the code (Article 2219) as a way of acquiring or discharging oneself at the end of a certain period and in accordance with the conditions determined by the law, so the provisions on prescription and usucaption are mixed in the twentieth title.

The twentieth title contains: general provisions (the first chapter), possession (the second chapter), causes that prevent prescripton (the third chapter), causes that interrupt or suspend the course of prescription (the fourth chapter) and the time required in order to prescribe (the fifth chapter).

742 In the CMBC (1756) possession is settled in the fifth chapter of the second book on *ius in re*.

In the Prussian *Landrecht* (1794) the seventh title (in the first part) includes detention and possession.

In the ABGB (1811) possession is situated in the first chapter (the second book on *ius rerum*, the first division on *ius in re*).

743 Currently, in the CC the twentieth title (of the third book on different ways of acquiring ownership) refers to prescription *(prescription extinctive)*. The twenty-first title of the third book concerns possession and usucaption *(prescription acquisitive)*.

The fourth book was extracted to ensure the transparency of the code. The title of the fourth book in French is *des sûretés*. This is a very wide term, designating safety, security, surety or guarantee. Institutions applicable to pledges and mortgages are arranged in this area.

the perspective gained by the passage of time, the systematization of a code is not considered to be the most successful, it embodies a full legislative vision, similar to the snapshot captured by a photograph. Once taken, the photograph remains; the same principle applies to the systematic patterns implemented in the civil codes.

3. *Ius in re* in the structure of the ABGB (1811)

In the ABGB the second book refers to *ius rerum (res)*. *Res* are all regulations of the substantive private law regarding property. Those are *ius in re*, inheritance law, obligations and matrimonial property law[744]. The second book (on *ius rerum*) is divided into two areas. The first concerns rights relating to objects (*ius in re*), whereas the second division approaches personal rights (obligations). Usucaption is arranged outside *ius in re*, in the final, third, book including provisions common to personal rights and *ius in re*, and it is arranged together with prescription. Both institutions are situated in the final, fourth chapter of the third book, at the end of the code. At this time usucaption was inherently systematically connected with prescription – legal effects of the passage of time were settled together, no matter the area of private law.

4. Second element of the Gaius model (*res*) in the structure of the verified codes

Following the outline of the arrangement of *ius in re* in the codes based on the Gaius scheme, this section now lists the similarities and differences in systematizing *res* in the codes. *Ius in re* and *res* are closely connected concepts, but they are not synonyms. *Ius in re* is the designation of the branch of private law, whereas *res* are things or objects. *Res* also indicates the second component of the Gaius model. In the codes based on the composition of Gaius perceived differently *res* prevails in their structure. In the CMBC (1756) *ius in re* and inheritance law together constitute *res*. In the CC (1804) *res* are goods and different modifications of ownership.

The legal category of ownership is crucial in the system of the CC, where the private law regarding property is viewed either as goods or possible modifications of ownership (the second book – *res*), or as one way of acquiring ownership (the third book – *actiones*). In the CC, ownership is the most significant compound of the system, replacing the Gaian *res* and encompassing the whole code. In codes founded on the Gaius model one consequence of the domination of *res* (*ius in re*)

---

744 In the ABGB (1811) in the first division (of the second book on *ius rerum*) *ius in re* (chapters from the first to the seventh) and succession law (chapters from the eighth to the fifteenth, but in the sixteenth chapter co-ownership *[von der des Eigentums und anderer dinglichen Rechten]* is put) are situated. The second division of the second book considers personal rights. That is the law of obligations (chapters from the seventeenth to the thirtieth). Matrimonial property law is contained in the twenty-eighth chapter of the second division, among the particular contracts.

is that the law of obligations is neglected in the systems of the codes. Only in the CMBC (1756) they are arranged in a separate book.

II. *Ius in re* in the structure of the Prussian *Landrecht* (1794)

The Prussian *Landrecht* is divided into two parts, both untitled. The first part contains *res* (substantive private law regarding property). The beginning of the first part follows the Gaius scheme (*personae – res – actiones*) and things are discussed i.a.[745] Subsequently, there are other institutions, which together with the Gaius model constitute the general part[746].

The seventh title considers detention and possession. The eighth title includes ownership. Following the eighth title, multiple institutions of the substantive private law are arranged, in the *Landrecht* perceived in connection with ownership, and in Prussia associated with *res*[747]. The nineteenth title comprises property rights and personal rights to the property of another (*von dinglichen und persönlichen Rechten auf fremdes Eigenthum überhaupt*). In the twentieth title are rights to the substance of a thing belonging to another (*von dem Rechte auf die Substanz einer fremden Sache*). The twenty-first title contains rights to the use of property belonging to another (*von dem Rechte ze dne*). The twenty-second title considers rights of land plots against other land plots (*von Gerechtigkeiten der Grundstücke gegen einander*).

The Prussian systematization impacted the French arrangement. Both in the *Landrecht* and in the CC (1804), ownership is one of the most important systematic components in the structure of the code. In the CC, the Gaius model was applied to the exterior divisions. The first book of the CC concerns persons. The second book considers goods and different modifications of ownership. The third book deals with different ways of acquiring ownership.

---

745 In the Prussian *Landrecht* (1794) the first title (of the first part) considers persons and their rights in general, the second title things and their rights in general, whereas the third title (legal) concerns actions and thus originating rights.

746 The fourth title concerns declarations of will. The fifth title: contracts. The sixth title: duties and rights arising from unlawful acts.

747 The ninth title comprises the acquisition of ownership in general and the immediate ways of acquisition in general. The tenth title: indirect acquisition of ownership. The eleventh title: titles of acquiring ownership, resulting from contracts between the living partners. The twelfth title: titles of acquiring ownership arising from dispositions in the case of death. The thirteenth title: acquisition of ownership of things and rights by a third party. The fourteenth title: conservation of ownership and rights. The fifteenth title: pursuit of ownership. The sixteenth title contains the ways in which rights and obligations cease. Further there are: in the seventeenth title co-ownership and in the eighteenth title shared ownership.

III. Pandect systematization

In the Pandect codes *ius in re* is settled in a separate book[748]. In the Pandect structure the divisions of the code into books are accordant with the respective books of the code[749]. The code may include a general part.

First, we discuss the arrangement of *ius in re* in codes that fully extract *ius in re* in their structure, and which do not contain a general part (Switzerland 1907; Hungary 1928, 1959, 2013). Second, this section addresses systematization in bourgeois codes that comprise a general part (Saxony – 1863, Germany – 1896, Russia – 1905, Czechia – 2012). We then deal with the composition of *ius in re* in the socialist civil codes; most of these include a general part at the opening of the code. Their distinctive feature is that they introduce the main framework of ownership, which strongly affects the systematization of *ius in re*. In the second socialist Czechoslovak civil code (1964) and in the East German civil code the arrangement of *ius in re* is the most extensively modified. As the current Russian civil code (1994 – 2006) replicates the systematization of the second socialist Russian civil code (1964), its arrangement is depicted among the socialist civil codes.

1. *Ius in re* in the structure of the codes that fully separate it

This section first considers the arrangement in codes that fully separate *ius in re* in their structure and which do not contain a general part. This systematization resembles the CMBC the most, where all the content applicable to *ius in re* is arranged in the second book on *ius in re*.

a) Swiss civil code (1907)

After the CMBC (1756), *ius in re* was first fully isolated in the structure of the Swiss civil code (1907). *Ius in re* is placed in the fourth book (*des droits réels*). The sequence in the code is: law of persons – family law – inheritance law – *ius in re*. Obligations are set in the Code of obligations (1911). Law of persons and family law together are *personae*, inheritance law and *ius in re* constitute *res*, whereas obligations set in a separate code are *actiones*.

b) Hungary

The Hungarian draft (1928) and codes (1959, 2013) follow this order: law of persons and family law (*personae*) – *ius in re* (*res*) – obligations and inheritance law (*actiones*)[750]. Due to the influence of socialist ideology, the title of the second book in the code of 1959 is ownership instead of *ius in re*.

---

[748] At the same time, an individual can enjoy his or her freedom in private law in two fields: *res (ius in re)* and *actiones* (obligations).

[749] Those are *personae* (law of persons and family law), *ius in re*, inheritance law and law of obligations.

[750] In this shape both Austrian and Swiss inspiration are visible. Hungary is traditionally with in the sphere of Austrian influence.

2. Bourgeois civil codes including a general part

In codes that include a general part, *ius in re* is inserted in a distinct book, whereas objects (*res*) are transferred to the general part. The systematization in the bourgeois civil codes is now outlined here. The general part comes first, and then the sequence of further books may vary. They are: *ius in re*, law of obligations, family law and law of succession. Next the composition of the socialist civil codes is analyzed. They must be settled separately due to significant differences in the arrangement of *ius in re* between bourgeois and socialist codifications.

a) Saxon civil code (1863)

The first option is to arrange *ius in re* after the general part. This composition is present in the Saxon civil code (1863): general part – *ius in re* – law of claims (obligations) – family law – inheritance law. *Res* (*ius in re*) prevails in the overall structure of the code. The Saxon civil code is the first codification that follows the Pandect systematization and which comprises a general part.

b) German BGB (1896)

Another solution is discernible in the German BGB, where *ius in re* (*res*) is included in the third book, after the law of obligations (*actiones*). The sequence of books is: general part – law of obligations – *ius in re* – family law – law of succession. In Germany *actiones* (obligations) dominate the systematization of the code.

c) Arrangement of *ius in re* in codes that include a general part and which follow the Gaius scheme (Russia – 1905, Czechia – 2012)

It is also possible to find a compromise between the Gaius model and the Pandect systematization with a general part. First, *personae* are settled (they are the general part and family law), followed by *res* (*ius in re* and succession law), and finally *actiones*. This systematization is visible in the Russian draft (1905) and in the current Czech civil code (2012). There is a slight difference in the arrangement of both codes: in the Russian draft (1905) *ius in re* and inheritance law are situated in

---

In the Hungarian draft (1928) the sequence of books is: law of persons and family law – *ius in re* – law of obligations – law of succession.

In the socialist Hungarian civil code (1959) the books are: introductory provisions – persons – right of ownership – law of obligations – succession law.

In the current Hungarian civil code (2013) there are: introductory provisions – man as a subject of law – legal entity – family law – *ius in re* – law of obligations – succession law.

distinct books[751], whereas in the Czech code (2012) *ius in re* and succession law are set in one book[752].

IV. Socialist civil codes

In socialist codifications family law is settled outside the civil code. The socialist Hungarian civil code (1959) does not include a general part, preferring to follow the systematization based on the sequence of *Institutes*. For this reason, it is the first code discussed. We then move to the composition of *ius in re* in the socialist codes with a general part. The most typical sequence of books is: general part – *ius in re* (*res*) – law of obligations (*actiones*) – inheritance law. We first consider the systematization in Russia (1922, 1964, 1994 – 2006), followed by the Czechoslovak (1950) and Polish (1964) codes. Finally, we discuss the arrangement in the Czechoslovak (1964) and East German (1975) civil codes. Their systematization differs significantly from that of all other codifications.

1. Hungary (1959)

In the socialist Hungarian civil code the order of books is: persons – right of ownership – obligations – inheritance law[753]. Instead of *ius in re* the central construct is ownership. Among the content applicable to *ius in re* only pledges are transferred to the book on obligations[754].

2. Russia (1922, 1964, 1994 – 2006)

In the first socialist Russian civil code (1922) the books are: general part – *ius in re* – obligations – inheritance law[755]. The same sequence is visible in two la-

---

751 The Russian draft (1905) includes: a general part – family law – inheritance law – *ius in re* – law of obligations.

The Russian systematization is almost identical to the Swiss arrangement, but in Switzerland there is no general part and Gaius scheme is replicated in the exterior divisions.

The Swiss civil code (1907) includes: law of persons – family law – inheritance law – *ius in re*. Law of obligations is settled in the Code of obligations (1911).

In the Swiss civil code law of persons and family law are *personae*, inheritance law and *ius in re res*, whereas obligations are *actiones*.

752 The Czech civil code (2012) contains: a general part – family law – absolute property rights (*res*) – relative property rights (law of obligations and concurrently *actiones*).

The second book determining absolute property rights consists of three titles. The first title includes the general provisions, the second title *ius in re,* and the third title succession law.

The Czech composition is the result of the strong attachment to the ABGB (1811), where *ius in re* and law of succession are arranged together in the second book on *ius rerum* (the first division on *ius in re*).

753 The socialist Hungarian civil code (1959) includes: introductory provisions – persons – right of ownership – law of obligations – inheritance law.

754 In the socialist Hungarian civil code (1959) pledges are placed in the fourth book on obligations, in the twenty-third chapter concerning accessory obligations securing a contract (§§ 251 – 269).

755 The mentioned shape resembles the first code based on the Pandect systematization (the Saxon civil code – 1863), where the arrangement is: a general part – *ius in re* – law of claims (obligati-

ter Russian codes[756] (1964, 1994 – 2006). There are nevertheless also differences; additional books were implemented in both codes, and the central construct is different. In the Russian code of 1964 the second book concerns the right of ownership, whereas in the current Russian code (1994 – 2006) the second book considers the right of ownership and other rights of estate.

The fundamental concept (*ius in re* or ownership?) determines the arrangement of the codes. In the first socialist Russian civil code (1922) the entirety of the content applicable to *ius in re* is situated in the second book on *ius in re*[757]. In the second socialist Russian civil code (1964) the second book regards ownership, and pledges are transposed among the law of obligations[758]. In the current Russian civil code (1994 – 2006) *ius in re* is settled in the second book on the right of ownership and other rights of estate, but pledges are placed in the third book concerning the general part of obligations[759].

The form of both codifications is similar, but their content is very different. In the current Russian code (1994 – 2006) there are many traditional institutions of *ius in re*, such as possession or servitudes[760]. The current Russian code also contains institutions that cannot be found in the bourgeois civil codes, such as the right of economic management and the right of operational management[761]. The

---

ons) – family law (including guardianship law) – law of succession.

The only difference is the lack of family law in the first socialist Russian civil code (1922).

756 The sequence in the Russian civil code from 1964 is: a general part – *ownership* – obligations – copyright law – right of discovery – patent law – succession law – international private law.

The order in the current Russian civil code (1994 – 2006) is: general provisions – *right of ownership and other rights to estate* – general part of obligations – particular kinds of obligations – inheritance law – international private law – rights to results of intellectual activities and means of individualisation.

757 In the first socialist Russian civil code (1922) the first chapter (of the second book on *ius in re*) concerns ownership, the second chapter the right of construction, and the last, third, chapter pledges.

Provisions on things are approached in the third chapter of the general part including objects of rights (goods).

758 In the second socialist Russian civil code (1964) pledges are put in the seventeenth chapter regarding securing of the performance of obligations (Articles 192 – 202), in the third book on obligations.

759 Pledges are located in the third book containing the general part of obligations (the first subsection of the third book, dealing with the general provisions on obligations), in the twenty-third chapter referring to providing for the discharge of obligations, in the third paragraph (§ 3).

760 Possession is recalled in the code repeatedly (e.g. in Article 209 or Article 212). Servitudes are present in the second book (referring to the right of ownership and the other rights of estate), in the seventeenth chapter (on the right of ownership and other real rights to land), in Article 274 and the subsequent provisions. In the Russian civil code putting servitudes in the second book (and also the further content) implies that this volume is subordinate to the central construct (ownership). Servitudes are perceived as rights lesser than ownership.

761 In the second book (on the right of ownership and other rights of estate) there is the nineteenth chapter, including the right of economic management and the right of operation management.

systematization of the second book (on the right of ownership and other rights of estate) is described in the footnote reference[762].

3. Czechoslovakia – 1950, Poland – 1964

The Czechoslovak civil code (1950) follows an identical order to the first socialist Russian civil code[763] (general part – *ius in re* – obligations – law of succession). In Poland the sequence is uniform, but the title of the second book is ownership and other *ius in re*[764]. Both the Czechoslovak and Polish codes include a wide catalogue of *ius in re*, and the entire volume applicable to *ius in re* is settled in the book on *ius in re*. The footnote reference outlines *ius in re* included in both codifications[765].

According to Article 294 (mentioning the right of economic management), the state or the municipal unitary enterprise which owns the property by the right of economic management shall possess, use and dispose of this property with in the limits defined in conformity with the present Code.

The citation of this provision clearly shows that the current Russian civil code (1994 – 2006) comprises the instruments enabling the management of state property, similar to state management in the socialist economy.

762 The second book concerns the right of ownership and other rights of estate.

At the beginning of the second book there is the thirteenth chapter, including the general provisions. The fourteenth chapter: the acquisition of the right of ownership. The fifteenth chapter: the cessation of the right of ownership. The sixteenth chapter: common property. The seventeenth chapter: the right of ownership and other real rights to land. The eighteenth chapter: the right of ownership and the other rights of estate to living quarters. The nineteenth chapter: the right of economic management and the right of operation management. The twentieth chapter: the protection of the right of ownership and of the other rights of estate.

While looking at the systematization of the Russian code, it is clear that ownership is very deeply ingrained in the table of contents.

It is in the middle of the second book, other institutions seem only to be forcefully implemented. It seems as if the whole content of the second book was secondary to the main construct, which is ownership.

763 In the divisions of the first socialist Czechoslovak civil code (1950) the introductory provisions were extracted as a separate book. For this reason the code includes: introductory provisions – a general part – *ius in re* – law of obligations – law of succession.

764 The Polish civil code (1964) includes: a general part – ownership and other *ius in re* – law of obligations – inheritance law.

765 The first socialist Czechoslovak code (1950) contains: ownership (the seventh chapter, the third book on *ius in re*), ownership of a construction and the right of construction (the eighth chapter), realty charges (the ninth chapter), usufruct (among the provisions on realty charges, Article 172 and subsequent provisions) as well as the right of pledges and the law of retention (the tenth chapter).

Among the provisions on ownership (the third book on *ius in re*, the eighth chapter: ownership) possession is contained (Articles 142 – 154) but not visible in the table of contents. The eighth chapter on ownership comprises Articles 100 – 154.

The Polish civil code (1964) encompasses: ownership (the first title of the second book on ownership and other *ius in re*), perpetual usufruct (the second title), limited property rights (the third title) and possession (the fourth title).

Among the limited property rights in the third title there are: general provisions (the first sub-

4. Czechoslovakia (1964)

Following the first socialist Czechoslovak civil code (1950) legislative work was still in process, and the second socialist Czechoslovak civil code (1964) was soon adopted. The first book is the general part. The second book refers to socialist collective ownership and personal ownership (§§ 123 – 151). The third book considers the personal use of dwelling units, other living spaces, and tracts of land (§§ 152 – 221); this volume applies to limited property rights. The second and third books together include content relevant to *ius in re*.

Obligations are settled in the fourth book (on services), the fifth book (on rights and duties from other juridical acts) and the sixth book (on responsibili-

division of the third title), usufruct (the second subdivision), servitudes (the third subdivision) and pledges (the fourth subdivision).

Not included in the code but recalled in the Article 244 comprising the catalogue of limited property rights, there are also mortgages and the right to premises of a cooperative member.

ty for damage and unjust enrichment). Inheritance law is arranged in the seventh book[766]. Despite modifications introduced to its external divisions, the Czechoslovak code follows the arrangement most typical for the socialist civil codes (general part – *ius in re* / ownership – obligations – succession law). Interestingly, some institutions of *ius in re* can be found in the final, eighth, book of the code, including the final provisions. They can easily be bypassed while reading the code. This area contains the regulation of institutions that are not welcome in the socialist state. They include individual (private) ownership[767] (§ 489), pledges and realty charges[768] (§ 495). Deliberations on the arrangement of the eighth book require a separate reference[769].

---

[766] The seventh book of the Czechoslovak civil code (1964) considers the inheritance of property constituting personal ownership.

[767] The main feature of the socialist civil codes is the differentiation of ownership. One possible distinction depends on the issue of who an owner is.

The primary rule of the socialist civil codes is the protection of socialist ownership, belonging to the state.

As the rights of individuals are restricted, in most cases they may only own that which is necessary for their basic needs. Those are the means of consumption. In this case the right of individuals is designated as personal ownership.

Individuals are not free to own the means of production (e.g. land). That is individual ownership, usually forbidden in the last socialist codifications (Russia – 1964, Czechoslovakia – 1964, East Germany – 1975).

In the Czechoslovak civil code (1964) the regulations of individual ownership were hidden in the final, eighth, book, which included the final provisions.

[768] The mention of individual ownership among the final provisions is not surprising – this type of ownership is forbidden in socialism. The same claim also applies to realty charges: being strongly connected with land, they are not in line with socialist ideology.

What is truly astonishing is that pledges are situated among the final provisions. That which was present in other definitive socialist codifications (Russia – 1964, East Germany – 1975) was not welcome in Czechoslovakia.

[769] The first division (of the eighth book on the final provisions) concerns the regulation of other private law relationships (§§ 488 – 497). The second division of the eighth book (on final provisions) comprises the transitional and final provisions.

The content of the second division does not create any doubts. The problem comes when the first division (regulation of other private law relationships) is considered.

There are two main possibilities. It could potentially apply to the private law relationships established before the code was adopted. That is the first option.

But § 489 states that private law relationships also arise from the individual ownership of things, which are not the objects of personal ownership (private ownership); this ownership is also protected from unlawful attacks.

The content of this section (as well as the systematization, the title of the second division [the regulation of other private law relationships] presumes the functioning of two legal realities, the socialist one and the capitalist one) implies that in the definitive socialist codification the institutions not recognized in the socialist state can operate to a certain (limited) extent.

5. East Germany (1975)

Finally, we consider the arrangement of *ius in re* in the East German civil code. It is the furthest from bourgeois constructs of any of the codes researched for this study[770]. The arrangement of the East German civil code was significantly influenced by the second socialist Czechoslovak civil code. The East German civil code was also supposed to be a negation of the Pandect systematization, elaborated in the German BGB[771] (1896).

The second book, concerning socialist ownership and personal ownership, shows a trace of *res*. The fourth book includes the use of real estate and buildings for residential and recreational purposes[772]. It contains content relevant to *ius in re*, corresponding with the legal relationships applicable to land[773]. The fourth book comprises, among other elements, the regulation of personal ownership[774] and servitudes[775]. The institutions of *ius in re* that can be classified among non-contractual sources of obligations are arranged in the fifth book (concerning the protection of life, health and property from damage). They are: nuisance towardsneighbours[776] (§ 329) and the obligation to return found items[777]. Pledges and mortgages are

---

770 The East German civil code (1975) includes: fundamental principles of socialist private law (the first book) – socialist ownership and personal ownership (the second book) – contracts relating to the material and cultural life (the third book) – use of the real estate and buildings for residential purposes and leisure (the fourth book) – protection of life, health and property from damage (the fifth book) – inheritance law (the sixth book) – specific provisions of the respective relationships of private law (the seventh book).

771 SOŚNIAK M., *Zasady kodeksu cywilnego Niemieckiej Republiki Demokratycznej* [Principles of the civil code of the German Democratic Republic], in: *Kodeks cywilny Niemieckiej Republiki Demokratycznej* [Civil code of the German Democratic Republic], Wrocław/ Warszawa/ Kraków/Gdańsk 1979, p. 16.

772 The systematization of the fourth book of the East German civil code is described more precisely among the specific issues regarding the structure of *ius in re* in the socialist civil codes.

773 This idea resembles the Russian solution, where the regulations referring to land occupy a separate branch of law. In East Germany land law was arranged in a book of the code, and in Russia it was placed in specific legislation.

The identification of land law as a branch distinct from private law is mentioned here: IGNATOWICZ J., *System Prawa Cywilnego. Prawo własności i inne prawa rzeczowe* [System of Private Law. The right of ownership and other *ius in re*], Wrocław/ Warszawa/ Kraków/Gdańsk 1977, p. 636.

774 That is the fourth chapter of the fourth book, regarding personal ownership of immovables and buildings.

775 In the East German civil code servitudes are designated as the rights of common use towards premises *(Mitbenutzungsrechte an Grundstücken)*. They are located at the end of the sixth chapter (the relationships between the users of neighboring immovables; §§ 321 – 322) of the fourth book concerning the use of real estate and buildings for residential and recreational purposes.

776 In the first chapter (preventing damage) of the fifth book (on the protection of life, health and property from damage) the second subdivision concerns claims arising from violations and disturbances (§§ 327 – 329). Nuisance towards neighbours is settled in § 329.

777 The last, fourth, chapter of the fifth book (on the protection of life, health and property from damage) contains the obligation of returning found items.

arranged in the seventh book (on the specific provisions of the respective relationships of private law), constituting an equivalent of the general part[778].

V. Conclusions

The first tendency visible in bourgeois codifications is the elaboration of the Pandect model. Its main merit is the clarity of the code: in the system of the books there is a book on *ius in re*. In the first codifications the content of *ius in re* was dispersed across the structure of the code. Only the CMBC (1756) contains a book on *ius in re*, comprising regulations exclusively of *ius in re*[779]. Later, among bourgeois civil codes the prevailing solution was to extract a book on *ius in re*, and which included only *ius in re*. A thing may be put in the general part (if a code has one) or in the opening of *ius in re* (if there is no general part in a code). Among bourgeois codifications the code that modifies the typical arrangement most significantly is the CC (1804). Such systematization results from settling the structure of the code on ownership. Similar reasoning is visible in the *Landrecht* (1794).

The most significant disparities in arranging *ius in re* are visible in the socialist civil codes themselves. Socialist civil codes may replicate the traditional arrangement (Russia – 1922, Czechoslovakia – 1950, Hungary – 1959, Poland – 1964), or elaborate the new socialist systematization of the civil codes, resulting in the redistribution of *ius in re* between different books (Czechoslovakia – 1964, East Germany – 1975). The socialist arrangement of *ius in re* was mainly inspired by the CC (1804) and its central construct of ownership. Attempts to elaborate the socialist structure of the civil codes turned out to be successful only in Russia, where socialist concepts are still evident (the second book regards the right of ownership and other rights of estate). In the former East Germany the German BGB (1896) was reintroduced after German reunification. In Czechia there was a radical break with socialist ideology. The result of this shift was the adoption of the new Czech civil code (2012), which was strongly inspired by Austrian concepts.

---

778 In the East German civil code (1975) the content of the general part was isolated between two books. Those are the first book (on the fundamental principles of socialist private law) and the last, seventh, book (including the specific provisions of the respective relationships of private law).

The first subdivision (of the third chapter on securing claims) concerns pledges, the second subdivision guarantees and the third subdivision mortgages.

The fourth subdivision of the third chapter comprises the protection of socialist property *(Eigentum)* in the case of construction works conducted on the immovables entrusted to use on the basis of a contract.

779 The second book of the ABGB (1811) also regards *ius rerum*, but in this case those are the regulations of substantive private law regarding property *(res)*. The second book contains the first division on *ius in re* (*ius in re* is settled in the chapters from the first to the seventh, inheritance law comes after in chapters from the eighth to the fifteenth). The second division (of the second book on *ius rerum*) considers personal rights (obligations).

F) Arrangement of the main systematic segments of *ius in re* in the codes

This section outlines the arrangement of the main systematic components of the codes researched for this study. They are ownership, limited property rights and possession. Why are these components significant to the civil codes? Ownership is the fundamental right of an individual in relation to his own possessions. Limited property rights are the encumbrances which can be levied against the property of another. Possession ensures protection to all *ius in re*. These three elements are the essence of *ius in re*. This section introduces the systematization of respective rights in relation to objects, which is examined in greater detail here. As the central construct (ownership or *ius in re*?) is the greatest determining factor in the arrangement of *ius in re*, the divisions of this section follow the main framework of *ius in re*.

I. Plan of the section

The composition in the codes with the main framework of *ius in re* is discussed first, followed by the codes settled on ownership. In a code arranged around *ius in re*, all components are located in a single book of the code. Choosing ownership as the central construct results in redistributing the elements between different books of the code. We first discuss the simpler systematization (with *ius in re*). Codes based on ownership usually modify the systematic patterns that can be found in the prior codifications.

II. Arrangement of the main systematic components in the codes settled on *ius in re*

1. Possible ways of arranging the components in the codes

Ownership is always placed at the beginning of *ius in re*, followed by limited property rights. Possession, meanwhile, is distributed to different places among *ius in re*. It may be situated before ownership and limited property rights. The composition, in that case, is: possession – ownership – limited property rights. The second option is to place possession after ownership and before limited property rights. As a result, the sequence is: ownership – possession – limited property rights. The final option available is to place possession at the back of *ius in re*, after ownership and limited property rights, resulting in the sequence: ownership – limited property rights – possession. As possession is a "travelling" component, the analysis here is conducted from the perspective of its location among the elements of the system of *ius in re*.

2. Composition: possession, ownership, limited property rights

The first arrangement is: possession – ownership – limited property rights. As possession is placed before ownership, the strongest element among *ius in re*, it is therefore emphasized in the shape of *ius in re*. This systematization was first applied in the ABGB[780] (1811). It was later introduced in the Saxon[781] (1863) and German[782] (1896) civil codes. This arrangement is also present in Czechia[783] (1937, 2012), due to the strong influence of the Austrian model. The same sequence is also visible in the current Hungarian civil code[784] (2013). All codifications with this composition demonstrate the impact of Austrian concepts. Its systematic patterns are often reproduced, especially in legal systems that use the same language.

3. Composition: ownership, possession, limited property rights

Another option is to place ownership first, then possession, and finally limited property rights. According to this order, possession is viewed as a derivative of ownership. The systematization discussed here can be found both in bourgeois and in socialist codifications: the CMBC[785] (1756), the Russian draft[786] (1905), the Hungarian draft[787] (1928) and the first socialist Czechoslovak civil code[788] (1950). This systematic pattern can be viewed both as neutral and as coherent with socialist ideology. Ownership, the most important among *ius in re*, is emphasized. In bourgeois codifications possession is perceived as one of the rights of an owner. This arrangement is convenient for socialist legislators. Possession, viewed unfa-

---

780 In the ABGB (1811) possession is settled at the beginning of *ius in re*, in the first chapter (of the first division on *ius in re*, in the second book on *ius rerum*). Ownership: the second to the fifth chapters. Limited property rights: sixth and seventh chapters.

781 In the Saxon civil code (1863) possession is put in the first division (of the second book on *ius in re*). Ownership: second division. Limited property rights: third, fourth and fifth divisions.

782 In the German BGB possession is positioned in the first chapter (of the third book on *ius in re*). Ownership: third chapter. Limited property rights: from the fourth to the eighth chapters.

783 In the Czechoslovak draft (1937) possession is settled in the opening of *ius in re*, in the fifth section (the second book on property law, the first division on *ius in re*). Ownership: from the sixth to the tenth sections. Limited property rights: from the eleventh to the fourteenth sections.

In the Czech civil code (2012) first possession is arranged, in the second chapter (the third book on absolute property rights, title II: *ius in re*). The third chapter: ownership. (The fourth chapter: co-ownership.) The fifth chapter: limited property rights.

784 In the current Hungarian civil code (2013) possession is put in the first division (of the fifth book on *ius in re*). Ownership: second division. Limited property rights: third division.

785 In the CMBC (1756) ownership is placed in the second chapter (of the second book on *ius in re*). Possession is located in the fifth chapter, after the content belonging to ownership (the third chapter: ways of acquiring ownership, the fourth chapter: prescription). Further chapters of the fourth book (from the sixth to the eleventh) comprise limited property rights.

786 In the Russian draft (1905) ownership is settled in the second division (of the fourth book on *ius in re*). Possession: third division. Limited property rights: fourth and fifth divisions.

787 In the Hungarian draft (1928) ownership is arranged in the first title (of the second book on *ius in re*). Possession is set among precepts relevant to ownership, but there is no one systematic division specifically approaching possession. Limited property rights: second title.

788 In the first socialist Czechoslovak civil code (1950) ownership is allocated at the beginning of the third book on *ius in re* (the seventh chapter; Articles 100 – 154). Possession is concluded among the precepts relevant to ownership (Articles 142 – 154). Limited property rights: from the eighth to the tenth chapters.

vourably by socialism, is diminished in the structure of *ius in re*. As a result, this systematization can be found in the first socialist Czechoslovak civil code (1950).

A very similar composition can be found in the first socialist Russian civil code (1922). Ownership is placed first, followed by limited property rights[789]. Possession is only mentioned in the code, but not extracted in its arrangement (Articles 58, 59 and 62). As this does not accord with socialism, it is diminished in the system of the code. Concurrently, the systematization in the first socialist Russian civil code (1922) was probably inspired by the arrangement of the Russian draft (1905), where possession is placed after ownership. The first socialist Czechoslovak civil code (1950) could have been influenced by the composition of the first socialist Russian civil code (1922).

4. Composition: ownership, limited property rights, possession

A further option is to place ownership at the beginning. Limited property rights are the second systematic compound in the sequence, whereas possession is the final element. This composition was first introduced in the Swiss civil code[790] (1907), then in the Polish draft on *ius in re*[791] (1937) and in the Polish civil code[792] (1964). Even though the Polish civil code applies a mixed systematization (the main framework is determined by the title of the second book, which considers ownership and other *ius in re*), including both bourgeois and socialist features, its form resembles other bourgeois codes based on *ius in re* much more closely than socialist civil codes founded on ownership[793].

---

789 In the first socialist Russian civil code (1922) the first chapter (of the second book on *ius in re*) considers ownership, the second the right of construction, and the third chapter pledges.

790 In the Swiss civil code (1907) ownership is located at the opening of the fourth book on *ius in re* (from the eighteenth to the twentieth titles). Limited property rights: from the twenty-first to the twenty-third titles. Possession: twenty-fourth title.

791 In the Polish draft on *ius in re* (1937) firstly ownership is arranged: second title. Limited property rights: from the third to the sixth titles. Possession: eighth title. The seventh title comprises regulations of the real estate register.

792 In the Polish civil code (1964) ownership is positioned in the first title (of the second book on ownership and other *ius in re*). The second title: perpetual usufruct. The third title: limited property rights. The fourth title: possession.

793 In the Polish civil code (1964) among the fourth titles of the second book on ownership and other *ius in re* (the first title: ownership, the second title: perpetual usufruct, the third title: limited property rights, the fourth title: possession) only the first title recalls ownership.

As a result, the systematization adopted in the Polish civil code (1964) is only a slight modification of the bourgeois arrangement with the sequence: ownership – limited property rights – possession.

Introducing the second title (perpetual usufruct) is connected with the impact of socialist ideology.

III. Arrangement in the codes based on ownership

We now examine codes settled on ownership. In codes arranged around ownership, systematic components of *ius in re* are extracted and arranged among further books of the code.

The first code with this composition is the French *Code civil* (1804). This shape was later adopted in socialist civil codes. It can be found in the socialist Hungarian civil code (1959), the second Czechoslovak civil code (1964), the second socialist Russian civil code (1964), and the East German civil code (1975). Due to its resemblance to the Russian code from 1964, the current Russian civil code (1994 – 2006) is also mentioned in this group.

1. French *Code civil* (1804)

In the CC the sequence of compounds is: ownership – limited property rights – possession. Elements are distributed between two books of the code: the second book (on goods and different modifications of ownership) and the third book (on different ways of acquiring ownership). The French systematization resembles the structure of codes that are based on *ius in re* (ownership – limited property rights – possession), but in France the components are settled in two books instead of one. Ownership is placed in the second book (comprising goods and different modifications of ownership), in the second title. Limited property rights are redistributed between the second book (on goods and different modifications of ownership) and the third book (on different ways of acquiring ownership).

Accordingly, with the titles of the books, limited property rights relating to modifications of ownership (usufruct and servitudes) are placed in the second book (after ownership)[794], whereas limited property rights resulting in the loss of ownership (pledges and mortgages) are settled near the end of the third book[795]. The loss of ownership by one person results in the acquisition of ownership by another. At the end of the third book, possession is situated after limited property rights[796]. It is set in the twentieth title concerning prescription.

In the French structure all components of *ius in re* act as systematic derivatives of ownership. This applies both to limited property rights and to possession. The French arrangement set the standard for subsequent codifications based on ownership; rights that can be placed next to ownership (usufruct and servitudes)

---

[794] In the CC (1804) usufruct is set in the third title of the second book on goods and different modifications of ownership. Servitudes are allocated afterwards, in the fourth title.

[795] Pledges are placed in the seventeenth title of the third book on different ways of acquiring ownership. The eighteenth title (of the third book) includes privileges and mortgages.

[796] Possession is arranged in the second chapter of the twentieth title (prescription) of the third book (on different ways of acquiring ownership).

At this point, the legal effects of the passage of time were settled together, regardless of the area of private law (law of obligations or *ius in re*). Possession is viewed as one of the necessary requirements for usucaption, constituting one of the ways of acquiring ownership.

and those that must be arranged outside the book on ownership (pledges and mortgages).

2. Arrangement in socialist civil codes based on ownership

In this section, we consider the arrangement of the components in the socialist civil codes based on ownership. We first analyze the systematization of the socialist Hungarian civil code (1959), because of all the socialist codes based on ownership it is the only code that admits possession. We then address the arrangement of the socialist civil codes based on ownership and not comprising possession (Russia – 1964, Czechoslovakia – 1964, East Germany – 1975).

a) Hungarian civil code (1959)

In the socialist Hungarian civil code, the third book concerns ownership. Regulations of ownership are settled in the first two titles of the third book on ownership: the first title deals with the general provisions on ownership, and the second title the special provisions concerning socialist ownership. Possession is arranged afterwards, in the third title of the third book. However, as possession constitutes one of the rights of an owner (*ius possidendi*), it might be claimed that ownership covers the entire book on ownership. This approach makes the Hungarian systematization more logical.

Limited property rights are divided between the third book (including the right of ownership) and the fourth book (comprising the law of obligations). The right of construction (lasting use of land), usufruct and land servitudes are located in the third book, among the rights of use[797], whereas pledges are placed in the fourth book, on obligations[798]. Pledges are perceived as a way of securing contracts. The Hungarian classification of limited property rights resembles the French arrangement; there is a differentiation of limited property rights, depending on whether or not they might considered to be derivatives of ownership.

b) Codes not including possession (Russia – 1964, Czechoslovakia – 1964, East Germany – 1975)

In the second socialist Russian code (1964), the second socialist Czechoslovak code (1964), and the East German civil code (1975) there is no possession. Consequently, there are only two systematic components: ownership and limited property rights. In all the above-mentioned codes, ownership is placed in the second book on ownership[799]. At the same time ownership is the only systematic com-

---

[797] In the socialist Hungarian civil code (1959), the third book on ownership, the first title, including the general provisions on ownership, the thirteenth chapter regarding the rights of use.
The right of construction [lasting use of land] (§§ 150 – 154), usufruct (§§ 157 – 165), land servitudes (§§ 166 – 170).

[798] Pledges are located in the twenty-third chapter (regarding accessory obligations securing a contract), in §§ 251 – 269, in the fourth book on obligations.

[799] In the second socialist Russian civil code (1964) that is in the second book on ownership, in the

pound present in the second book, whereas limited property rights are settled outside the book on ownership. Additionally, limited property rights are restricted: there are fewer than in bourgeois civil codes.

The first option is to reduce limited property rights in the code almost to a minimum. This composition is evident in the second socialist Russian civil code (1964). Pledges are the only limited property right included in the civil code, placed in the third book including the law of obligations[800]. In the second socialist Czechoslovak code (1964) the third book (which follows the second book on socialist collective ownership and personal ownership) includes the personal use of dwelling units, other living spaces, and tracts of land. Settling limited property rights after ownership is a typical arrangement. In the East German civil code (1975), servitudes[801] are located in the fourth book (on the use of real estate and buildings for residential and recreational purposes), whereas pledges and mortgages are situated in the last, seventh, book[802] (comprising the particular relationships of the respective relationships of private law).

c) Russian civil code (1994 – 2006)

The arrangement of the systematic components in the current Russian civil code is the last codification discussed here. Its composition was strongly inspired by the second socialist Russian civil code (1964). The second book of the current Russian code concerns the right of ownership and other rights of estate. Ownership appears repeatedly in the divisions of the second book[803]. The content of *ius in re* is reduced to being secondary to ownership, but the reference to "other rights of

---

second Czechoslovak civil code (1964) in the second book on socialist collective ownership and personal ownership, whereas in the East German code (1975) in the second book on socialist ownership and personal ownership.

800 In the second socialist Russian civil code (1964) pledges are set in the seventeenth chapter (the third book on obligations) referring to securing the performance of obligations, in Articles 192 – 202.

The further content applicable to limited property rights is settled outside the civil code.

801 In the East German civil code servitudes are designated as the rights of common use towards premises *(Mitbenutzungsrechte an Grundstücken)*. They are situated at the end of the sixth chapter (the relationships between the users of neighbouring immovables; §§ 321 – 322) of the fourth book regarding the use of real estate and buildings for residential and recreational purposes.

802 In the East German civil code pledges and mortgages are put in the third chapter (securing claims) of the seventh book (concerning the specific provisions of the respective relationships of private law).

803 The second book of the current Russian civil code (1994 – 2006) refers to the right of ownership and the other rights of estate. In the second book there are: general provisions (the thirteenth chapter), the acquisition of the right of ownership (the fourteenth chapter), cessation of the right of ownership (the fifteenth chapter), common property (the sixteenth chapter), right of ownership and other real rights to land (the seventeenth chapter), right of ownership and the other rights of estate to living quarters (the eighteenth chapter), right of economic management and right of operation management (the nineteenth chapter), and protection of the right of ownership and of the other rights of estate (the twentieth chapter).

estate" in the title of the second book implies that the other *ius in re* also receive the protection applicable to *ius in re*. Possession or servitude are mentioned in the text of the code[804]. Just as with other codifications based on ownership, pledges are transferred to the law of obligations[805].

IV. Conclusions

The analysis in this section has shown that the most significant modifications in arranging the systematic components of *ius in re* result from implementing the main framework of ownership in the code. In bourgeois civil codes only some systematic patterns can be observed in all codifications. They are: possession – ownership – limited property rights or ownership – possession – limited property rights or ownership – possession – limited property rights.

Socialist ideology also determine show the elements of the system are organized, but socialist civil codes based on *ius in re* typically have only a few alterations. This implies that the construct of ownership is a factor that alters the arrangement of *ius in re* more determinedly than socialism itself. The most visible changes are present in codes impacted by both factors: socialism and the central construct of ownership. Those codes were mainly inspired by the composition of the CC (1804), introduced after the French bourgeois Revolution. In the CC all institutions of *ius in re* are secondary to the central concept of the code, which is ownership.

The glorification of socialism results in the elimination of one of the systematic compounds, which is possession[806] (Russia – 1964, Czechoslovakia – 1964, East Germany – 1975). Those are the last socialist civil codes to have been established. Interestingly, their systematization of the components of *ius in re* is very simple: ownership is the only compound settled in the book on ownership, whereas limited property rights are placed outside the book on ownership.

G) Arrangement of *ius in re* in the systems of the codes

After outlining the definitions of a thing (*res*), we discussed the arrangement of *ius in re* in the divisions of the analyzed codes, as well as the systematization of the main components of *ius in re*. It is now necessary to examine some issues in

---

804 In the current Russian civil code (1994 – 2006) possession is recalled (e.g. in Article 209, Article 224 or Article 247). Servitudes are set in the second book (on the right of ownership and the other rights of estate), in the seventeenth chapter concerning the right of ownership and other real rights to land (Article 274 and the subsequent provisions).

805 Pledges are put in the third book including the general part of obligations (the first subsection of the third book, comprising the general provisions on obligations), in the twenty-third chapter considering providing for the discharge of obligations, in the third paragraph (§ 3).

806 Among the socialist codifications based on ownership only the socialist Hungarian civil code (1959) includes possession, but it was the first socialist civil code based on ownership. The inclusion of possession is one of its bourgeois features.

greater detail, i.e. the composition of the particular *iura in re* in the structure of the codes researched in this study. As ownership is the most significant among *iura in re*, it is therefore the first institution discussed. The arrangement of limited property rights is subsequently analyzed, followed by possession.

I. Ownership (*ius in re sua*) and its place in the structure of *ius in re*

Ownership is the most powerful right of an individual in relation to an object constituting his property (*ius in re sua*). Among the most important privileges of an owner are: use (*ius utendi*), possession (*ius possidendi*) and disposing a thing (*ius disponendi*). Ownership is indivisible and an owner himself is master of his thing. Due to its significance, it is placed at the beginning of *ius in re*. Ownership is a uniform legal concept, but it can be divided into systematic subcategories in the codes.

1. Arrangement of ownership in codes founded on *ius in re*

In codes founded on *ius in re* there are only two options for arranging ownership. Either it is positioned as the first component in the book on *ius in re* or it is preceded by possession.

a) Ownership as the first *ius in re* in sequence

In codes based on *ius in re*, ownership is positioned at the beginning of the book on *ius in re*. This systematization is visible both in the bourgeois codifications[807] and in the socialist civil codes settled on *ius in re*[808]. This composition can be considered neutral: as ownership is the most significant among *ius in re*, then where else could it be situated? At the same time, if ownership is set in the opening of *ius in re*, then it is also emphasized. Such an arrangement is accordant with socialism, because ownership is highlighted in the system of the code. This systematization is applied in the first socialist civil codes (Russia – 1922, Czechoslovakia – 1950). The same composition is also visible in the Polish civil code (1964), which is

[807] In the Swiss civil code (1907) ownership is set in the first division of the fourth book on *ius in re*. This arrangement is visible in the text of the code. The first division comprises: general provisions (the eighteenth title), ownership of immovables (the nineteenth title) and ownership of movables (the twentieth title).

In the Russian draft (1905) ownership is allocated in the second division of the fourth book on *ius in re*, after precepts relating to real estate property *(Liegenschaftsrecht)*.

In the Hungarian draft (1928) ownership is placed in the first title of the second book on *ius in re*.

[808] In the first socialist Russian civil code (1922) ownership is settled in the first chapter (of the second book on *ius in re*).

In the first socialist Czechoslovak civil code (1950) ownership is classified in the seventh chapter (of the third book on *ius in re*). That is the first chapter in the third book.

based on ownership and other *ius in re*[809]; elaborating socialist legal science later resulted in adopting codes with systems based on ownership instead of *ius in re*[810].

In the bourgeois codifications ownership can be preceded by a systematic unit regarding objects[811]. Such an arrangement is not typically found in codes that include a general part, where objects (*res*) are transposed to the general part. In the composition discussed here ownership is not emphasized in the system of *ius in re*. For this reason, this systematization would not cohere with a socialist civil code. The socialist Hungarian civil code (1959) does not contain a general part and the provisions on things are placed at the beginning of the provisions of the third book, but in Hungary things constitute a systematic subset of ownership and they are not an independent systematic factor[812].

b) Locating ownership after possession: ownership as the second *ius in re* in sequence

The second option for systematization in codes based on *ius in re* is to situate ownership after possession[813]. If possession positioned first, then it is emphasized

---

809 In the Polish civil code (1964) the first title (of the second book on ownership and other *ius in re*) regards ownership.

810 In the socialist Hungarian civil code (1959) the third book refers to the right of ownership.

In the second socialist Russian civil code (1964) the second book concerns the right of ownership.

In the second socialist Czechoslovak civil code (1964) the second book regards socialist collective ownership and personal ownership.

In the East German civil code (1975) the second book considers socialist ownership and personal ownership.

811 In the CMBC (1756) precepts on ownership are positioned directly after provisions relevant to *res*, in the second chapter of the second book on *ius in re*.

In the Polish draft on *ius in re* ownership is located in the second title, after an object of *ius in re* (the first title).

812 In the socialist Hungarian civil code (1959) the first title of the third book comprises the general provisions of ownership. The ninth chapter of the code (the second chapter included in the first title of the third book) refers to the objects of ownership.

813 In the ABGB (1811) the first chapter (of the second book on *ius rerum*, the first division on *ius in re*) concerns possession. The second chapter: ownership.

In the Saxon civil code (1863) the first division (of the second book on *ius in re*) regards possession of things. The second division: ownership.

The Saxon arrangement is very similar to the Austrian systematization.

In the German BGB (1896) ownership is situated in the third chapter of the third book on *ius in re*, after possession (the first chapter) and the general provisions regarding rights over land (the second chapter).

In the Czechoslovak draft (1937) ownership is settled in the sixth section of the second book on property law *(droits patrimoniaux*; the first division of the second book considering *ius in re*), right after possession (the fifth section).

In the current Czech civil code (2012) the first chapter includes the general provisions. The second chapter: possession. The third chapter: ownership. The chapters are placed is the third book on absolute property rights, title II: rights *in rem*.

among *ius in re*. This composition was not observed in the socialist civil codes. Such an arrangement is very unlikely to be found in a socialist civil code because it would suggest that possession is more significant than (socialist) ownership.

2. Arrangement of ownership in the codes separating a book on ownership

If a legislator establishes a separate a book on ownership in the structure of a civil code, then ownership is embedded in it. The first code to apply this systematic pattern is the French *Code civil*. This systematization was subsequently widely adopted in socialist civil codes.

a) French *Code civil* (1804)

In the CC ownership is mentioned in the titles of its two (of three) books. The second book concerns goods and different modifications of ownership, whereas the third book comprises different ways of acquiring ownership. Ownership is an element that prevails in the overall structure of the code. It is a central construct, and the most important determinant of private law in the French codification[814]. In the CC ownership is set in the second title of the second book, after goods and before limited property rights[815].

b) Socialist civil codes

In socialism the legal category of *ius in re* is displaced by ownership. The system of the code is settled on ownership in Hungary (1959), Russia (1964), Czechoslovakia (1964) and East Germany (1975).

In the socialist Hungarian civil code (1959), apart from ownership, other *ius in re* (right of construction [enduring use of land], usufruct and servitudes) are also contained in the book on ownership[816], whereas in later socialist codes based

In the current Hungarian civil code (2013) possession is put in the first division (of the fifth book on *ius in re*). Ownership: second division.

814 There is a significant difference between the main frame of ownership in the French codification and other (socialist) civil codes based on ownership.

In other codifications, ownership is (usually) the title of the second book; in France the second book concerns goods and different modifications of ownership, and the third book considers different ways of acquiring ownership.

Contrary to other codes, the CC is arranged around ownership and not based on ownership. In the structure of the French code, ownership is the factor that encompasses the entirety of private law.

815 In the CC (1804) ownership is located in the second title of the second book (Article 544 – 577), after the first title regarding the distinction of goods and in front of the third title containing usufruct, use and habitation.

816 The third book of the socialist Hungarian civil code (1959) concerning ownership is divided into three titles. The first title: general provisions on ownership. The second title: special provisions regarding socialist ownership. The third title: possession.

The right of construction [lasting use of land] (§§ 150 – 154), usufruct (§§ 157 – 165) and servitudes (§§ 166 – 170) are included in the thirteenth chapter (rights of use), in the first title (general provisions on ownership), in the third book on ownership.

on ownership (Russia – 1964, Czechoslovakia – 1964, East Germany – 1975), ownership is the only *ius in re* included in the book on ownership. In the Hungarian systematization limited property rights are the systematic subsets of ownership; the thirteenth chapter, where they are located, concerns the rights of use. Furthermore, in this composition limited property rights (except pledges, which are settled elsewhere) adhere to the main right in the structure of the code: ownership. They are the most significant components of ownership among *ius in re*. The structure of the book on ownership in the socialist Hungarian civil code (1959) demonstrates the passage between socialist civil codes based on *ius in re* and the last socialist codifications. The first title of the third book on ownership contains the general provisions on ownership. The second title comprises special provisions regarding socialist ownership. The third title includes possession. The first two titles concern ownership. The third title (on possession) can be viewed as the extension of the rights of an owner *(ius possidendi)*.

In the last socialist civil codes (Russia – 1964, Czechoslovakia – 1964, East Germany – 1975) ownership is the only systematic compound in the book on ownership. The systematic categories in the book on ownership constitute different kinds of ownership. This issue is described below.

3. Systematic differentiations of ownership in the researched civil codes

The next problem analyzed here concerns the systematic distinctions of ownership in the civil codes. We first discuss socialist codifications, followed by bourgeois codes.

a) Systematic differentiations of ownership in the socialist civil codes

In the socialist civil codes there are many kinds of ownership, depending on the legal subject (state, individual) performing a right as well as on its destination. This problem is expressed in the systematization of the researched codifications. The applicable terms are further explained in this section, alongside the specific issues regarding the structure of *ius in re* in the socialist civil codes. Here, the examination is restricted to the arrangement of different kinds of ownership in the socialist civil codes. The first option is to locate them at the beginning of the precepts on *ius in re*[817]. This arrangement is visible in the first socialist civil codes

---

[817] In the Russian (1922) and Czechoslovak (1950) civil codes the systematic differentiations of ownership are mentioned at the beginning of the book on *ius in re*, in the opening of the precepts on ownership. In both codifications the first chapter in the book on *ius in re* refers to ownership.

In the first socialist Russian civil code (1922) in Article 52 [the second book on *ius in re*, the first chapter: ownership; Article 52 is the first provision of the second book] state ownership *(propriété publique)*, cooperative ownership and private ownership are recalled.

In the Russian code there are no specific systematic divisions approaching different kinds of ownership.

In the first socialist Czechoslovak civil code (1950) in the seventh chapter regarding ownership (the first chapter included in the third book on *ius in re*) in the text there are visible

(Russia – 1922, Czechoslovakia – 1950) and in the Polish civil code (1964). The same composition can be found in the socialist Hungarian civil code (1959), but there is a separate chapter in the code, dealing with the forms of ownership[818]. That is a systematic amendment, enabling a clearer orientation in the content of the code.

The second option is evident in the last socialist codifications to have been established, where the differentiations of ownership constitute the divisions in a book on ownership. If a socialist civil code addresses the needs of citizens (Czechoslovakia – 1964, East Germany – 1975), then only two kinds of ownership are extracted: first ownership of the state, followed by personal ownership[819].

The second socialist Russian civil code (1964) follows the unity of private law. Apart from the needs of socialist citizens, it also regulates the sector of the planned economy. The general principles are settled first, and then state ownership and ownership of different socialist units. Ownership of an individual (personal ownership) is positioned at the end[820]. Among the last socialist codifications it seems that the unity of private law is the most important factor determining the divisions of the (second) book on ownership. In the second socialist Russian civil

---

sections corresponding to different kinds of ownership. Those are: socialist ownership (Articles 100 – 104), personal ownership (Article 105) and private ownership (Article 106).

In the Polish civil code (1964) the first subdivision comprising the general provisions includes: socialist ownership (Articles 126 – 129), individual (private) ownership (Articles 130 – 131) and personal ownership (Articles 132 and subsequent provisions). This content is arranged in the second book on ownership and other *ius in re*, in the first title on ownership.

The discussed provisions were present only in the original version of the Polish civil code. After the fall of socialism they were removed from the system of the code.

818 In the socialist Hungarian civil code (1959) that is the first chapter in the third book on ownership, titled: forms of ownership. In the structure of the socialist Hungarian civil code (1959) that is the eighth chapter, included in the first title of the third book. The first title (of the third book) comprises the general provisions on the right of ownership.

819 In the second socialist Czechoslovak civil code (1964) the second book considers socialist collective ownership and personal ownership. The first division of the second book concerns socialist collective ownership and meeting the needs of citizens. The second division refers to personal ownership.

In the East German civil code (1975) the second book deals with socialist ownership and personal ownership.

Socialist ownership is included in the first chapter of the second book, whereas personal ownership is contained in the second chapter. Additionally, in the East German civil code (1975) part of the precepts on ownership is placed in the fourth chapter (personal ownership of immovables and buildings) of the fourth book (on the use of real estate and buildings for residential and recreational purposes).

820 The seventh chapter of the Russian civil code from 1964 (that is the first chapter of the second book on ownership) comprises the general principles. The eighth chapter concerns state ownership. The ninth and tenth chapters distinguish ownership of different socialist units (the ninth chapter: ownership of kolkhozs and other cooperative organizations and their associations, the tenth chapter: ownership of trade unions and other social organisations). The eleventh chapter refers to personal ownership.

code (1964) there are more forms of ownership than in the Czechoslovak (1964) and East German (1975) civil codes, which include only what is necessary for citizens.

b) Systematic distinctions of ownership in the bourgeois civil codes

In the bourgeois civil codes ownership is a uniform concept, but it can be divided into systematic subcategories. The most popular among them is differentiation depending on the object of ownership (Switzerland – 1907, Hungary – 1928). If that composition is applied, then ownership of immovables is placed first, followed by ownership of movables[821].

c) Systematization of co-ownership in the researched civil codes

Co-ownership is another differentiation introduced in the civil codes, evident in both bourgeois and socialist codifications. Co-ownership is usually placed among the precepts relevant to ownership[822]. The Austrian arrangement varies from other civil codes. In the ABGB (1811) co-ownership can be found twice. First, there is a single provision on co-ownership in the chapter on ownership (§ 361). Second, co-ownership is used as a binder between *ius in re* and inheritance law, both classified in the first division (on *ius in re*) of the second book on *ius rerum*[823]. The exact title of the sixteenth chapter, including co-ownership, is *von der Gemeinschaft des Eigentums und anderer dinglichen Rechte*. This title implies that co-ownership applies not only to ownership, but also to other *ius in re*. As in Austria, inheritance law is classified among *ius rerum*, co-ownership also complies with succession law. The division on *ius in re* (*res*) and the law of obligations (*actiones*) is the foundation of private law. In the ABGB both areas of private law are included in the second book regarding *ius rerum res*). Placing co-ownership between them, as the common factor in private law, establishes the unity of the second book. Co-ownership together with a thing are the pillars of the second book.

---

821 In the Swiss civil code (1907) the nineteenth title (in the fourth book on *ius in re*) includes the ownership of immovables, whereas the twentieth title includes ownership of movables.

In the Hungarian draft (1928) the first title (of the second book on *ius in re*) regards ownership. The first chapter (of the first title) contains the general provisions. The second chapter: ownership of immovables. The third chapter: ownership of movables.

822 This systematization is visible, e.g. in the German BGB (1896), where co-ownership is arranged in the fifth title (of the third chapter regarding ownership), in the third book on *ius in re*.

In the East German civil code (1975) co-ownership is settled in the last, fourth, chapter of the second book on socialist ownership and personal ownership.

823 In the ABGB (1811) the first division (of the second book on *ius rerum*) concerns *ius in re*, whereas the second division contains the personal rights (obligations).

The last, sixteenth, chapter (of the first division on *ius in re*) considers co-ownership. *Ius in re* is settled from the first to the seventh chapter of the first division; inheritance law is regulated from the eighth to the fifteenth chapter.

d) Arrangement of ways of acquiring ownership

Different ways of acquiring ownership are usually settled among provisions relevant to ownership (e.g. Saxony[824] – 1863) or in a distinct systematic unit after ownership[825]. Acquisition of ownership may also form the basis for arranging the code. That is the composition in the French *Code civil* (1804) and in the Prussian *Landrecht* (1794). This systematization was primarily inspired by the *Institutes* of Gaius, where *res* comprise different ways of acquiring ownership. As Gaius classified most substantive private law (*ius in re*, inheritance law, matrimonial property law and law of obligations) among *res*, it is not surprising that this composition also exerted an impact on the systematization of the codifications.

In the Prussian *Landrecht* the impact of *Institutes* is evident in how the content of private law is settled according to the titles of ownership. Methods of acquiring ownership following the provisions of ownership:this content is typical of the acquisition of ownership[826]. Further, there are the particular contracts (the eleventh title of the first part concerns the titles relating to the acquisition of ownership, resulting from contracts between living partners) and inheritance law (the twelfth title, which includes titles relating to ownership acquistion arising from ordinances in the case of death). Ownership is one of the main determinants of substantive private law in the Prussian *Landrecht*, and many institutions of private law in the system of *Landrecht* are perceived in relation to ownership.

In the CC the third book considers different ways of acquiring ownership, including inheritance law, matrimonial property law, the law of obligations and institutions of *ius in re* resulting in the extinction of ownership[827]. The French

824 The second division of the second book on *ius in re* of the Saxon civil code (1863) regards ownership. In the first chapter there are the general provisions. The second chapter regards the acquisition of ownership of movables, whereas the third chapter refers to the acquisition of immovables.

825 This arrangement is present in the CMBC (1756), where ways of acquiring ownership are positioned after ownership. The second chapter of the second book on *ius in re* regards ownership and the third chapter regards the ways of acquiring ownership *(Art und Weise, das Eigentum zu erlangen)*.

826 In the Prussian *Landrecht* (1794) the eighth title (of the first part) considers ownership. The ninth title regards the acquisition of ownership in general and the immediate ways of acquisition in general. The tenth title concerns the indirect acquisition of ownership.

827 In the CC (1804) the third book regards different ways of acquiring ownership. Precepts on acquiring ownership (designated as the general provisions) are placed at the beginning of third book, in Articles 711 – 717).

The third book comprises inheritance law, matrimonial property law, obligations and some institutions of *ius in re*. The first title of the third book: successions. The second title: donations *inter vivos* and wills. The third title: contracts and conventional obligations in general. The fourth title: commitments formed without an agreement.

Titles from the fifth to the fifteenth: particular contracts (the fifth title includes matrimonial property law). Finally there are the systematic compounds connected the most with *ius in re*. The sixteenth title: personal arrest in a private law matter. The seventeenth title: pledges. The

arrangement was impacted both by the *Institutes* of Gaius and the Prussian *Landrecht* prior to the CC. Additionally, this systematization is in line with the ideology of the French Revolution, which privileges an individual's right to ownership and his natural and secular rights. Both in Prussia and France a significant volume of private law is perceived in terms of the acquisition of ownership.

e) Arrangement of usucaption in the civil codes

Usucaption is one ways in which ownership is acquired, but it has a significant systematic function in the civil codes. Even though that is one way in which ownership can be acquired, due to its systematic relevance it must be approached separately. It is now usually classified among *ius in re*, but that was not always the case. In Roman law all consequences of the expiration of time are settled together, regardless of the area of private law in which an event occurs. This viewpoint has impacted the systematization of civil codes; prescription and usucaption are positioned next to each other in the oldest codifications[828]. When the Pandect systematization was established, usucaption and prescription were systematically separated from each other for the first time. As a result, the new rule became that prescription was arranged in the general part and usucaption among *ius in re*. This composition was first introduced in the Saxon civil code[829] (1863). Later, it

---

eighteenth title: privileges and mortgages. The nineteenth title: forced expropriation and orders between creditors. The twentieth title: prescription.

828 In the CMBC (1756) prescription and usucaption are placed in the fourth chapter (concerning prescription) of the second book on *ius in re*, right after different ways of acquiring ownership (the third chapter) and before possession (the fifth chapter). In Bavaria prescription was classified among *ius in re*.

In the CC (1804) provisions relevant to usucaption were mixed with precepts on prescription in the twentieth title (on prescription) of the third book on different ways of acquiring ownership. This arrangement was amended in 2008.

From now, on the twentieth title of the third book concerns prescription, and the newly established twenty-first title refers to possession and usucaption.

In the Prussian *Landrecht* (1794) the ninth title (of the first part) refers to the acquisition of ownership in general and the immediate ways of acquisition in general. The last, ninth, chapter (of the ninth title) concerns prescription.

In the ABGB (1811) usucaption is arranged together with prescription in the last, fourth, chapter of the third book (including provisions common to personal rights and *ius in re*). The fourth chapter on prescription and usucaption is set right after the third chapter regarding cancellation of rights and obligations.

829 In the Saxon civil code (1863) prescription is placed in the general part, in the fifth subsection (ending of lawsuits) of the last, sixth, division regarding the securing, preservation and pursuit of rights (§ 150 and the subsequent provisions).

Usucaption of movables is settled among *ius in re* (the second book on *ius in re*, the second division considering ownership, the second chapter regarding the acquisition of ownership of movables, the last, eighth, subsection on usucaption).

was propagated by the German BGB[830] (1896), and became a rule in the codes researched for this study[831].

4. Conclusions

In bourgeois codes ownership is arranged at the beginning of *ius in re*. It might be the first *ius in re* in sequence, or it might be preceded by possession. Arrangement of ownership is modified most significantly in the codes founded on ownership. The first among them was the CC (1804). Its second book regards goods and different modifications of ownership, and the third book concerns different ways of acquiring ownership. In the socialist civil codes based on *ius in re* ownership is set in the opening of the book on *ius in re*, whereas in the last socialist civil codes to be established the main framework of ownership is present. Other institutions (such as co-ownership or different ways of acquiring ownership) act as the systematic subsets of ownership. Sometimes they might gain significance and become the foundation of the structure of the code. In the socialist civil codes ownership becomes the central feature of the code; it captures the place normally admitted to *ius in re*.

II. Arrangement of limited property rights in the researched codes

The next issue to consider is the arrangement of limited property rights. Ownership is a right performed in relation to one's own thing (*ius in re sua*). Limited property rights are designated in Latin as *iura in re aliena* (rights performed in relation to the object of another). Contrary to ownership, the fullest right to property, limited property rights give the beneficiary of a right only a partial, restricted use of an object. Limited property rights allow us to execute, with in the limits of statutes, our rights on things that do not belong to us. Limited property rights cannot function on their own and they are "fastened" to a thing belonging to another[832]. The civil codes acknowledge the systematic isolation of ownership from *iura in re aliena*. As the most powerful right, ownership is placed at the beginning of *ius in re*. Being weaker rights, limited property rights are positioned after ownership.

---

830 In the German BGB (1896) the fifth chapter of the general part refers to prescription. Usucaption is a distinct systematic category among the precepts on the acquisition and loss of movable property (the third book on *ius in re*, the third chapter regarding ownership, the third title referring to acquisition and loss of movable property, the second subdivision on usucaption).

831 This arrangement is visible, e.g. in the Polish civil code (1964). The sixth title of the general part considers the limitation of claims.

Usucaption is regulated among *ius in re* [the second book on ownership and other *ius in re*, the first title on ownership, the third division regarding the acquisition and loss of ownership, the second chapter including usucaption (Articles 172 – 176)].

832 In exceptional situations it is possible to have a limited property right to our object.

E.g. § 1163 (1) of the German BGB (1896): If the claim for which the mortgage is granted has failed to come into existence, the mortgage belongs to the owner. If the claim is extinguished, the owner acquires the mortgage.

1. Main framework of the *ius in re* versus arrangement of limited property rights

Here we consider the relation between the main framework of *ius in re* and the distribution of limited property rights in the books of the civil codes. That is one of the most important factors determining the systematization of limited property rights. If a legislator settles *ius in re* around *ius in re*, then limited property rights are located in a single book[833]. If ownership is the central concept of the system, then limited property rights are redistributed between different books of the code. That impacts the arrangement of pledges, but other limited property rights might also be transposed to other books. This composition is visible both in the bourgeois civil codes (the CC – 1804) and in the socialist codifications based on ownership[834].

2. Arrangement of limited property rights in the codes that adopt the main framework of *ius in re*

Before we analyze the systematization of limited property rights in the civil codes, this section outlines their arrangement. The composition of limited property rights is impacted by the main framework of *ius in re* as applied in the codes, as well as the background of the system: capitalism or socialism. First, the arrangement of limited property rights in the codes with the main framework of *ius in re* is presented. In this composition all limited property rights are settled in a single book of the code regarding *ius in re*. The codes set on *ius in re* are divided into two groups. The composition of limited property rights in German-speaking countries is first discussed, followed by the systematization of limited property rights in the bourgeois codifications (and drafts) based on *ius in re* in non-German speaking countries. The systematization of limited property rights in the codes principally built on the framework of ownership, and in the socialist civil codes is subsequently analyzed. In codes based on ownership, limited property rights are redistributed between the books of the code.

[833] This composition is present in: the CMBC (1756), the ABGB (1811), the Saxon civil code (1863), the German BGB (1896), the pre-revolutionary Russian draft (1905), the first socialist Russian civil code (1922), the Czechoslovak draft (1937), the first socialist Czechoslovak civil code (1950), the Czech civil code (2012), the Hungarian draft (1928), the Hungarian civil code (2013), the Polish draft on *ius in re* (1937) as well as the Polish civil code (1964), impacted by socialism.

[834] The Hungarian civil code (1959), the Czechoslovak civil code (1964), the Russian civil codes (1964, 1994 – 2006) and the East German civil code (1975).

3. Arrangement of limited property rights in codes based on *ius in re* in German-speaking countries

We first examine codes in German-speaking countries that adopt the main framework of *ius in re*. They are: the CMBC (1756), the ABGB (1811), the Saxon civil code (1863), the German BGB (1896) and the Swiss civil code (1907).

a) CMBC (1756)

In the CMBC limited property rights are settled in the second book on *ius in re*, from the sixth to the ninth chapters. The sixth chapter concerns pledges. The seventh chapter refers to servitudes in general. The eighth chapter contains all specific kinds of servitudes (*von Haus- und Feld-Dienstbarkeiten und anderen ähnlichen Gerechtigkeiten*). The ninth chapter considers usufruct.

b) ABGB (1811)

In the ABGB limited property rights are arranged in the first division (*ius in re*) of the second book on *ius rerum*, in the sixth and the seventh chapters. The sixth chapter concerns pledges, and the seventh chapter servitudes.

c) Saxon civil code (1863)

In the Saxon civil code limited property rights are placed in the third, fourth and fifth systematic divisions of the second book on *ius in re*. The third division concerns pledges, the fourth division realty charges, and the fifth division servitudes.

d) German BGB (1896)

In the German BGB limited property rights are located in the third book on *ius in re*, from chapters four to eight[835]. The fourth chapter contains servitudes. The fifth chapter concerns right of pre-emption. The sixth chapter addresses realty charges. The seventh chapter deals with mortgages, land charges and annuity charges. Pledges on movable things and on rights are presented at the end of *ius in re* (in the eighth chapter).

e) Swiss civil code (1907)

In the Swiss civil code limited property rights are arranged in the fourth book on *ius in re*, from the twenty-first to the twenty-third title. The twenty-first title

---

[835] In the German BGB the arrangement of the limited property rights was reformed. Due to the fact that the hereditary building rights (put in the fourth chapter) were considered to be an insignificant compound of *ius in re*, they were removed.

Previously, there had been: hereditary building rights (the fourth chapter), servitudes (the fifth chapter), the right of pre-emption (the sixth chapter), realty charges (the seventh chapter), mortgages, land charges and annuity charges (the eighth chapter), as well as pledges on movable things and other rights (the ninth chapter).

This area of the BGB is one of the few cases in which in this study takes the later systematization into account and discusses it as if it were original.

regards servitudes and realty charges. The twenty-second title concerns pledges on immovables. The twenty-third title, pledges on movables.

4. Bourgeois codifications in non-German speaking countries that adopt the main framework of *ius in re*

Next, we move to the bourgeois codes (and drafts) based on *ius in re* from non-German speaking countries. We consider the systematization of limited property rights first in the drafts (Russia – 1905, Hungary – 1928, Czechoslovakia – 1937, Poland – 1937) and then in the civil codes (Czechia – 2012, Hungary – 2013)

a) Russian draft (1905)

In the Russian draft limited property rights are placed after ownership (the second division of the fourth book on *ius in re*) and possession (the third division). The next two divisions (the fourth and fifth divisions of the fourth book) concern limited property rights.

The fourth division is titled limited property rights (*Rechte an fremden Sachen*). It includes the general provisions in its opening (the first line), followed by the right of interests to inheritance (*Erbzinsrecht*) in the second line, and then (in the third line) the right of extracting minerals. In the final, fourth, line usufruct, servitudes and realty charges are arranged.

The fifth division comprises mortgages and pledges[836].

b) Hungarian draft (1928)

In the Hungarian draft the second title (of the second book on *ius in re*) concerns limited property rights. These are, in order: land servitudes (the first chapter), personal servitudes (the second chapter), the right of construction (*Baurecht*; the third chapter), realty charges (the fourth chapter), mortgages (*Grundpfandrecht*;

---

[836] In the Russian draft (1905) there are three more divisions, set in the fourth book on *ius in re*. The sixth division comprises the specific kinds of land ownership. These are institutions typical for pre-revolutionary Russian private law.

The sixth and seventh divisions are more interesting if the arrangement of the later Russian codes (1964, 1994 – 2006) is considered. The sixth division refers to copyright law *(Autorrecht)*. The seventh division deals with the right to inventions, trademarks and companies *(Recht auf Erfindungen, auf Warenzeichen und auf eine Firma)*.

The second socialist Russian civil code (1964) includes: general principles – ownership – law of obligations – *copyright law – right of discovery – patent law* – succession law – international private law.

In the current Russian civil code (1994 – 2006) there are: general provisions – right of ownership and other rights to estates – general part of obligations – particular kinds of obligations – inheritance law – international private law – *rights to the results of intellectual activities and means of individualisation*.

Arranging the regulations of copyright law (and related areas of private law) in the Russian draft (1905) inspired the later Russian codes, where the discussed volume was arranged and put in distinct books.

the fifth chapter), pledges on movables (the sixth chapter) and pledges on claims and other rights (the seventh chapter).

c) Polish draft on *ius in re* (1937)

In the Polish draft on *ius in re* limited property rights are positioned after ownership (the second title). The third title deals with servitudes; the fourth title, the law of retention; and the fifth title, pledges. The final systematic category concerning limited property rights are realty charges (the sixth title).

d) Czechoslovak draft (1937)

In the Czechoslovak draft limited property rights are settled from sections eleven to fourteen in the first division (*ius in re*) of the second book on *ius in re*. The eleventh section addresses the right of construction. The twelfth section concerns servitudes. The thirteenth section handles pledges. The final, fourteenth, section looks at realty charges.

e) Czech civil code (2012)

In the Czech civil code limited property rights are positioned in the fifth chapter (the third book comprising absolute property rights, title II: *ius in re*). The right of superficies (the right of construction) is placed in the first division (of the fifth chapter). The second division concerns easements (servitudes). Pledges are located in the third division; right of retention is in the fourth division. Following limited property rights, the sixth chapter considers the administration of the property of others, and also deals with trusts (the fourth division of the sixth chapter).

f) Hungarian civil code (2013)

In the Hungarian civil code limited property rights are set in the third division of the fifth book on *ius in re*. The seventh title of the fifth book on *ius in re* (the first title in the third division) regards liens, mortgages and other pledges. The eighth title concerns the rights of use (usufruct). The final, ninth, title considers rights of access and use for public purposes (servitudes).

5. Arrangement of limited property rights in the socialist civil codes based on *ius in re*

This section outlines the arrangement of limited property rights in socialist codes settled on *ius in re*. They are the first socialist Russian civil code (1922) and the first socialist Czechoslovak civil code (1950). The Polish civil code (1964) was also classified in this group; even though its central construct is ownership and other *ius in re*, its composition is almost identical to that of codes based on *ius in re*. The socialist civil codes based on ownership are mentioned later.

a) Russian civil code (1922)

In the first socialist Russian civil code there are only two limited property rights. In the second chapter (of the second book on *ius in re*) the right of construction[837] is placed, and in the third chapter pledges.

b) Czechoslovak civil code (1950)

In the first socialist Czechoslovak civil code limited property rights are arranged in the third book on *ius in re* from chapters eight to ten. Chapter eight concerns the ownership of a construction and the right of construction. In the ninth chapter realty charges are settled[838]. The tenth chapter concerns pledges and the law of retention.

c) Polish civil code (1964)

In the Polish civil code the third title (of the second book on ownership and other *ius in re*) refers to limited property rights. The first subdivision of the third title contains the general provisions; in their opening in Article 244 there is a list of limited property rights. They are: usufruct, servitudes, pledges, cooperative ownership rights to premises, and mortgages (Article 244 § 1). According to Article 244 § 2, the latter two are settled in separate legislation[839].

---

837 Article 71 of the first socialist Russian civil code from 1922 concerns the right of construction.

Article 71 Les contrats concernant la concession des parcelles municipales de terrains à bâtir sont conclus par les sections communales avec les groupements coopératifs et les autres personnes juridiques de même qu'avec de simples citoyens pour une durée de quarante-neuf ans, s'il s'agit de constructions de pierres, et de vingt ans pour les autres constructions.

Remarque. – Le contrat relative au droit de construction peut s'étendre à un terrain, qui n'est pas directement destiné à la construction, mais la dessert au point de vue économique.

The cited provision shows that the right of construction in the first socialist Russian civil code can be classified among *iura in re aliena*.

More about the right of construction in the Soviet Russia and in other socialist jurisdictions can be found in the third chapter of the monograph of: WINIARZ J., *Użytkowanie wieczyste* [Perpetual usufruct], Warszawa 1967, pp. 104 – 177.

The chapter considers the social and economic function of the perpetual usufruct (right of construction) in connection to the functions performed by the similar legal forms in some socialist states.

838 Additionally, in the first Czechoslovak civil code (1950) there is the regulation of usufruct, hidden among the ninth chapter regarding realty charges. The ninth chapter comprises Articles 166 – 187; usufruct is put in Articles 172 – 180.

839 That is the effect of the specific legislative technique used in the Polish civil code (1964). Both cooperative ownership rights to premises and mortgages needed to be mentioned in the code. The socialist authority favoured cooperative ownership rights to premises (which most lawyers who adopted a more bourgeois approach did not follow), whereas lawyers in these socialist contexts had a preference for capitalist mortgages, despised by the socialist authorities.

The mentioned limited property rights are at the same time present and not included in the code. They are recapitulated in Article 244, but could be crossed out and completely erased from the code at any time.

The second subdivision of the third title concerns usufruct. The third subdivision is on servitudes. The final, fourth, subdivision of the third title deals with pledges. The second title of the second book precedes the third title, and addresses perpetual usufruct (right of construction).

6. Civil codes based on ownership – the French *Code civil* (1804) and socialist codifications

Finally, this section addresses the civil codes based on the main framework of ownership. The central construct of ownership affects the systematization of limited property rights. The systems of socialist civil codes are often based on ownership. Regardless of the central concept of the code, the catalogue of limited property in socialist civil codes is restricted. First, we consider the composition of limited property rights in the CC (1804). That is the only (fully) bourgeois codification that bases its system on ownership. Subsequently, we address the arrangement of limited property rights in the socialist civil codes.

This section then moves to codes based on ownership (Hungary – 1959, Russia – 1964, Czechoslovakia – 1964, East Germany – 1964). Finally, we analyze the systematization of limited property rights in the current Russian civil code (1994 – 2006). Its second book considers the right of ownership and the other rights of estate. Its composition is very similar to that of codes founded on ownership.

a) French *Code civil* (1804)

In the CC limited property rights are separated into two books. Usufruct, use and habitation are settled in the third title of the second book (on goods and different modifications of ownership). Servitudes and land services are located subsequently in the fourth title. Pledges and mortgages are placed at the end of the third book (regarding different ways of acquiring ownership). Pledges are positioned in the seventeenth title and mortgages in the eighteenth title.

Subsequently, the systematization of limited property rights in the socialist civil codes that adopt the main framework of ownership is examined. They are: the Hungarian civil code (1959), the second socialist Russian civil code (1964), the second socialist Czechoslovak civil code (1964), the East German civil code (1975), and the current Russian civil code (1994 – 2006).

b) Hungarian civil code (1959)

In the Hungarian civil code the right of construction [lasting use of land] (§§ 150 – 154), usufruct (§§ 157 – 165) and land servitudes (§§ 166 – 170) are arranged in the thirteenth chapter (rights of use), in the first title (general provisions on ownership) of the third book on ownership. Pledges are settled in the fourth book on obligations, in the twenty-third chapter, concerned with accessory obligations securing a contract (§§ 251 – 269).

c) Russian civil code (1964)

In the Russian civil code pledges are the only limited property right[840], locted in the seventeenth chapter of the third book (obligations) regarding security in performing obligations (Articles 192 – 202). The second book on ownership comprises only the regulation of ownership.

d) Czechoslovak civil code (1964)

In the fifth division (securing rights and duties) of the general part the limitation of the transfer of an immovable (§§ 58 – 61) is settled. That is a legal form of securing claims that was introduced instead of mortgage[841]. The second book, which concerns socialist collective ownership and personal ownership, does not include any limited property rights. The third book of the code deals with the personal use of dwelling units, other living spaces, and tracts of land. Pledges and realty charges are handled in the final, eighth, book, containing final provisions, in § 495.

e) East German civil code (1975)

In the East German civil code, the second book concerning socialist ownership and personal ownership only concludes the provisions on ownership. Servitudes (rights of common use – *Mitbenutzungsrechte an Grundstücken*) are situated at the end of the final, sixth, chapter (which concerns the relationships between the users of neighbouring immovables) of the fourth book (regarding the use of real estate and buildings for residential and recreational purposes), in §§ 321 – 322. The third chapter of the final, seventh, book (which concludes the specific provisions of the respective relationships of private law) concerns securing claims. Pledges are arranged in the first subdivision (of the third chapter) and mortgages in the third subdivision.

f) Russian civil code (1994 – 2006)

The current Russian civil code differs from the other civil codes discussed here. Our examination is limited to servitudes and pledges. Servitudes are placed in the

---

840 The systematization of limited property rights in the second socialist Russian civil code (1964) is explained by reducing the catalogue present in the first socialist Russian civil code (1922), where only the rights of construction and pledges were included.

In 1948 (decree of the Presidium of the Supreme Soviet of 26.08.1948) the right of construction was replaced by the personal ownership of a residential house.

The arrangement of the Russian code of 1964 consequently emerged from these changes in the legislation. As the right of construction was erased from the catalogue of limited property rights, the only limited property right that had to be included in the code of 1964 were pledges.

WASILKOWSKI J., *Zarys prawa rzeczowego* [An introduction to *ius in re*], Warszawa 1963, p. 18.

841 VONDRACEK TH. J., *Commentary on the Czechoslovak civil code* , Dordrecht/ Boston/ Lancaster 1988, pp. 78 – 79.

second book (which refers to the right of ownership and the other rights of estate) in the seventeenth chapter, which concerns the right of ownership and other real rights to land (Article 274 and the subsequent provisions). Pledges are situated in the third book containing the general part of obligations (the first subsection of the third book, dealing with the general provisions on obligations), in the twenty-third chapter concerning providing for the discharge of obligations, in the third paragraph (§ 3).

7. Principles of arranging limited property rights in the codes (based on ownership)

Next, the discussion moves to analyzing the arrangement of respective limited property rights. Each limited property right is a charge placed on ownership. From the systematic point of view, the main problem is the sequence of charges arranged among limited property rights. The order of limited property rights is mainly determined by their gravity. Legislators usually first settle lighter charges (servitudes) and then heavier ones (pledges). Pledges are the heaviest charge; if a creditor satisfies his claims, then it might result in the extinction of ownership. Nonetheless, that occurs only if a debtor does not fulfil his obligation and the pledged thing has to be sold. Servitudes are lighter than pledges. Realty charges are between pledges and servitudes. We first discuss the composition of servitudes. Closely connected with ownership, they are settled at the beginning of limited property rights. We then analyze realty charges, and finally pledges. In the case of each limited property right the discussion considers the impact of the main construct applied in the code (ownership or *ius in re*) on its arrangement.

8. Servitudes

Servitudes increase the usability of a different real estate or satisfy the needs of a particular person. Like all other limited property rights, they are located after ownership. First, this section discusses the influence of the main framework of *ius in re* on the arrangement of servitudes. Next, it describes the arrangement in which servitudes are situated before pledges (the second point), followed by the resolution in which pledges come first (the third point). The systematization of usufruct is subsequently depicted: first, its arrangement in the bourgeois civil codes (the fourth point), and then in the socialist civil codes (the fifth point). These deliberations raise the question of whether land servitudes are admitted in socialist civil codes (the sixth point). The seventh point portrays the systematization of land servitudes in the East German civil code (1975). Their peculiar arrangement is thoroughly assessed in the seventh point. The unusual systematic pattern of the East German code also provides a good opportunity to show the specifics of this codification, which varies from other the socialist civil codes researched here (the eighth point). Finally, this section presents the conclusions drawn from studying the arrangement of servitudes (the ninth point).

a) Impact of the main framework of *ius in re* on the arrangement of servitudes

In codes based on *ius in re*, servitudes are placed in the book on *ius in re*[842]. Like all other limited property rights, they are situated after ownership. If servitudes can be found in codes based on ownership, then they are arranged in the same book as ownership[843]. This systematic pattern is replicated in the codes based on ownership and other *ius in re*[844]. Socialist civil codes settled on ownership (Russia – 1964, Czechoslovakia – 1964) are not likely to include servitudes. In both jurisdictions, servitudes had already been removed from the preceding codifications (Russia – 1922, Czechoslovakia – 1950). Their absence results from the introduction of socialist ideology.

---

842 This systematization can be found, e.g. in the Saxon civil code (1863) and the German BGB (1896).

In the Saxon civil code (1863) the last, fifth, division (of the second book on *ius in re*) regards servitudes.

In the German BGB (1896) the fourth chapter (in the third book on *ius in re*) refers to servitudes.

843 In the CC (1804) servitudes are settled in the fourth title (of the second book on goods and different modifications of ownership). Ownership: second title.

In the socialist Hungarian civil code (1959) land servitudes are contained in the third book on ownership (the first title: general provisions on ownership), in the thirteenth chapter (rights of use), in §§ 166 – 170.

In the East German civil code (1975) servitudes are designated as the rights of common use towards premises *(Mitbenutzungsrechte an Grundstücken)*. They are located at the end of the sixth chapter (the relationships between the users of neighbouring immovables; §§ 321 – 322) of the fourth book (on the use of real estate and buildings for residential and recreational purposes).

In the East German civil code there is the second book (on socialist ownership and personal ownership), as well as the regulation on personal ownership in the fourth book (on the use of real estate for residential and recreational purposes); the fourth chapter of the fourth book deals with the personal ownership of immovables and buildings.

As a result, in the East German civil code ownership and servitudes are set in the same (fourth) book.

844 The Polish civil code (1964) preserves the arrangement typical for the bourgeois civil codes. The second book on ownership and other *ius in re* includes four titles: ownership (the first title), perpetual usufruct (the second title), limited property rights (the third title) and possession (the fourth title). Servitudes are placed in the third subdivision (the second book on ownership and other *ius in re*, the third title: limited property rights).

In the current Russian civil code (1994 – 2006) the second book concerns the right of ownership and other rights of estate. There are: general provisions (the thirteenth chapter), the acquisition of the right of ownership (the fourteenth chapter), the cessation of the right of ownership (the fifteenth chapter), common property (the sixteenth chapter), the right of ownership and other real rights to land (the seventeenth chapter).

Servitudes are included in the seventeenth chapter (the right of ownership and other real rights to land), in Article 274 and the subsequent provisions.

b) Which institution should be settled first – servitudes or pledge? Situating servitudes first

The next problem is where to locate servitudes among limited property rights. Servitudes are most likely to be situated after ownership, before pledges (ownership – servitudes – pledges). In such a systematization, servitudes act as the rights coherent with ownership. This arrangement is visible in most of the jurisdictions analyzed in this study: France[845] (1804), Germany[846] (1896), Switzerland[847] (1907), Russia[848] (1905, 1994 – 2006), Hungary[849] (1928, 1959), Czechia[850] (1937, 2012),

---

845 In the CC (1804) servitudes are settled in the fourth title of the second book (concerning goods and different modifications of ownership). The second title (of the second book) regards ownership.

From the systematic point of view, servitudes are viewed as one of the possible ways of modifying ownership.

Pledges are arranged in the seventeenth title (of the third book on different ways of acquiring ownership). Mortgages come afterwards, in the eighteenth title.

846 In the German BGB (1896) servitudes are arranged in the fourth chapter (of the third book on *ius in re*), after ownership (the third chapter). The seventh chapter: mortgages, land charges and annuity charges are settled. The eighth chapter: right of pledge on movable things and on rights.

847 In the Swiss civil code (1907) servitudes are located after ownership (set in the fourth book on *ius in re*, in the eighteenth to the twentieth titles). Servitudes and realty charges: twenty-first title. The twenty-second title concerns pledges on immovables, and the twenty-third deals with pledges on movables.

848 In the Russian draft (1905) the sequence of institutions is: ownership – servitudes – pledges.

Ownership: second division (of the fourth book on *ius in re*). Servitudes: fourth division *(Rechte an fremden Sachen)*. Pledges and mortgages: fifth division.

In the current Russian civil code (1994 – 2006) servitudes are put in the second book (on the right of ownership and other rights of estate), in the seventeenth chapter (on the right of ownership and other real rights to land), in Article 274 and subsequent provisions.

Pledges are set in the third book (containing the general part of obligations), in the first subsection of the third book (general provisions on obligations), in the twenty-third chapter (providing for the discharge of obligations), in the third paragraph (§ 3), in Articles 334 – 358.

849 In the Hungarian draft (1928) the consecution is: ownership – servitudes – pledges.

Ownership: first title (of the second book on *ius in re*). The second title concerns limited property rights. Servitudes: the first and second chapters (of the second title). Pledges: the fifth, sixth and seventh chapters.

In the socialist Hungarian civil code (1959) servitudes are located in the third book (ownership), whereas pledges are in the fourth book (law of obligations).

Land servitudes can be found in the first title of the third book (the first title: general provisions on ownership), in the thirteenth chapter (rights of use), in §§ 166 – 170.

Pledges are positioned in the fourth book on obligations, in the twenty-third chapter concerning the accessory obligations securing a contract, in §§ 251 – 269.

850 In the Czechoslovak draft (1937) servitudes are situated in the twelfth section (the second book on property law, the first division [of the second book] regarding *ius in re*). Servitudes are put after ownership (from the sixth to the tenth sections) and before pledges (the thirteenth section).

In the Czech civil code (2012) ownership is set in the third chapter (of the third book considering absolute property rights, title II: *ius in re*). The fourth title: co-ownership. The fifth chapter: limited property rights. In the second subdivision (of the fifth chapter) servitudes are set, and in

Poland[851] (1937, 1964) and East Germany[852] (1975). This systematic pattern is visible in the codes based on *ius in re* (e.g. the German BGB – 1896), ownership (the French CC – 1804, the socialist Hungarian civil code – 1959, the East German civil code – 1975) or ownership and other *ius in re* (the Polish civil code – 1964; the Russian civil code 1994 – 2006).

c) Locating servitudes after pledges

Another option is to position servitudes after pledges[853] (Bavaria – 1756, Austria – 1811, Saxony – 1863, Hungary – 2013). This systematization is uncommon and typical of the first codifications, but later disappeared. In the twentieth and twenty-first centuries this arrangement appeared only once, in the current Hungarian civil code (2013).

This systematic pattern cannot be found in codes based on ownership. The order ownership – pledges – servitudes in a code based on ownership is unlikely to occur or to integrate well. Not being a neutral compound of the system, the main framework of ownership determines the systematization of pledges, positioning them outside the book on ownership. If ownership, a subjective legal category, de-

---

the third pledges.

[851] In the Polish draft on *ius in re* (1937) ownership is put in the second title. Servitudes: third title. Pledge rights: fifth title.

In the Polish civil code (1964) the first title (of the second book on ownership and other *ius in re*) considers ownership. Servitudes: third subdivision (of the third title: limited property rights). Pledges: fourth subdivision.

[852] In the East German civil code servitudes are placed in front of pledges. Both institutions are arranged in different books, but servitudes (the fourth book) are set in front of pledges (the seventh book).

Servitudes are designated as the rights of common use *(Mitbenutzungsrechte an Grundstücken)* and they are positioned at the end of the sixth chapter (relationships between the users of neigbouring immovables; §§ 321 – 322) of the fourth book (on the use of real estate and buildings for residential and recreational purposes).

Pledges and mortgages are arranged in the last, seventh, book (specific provisions of the respective relationships of private law), in the third chapter concerning securing claims.

[853] In the CMBC (1756) pledges: the sixth chapter of the second book (on *ius in re*). The seventh chapter: servitudes in general. The next, eighth, chapter concerns all further specific kinds of servitudes (*von Haus- und Feld-Dienstbarkeiten und anderen ähnlichen Gerechtigkeiten*. The ninth chapter: usufruct.

In the ABGB (1811) pledges: sixth chapter (the second book on *ius rerum*, the first division on *ius in re*). Servitudes: seventh chapter.

In the Saxon civil code (1863) pledges: third division (of the second book on *ius in re*). Realty charges: fourth division. Servitudes: fifth division.

In the Hungarian civil code (2013) the seventh title (the third division: limited property rights, the fifth book on *ius in re*) concerns liens, mortgages and other pledges. Servitudes are settled after pledges; the eighth title considers the rights of use, and the ninth title the rights of access and use for public purposes.

In the ninth title there are: easements (the thirty-third chapter) and use for public purposes (the thirty-fourth chapter).

signates the standards of the code, then the system would probably be overloaded, and the framework of the code could break down. If such a composition were to be applied, then both pledges and servitudes would be placed outside the book on ownership. Servitudes are always positioned in the same book as ownership. The most representative composition can be observed even in codes that modify the arrangement of *ius in re* the most significantly (East Germany[854] – 1975, Russia[855] 1994 – 2006).

d) Usufruct in the bourgeois civil codes

Usufruct is a personal servitude. A person who performs usufruct might use an object and collect fruits from it. A usufructuary is not allowed to change the substance of a thing on which he or she performs the right. In the codes analyzed

---

854 In East Germany (1975) the content of the general part is divided between the first book (the fundamental principles of socialist private law) and the seventh book (specific provisions of the respective relationships of private law), but the traditional sequence ownership – servitudes – pledges is retained.

Ownership is settled in the code twice; the most prominent occurrence in the divisions of the code is in the second book (on socialist ownership and personal ownership), but there is also a regulation on ownership in the fourth chapter (personal ownership of immovables and buildings) of the fourth book (use of real estate and buildings for residential and recreational purposes).

The East German civil code is deeply rooted in the Pandect model, approaching the most general issues first followed by more specific ones.

The second book, concerning socialist ownership and personal ownership, designates the direction of the code; that is its main task. For this reason, more precise regulations, necessary for socialist citizens, are placed in the fourth book (in the fourth chapter on the personal ownership of immovables and buildings).

Just as its name indicates (use of real estate and buildings for residential and recreational purposes), the fourth book is an area where socialist citizens can find all content concerning the use of immovables.

Situating the provisions on ownership in the fourth book ensures a greater balance in the system of the code.

In the East German civil code servitudes are designated as the rights of common use towards premises (*Mitbenutzungsrechte an Grundstücken*). They are positioned at the end of the sixth chapter (the relationships between the users of neighbouring immovables; §§ 321 – 322) of the fourth book (on the use of real estate and buildings for residential and recreational purposes).

Pledges and mortgages are positioned in the third chapter (securing claims) of the final, seventh, book (specific provisions of the respective relationships of private law).

The code furthest from all bourgeois civil codes in its systematization transforms the traditional systematic patterns in an interesting way.

855 In the current Russian civil code (1994 – 2006) servitudes are settled in the second book (on the right of ownership and the other rights of estate, in the seventeenth chapter (on the right of ownership and other real rights to land), in Article 274 and subsequent provisions.

Pledges are positioned in the third book (comprising the general part of obligations), in the first subsection of the third book (the general provisions on obligations), in the twenty-third chapter (providing for the discharge of obligations), in the third paragraph (§ 3), in Articles 334 – 358.

here, usufruct is mostly settled among servitudes[856], or it is a separate *ius in re* placed after servitudes[857].

In bourgeois civil codes usufruct may be placed before servitudes, but this is not a typical arrangement. It can be found only in the CC (1804) and in the current Hungarian civil code (2013). In the CC ownership was "taken" mildly and the charges on ownership are organized from the lightest to the heaviest[858]. Usufruct, the lightest possible charge, is situated directly after ownership. In the current Hungarian civil code (2013), just asin the socialist Hungarian civil code (1959), usufruct is placed before servitudes[859].

[856] This composition is the most common among the researched codes.

It is visible, e.g. in the ABGB (1811), where usufruct is placed among servitudes [the seventh chapter (the second book on *ius rerum*, the first division on *ius in re*)]. In the ABGB servitudes are arranged from § 472 to § 530. Usufruct is set from § 509 to § 520.

In the German BGB (1896) servitudes are arranged in the fourth chapter (of the third book on *ius in re*). The first title of the fourth chapter regards easements, and the second usufruct.

[857] In the CMBC (1756) usufruct is settled in the ninth chapter (of the second book on *ius in re*). The seventh chapter concerns servitudes in general. The eighth chapter comprises all specific kinds of servitudes *(von Haus- und Feld-Dienstbarkeiten und anderen ähnlichen Gerechtigkeiten)*.

[858] In the CC (1804) ownership: the second title (of the second book on goods and different modifications of ownership). Usufruct, use and habitation: third title. Servitudes and land services: fourth title. The fourth title is the last title of the second book.

The third book of the CC considers different ways of acquiring ownership. The first title of the third book includes the law of succession, the second title donations *inter vivos* and wills. Further, the regulations of the law of obligations come. All described aspects of the system can be viewed in terms of the acquisition of ownership.

Afterwards, there are institutions of *ius in re* which may result in the loss of ownership of an individual. Those are pledges (the seventeenth title of the third book) as well as privileges and mortgages (the eighteenth title). The nineteenth title regulates forcible ejection and the order among creditors.

In the last, twentieth, title prescription is situated. When the CC was adopted, systematizing usucaption and prescription together was common. If effective, usucaption results in the loss of ownership.

[859] In the current Hungarian civil code (2013) the eighth title (the fifth book on *ius in re*, the third title: limited property rights) considers the rights of use (usufruct). The ninth title regards the rights of access and use for public purposes. The first content visible in the ninth title are easements (servitudes), set in the thirty-third chapter.

This arrangement resembles the composition present in the socialist Hungarian civil code (1959), where land servitudes (§§ 166 – 170) are set after usufruct [lasting use of land] (§§ 157 – 165). Both institutions can be found in the third book on ownership, the first title: general provisions on ownership, the thirteenth chapter: rights of use.

e) Usufruct in socialist civil codes

Both usufruct and land servitudes are rarely present in socialist civil codes, but if they are included[860], then usufruct is placed before land servitudes[861]. In socialist legal systems usufruct is preferred to land servitudes. In bourgeois civil codes usufruct mainly serves the purpose of maintenance. Usufruct has become a crucial element of the socialist *ius in re*, fulfilling an important role in the productivity of the land[862]. If most land becomes the property of the state, then the state cannot itself use the land it owns. In a socialist state a usufructor may change the purpose of the used thing as well as violate its substance; without introducing modifications it would be almost impossible to generate production on the land[863].

---

[860] In both socialist Russian civil codes (1922, 1964) there is no regulation of usufruct.

Rights of use are mentioned in the systematization of the Czechoslovak (1964) and East German (1975) civil codes. In the Czechoslovak civil code that is the third book regarding the personal use of dwelling units, other living space, and tracts of land, whereas in the East German civil code this is the fourth book concerning the use of real estate and buildings for residential and recreational purposes.

The East German legislator broke with the capitalist terminology deriving from the German BGB. In the East German code only the term *Nutzung* (or *Nutzungsrechte*) is applied; the bourgeois construct of *Niessbrauch* has been rejected.

SOŚNIAK M., *Zasady kodeksu cywilnego Niemieckiej Republiki Demokratycznej* [Principles of the civil code of the German Democratic Republic], in: *Kodeks cywilny Niemieckiej Republiki Demokratycznej* [Civil code of the German Democratic Republic], Wrocław 1979, p. 20.

[861] In the socialist Hungarian civil code (1959) usufruct is arranged in front of land servitudes (the third book: right of ownership, the first title: general provisions on ownership, the thirteenth chapter: rights of use).Usufruct is situated in §§ 157 – 165 and land servitudes in §§ 166 – 171.

In the Polish civil code (1964) usufruct: second subdivision (of the third title on limited property rights; the third title is set in the second book on ownership and other *ius in re*). Servitudes: third subdivision.

[862] IGNATOWICZ J., *Obrót nieruchomościami miejskimi* [Municipal property trade], Zeszyty Problemowo-Analityczne [Problem-Centred and Analytical Bulletin] 1971, no. 21, p. 57.

[863] *Ibidem*, pp. 57 – 58.

The importance of usufruct is evident in the systematization of the Polish civil code[864] (1964), where usufruct is an independent *ius in re*, situated before land servitudes[865]. The shift in the sequence results from the fact that usufruct was favoured over servitudes[866]. Even though usufruct was central for Russian *ius in re*, it cannot be found in the Russian socialist civil codes (1922, 1964). In Russia the regulations regarding land were settled outside the civil code[867] and usufruct is not a part of *ius in re*, but of land law (*Bodenrecht*), settling the legal relationships applicable to land[868].

f) Arrangement of land servitudes in socialist civil codes

In socialist civil codes land servitudes are restricted – they cannot be found in Russia (1922, 1964) and Czechoslovakia (1950, 1964). Land servitudes have an important function in every legal system where there are many landowners[869]. In socialist legal systems land is one of the means of production, and it can be the sole property of the state; individuals are only allowed to own the means of consumption. In the conflict of values (protecting state ownership versus the rights of individuals) the state eliminates permanent charges on its property. Typically, servitudes can be found only in socialist civil codes that allow ownership of land by

864 In the Polish civil code (1964) usufruct comes in front of land servitudes. The third title (of the second book on ownership and other *ius in re*) comprises, in sequence: the general provisions (the first subdivision), usufruct (the second subdivision), servitudes (the third subdivision) and pledges (the fourth subdivision).

865 IGNATOWICZ J., *System Prawa Cywilnego. Prawo własności i inne prawa rzeczowe* [System of Private Law. The right of ownership and other *ius in re*], Wrocław/ Warszawa/ Kraków/ Gdańsk 1977, p. 635.

866 As, in socialism, land servitudes are considered to be connected mainly with individual ownership (which should eventually disappear as irrelevant in a socialist reality), then settling usufruct before land servitudes is a logical consequence in the shift of the system.
The mention of the relation of land servitudes with individual (private) ownership is here: WASILKOWSKI J., *Zarys prawa rzeczowego* [An introduction to *ius in re*], Warszawa 1963, p. 19.

867 IGNATOWICZ J., *System Prawa Cywilnego. Prawo własności i inne prawa rzeczowe* [System of Private Law. The right of ownership and other *ius in re*], Wrocław/ Warszawa/ Kraków/ Gdańsk 1977, pp. 636–637.

868 *Ibidem*, p. 636.

869 *Ibidem*, p. 678.

individuals[870] (Hungary – 1959, Poland – 1964). If land servitudes are contained in a socialist civil code, then they are placed after usufruct[871].

[870] Both the Hungarian (1959) and Polish (1964) civil codes approach individual ownership in their provisions.

In the socialist Hungarian civil code (1959) it is located in § 93.

According to first section of § 93, those means of production that the written law does not recognize as exclusive state ownership can belong to private ownership. The state defines the private ownership of small producers who fulfil a socially useful economic activity.

According to Article 130 of the Polish civil code (1964), lands, buildings and other means of production that are not exclusive to socialist ownership can, on the basis and with in the limits of statutes, be an object of the ownership of natural persons (individual ownership).

Article 131 states that when translating and applying the provisions of this code, the care of the Polish People's Republic towards the individual farms of labouring peasant farmers should be considered.

In the socialist Hungarian civil code (1959) land servitudes are settled in the third book on ownership, in §§ 166 – 170 (the first title of the third book concerns general provisions on ownership, and the thirteenth chapter addresses rights of use).

In the Polish civil code (1964) land servitudes are placed in the third subdivision (the third title on limited property rights, in the second book on ownership and other *ius in re*).

Land servitudes are perceived as "an inevitable correlate" of individual (private) ownership of land, which is especially crucial in rural relations.

WASILKOWSKI J.., *Zarys prawa rzeczowego* [An introduction to *ius in re*], Warszawa 1963, p. 19.

[871] In the socialist Hungarian civil code (1959) firstly usufruct [lasting use of land] is arranged (§§ 157 – 165) and then land servitudes (§§ 166 – 170). Both institutions are settled in the third book on ownership (the first title: general provisions on ownership, the thirteenth chapter: rights of using objects).

In the Polish civil code (1964) the second subdivision (the second book on ownership and other *ius in re*, the third title: limited property rights) concerns usufruct. The third subdivision includes servitudes.

g) Land servitudes in the East German civil code (1975)

Among the socialist civil codes, the most interesting systematization of land servitudes is found in the East German civil code (1975), where they are reformulated and designated as rights of common use (*Mitbenutzungsrechte an Grundstücken*). In East Germany, servitudes are viewed as one aspect of the legal relationship between the users of neighbouring immovables[872]. The presence of servitudes can be justified with a philosophy different to that found in other last socialist codifications (Russia – 1964, Czechoslovakia – 1964). Comprising bourgeois freedom of contract[873], the rephrased land servitudes are also included in the code.

h) Remarks on the specifics of the system of the East German civil code (1975), in relation to the composition of land servitudes

Having outlined land servitudes in the East German civil code, this section makes some remarks on the specifics of the codification. East German lawyers recognized the value of some bourgeois institutions and chose to include them in the code. More typically, such capitalist compounds are removed from socialist civil codes. In East Germany, for many years lawyers discussed and elaborated the system of socialist private law, resulting in the East German civil code (1975). The disadvantage of the East German code is its bizarre arrangement[874], alongside the considerable effort it made to negate its bourgeois model, the German BGB[875] (1896).

Among the last socialist codifications to have been devised, lawyers probably deliberated most extensively on the East German civil code. Thirty years passed between the implementation of socialism in East Germany and the introduction of the East German civil code (1975). The East German civil code admits personal ownership – individuals are allowed only to own the means of consumption, and owning the means of production (especially land) is forbidden to them. Subsequently, the current Russian civil code (1994 – 2006) was devised, incorporating

[872] That is the title of the last, sixth, chapter of the fourth book (on the use of real estate and buildings for residential and recreational purposes) of the East German civil code (1975), where servitudes are located, in § 321 and § 322.

[873] According to the second part of § 8 of the East German civil code (1975), with in the limits of this bill citizens are authorized to enter into any contracts which are supposed to satisfy their material and cultural needs.

[874] The East German civil code (1975) includes: fundamental principles of socialist private law – socialist ownership and personal ownership – contracts relating to material and cultural life – use of real estate for residential and recreational purposes – protection of life, health and property from damage – inheritance law – specific provisions of the respective relationships of private law.

[875] SOŚNIAK M., *Zasady kodeksu cywilnego Niemieckiej Republiki Demokratycznej* [Principles of the civil code of the German Democratic Republic], in: *Kodeks cywilny Niemieckiej Republiki Demokratycznej* [Civil code of the German Democratic Republic], Wrocław/ Warszawa/ Kraków/ Gdańsk 1979, p. 16.

both socialist and bourgeois features (but without a clear rationale). Like the East German civil code, it also contains servitudes, but they are not listed in the table of contents[876].

i) Conclusions

In bourgeois civil codes based on *ius in re* servitudes are always present, typically located after ownership and before pledges. The sequence ownership – pledges – servitudes can be found in older codifications. In socialist civil codes that solely allow personal ownership servitudes are eradicated (Russia, Czechoslovakia), but they could also be reformulated and included in a later socialist codification (East Germany – 1975). Interestingly, the central construct in the code (ownership of *ius in re*) is the secondary factor in the arrangement of servitudes. In all the codes researched for this study the regulation of servitudes can be found in the same book as ownership. In socialist civil codes, usufruct may be given a new function. Servitudes are one area that demonstrates the impact of socialist ideology on private law.

9. Realty charges

A realty charge is related to the repeated duty of benefit (*Leistung, prestation*) that every owner of a charged immovable must pay towards every owner of another immovable. Realty charges are not as significant in the system of *ius in re* as servitudes or pledges, but my analysis has revealed some interesting tendencies in their systematization. In the civil codes examined here, realty charges can be found almost exclusively in the codes based on *ius in re*[877]. The codes based

[876] In the current Russian civil code (1994 – 2006) servitudes are arranged in the second book (on the right of ownership and other rights of estate), in the seventeenth chapter concerning the right of ownership and other real rights to land (Article 274 and the subsequent provisions).

[877] In the Saxon civil code (1863) realty charges are included in the fourth division of the second book on *ius in re*.

In the German BGB (1896) the sixth chapter (of the third book on *ius in re*) comprises realty charges.

In the Russian draft (1905) the fourth book regards *ius in re*. The fourth division (of the fourth book) contains limited property rights *(Rechte an fremden Sachen)*. The last, fourth, line of the fourth division includes usufruct, servitudes and realty charges.

In the Swiss civil code (1907) the twenty-first title (of the fourth book on *ius in re*) concludes servitudes and realty charges.

In the Hungarian draft (1928) realty charges are arranged in the fourth chapter, of the second title on limited property rights, in the second book on *ius in re*.

In the Polish draft on *ius in re* (1937) the sixth title considers realty charges.

In the Polish decree on *ius in re* (1946) realty charges are positioned in the ninth title.

In the Czechoslovak draft (1937) realty charges are situated in the fourteenth section, of the first division (considering *ius in re)* of the second book on property law.

In the first socialist Czechoslovak civil code (1950) the ninth chapter (of the third book on *ius in re*) refers to realty charges.

In the Czech civil code (2012) realty charges (real burdens) are classified among servitudes.

on ownership (or ownership and other *ius in re*) do not contain realty charges; there is a single mention of realty charges among the final provisions (in § 495) of the second socialist Czechoslovak civil code, based on ownership[878]. Before the adoption of socialism, realty charges were introduced into all drafts in Central and Eastern Europe[879]. Realty charges are also included in the first socialist Czechoslovak civil code[880] (1950). Interestingly, the regulation of realty charges was present in Poland until the Polish civil code (1964) was adopted[881]. Among the post-socialist jurisdictions discussed in this study, currently they are present only in Czechia[882] (2012). The Czech attachment to realty charges, which are always present (1937, 1950, 1964, 2012), is surprising, but it seems to be a national characteristic.

Having listed the codifications where realty charges are present, it is now necessary to identify the systematic patterns we can observe across them. In the civil codes realty charges usually belong in a separate systematic category[883]. Another option is to settle realty charges in one section with servitudes[884] or to make them a systematic subset of servitudes[885]. Additionally, usufruct might also be situated among the provisions on realty charges[886]. One conclusion we can draw from the

---

Servitudes are situated in the second division [the third book: absolute property rights, title II: rights *in rem*, the fifth chapter: limited property rights (rights *in rem* in things of others)].

The second division (of the fifth chapter) comprises easements (servitudes). At the end of the second division, there is the seventh subdivision, comprising realty charges.

878 In the second socialist Czechoslovak civil code (1964) the second book concerns socialist collective ownership and personal ownership.

879 The Russian draft (1905), Hungarian draft (1928), Czechoslovak draft (1937) and Polish draft on *ius in re* (1937).

880 In the first socialist Czechoslovak civil code (1950) the ninth chapter (placed in the third book on *ius in re*) regards realty charges.

881 In the Polish decree on *ius in re* (1946) the ninth title deals with realty charges.

882 Realty charges cannot be found in the current Russian civil code (1994–2006), the current Hungarian civil code (2013), or the Polish civil code (1964).

883 The Saxon civil code (1863), the German BGB (1896), the Hungarian draft (1928), the Polish draft on *ius in re* (1937), the Czechoslovak draft (1937) and the first socialist Czechoslovak civil code (1950).

884 In the Swiss civil code (1907) the twenty-first title (the fourth book on *ius in re*) considers servitudes and realty charges.

A very similar composition is visible in the Russian draft (1905). There usufruct, servitudes and realty charges are included in one section [the fourth book on *ius in re*, the fourth division deeming the rights on the thing of another *(Rechte an fremden Sachen)*], the fourth line comprising usufruct, servitudes and realty charges).

885 In the Czech civil code (2012) realty charges (real burdens) are set among servitudes.

Servitudes are placed in the second division [the third book: absolute property rights, title II: rights *in* rem, the fifth chapter: limited property rights (rights *in rem* in things of others)].

The second division (of the fifth chapter) includes easements (servitudes). The seventh subdivision (put at the back of the second division on easements) contains realty charges.

886 In the first socialist Czechoslovak civil code (1950) the ninth chapter (the third book on *ius in re*) contains realty charges (Articles 166–187).

systematization of realty charges concerns their pronounced systematic relation with servitudes and usufruct.

Another tendency found in the codifications is that they apply a consecutive sequencing based on the charges of ownership. In this systematization, realty charges are positioned between servitudes and pledges. If, first, the lightest charges are located (servitudes), then the order of the institutions is: servitudes – realty charges – pledges[887]. If the heaviest charges come first (pledges), realty charges are placed after pledges and before servitudes[888] (pledges – realty charges – servitudes). In both systematic patterns (situating realty charges among servitudes, next to servitudes, or applying the sequence, servitudes – realty charges – pledges/pledges – realty charges – servitudes) the connection between realty charges and servitudes is visible. The final option in the systematization is to place realty charges at the end of limited property rights, after pledges[889].

10. Pledges

This section addresses the systematization of pledges from several angles. First, we consider the influence that the main construct (ownership or *ius in re*?) applied in the code exerts on their composition. Subsequently, this section addresses which institution should be positioned first – servitudes or pledges? As settling the system of the code on ownership results in situating pledges outside the book on ownership, this issue is described in the third point. The fourth point deals with

In the chapter there is a subsection, not extracted in the table of contents, comprising provisions on usufruct (Articles 172 and further provisions).

The systematization of this chapter is not very clear.

887 In the German BGB (1896) the consecution of the institutions is: servitudes – realty charges – pledges.

The fourth chapter (of the third book on *ius in re*) concerns servitudes. The fifth chapter: right of pre-emption. The sixth chapter: realty charges. The seventh chapter: mortgages, land charges and annuity charges. The eighth chapter: right of pledges on movable things and rights.

In the Hungarian draft (1928) the sequence is identical to the German BGB: servitudes – realty charges – pledges.

The second title (of the second book on *ius in re*) regards limited property rights. In the first two chapters of the second title servitudes are situated. The third chapter: construction (*Baurecht*). The fourth chapter: realty charges. Pledges are arranged in the fifth to the seventh chapters.

888 This arrangement is present in the Saxon civil code (1863).

The second book on *ius in re* comprises five divisions. They are, in order: possession – ownership – pledges – realty charges – servitudes.

889 In the Polish draft on *ius in re* (1937) the sixth title includes realty charges. Pledge rights (the fifth title) come before realty charges.

In the Czechoslovak draft (1937) realty charges are located in the fourteenth section (the second book on property law, the first division concerning *ius in re*), after pledge rights (the thirteenth section).

Both in the Polish and Czechoslovak drafts realty charges are the last limited property right in the sequence.

the systematic differentiations of pledges. Finally, this section presents its conclusions (the fifth point).

a) Impact of the main framework of *ius in re* on the arrangement of pledges

Apart from ownership, pledges are the only systematic compound of the system of *ius in re* that can be found almost everywhere[890]. The factor that impacts its arrangement most forcefully is the main framework of *ius in re*. In codes based on *ius in re*, pledges are situated in the book on *ius in re*[891]. If a code is settled around ownership, then pledges are located outside the book on ownership, constituting a static element in the system of the code[892] (*res*). In codes founded on ownership and other *iura in re* the systematization of pledges is determined by the choice of the legislator – if the code is more similar to codes based on *ius in re*, then pledges are placed among *ius in re*[893]. If the second book more closely resembles codes

---

[890] The only codification where the presence of pledges can be questioned is the second socialist Czechoslovak civil code (1964). Pledges are solely recalled in the last, eighth, book (containing the final provisions), in § 495.

In the general part (the fifth division on securing rights and duties) there is a subsection, mentioning the limitation of the transfer of an immovable (§§ 58 – 61).

[891] This arrangement is visible, e.g. in the Saxon civil code (1863) or in the German BGB (1896).

In the Saxon civil code (1863) the third division (in the second book on *ius in re*) concerns pledges.

In the German BGB (1896) the seventh chapter (of the third book on *ius in re*) regards mortgage, land charges and annuity charges. The eighth chapter includes the right of pledges on movable things and rights.

[892] In the CC (1804) pledges are set at the back of the third book (on different ways of acquiring ownership), in the seventeenth title. Mortgages are included in the eighteenth title.

In the CC ownership is set in the second title (of the second book on goods and different modifications on ownership).

In the socialist Hungarian civil code (1959) pledges are situated in the fourth book on obligations, in the twenty-third chapter referring to the accessory obligations securing a contract (§§ 251 – 269).

In the Hungarian code the third book deals with the right of ownership.

In the second socialist Russian civil code (1964) pledges are located in the third book on obligations, in the seventeenth chapter (security of performing obligations), in Articles 192 – 202.

In the Russian code the second book concerns ownership.

In the East German civil code (1975) pledges are settled in the last seventh book (specific provisions of the respective relationships of private law), in the third chapter (securing claims). The first subdivision of the third chapter contains pledges and third mortgages.

In the East German code the second book regards socialist ownership and personal ownership.

[893] In the Polish civil code (1964) the second book concerns ownership and other *ius in re*. The first title of the second book contains ownership, the second perpetual usufruct (law of construction), the third limited property rights, and the last, fourth, possession.

Even though the Polish civil code was impacted by socialism, its arrangement does not vary significantly from the divisions which can be found in the bourgeois civil codes. For this reason, just like other *ius in re*, pledges are set in the second book.

arranged around ownership, then pledges are situated outside the second book and transferred to the law of obligations[894].

b) What comes first – servitudes or pledges?

In the civil codes the most typical sequence is: ownership – servitudes – pledges. It is visible in: France[895] (1804), Germany[896] (1896), Switzerland[897] (1907), Czechia[898] (1937, 2012), Poland[899] (1937, 1964), Hungary[900] (1928, 1959) and Ru-

---

In the Polish civil code (1964) the last, fourth, subdivision (of the second book on ownership and other *ius in re*, the third title: limited property rights) comprises pledges.

894 In the current Russian civil code (1994 – 2006) the second book refers to the right of ownership and other rights of estate. At the beginning of the second book there is the thirteenth chapter, concerning the general provisions. The fourteenth chapter: the acquisition of the right of ownership. The fifteenth chapter: the cessation of the right of ownership. The sixteenth chapter: common property. The seventeenth chapter: the right of ownership and other real rights to land. The eighteenth chapter: the right of ownership and the other rights of estate to living quarters. The nineteenth chapter: the right of economic management and the right of operation management. The twentieth chapter: the protection of the right of ownership and of the other rights of estate.

The brief analysis of the divisions of the second book of the current Russian civil code shows that its composition is very different from the codes settled on *ius in re*.

Putting in the centre of its system ownership, it follows the systematization typical for the codes based on ownership, where pledges are transposed among the law of obligations.

In the current Russian civil code (1994 – 2006) pledges are set in the third book including the general part of obligations (the first subsection of the third book, comprising the general provisions on obligations), in the twenty-third chapter considering providing for the discharge of obligations, in the third paragraph (§ 3).

895 In the CC (1804) servitudes are arranged in the fourth title (of the second book on goods and different modifications of ownership).

Pledges: seventeenth title (of the third book on different ways of acquiring ownership). Mortgages: eighteenth title.

896 In the German BGB (1896) servitudes: fourth chapter (of the third book on *ius in re*). The seventh chapter: mortgages, land charges and annuity charges. The eighth chapter: rights of pledges on movables and on rights.

897 In the Swiss civil code (1907) servitudes: twenty-first title (the fourth book on *ius in re*, the second division: limited property rights) in the second division (limited property rights). Pledges: twenty-second and twenty-third titles.

898 In the Czechoslovak draft (1937) servitudes: twelfth section (of the first division on *ius in re*, placed in the second book on property lw). Pledges: thirteenth section.

In the Czech civil code (2012) servitudes: second division (the third book on absolute property rights, title II: *ius in re*, the fifth chapter: limited property rights). Pledges: third division.

899 In the Polish draft on *ius in re* (1937) servitudes: third title. Pledge rights: fifth title.

In the Polish civil code (1964) servitudes: third subdivison (the second book on ownership and other *ius in re*, the third title: limited property rights). Pledges: fourth subdivision.

900 In the Hungarian draft (1928) servitudes: first and second chapters (the second book on *ius in re*, the second title: limited property rights). Pledges cover the last three chapters of the second title (fifth, sixth and seventh).

In the socialist Hungarian civil code (1959) servitudes are settled in front of pledges.

ssia[901] (1905, 1994 – 2006). This arrangement is visible in codes based on *ius in re* (e.g. the German BGB – 1896), on ownership (the CC – 1804, the socialist Hungarian civil code – 1959, the East German civil code – 1975), and in the Polish civil code (1964), which is based on ownership and other *ius in re*. In the socialist civil codes founded on *ius in re* and that do not include servitudes, pledges are the final *ius in re*[902] (Russia – 1922, Czechoslovakia – 1950). As there are no servitudes, the only available order is ownership – pledges. The sequence of the compounds might also be: ownership – pledges – servitudes. This can be found in Bavaria[903] (1756), Austria[904] (1811), Saxony[905] (1863) and Hungary[906] (2013).

c) Place of pledges in the codes based on ownership

In codes based on ownership, the divisions are not aligned with the branches of private law (*ius in re*, obligations), but are adapted to the central construct of the code: ownership. Ownership is perceived in relation to the one to whom it be-

---

Land servitudes are located in the third book on ownership (the first title: general provisions on ownership, the thirteenth chapter: rights of use, §§ 166 – 170).

Pledges are situated in the fourth book on obligations, in the twenty-third chapter (accessory obligations securing a contract), in §§ 251 – 269.

901 In the Russian draft (1905) servitudes: fourth division (the fourth book on *ius in re*). Pledges and mortgages: fifth division.

In the current Russian civil code (1994 – 2006) servitudes come in front of pledges.

Servitudes can be found in the second book (the right of ownership and other rights of estate), in the seventeenth chapter (considering the right of ownership and other real rights to land), in Article 274 and the subsequent provisions.

Pledges are arranged in the third book containing the general part of obligations (the first subsection of the third book comprising the general provisions on obligations), in the twenty-third chapter considering providing for the discharge of obligations, in the third paragraph (§ 3).

902 In the first socialist Russian civil code (1922) ownership: first chapter (of the second book on *ius in re*). Pledges are put in the last, third, chapter of the second book.

In the first socialist Czechoslovak civil code (1950) pledges are positioned in the last, tenth, chapter of the second book on *ius in re*. That is the last systematic division included in the second book.

Ownership is placed in the seventh chapter.

903 In the CMBC (1756) pledge: the sixth chapter (of the second book on *ius in re*). The seventh chapter: servitudes in general. The eighth chapter comprises all further specific kinds of servitudes *(von Haus- und Feld-Dienstbarkeiten und anderen ähnlichen Gerechtigkeiten)*.

904 In the ABGB (1811) pledges: sixth chapter [the first division (on *ius in re*) of the second book on *ius rerum*]. Servitudes: seventh chapter.

905 In the Saxon civil code (1863) pledges: third division (of the second book on *ius in re*). Realty charges: fourth division. Servitudes: fifth division.

906 In the Hungarian civil code (2013) the second division (of the fifth book on *ius in re*) regards ownership. The third division comprises limited property rights.

At the beginning of limited property rights there is the seventh title concerning liens, mortgages and other pledges. The eighth title regards usufruct (rights of use). The ninth title concerns the rights of access and use for public purposes. At the opening of the ninth title the thirty-third chapter including easement (servitudes) comes.

longs. In the French CC that is the ownership of an individual[907], whereas the socialist civil codes pay the most attention to socialist ownership (ownership of the state). No matter what form of ownership is privileged in the code, the systematic outcome is the same. Such a composition results in the "flexure" of the system. Ownership is "heavier" than neutral *ius in re*. To maintain a balance, pledges are placed outside the book on ownership. If ownership is the main legal category designating the direction of the system of private law in a civil code, then only the content of *ius in re* (e.g. servitudes) ancillary to ownership can be arranged in the book on ownership. Pledges, being a form of securing claims, cannot be considered in these terms and must "move out" from the book on ownership. In the CC (1804), pledges are placed near the end of the third book (on different ways of acquiring ownership[908]). In socialist civil codes based on ownership the most typical solution is to arrange pledges in the general part of obligations[909] (Hungary – 1959; Russia – 1964, 1994 – 2006), where they are perceived as one way of securing obligations[910]. In socialist civil codes pledges can be situated in the general part, to locate them in the context of giving security[911] (Czechoslovakia – 1964,

[907] *Article 544 La propriété est le droit de jouir et disposer des choses de la manière la plus absolue, pourvu qu'on n'en fasse pas un usage prohibé par les lois ou par les réglemens.*

[908] In the CC (1804) pledges are located in the seventeenth title (of the third book on different ways of acquiring ownership). Mortgages: eighteenth title.

The second book refers to goods and different modifications of ownership. Ownership is included in the second title of the second book.

[909] In the socialist Hungarian civil code (1959) pledges are arranged in the twenty-third chapter (accessory obligations securing a contract) in the fourth book on obligations (§§ 251 – 269).

The third book regards the right of ownership.

In the second socialist Russian civil code (1964) pledges are established in the seventeenth chapter, concerning the securing of performance of obligations (Articles 192 – 202), in the third book on obligations.

The second book deals with ownership.

In the current Russian civil code (1994 – 2006) pledges are placed in the third book comprising the general part of obligations (the first subsection of the third book containing general provisions on obligations), in the twenty-third chapter (providing for the discharge of obligations), in the third paragraph (§ 3).

The second book of the current Russian code contains the right of ownership and the other rights of estate.

The systematization in the current Russian civil code (1994 – 2006) is very similar to the arrangement in the second socialist Russian civil code (1964).

[910] In the socialist Hungarian civil code (1959) pledges are put in the twenty-third chapter, on the accessory obligations securing a contract.

In the second socialist Russian civil code (1964) pledges are arranged in the seventeenth chapter, on the securing of performance of obligations.

In the current Russian civil code (1994 – 2006) pledges are set in the twenty-third chapter, comprising providing for the discharge of obligations.

[911] In the second socialist Czechoslovak civil code (1964) the fifth division of the general part regards giving security to rights and duties. In the fifth division there is a section referring to the restriction of the transmission of an immovable (§§ 58 – 61).

East Germany – 1975). In the civil codes provisions on pledges may be fragmented – the provisions on pledge and on a contract establishing pledge are arranged separately[912].

d) Systematic differentiations of pledge in the researched codes

Divisions in a code are mainly determined by the object of pledge, but that is not the only option; there are different possibilities for formulating a pledge[913]. If there are no such distinctions, then pledge is a uniform construct[914]. Another option is to separate pledge from mortgage[915]. Pledge may also be isolated into mortgage,

---

In the East German civil code (1975) the content of the general part is divided between the first book (including the fundamental principles of socialist private law) and the last, seventh, book (comprising the particular provisions on the respective relationships of private law).

The third chapter of the seventh book concerns securing claims. In the first subsection of the third chapter pledges are arranged, and in the third subsection mortgages. Between them, in the second section, guarantees are put.

[912] In the ABGB (1811) the sixth chapter (the second book on *ius rerum*, the first division on *ius in re*) concerns pledges. The contract of pledges is arranged in the third book comprising the institutions common to *personae* and *res*, in the first chapter on the security of rights and obligations (§§ 1368 – 1374).

In the first socialist Czechoslovak civil code (1950) the tenth chapter (in the third book on *ius in re*) considers the right of pledges and the law of retention. Concurrently, the regulation of the pledge agreement is visible in the fourteenth chapter (set in the fourth book on the law of obligations) referring to the securing of obligations, in Article 293.

[913] More in: IGNATOWICZ J., *System Prawa Cywilnego. Prawo własności i inne prawa rzeczowe* [System of Private Law. The right of ownership and other *ius in*], Wrocław/ Warszawa/ Kraków/ Gdańsk 1977, pp. 804 – 806.

[914] This systematization was introduced for the first time in the CMBC (1756), where the sixth chapter of the second book on *ius in re* regards pledge.

It is present also in the ABGB (1811), where all kinds of pledge are settled together in the sixth chapter of the first division (on *ius in re*) of the second book on *ius rerum.*

The mentioned arrangement is typical also for Russia (1922, 1964, 1994 – 2006). In all recalled codes there are no systematic differentiations of pledge. Additionally in those Russian codes there is a precept stating that pledge can be established on all goods.

In the code from 1922 that is Article 87. In the code from 1964 this is Article 194, and in the current code (1994 – 2006) Article 336.

The same composition is typical for Czechia. The most probably Czech systematization is the result of replicating the Austrian arrangement.

In the Czechoslovak draft (1937) pledge is included in the thirteenth section of the first division *(ius in re)* of the second book on property law. In the first provision of the thirteenth section (§ 325) it is stated that a pledge can be established for all things.

In the current Czech civil code from 2012 (the third book on the absolute property rights, title II: *ius in re*, the fifth chapter on the limited property rights, the third division: pledge) the first part of section 1310 states that any marketable thing can be pledged.

Pledge as a uniform construct is visible also in the Hungarian civil code (2013); in the division (the third division of the fifth book on *ius in re*) regarding limited property rights there is the seventh title on liens, mortgages and other pledges.

[915] In the CC (1804) the seventeenth title (of the third book on different ways of acquiring ownership) regards pledge. Mortgage is included in the eighteenth title of the third book.

pledge on movables and pledge on rights[916]. In addition to this differentiation, a distinction between pledge on immovables and on movables can be introduced[917].

e) Conclusions

Apart from ownership, pledge is the most widespread institution of *ius in re*, included in both bourgeois and socialist civil codes. The most typical sequence is ownership – servitudes – pledge, whereas the sequence of ownership – pledge – servitudes is rather rare. The central construct of the code (ownership or *ius in re*?) exerts the most pronounced effect on the arrangement of pledge; in codes based on ownership, pledge is placed outside the book on ownership.

III. Possession in the systematization of the civil codes

As it is the final systematic component of *ius in re*, possession is described after ownership and limited property rights. Possession can be set at the beginning of *ius in re* (before ownership), after ownership or at the end of *ius in re*. The first point in this section presents the location of possession as the first among *ius in re*. The second point addresses the arrangement whereby possession is a derivative of ownership. In the third point, we consider the location of possession at the end of *ius in re*. The systematization of possession in the CC (1804) is examined in the fourth point because it varies from that found in other codifications. The fifth point depicts the composition of possession in the socialist civil codes. Finally, this section draws conclusions from the preceding analysis.

In the Russian draft (1905) mortgage and pledge are distinguished in the table of contents (the fifth division of the fourth book on *ius in re*).

In the East German civil code (1975) pledge and mortgage are situated in the third chapter (securing claims) of the seventh book (particular provisions on the respective relationships of private law). Pledge is put in the first section (of the third chapter) and mortgage in the third section.

916 In the German BGB (1896) the eighth title of the third book on *ius in re* includes mortgage, land charge and annuity charge. The ninth chapter refers to right of pledge on movables and on rights.

In the Hungarian draft (1928) pledge is extracted into three systematic categories: mortgage, settled in the fifth chapter (of the second title of the second book on *ius in re*), pledge on movables (the sixth chapter) and pledge on claims and other rights (the seventh chapter).

In the Polish civil code (1964) mortgage is mentioned in the catalogue of the limited property rights included in Article 244, but it is set outside the civil code. Pledge is placed at the end of the limited property rights (the last fourth subdivision of the third title regarding limited property rights, in the second book on ownership and other *ius in re*).

The first chapter of the fourth subdivision: pledge on movables. The second chapter: pledge on rights.

917 In the Swiss civil code (1907) the twenty-second title of the fourth book on *ius in re* concerns the pledge on immovables (*du gage immobilier*), whereas the twenty-third title mentions the pledge on movables *(du gage mobilier)*.

1. Possession as the first among *ius in re*, settled before ownership

If possession is placed at the beginning of *ius in re*, then it is viewed as the most important among *ius in re*. This composition corresponds with its function in the system of *ius in re* – it protects all legal statuses that encompass *ius in re*. This arrangement is present in: Austria[918] (1811), Saxony[919] (1863), Germany[920] (1896), Czechia[921] (1937, 2012) and Hungary[922] (2013). In Czechia this arrangement results from the notable influence of Austrian concepts. The Saxon civil code was also inspired by the ABGB.

In Germany, this composition results from the introduction into legislation of the idea that what can be taken in hand should be placed at the opening of *ius in re*; it is connected with the actual power of a human over a corporeal object (*tatsächliche Gewalt*)[923]. In the German BGB (1896), possession is viewed as the most general among the content included in the third book on *ius in re*. At the same time, it should not surprise us that the BGB has such a systematization; the placement of possession before ownership had already been introduced in three written laws in German-speaking jurisdictions[924]. The systematic pattern discussed here cannot be found in the socialist civil codes; possession cannot precede ownership,

---

918 In the ABGB (1811) possession: first chapter of the first division (on *ius in re*) of the second book on *ius rerum*. Ownership: second chapter.

919 In the Saxon civil code (1863) possession of things: first division (of the second book on *ius in re*). Ownership: second division.

920 In the German BGB (1896) possession is arranged in the first chapter of the third book on *ius in re*. The second chapter: general provisions on rights in land. The third chapter: ownership.

921 In the Czechoslovak draft (1937) possession is put in the fifth section of the first division *(ius in re)* of the second book on property law *(droits patrimoniaux)*. The fifth section opens the first division regarding *ius in re*. The sixth section: ownership and its protection.

In the current Czech civil code (2012) possession is arranged in the second chapter (the third book on absolute property rights, title II: rights *in rem*, the second chapter: possession). Possession is placed between the general provisions (the first chapter) and ownership (the third chapter).

922 In the current Hungarian civil code (2013) the first division (of the fifth book on *ius in re*) considers possession.

In the structure of the fifth book on *ius in re* in the Hungarian code possession is underlined, by becoming one of the four compounds of the book on *ius in re*.

Those are: possession (the first division), ownership (the second division), limited property rights (the third division) and the real estate register (the fourth division).

923 ZOLL F., *Prawa rzeczowe na ziemiach polskich* [*Ius in re* on the Polish lands], Warszawa/Kraków 1920, p. 86.

BETTI E., *Le système du code civil allemand*, Milano 1965, p. 99.

924 In the Prussian *Landrecht* (1794) the seventh title (in the first part) includes detention and possession. Ownership comes in the eighth title.

In ABGB (1811) possession is set in the first chapter (the second book on *ius rerum*, the first division on *ius in re*). The second chapter concerns ownership.

In the Saxon civil code (1863) the first division (of the second book on *ius in re*) contains the possession of things. The second division comprises ownership.

because that would imply that in the hierarchy of *ius in re* possession overtakes ownership. The supremacy of (socialist) ownership is a central principle of socialist civil codes.

2. Possession as a derivative of ownership

Another option is to locate possession after ownership. Such a systematization results from the fact that it is treated as one of the rights of an owner (*ius possidendi*). This arrangement emphasizes the relation between ownership and possession. Possession can be located in a separate systematic unit after ownership[925] (Bavaria – 1756, Russia – 1905) or it might also be distributed among the precepts on ownership[926] (Hungary – 1928, Czechoslovakia – 1950). If possession is arranged in a separate section after ownership, then it is more significant than in an arrangement where it is only placed among the provisions on ownership. The second systematic pattern results in its disappearance from the table of contents. In the first socialist Czechoslovak civil code (1950) this systematization was very convenient for the socialist legislator – bourgeois possession was less evident in the code. Possession might also be mentioned only in the text of the code. This systematization is visible in Russia[927] (1922, 1994 – 2006).

3. Possession at the end of *ius in re*

The last option is to position possession at the end of *ius in re*. Possession may constitute the final systematic compound in the structure of *ius in re*[928] or it may

---

[925] In the CMBC (1756) possession is arranged in the fifth chapter (of the second book on *ius in re*). It is located right after the compounds relevant to ownership (the second chapter: ownership, the third chapter: different ways of acquiring ownership, the fourth chapter: prescription) and in front of limited property rights (the sixth chapter: pledges).

In the Russian draft (1905) possession is located in the third division (of the fourth book on *ius in re*), after ownership (the second division) and in front of limited property rights *(Rechte an fremden Sachen)*, located in the fourth division.

[926] In the Hungarian draft (1928) possession is mentioned in the table of contents, among the provisions of ownership (the first title of the second book on *ius in re*). There is no separate chapter approaching possession, but there are sections, e.g. the legal meaning of possession in general (§§ 443 – 447).

Possession is included in the first socialist Czechoslovak civil code (1950), but it is not extracted in the table of contents. It is set at the end of provisions relevant to ownership (Articles 100 – 154), in Articles 142 – 154.

The seventh chapter of the code (the first chapter in the third book on *ius in re*) regards ownership.

[927] In the first socialist Russian civil code (1922) possession is recalled in Articles 58, 59 and 62.

In the current Russian civil code (1994 – 2006) possession can be noticed in many provisions (e.g. in Article 209, Article 224 or Article 247).

[928] In the Polish draft on *ius in re* (1937) possession is included in the last, eighth, title, right after the real estate register (the seventh title).

In the Polish civil code (1964) possession is positioned in the last, fourth, title (of the second book on ownership and other *ius in re*). The third title refers to limited property rights.

be preceded by the real estate register[929]. There is a significant difference between both systematic patterns. If possession can be found at the end of *ius in re*, then it is strongly visible in the table of contents. Encompassing all *ius in re*, it implies its important systematic function, protecting all *ius in re*. If the real estate register comes after possession, then possession is not emphasized in the structure of *ius in re*; it is also not marginalized.

Underlining possession by placing it at the end of *ius in re* is a feature of the Polish systematization – the same composition is present in the Polish draft on *ius in re* (1937) and the Polish civil code (1964), which were both impacted by socialism. The socialist Hungarian civil code (1959) applied the same arrangement. Isolating possession in the structure of the socialist civil codes (Hungary – 1959, Poland – 1964) implies that those codifications are not fully socialist.

4. Bourgeois system that most marginalizes possession (France – 1804)

The location of possession in the CC differs from that in other codifications. It is placed in the second chapter of the twentieth title regarding prescription, at the end of the code in the third book (which concerns different ways of acquiring ownership). In the original version of the CC the twentieth title constitutes the final systematic division in the code. In the CC possession is one of the necessary conditions for obtaining the ownership of an object, based on usucaption[930]. When the CC was adopted, it was common to arrange prescription together with usucaption, but in other codes possession is viewed as an independent institution, not just as a state of fact, resulting in usucaption. The second book of the CC concerns goods

---

In the socialist Hungarian civil code (1959) possession is located in the last, third, title of the third book on ownership.

The first title: general provisions on ownership. The second title: respective provisions regarding socialist ownership.

929 In the Swiss civil code (1907) possession is the last *ius in re*, located in the twenty-fourth title of the fourth book on *ius in re*. It is settled after the pledge on movables (the twenty-third title). The last, twenty-fifth, title (of the fourth book) contains the regulation of the real estate register.

Here the arrangement of possession in the Swiss civil code (1907) is considered. The fourth book on *ius in re* of the Swiss civil code apart from titles also comprises divisions. The first division: ownership. The second division: limited property rights. The third division: possession and real estate register.

It seems to me that arranging together possession and real estate register in the same division is related to a need of settling together the remaining institutions of *ius in re*.

930 ZOLL F., *Prawa rzeczowe na ziemiach polskich* [*Ius in re* on the Polish lands], Warszawa/Kraków 1920, p. 83.

Provisions on usucaption are distributed between different places in the CC; possession is arranged in the second chapter (of the twentieth title on prescription), in Articles 2228 – 2235. The third chapter of the twentieth title considers the causes which prevent prescripton. Articles 2236 and further provisions also include content regarding possession.

Additionally, in the second book (on goods and different modifications of ownership) in the first title (on the distinction of goods), there is the last, third, chapter, concerning goods in relation to those who possess them *(des biens dans leur rapport avec ceux qui les possèdent)*.

and different modifications of ownership. Enabling the acquisition of ownership possession (by usucaption) does not fit this set of ideas. In the CC further *ius in re* are set at the end of the third book, on different ways of acquiring ownership. As with socialist codifications, in France ownership also erodes its rival. Regardless of whether we are dealing with a socialist or a bourgeois civil code founded on ownership, ownership acts similarly.

5. Possession in the systems of the socialist civil codes

As possession protects the rights of individuals, it does not cohere with socialism. As a result, it is not present in the last socialist codifications to have been devised (Russia – 1964, Czechoslovakia – 1964, East Germany – 1975). In the first socialist Russian civil code (1922) possession is only mentioned in the text of the code[931] (e.g. Article 58), whereas in the first socialist Czechoslovak civil code (1950) it is settled among precepts relevant to ownership[932]. In such a systematization possession is overlooked in the system of the code, but it can still be applied by the courts. The Russian (1922) and Czechoslovak (1950) codes are the first socialist civil codes. Even then it was clear that possession was an institution that was not welcome in the socialist reality. For this reason, it does not appear in the table of contents. Subsequently, possession disappears in the second socialist Russian civil code (1964), the second socialist Czechoslovak civil code (1964) and the East German civil code (1975).

The final systematic opportunity was applied in the Polish (1964) and Hungarian (1959) civil codes. Their philosophy differs from other socialist codifications: these two codes admit capitalist institutions, such as ownership of land by individuals. In both codes possession was explicitly isolated in the table of contents by its location at the end of *ius in re*[933]. In Hungary and Poland possession may act as the identifying mark of a bourgeois civil code in the socialist reality. Typically, the capitalist arrangement in which possession is placed before ownership wasnot possible during periods of socialism. Such a despised element of the system could not dethrone glorified (socialist) ownership.

---

[931] The same composition is visible in the current Russian civil code (1994 – 2006), where possession is solely recalled in the text of the code (e.g. in Article 209).

The current Russian civil code is composed of both socialist and bourgeois features.

[932] In the first socialist Czechoslovak civil code (1950) ownership is located in the first chapter (of the third book on *ius in re*) regarding ownership (Articles 100 – 154). Possession is arranged at the end of provisions on ownership (Articles 142 – 154).

Divisions in the table of contents of the Czechoslovak code expose only books and chapters. As a result, possession is not visible in the table of contents.

[933] In the socialist Hungarian civil code (1959) the last, third, title (of the third book on ownership) includes possession.

In the Polish civil code (1964) the last, fourth title (of the second book on ownership and other *ius in re*) considers possession.

6. Conclusions

Possession is a primary compound of *ius in re*. The analysis in this sections hows that it is usually placed at the opening of *ius in re*, directly after ownership (acting as *ius possidendi*) or after limited property rights. It is never settled among limited property rights. All codifications preserve the systematic differentiation between ownership, possession and limited property rights. In codifications impacted by a state ideology possession can be diminished in the structure of *ius in re* or even erased from the civil code. The bourgeois revolution is only able to diminish possession. That is the arrangement in the CC (1804); even if the central construct of ownership is not "happy" with possession, it must still be present in the code, because a system that protects the rights of individuals (and their ownership) cannot negate it. In socialism the approach was different; the system of private law, which promoted (state) ownership, erased the numerous institutions of *ius in re* connected to the use of land by individuals, among others, possession. The removal of possession from socialist civil codes was caused by two factors: both the main framework of ownership and socialist ideology.

H) Structure of *ius in re* in the socialist civil codes

This part of the chapter on *ius in re* examines further problems relating to the arrangement of *ius in re* in the socialist civil codes. First, it addresses whether a socialist civil code includes the systematic distinction between *ius in re* and the law of obligations. If the written laws contain the classification of *ius in re* and law of obligations, then the right of construction is included. The arrangement of the last socialist codifications is then discussed, followed by ownership pertaining to an individual in the socialist civil codes. Subsequently, this section considers what kind of ownership can be inherited in socialist civil codes, and, in due course, whether the division between relative and absolute property rights also applies to socialist civil codes. Finally, this section draws conclusions from this area of the analysis.

I. Does a socialist civil code contain a systematic division between *ius in re* and obligations?

Do socialist civil codes preserve the systematic distinction between *ius in re* and the law of obligations? First, this section describes the codifications where such an arrangement results from the fact of being the first socialist civil codes (Russia – 1922, Czechoslovakia – 1950). Both jurisdictions later adopted the definitive socialist codes (Russia – 1964, Czechoslovakia – 1964). We subsequently discuss civil codes in which the intention of the legislators was to implement socialism only partially (Hungary – 1959, Poland – 1964).

1. Yes, because there was no other option at this time (Russia – 1922, Czechoslovakia – 1950)

The first socialist civil codes (Russia – 1922, Czechoslovakia – 1950) maintain the *ius in re* and law of obligations classifications[934]. At that point, the most natural and obvious option was to base the system on *ius in re*. Both codifications are too short and their provisions are too general[935]. These characteristics allowed socialism to be introduced; the courts could interpret the provisions differently, according to need.

2. Yes, because that was the legislative choice (Hungary – 1959, Poland – 1964)

Among the later codifications, a systematic distinction of *ius in re* and the law of obligations is apparent in Hungary (1959) and Poland (1964). This arrangement is not necessarily manifest in their exterior divisions: the third book of the Hungarian code considers the right of ownership, whereas the second book of the Polish civil code refers to ownership and other *ius in re*. In both countries there was a preference for a more bourgeois arrangement, illustrated by the inclusion of possession, which was not embraced by socialism[936], and in the admittance of individual ownership[937] (individuals owning means of production, especially land).

There is a significant difference between the Hungarian civil code (1959) and the Polish civil code (1964). After removing some socialist provisions after the fall of the socialist system, the Polish civil code serves as a bourgeois civil code[938]. Socialism did not affect its spirit, and the entire content applicable to *ius in re* is arranged in a single book. The core of the socialist Hungarian civil code is shaped

---

934 In the first socialist Russian civil code (1922) the second book considers *ius in re*. The third book: law of obligations.

In the first socialist Czechoslovak civil code (1950) the third book refers to *ius in re*. The fourth boo k: law of obligations.

935 KNAPP V., *Les principes du nouveau droit civil*, Bulletin de Droit Tchécoslovaque 1951 no. 1 – 2, p. 9.

936 In the socialist Hungarian civil code (1959) the last third title (of the third book on ownership) deals with possession.

In the Polish civil code (1964) the fourth title (of the second book on ownership and other *ius in re*) concerns possession.

937 In the socialist Hungarian civil code (1959) this issue is mentioned in § 93, whereas in the Polish civil code (1964) it appears in Article 130.

938 When the Polish civil code (1964) entered in force, the most significant amount of socialist provisions were included in Articles 126 – 139 (the second book on ownership and other *ius in re*, the first title: ownership, the first division: general provisions).

Currently the most significant remnant of socialism in the Polish civil code is Article 140: Within the limits specified by statutes and the principles of community coexistence the owner may, to the exclusion of other persons, use the thing in conformity with the social and economic purpose of his right, in particular he may collect profits and other proceeds from the thing. He may dispose of the thing with in the same limits.

by socialism. The additional specifics of the codification that distinguish it from other codes require a separate reference[939].

II. If so, then the right of construction is included among limited property rights

Even though the right of construction is only a systematic detail, it is discussed separately here due to its significance to the systematization of *ius in re* in the socialist civil codes. Socialist codifications that preserve the division between the law of obligations and *ius in re* include the right of construction. In the Polish civil code (1964) it is designated as perpetual usufruct. Construction concerns the legal situation in which the owner of a construction and of land under construction are different persons. In the capitalist reality it only applies to the construction of a building on the land belonging to another person; its use is restricted to immovables with special purposes[940]. Construction is an institution of the Germanic law, breaking with the Roman *superficies solo cedit*. In Germany construction is designated as *Erbbaurecht* (hereditary building rights)[941]. For the use of land, a

---

[939] Two codes with a mixed systematization were mentioned – those are the Polish civil code (1964) and the current Russian civil code (1994 – 2006). The second book of the Polish civil code considers ownership and other *ius in re*, whereas the second book of the Russian code refers to the right of ownership and the other rights of estate.

The socialist Hungarian civil code (1959) also belongs to this group due to the peculiarity of its arrangement. The first title of the third book on ownership comprises the general provisions on ownership, the second title the special provisions concerning the socialist ownership and the last third title possession. The first title is neutral, the second title is socialist and the last third title is bourgeois. Underlining possession in the table of contents could be explained by the fact that possession is one of the rights of an owner *(ius possidendi)*.

[940] IGNATOWICZ J., *System Prawa Cywilnego. Prawo własności i inne prawa rzeczowe* [System of Private Law. The right of ownership and other *ius in re*], Wrocław/ Warszawa/ Kraków/ Gdańsk 1977, p. 546.

[941] More about *Erbbaurecht* in Germany here:

WIELING H.J., FINKENAUER T., *Sachenrecht*, Berlin 2020, pp. 488 – 490.

In the original version of the German BGB (1896) there was the regulation of *Erbbaurecht*. It was put in the fourth chapter of the third book on *ius in re*.

§ 1012 Ein Grundstück kann in der Weise belastet werden, daß demjenigen, zu dessen Gunsten die Belastung erfolgt, das veräußerliche und vererbliche Recht zusteht, auf oder unter der Oberfläche des Grundstücks ein Bauwerk zu haben (Erbbaurecht).

§ 1013 Das Erbbaurecht kann auf die Benutzung eines für das Bauwerk nicht erforderlichen Theiles des Grundstücks erstreckt werden, wenn sie für die Benutzung des Bauwerkes Vor theil bietet.

§ 1014 Die Beschränkung des Erbbaurechts auf einen Theil eines Gebäudes, insbesondere ein Stockwerk, ist unzulässig.

§ 1015 Die zur Bestellung des Erbbaurechts nach §. 873 erforderliche Einigung des Eigenthümers und des Erwerbers muß bei gleichzeitiger Anwesenheit beider Theile vor dem Grundbuchamt erklärt werden.

§ 1016 Das Erbbaurecht erlischt nicht dadurch, daß das Bauwerk untergeht.

§ 1017 Für das Erbbaurecht gelten die sich auf Grundstücke beziehenden Vorschriften.

beneficiary of the right of construction (owner of a building) pays a remuneration, usually in the form of rent. Construction lasts for a limited number of years; after the passage of a designated period of time it becomes connected to the ownership of land[942].

Having sketched the background of the institution, we now consider its arrangement in the socialist civil codes. In the codes examined here, we can observe the sequence: ownership – right of construction – other limited property rights[943]. This order is visible in all socialist codes that maintain the division be-

---

Die für den Erwerb des Eigenthums und die Ansprüche aus dem Eigenthume geltenden Vorschriften finden auf das Erbbaurecht entsprechende Anwendung.

Currently the regulation of Erbbaurecht can be found in the statute on hereditary building rights Erbbaurechtsgesetz vom 15. Januar 1919 (Reichs-Gesetzblatt, p. 72, p. 122), lastly modified on 1st October 2013, Bundesgesetzblatt 2013 I, p. 3719.

§ 1 (1) Ein Grundstück kann in der Weise belastet werden, daß demjenigen, zu dessen Gunsten die Belastung erfolgt, das veräußerliche und vererbliche Recht zusteht, auf oder unter der Oberfläche des Grundstücks ein Bauwerk zu haben (Erbbaurecht).

(2) Das Erbbaurecht kann auf einen für das Bauwerk nicht erforderlichen Teil des Grundstücks erstreckt werden, sofern das Bauwerk wirtschaftlich die Hauptsache bleibt.

(3) Die Beschränkung des Erbbaurechts auf einen Teil eines Gebäudes, insbesondere ein Stockwerk ist unzulässig.

(4) Das Erbbaurecht kann nicht durch auflösende Bedingungen beschränkt werden. Auf eine Vereinbarung, durch die sich der Erbbauberechtigte verpflichtet, beim Eintreten bestimmter Voraussetzungen das Erbbaurecht aufzugeben und seine Löschung im Grundbuch zu bewilligen, kann sich der Grundstückseigentümer nicht berufen.

942 The right of construction could last between 30 and 80 years. The right of construction was introduced before the Great War (in Małopolska/ Austria), during a period of high prices, to enable the less affluent to build small houses. The transmission of the ownership of a construction does not change the period during which the right was determined.

ZOLL F., *Prawo cywilne opracowane głównie na podstawie przepisów obowiązujących w Małopolsce. Tom II Prawa rzeczowe i prawa rzeczowym podobne* [Private law elaborated mainly on the basis of the provisions binding in Małopolska. Volume II *Ius in re* and rights similar to *ius in re*], Poznań 1931, pp. 105 – 106.

In the interwar Polish draft on *ius in re* (1937) the right of construction was modified and temporal ownership was introduced. During the period of transference of the ownership of a land unit, the state (fisc), the regional authority or a person of public law may stipulate that after a certain period of time (between 30 and 100 years) the land should revert to its original owner (Articles 99 and 100). The ownership of land is transferred, but only for a limited period of time. In this way the state could maintain control of certain key areas.

The function of temporal ownership is different from the right of construction; construction supports those who have no money and enables them to build their own house. Temporal ownership does not perform a social, but rather an economic function.

Temporal ownership was invented by Ihering. On the basis of temporal ownership, an owner receives a right which is limited only by time.

WINIARZ J., *Użytkowanie wieczyste* [Perpetual usufruct], Warszawa 1967, p. 78.

943 In the first socialist Russian civil code (1922) the right of construction is one of three *ius in re*. It is set in the second book on *ius in re*, in the second chapter. The first chapter: ownership. The third chapter: pledge.

In the first socialist Czechoslovak civil code (1950) construction is placed in the eighth chap-

tween *ius in re* and the law of obligations (Russia – 1922, Czechoslovakia – 1950, Hungary – 1959, Poland – 1964). Compared with other socialist civil codes, the right of construction is foregrounded in the Polish code[944] (1964).

III. Arrangement in the last socialist codifications

We now consider the later socialist codifications (Russia – 1964, Czechoslovakia – 1964, East Germany – 1975). Their common feature is the main framework of ownership[945], and that they only recognize personal ownership[946], according to which individuals may only own the means of consumption. Ownership is related to *res* (*ius in re*). Socialist ownership is the most sacred element in the secular socialist temple. For this reason, the systematic arrangement (of the second) book on ownership must be flawless from the ideological perspective. This area of the code must be purer than the law of obligations, a merely technical branch of private law. *Ius in re* is an area of private law that is the most altered by socialist lawmakers[947].

ter (of the third book on *ius in re*). The seventh chapter: ownership. The ninth chapter: realty charges. The tenth chapter: pledge and the law of retention.

In the socialist Hungarian civil code the right of construction [lasting use of land] (§§ 150 – 154) is arranged in the thirteenth chapter (rights of use), in the first title (general provisions on ownership) of the third book on ownership. Usufruct is situated in §§ 157 – 165 and land servitudes in §§ 166 – 170. Pledges are put in the fourth book on obligations, in the twenty-third chapter concerning accessory obligations securing a contract (§§ 251 – 269).

In the Polish civil code (1964) the right of construction (designated as the perpetual usufruct *[użytkowanie wieczyste]*) is arranged in the second title of the second book on ownership and other *ius in re*. It is positioned after ownership (the first title) and before limited property rights (the third title).

944 In the Polish civil code the second title (of the second book on ownership and other *ius in re*) concerns the perpetual usufruct (right of construction). It is positioned between ownership (the first title) and limited property rights (the third title). The systematization of the second book indicates that construction is not one of the limited property rights. Perpetual usufruct is not recalled in Article 244, in the catalogue of limited property rights.

IGNATOWICZ J., *Obrót nieruchomościami miejskimi* [Municipal property trade], Zeszyty Problemowo-Analityczne [Problem-Centred and Analytical Bulletin] 1971, no. 21, p. 36.

945 In the second socialist Russian civil code (1964) the second book concerns the right of ownership.

In the second socialist Czechoslovak civil code (1964) the second book deals with socialist collective ownership and personal ownership.

In the East German civil code (1975) the second book considers socialist ownership and personal ownership.

946 In the divisions of the mentioned codes only personal ownership is mentioned.

In the second socialist Russian civil code (1964) the eleventh chapter (in the second book on ownership) concerns personal ownership.

In the second socialist Czechoslovak civil code (1964) the second book refers to socialist collective ownership and personal ownership. The second division of the second book deals with personal ownership.

In the East German civil code (1975) the second book regards socialist ownership and personal ownership. The second chapter of the second book considers personal ownership.

947 Not only the arrangement of *ius in re* changes, but its content is also modified. The protection

Institutions that are problematic for socialist legislators can be removed from the code, and either transferred to the law of obligations or reformulated.

In the last socialist civil codes to be devised, a significant volume relevant to *ius in re* was arranged outside the civil code (Russia – 1964) or situated in a distinct book concerning the use of immovables (Czechoslovakia – 1964, East Germany – 1975). The same classification, i.e. the land law (*Bodenrecht*), is applied in the codes. As with the divisions of the Czechoslovak (1964) and East German civil codes (1975), there is only a reference to immovables[948], while movables are neglected. The systems of the last socialist civil codes are founded on two concepts: (socialist) ownership and land law.

1. Settling the majority of the content of *ius in re* outside the civil code (Russia – 1964)

In the second socialist Russian civil code (1964), the second book on ownership includes only the provisions relevant to ownership. The content applicable to *ius in re* and the use of real estate are settled outside the civil code, in separate legislation. In the system of the code considerable attention is paid to lease, a contractual way of using objects[949]. Placed among the law of obligations, pledge was denied the attribute of being an absolute property right[950].

---

granted to *ius in re* is very strong. It is necessary in capitalism, but in the socialist reality the viewpoint changes – the rights of individuals do not require this kind of security. In the last socialist codifications, (socialist) ownership becomes the only *ius in re* that deserves the absolute protection of *ius in re*. As a result, the legal category of *ius in re* can disappear from the code – this systematization is visible in the latest socialist codifications.

948 In the second socialist Czechoslovak civil code (1964) the third book deals with the personal use of dwelling units, other living space, and tracts of land.

In the East German civil code (1975) the fourth book considers the use of real estate and buildings for residential and recreational purposes.

949 The second socialist Russian civil code (1964) dedicates considerable attention to lease. The twenty-seventh chapter (the third book on obligations) considers the lease of property (Articles 275 – 294) and the twenty-eighth chapter regards the lease of housing (Articles 295 – 341). That constitutes over 60 provisions in a written law consisting of 569 Articles.

If *iura in re* are erased from the code, then other institutions regulating the use of objects receive more attention. The most important issue is that citizens need to be supplied with real estate by the state.

An interesting provision is Article 57 of the Principles of the Civil Legislation of the USSR: until the costless use of housing units is established, a tenant is duly obliged to pay rent.

950 *Братусъ С. Н.*, *Предмет и* система совецкого гражданского права, Москва 1963, p. 186.

BRATUS S. N., *Predmet i sistema sovetskogo grazhdanskogo prava*, Moskva 1963, p. 186. [BRATUS S. N., *Subject and system of the Soviet private law*, Moskva 1963, p. 186.]

NOWICKI I. B., ŁUNC Ł. A., *Ogólna nauka o zobowiązaniach* [The general science of the law of obligations], Warszawa 1954, p. 48 and the subsequent pages.

2. Extracting a distinct book relating to the use of immovables in the table of contents (Czechoslovakia – 1964, East Germany – 1975)

The second socialist Czechoslovak civil code (1964) and the East German civil code (1975) are systematized according to the needs of citizens. In Czechoslovakia the entire volume of *ius in re* is placed in one area of the code (in the second book, on socialist collective ownership and personal ownership, and in the third book, which concerns the personal use of dwelling units, other living spaces, and tracts of land), whereas in East Germany two books on *ius in re* are isolated in the third book, concerning contracts (the second book relates to socialist ownership and personal ownership, the third book covers contracts relating to material and cultural life, and the fourth book deals with the use of real estate and buildings for residential and recreational purposes).

In the Czechoslovak code the third book regulates the personal use of dwelling units, other living spaces, and tracts of land. As with other late socialist codifications, the rights of a citizen in relation to his or her assets were perceived mainly in terms of personal ownership. In Czechoslovakia, the lease of flats was rejected; contractual regulation, granting the citizens only the temporary use of immovables, was considered unnecessary[951].

In East Germany the fourth book (concerning the use of real estate for residential and recreational purposes) includes a catalogue of how a citizen may use (*Nutzung*) land and buildings[952]. Contrary to the Czechoslovak code, in the East German code also considers the needs of citizens regarding leisure. The fourth book also includes the regulation of personal ownership[953]. The fourth book of the East German civil code could be criticized for not regulating lease; had it done so, then the fourth book would comprise all institutions concerning the use of real estate by citizens[954]. The reason for such an arrangement concerns real estate, mentioned in the title of the fourth book. Real estate involves immovables, which are in the centre of the fourth book, as is also the case for the third book of the BGB (1896), which considers *ius in re*. Furthermore, the system privileges personal ownership and not lease[955]. In East Germany, immovables must be used in accordance with their purpose, which is designated by the statutes[956].

---

[951] RYBÁRIK K., *Le droit d'usage personnel d'habitations*, Bulletin de Droit Tchécoslovaque 1973 no. 1 – 2, pp. 242 – 245.

[952] LÜBCHEN G. A., *Die Stellung des Zivilgesetzbuchs in der einheitlichen sozialistischen Rechtsordnung der DDR*, Neue Justiz 1975 no. 16, p. 470.

[953] In the East German civil code (1975) the fourth chapter (of the fourth book concerning the use of the real estate for the residential and recreational purposes) considers personal ownership of immovables and buildings.

[954] WESTEN K. (ed.), *Das neue Zivilrecht der DDR nach dem Zivilgesetzbuch von 1975*, Berlin 1977, p. 24.

[955] *Ibidem*, p. 25.

[956] *§ 284 (2) Die Nutzung des Bodens durch Bürger hat so zu erfolgen, daß sie mit den gesell-*

IV. Explaining different kinds of ownership in the socialist civil codes

The next issue concerns different kinds of ownership in the socialist civil codes. In the bourgeois civil codes, private ownership is a uniform concept. We are free to own almost anything provided that it is not *res extra commercium*. In a socialist reality, the situation is different. Here, the terms used in the chapter are explained (socialist ownership, personal ownership, individual ownership). The distinction of the right of ownership in the socialist reality is conditioned by two factors: subject and object criteria. Subject involves asking, who is an owner? If socialist ownership is prioritized, then individual ownership is undermined. In socialism, citizens are expected to work, and in return for their work their material and cultural needs are met. The state provides them with what is necessary to live, i.e. the means of consumption, such as clothes, food or a housing unit. The definition of personal ownership, which can be found in the Principles of the Civil Legislation of the USSR, was a point of reference for other socialist jurisdictions[957]. An individual may not own the means of production (which are reserved for the socialist state), among which the most important is land. This viewpoint is validated in the last socialist civil codes (Russia – 1964, Czechoslovakia – 1964, East Germany – 1975).

The distinction between socialist (state) ownership and ownership by an individual is present in all socialist codifications. The first socialist Russian civil code (1922) uses only the term "private ownership" (*propriété privée*), but the code

schaftlichen Erfordernissen übereinstimmt. Sie umfaßt die Pflege und den Schutz des Bodens als wichtige Voraussetzung für die Gestaltung der sozialistischen Umwelt- und Lebensbedingungen der Bürger. Grundstücke und Gebäude sind zweckgebunden zu nutzen. Eine den gesellschaftlichen Erfordernissen widersprechende Bodennutzung ist unzulässig.

957 Article 25 of the Principles of the Civil Legislation of the USSR:

The personal ownership of citizens may constitute property intended to fulfill their material and cultural needs. An object constituting the personal ownership of all citizens may be income and savings from their work, a residential house (or part thereof), an auxiliary household, household and everyday items as well as items of personal need and convenience. The property constituting personal ownership cannot be used to obtain non-work income.

An object constituting the personal ownership of a citizen may be only one residential house. Cohabiting spouses and their minor children can have only one residential house, constituting the personal ownership of one of them or co-ownership. The acceptable sizes of a residential house, which may constitute the personal ownership of a citizen, as well the conditions and the mode of leasing premises in such a house are determined by the legislation of the union republics. (…)

states that individuals are not allowed to possess land or any significant means of production[958]. The bourgeois presumption of freedom of ownership (according to which an individual may own almost anything) was denied. The most crucial property is owned by the state. The first Russian civil code (1922) established the approach followed subsequent socialist legislators. The term "private ownership" was used in the code because there was as yet no clear differentiation between personal and individual ownership.

A general principle was later implemented. It encompassed both personal ownership (ownership of the means of consumption, and of objects necessary to daily use) and private (or individual) ownership. Individual ownership was openly allowed in Hungary[959] (1959) and Poland[960] (1964). If other kinds of ownership are identified (socialist ownership, personal ownership and private/individual ownership), then the sequence is: socialist ownership – personal ownership – individual ownership (Hungary – 1959). The ownership of the state is placed first, followed by the rights of individuals[961]. The Polish civil code (1964) includes, in order: socialist ownership, individual ownership and finally personal ownership[962]. This

---

[958] *Article 53 Le sol, le sous-sol, les forêts, les eaux, les chemins de fer d'utilité générale, leur matériel roulant et les appareils volants peuvent être exclusivement propriété de l'Etat.*

Article 54 Peuvent être objet de propriété privée: les bâtiments non municipalisés, les enterprises commerciales, les enterprises industrielles qui occupent des ouvriers salariés dont le nombre n'excède pas les chiffres prévus par les lois spéciales, les instruments et moyens de production, l'argent, les valeurs mobilières et autres objets de valeur y compris les monnaies d'or et d'argent et les devises étrangères, les objets d'utilité domestique ou mènagère ou à usage personnel, les marchandises dont la vente n'est pas interdite par la loi et tous les biens non exclus du commerce privé.

Article 55 Les enterprises où le nombre des ouvriers salariés dépasse celui qui est prévu par la loi, le télégraphe et le radiotélégraphe, et les autres installations qui intéressent l'Etat, ne peuvent être objet de propriété privée que sur la base des concessions obtenues du gouvernement.

Les codes de la Russie Soviétique. Tome 1 Code de la famille Code civil, Paris 1925, pp. 137 – 138.

[959] In the socialist Hungarian civil code (1959) the individual (private) ownership is mentioned in § 93. According to first section of § 93, means of production, which the written law does not recognize as the exclusive ownership of the state, can be the objects of private ownership. The state allows the private ownership of small producers, serving socially useful economic activity.

[960] According to Article 130 of the Polish civil code (1964), lands, buildings and other means of production, which do not constitute the exclusive object of the socialist ownership, can be, on the basis and with in the limits of statutes, an object of ownership of natural persons (individual ownership).

Article 131 states that when translating and applying the provisions of this code, the care of the Polish People's Republic towards the individual farms of the working peasant farmers should be considered.

[961] In the socialist Hungarian civil code (1959), there are in sequence: socialist ownership (§ 88), state ownership (§ 89), co-operative ownership (§ 90), ownership of associations (§ 91), personal ownership (§ 92) and private (individual) ownership (§ 93).

[962] In the Polish civil code (1964) there are: socialist ownership (Articles 126 – 129), individual

arrangement expresses the hostility of lawyers towards socialism. Individual ownership precedes personal ownership.

V. What kind of ownership can be inherited in the socialist civil codes?

In the last socialist codifications only personal ownership can be inherited; this form of succession was considered to be fully coherent with socialist ideology[963]. The seventh book of the second Czechoslovak civil code (1964) considers the inheritance of property constituting personal ownership. This solution derives from Soviet Russia, where only personal ownership could be an object of ownership[964]. If in Soviet Russia a family (spouses and their underage children) acquired, in accordance with the legal provisions, the right of personal ownership to more than one residential house, then they had to choose one of them. They were obliged to sell, donate or dispose of the other house (s) with in one year[965]. If individuals are allowed to own the means of production (land) in socialist civil codes, then the system should implement the socialist rule, according to which the land should be the property of those who work on it[966]. This approach is manifested in the Polish civil code (1964).

VI. Does the division between relative and absolute property rights also apply to the socialist civil codes?

We now examine the division between absolute and relative property rights in the socialist civil codes. In socialist codifications based on *ius in re* their composition enforces applying the security applicable to *ius in re* to the institutions placed in the book on *ius in re*[967] (Russia – 1922, Czechoslovakia – 1950). In the last socialist codifications socialist ownership is the only absolute property right and the

---

(private) ownership (Articles 130 – 131) and personal ownership (Articles 132 and the subsequent provisions).

963 WESTEN K. (ed.), *Das neue Zivilrecht der DDR nach dem Zivilgesetzbuch von 1975*, Berlin 1977, p. 274.

964 CHAŁFINA R. O., *Prawo dziedziczenia w ZSRR* [The law of inheritance in the USSR], Warszawa 1952, p. 5.

965 That is Article 107 of the second socialist Russian civil code (1964).

966 The Polish civil code (1964): Article 131 states that when translating and applying the provisions of this code, the care of the Polish People's Republic towards the individual farms of the working peasant farmers should be considered.

In the Polish civil code the last tenth title (of the fourth book on inheritance law) includes the particular provisions on the inheritance of the farms. The right of succession to a farm was given to members of the family who were working farmers (Articles 1059 – 1062). If none of them had such qualifications, then the farm became the property of the State Treasury (Article 1063).

967 NOWICKI I. B., ŁUNC Ł. A., *Ogólna nauka o zobowiązaniach* [The general science of the law of obligations], Warszawa 1954, p. 47 and the subsequent pages.

Firstly the authors state that the first socialist Russian civil code (1922) include the division on absolute property rights *(ius in re)* and the relative property rights (obligations).

category of *ius in re* disappears, resulting in the transformation of other rights in relation to objects into relative property rights. Nonetheless, in East Germany the concept of *ius in re* was still present in legal science[968]. In Poland, the exterior divisions indicate the relevance of *ius in re* – the second book of the Polish civil code refers to ownership and other *ius in re*. In the socialist Hungarian civil code (1959), the third book concerns the right of ownership as well as other rights dealt with in the third book (such as possession, servitudes or usufruct) that are given the security of *ius in re*[969]. Arranged in the fourth book on obligations, pledge loses the attribute of an absolute property right[970].

VII. Conclusions

The analysis in this section has demonstrated the most significant systematic patterns evident in the socialist civil codes. Introducing the right of construction among *ius in re* is the most popular systematization present in codes that retain a systematic division between *ius in re* and the law of obligations. In the last socialist codifications, the prevailing classification concerns the differentiation of legal relationships regarding the use of land. This area of law can either be placed in a distinct book of the code (Czechoslovakia – 1964, East Germany – 1975) or isolated from a civil code (Russia – 1964). The construction of land law omits movables.

Nonetheless, despite changes in the axiology of the system of *ius in re* in socialist legal systems, even if *ius in re* is not visible in the civil codes, it can be still found in the legal science. The most accurate statement would be that rights relating to objects were modified, and that the division on *ius in re* and the law of obligations has become blurred. For citizens of a socialist state, personal ownership (that is, the ownership of objects of daily use) was preferred. In Hungary and Poland the ownership of the means of production, such as land, was also admitted.

In the second book on *ius in re* there are three *ius in re*. Those are ownership (the first chapter), right of construction (the second chapter) and pledge of goods (the third chapter).

In the subsequent pages authors raise various arguments why the right of construction and pledge should not be classified among the absolute property rights.

KNAPP V., *Př edmet a systém československého socialistického práva občanského* [Subject and system of the Czechoslovak socialist private law], Praha 1959, p. 250.

968 WESTEN K. (ed.), *Das neue Zivilrecht der DDR nach dem Zivilgesetzbuch von 1975*, Berlin 1977, pp. 69 – 70.

969 CSANÁDI Gy., *Das Eigentumsrecht im ungarischen Zivilgesetzbuch*, in: EÖRSI G., *Das ungarische Zivilgesetzbuch in fünf Studien*, Budapest 1963, p. 181.

("The third part of the code [regarding ownership] does not cover all rights *in rem*, but only the rights of ownership and besides some rights of use of an absolute character".)

970 *Ibidem*, pp. 119 – 120.

I) Conclusions drawn from the analysis of the arrangement of *ius in re*

The analysis in this section has shown that the systematization of *ius in re* is a set of complex rules, replicated in different jurisdictions. The systematic patterns for arranging *ius in re* are much more rigid than those for organizing the law of obligations. That is a result of the inflexibility of *ius in re*. Just as the catalogue of *ius in re* is fixed in each codification, so the rules for establishing *ius in re* are rather stiff. The definition of a thing clearly demonstrates the most significant dissimilarities between the codifications.

The second problem described is the main framework of *ius in re*. Here, the analysis drew a clear conclusion, stating that *ius in re* is the most universal solution, present in all codifications – except those in which state ideology interferes. They include the French *Code civil* (1804) and the codifications shaped by socialism. Ownership impacts the arrangement of *ius in re*, being responsible for most of the aberrations in the composition of *ius in re* found in the majority of the codes researched for this study. What may be noticed in the socialist codifications is a "marriage" of two factors influencing the system of *ius in re*. These "spouses" are socialist ideology and the main framework of ownership. This mixture results in very unusual systematic patterns. Their influence is discussed in the ensuing sections of this chapter. After the fall of socialism in the jurisdictions analyzed here, the most usual solution saw a return to the traditional arrangement of *ius in re*.

Ownership, possession and limited property rights are systematic components in the systematization of *ius in re*. Their composition is a vital issue in the structure of *ius in re*, and the civil codes apply their systematic distinction. The most marked differentiation concerns the split between ownership and limited property rights. Constituting *ius possidendi*, possession may be arranged among the provisions of ownership. No further interpenetration between the systematic factors occurs besides. Ownership comes before limited property lights. Possession can never be settled between the limited property rights.

A significant problem in the arrangement of *ius in re* is cause and its connection with the transfer of ownership. This issue is discussed in the chapter on the law of obligations (section F, considering cause in the researched civil codes). Cause expresses the systematic distinction between the law of obligations and *ius in re* in the civil codes analyzed here. It is related to the land registry. The location of the land and mortgage register is an interesting aspect, which was not mentioned in this chapter due to the limitations of this study.

Chapter 4: Law of persons and family law

A) Introduction

Omne autem ius, quo utimur, vel ad personas pertinet, vel ad res vel ad actiones. All private law refers either to persons (*personae*), things (*res*) or actions (*actiones*). In the first book of the *Institutes*, Gaius concentrates only on a person as a subject of law. Provisions on the property of an individual (and matrimonial property law) are settled in the second book of the *Institutes*, among *res*. In this chapter, we consider the systematization of the law of persons and family law (*personae*) in the systems of the civil codes researched for this book. As the sequence of its chapters corresponds to that of the German *Bürgerliches Gesetzbuch*, the chapter on family law and law of persons (*personae*) is placed after *ius in re* and before succession law. It constitutes the fifth chapter of this study.

This section first analyzes the systematization of the law of persons and family law in the codes inspired by the Gaius model. An individual is at the centre of the codes impacted by the Gaius scheme. This arrangement precedes the Pandect model. Second, we consider composition in codes that include a general part. One of the problems investigated is which element prevails in the structure of the codes: *persona* or *res*. This issue lies at the centre of the analysis, and it is related to different ways of reinterpreting the Gaius scheme in the systematization of the civil codes.

Before pursuing further considerations, it needs to be stated that the content of family law does not remain without systematic connections to other branches of private law. When entering into a matrimonial property agreement, we also apply the provisions on the conclusion of contracts located in the general part, and then the further provisions on agreements, situated in the book on the law of obligations. In order to settle a legal case, it is frequently necessary to apply the provisions located in various books of a civil code. As a result, the functioning of the entire system of private law requires all provisions. If family law is arranged outside a civil code, then accordingly the provisions set into two written laws are used. Nonetheless, it cannot be isolated from the civil code effectively; the provisions of family law are central to the succession of property. We may dispose of our property in the event of death by a will, or the matter can be settled by the provisions of inheritance law. The application of family law regulations is indispensable in this context, because kinship is settled by the provisions of family law.

As a result, blood relations and inheritance cannot be detached from each other. For this reason, every change in the basic concepts of family law (e.g. marriage) immediately creates legal consequences in terms of inheritance law, irreversibly changing the line of succession.

The classification of family law varies from that of other fields distinguished in the Pandect systematization. The general part, *ius in re* and the law of obligations are first and foremost abstract areas of private law. Family law and inheritance law are connected with a particular subject, visible in private law and social issues[971]; these typologies are more comprehensible to a regular citizen who is not a lawyer. The divisions of family law and inheritance law vary from those found in other Pandect classifications, because both are connected to a distinctive feature; in the case of inheritance law, the death of an individual, and in family law, marriage and kinship[972]. It should be underlined that the relation of family law to private law is inevitable; German lawyers attempted to separate these two areas, but the attempt proved to be impossible[973]. After all, the status of family law is irreversibly linked to the protection of private interests[974].

One feature of family law is that it involves a closed catalogue of family relationships found among groups of people. German legal doctrine refers to this as a *numerus clausus*[975]. Individuals can only situate themselves in the family relationships determined by the statutes and they are not free to designate new ones. In this respect family law somewhat resembles *ius in re*, which are characterized by the closed catalogue of rights in relation to objects, and from which individuals may choose. A change in legal regulations in this respect results from redefining the relationships of family law, which is possible, but it is also equivalent to introducing alterations to the basic concepts of private law.

My research has revealed that family law is the area of private law that has undergone the most significant reforms. Family law relationships are evidently very different now from those belonging to the period in which the CMBC (1756) was adopted, or the Prussian *Landrecht* (1794). The same applies to the German BGB (1896), the fourth book of which, on family law, has witnessed the most significant alteration of all its books[976]. In France, family law has been a stable area

---

971 MUSCHELER K., *Familienrecht*, München 2017, p. 7.
Conf . KOCH E., *Einleitung I: Familienrecht im System des Zivilrechts*, in: SCHMOECKEL M. (ed.), *Historisch-kritischer Kommentar zum BGB. Band IV Familienrecht §§ 1297 – 1921*, Tübingen 2018, p. 2.

972 MEDICUS D., *Schuldrecht I. Allgemeiner Teil*, München 2006, p. 13.

973 KOCH E., *Einleitung I: Familienrecht im System des Zivilrechts*, in: SCHMOECKEL M. (ed.), *Historisch-kritischer Kommentar zum BGB. Band IV Familienrecht §§ 1297 – 1921*, Tübingen 2018, p. 1.

974 DETHLOFF N., *Familienrecht. Ein Studienbuch*, München 2018, p. 2.

975 MUSCHELER K., *Familienrecht*, München 2017, p. 81.

976 DETHLOFF N., *Familienrecht. Ein Studienbuch*, München 2018, p. 11.

for over a century and a half since the adoption of the CC[977] (1804). In the past few decades, French family law has been considerably modified, the legal area that has experienced the most significant changes since the French Revolution. By comparison, the Polish legal system is somewhat different; since the adoption of the Polish family and guardianship code of 1964, Polish family law has not particularly changed. During the interwar period in Poland, social discussion concerning family law blocked the adoption of a civil code, meaning that Polish society restrained amendments to family law regulations.

Family law is the field of private law that is most susceptible to ideological influence, much more demonstrably than other branches of private law. In Central and Eastern Europe, the impact of socialism on private law has been particularly evident;it is only one of numerous legislative ideologies capable of modifying our family relationships and pushing them in new directions. The reason behind this is the strong relationship between family law and ethical rules. To divorce or not to divorce? This is only one of many possible questions in this domain, and the reply it invites will be different, depending on the choices taken by a lawmaker. Inheritance law primarily addresses those who inherit the property of a deceased person. As with other branches of private law, it targets those who are engaged in a specific area due to the property they own or the contracts they enter into. Those affected by the precepts of family law are families and their members[978].

B) Arrangement of *personae* in codes based on the Gaius scheme

After this introduction, we must move to analyzing the systematization of family law and the law of persons in the codifications covered in this study. The civil codes founded on the Gaius model are: the CMBC (1756), the French *Code civil* (1804) and the ABGB (1811). Their first book contains the law of persons[979]. In codes following the Gaius model two patterns of arranging *personae* can be observed. The first option is to arrange all content relevant to the law of persons and family law in the first book. That occurs in the CMBC, where the *res* element (ma-

---

The extensive list of the reforms of family law implemented into the German BGB (1896) can be found here:

MUSCHELER K., *Familienrecht*, München 2017, pp. 31 – 35.

977 MALAURIE P., FULCHIRON H., *Droit de la famille*, Paris 2018, p. 59.

978 HAIBACH U., *Familienrecht in der Rechtssprache. Die historische Entwicklung zentraler Ausdrücke des geltenden Familienrechts*, Frankfurt am Main 1991, p. 11.

979 In the CMBC (1756) the books are: legal rules in general and law of persons – *ius in re* – inheritance law – law of obligations.

The French *Code civil* (1804) contains: persons – goods and different modifications of ownership – different ways of acquiring ownership.

In the ABGB (1811) the first book comprises the law of persons, the second book *ius rerum*, and the last, third, book includes the provisions common to personal rights and *ius in re*.

trimonial property law) is placed in the first book[980]. The second systematic option is to replicate the Gaian arrangement of *personae*. As a result, non-property regulations on persons are included in the first book, whereas matrimonial property law is settled outside the first book, among the provisions on the property of an individual (*res*). In the French and Austrian codes matrimonial property law is situated among the law of obligations[981], constituting the part of the law regarding property. In Austria, matrimonial property law is only one of the particular contracts, whereas in France it is placed between general and particular obligations[982].

In the French and Austrian civil codes, the stress on *persona* results from the relationship between an individual and the surrounding world in the structure of the codes. In both codifications this connection is understood differently: in the CC it involves exercising the right of ownership[983], whereas in the ABGB it concerns the contradiction between a human being (*persona*) and his or her surroundings (*res*)[984]. If *persona* is highlighted in the systematization of codes founded on the Gaius model, then matrimonial property law is transferred to the provisions of property law. The result of applying the arrangement of the *Institutes*

---

[980] In the CMBC (1756) in the sixth chapter (of the first book concerning the legal rules in general and law of persons) regarding marriage in § 13 a dowry is mentioned.

[981] In the French CC (1804) the matrimonial property law is settled at the beginning of particular contracts, before sales.

Matrimonial property law is located in the fifth title [including prenuptial agreements and matrimonial regimes] of the third book on different ways of acquiring ownership. It is set between the commitments formed without an agreement (the fourth title) and sales (the sixth title).

In the ABGB (1811) matrimonial property is placed among the particular obligations, in the twenty-eighth chapter [the second division comprising the personal rights (obligations) of the second book on *ius rerum*], referring to prenuptial agreements and the entitlement to a dowry. It is situated between the partnership agreement (the twenty-seventh chapter) and the random agreements (the twenty-ninth chapter).

[982] Even though that matrimonial property law is the part of family law, in the first codifications its relation to *res* was the most significant feature of its arrangement. That is the systematization which can be found in the CC (1804) and the ABGB (1811) until nowadays, but in the German BGB (1896) matrimonial property law was classified in the fourth book on family law.

MAETSCHKE M., *§§ 1363–1557. Eheliches Güterrecht (I) Einführung: Regelungsgegenstand, -probleme und Lösungswege*, in: SCHMOECKEL M. (ed.), *Historisch-kritischer Kommentar zum BGB. Band IV Familienrecht§§ 1297–1921*, Tübingen 2018, pp. 583–584.

[983] In the CC (1804) the first book includes persons, the second book goods and different modifications of ownership, whereas the last, third, book comprises different ways of acquiring ownership.

Ownership of an individual is recalled in the titles of two among the three books of the code.

[984] In the ABGB (1811) the first book regards the law of persons and the second book *ius rerum*. The last, third, book includes the provisions common to personal rights and *ius in re*.

According to § 285, in the legal understanding, everything that is different from a person and serves a human use is a thing.

The central construct of the second book is an object, understood very widely.

to the legislation is that the regulations of non-property law are placed in the first book, whereas the rest are settled among *res*[985].

C) Structure of family law in newer codes with the Gaius model

In newer codifications that follow the order of the *Institutes* and which not containing a general part, *personae* are placed at the beginning of the code. This arrangement is present in Switzerland[986] (1907) and Hungary[987] (1928, 1959, 2013). In this systematization *personae* prevail in the divisions of the code. The first part of the Gaius model is concerned with all that refers to persons. Just asin the CMBC (1756), matrimonial property law is always settled among *personae*[988]. This arrangement is different from the *Institutes* of Gaius, where matrimonial property law is located among *res* instead of *personae*. Law of persons and family law can be situated in one book (Hungary – 1928)[989] or two books (Switzerland – 1907)[990]. Additionally, legal persons can be placed at the beginning of the code in a separate book (Hungary – 2013)[991]. A code that replicates the Gaius model and which does not include a general part may adopt an arrangement typical of socialist civil codes. As a result, family law is systematized outside the civil

[985] In the CC (1804) that is in the third book (on the different ways of acquiring ownership), whereas in the ABGB (1811) it is in the second book on *ius rerum*.

[986] The Swiss civil code (1907) embraces: law of persons – family law – inheritance law – *ius in re*. Law of obligations is settled outside the civil code, in the Code of obligations (1911).

[987] The Hungarian draft (1928) includes: law of persons and family law – *ius in re* – law of obligations – law of succession.

The socialist Hungarian civil code (1959) comprises: introductory provisions – persons – right of ownership – law of obligations – inheritance law.

The current Hungarian civil code (2013) contains: introductory provisions – individual as subject of law – legal persons – family law – *ius in re* – law of obligations – succession law.

[988] Among the preceding codifications, this composition is present only in the CMBC (1756), whereas in the CC (1804) and in the ABGB (1811) matrimonial property law is settled outside the first book.

In the Swiss civil code (1907) the sixth title (set in the second book on family law) considers matrimonial property law.

In the Hungarian draft (1928) the first book contains the law of persons and family law. The second title of the first book comprises marriage law. The third chapter of the second title deals with matrimonial property law.

As the socialist Hungarian civil code (1959) does not include family law, the regulation of matrimonial property law is arranged outside the civil code.

In the current Hungarian civil code (2013) the sixth title (of the fourth book concerning family law) deals with the rights in property arising out of a matrimonial relationship.

[989] The first book of the Hungarian draft (1928) includes the law of persons and family law.

[990] In the Swiss civil code (1907) the first book regards the law of persons and the second book contains family law.

[991] The current Hungarian civil code (2013) comprises: introductory provisions – individual as subject of law – legal persons – family law – *ius in re* – law of obligations – law of succession.

code, whereas the law of persons remains at the opening of the code (Hungary – 1959)[992]. In such arrangements *personae* are suppressed in the code.

D) Arrangement of family law in civil codes with a general part

In codes containing a general part, the precepts of the law of persons and family law are redistributed and separated from each other. Being part of the Gaius model (*personae – res – actiones*), persons are placed at the beginning of the code. This arrangement is visible in all codifications with a general part, regardless of whether they are bourgeois or socialist[993]. These regulations are significant to the entirety of private law (such as legal capacity, name or personal rights). Family law, meanwhile, is set in a separate book[994]. This systematic pattern derives from

---

[992] The socialist Hungarian civil code (1959) contains: introductory provisions – persons – right of ownership – obligations – succession law.

Apart from extracting family law, the exterior divisions of the socialist Hungarian civil code (1959) were not significantly affected by socialism.

[993] In the Saxon civil code (1863) the second division of the general part regards persons.

In the German *Bürgerliches Gesetzbuch* (1896) the first chapter of the general part comprises persons.

This systematization is also visible in all Russian civil codes (1905, 1922, 1964, 1994 – 2006).

In the Russian draft (1905) the first division of the general part contains persons.

In the first socialist Russian civil code (1922) the second chapter of the general part is titled: subjects of rights (persons).

In the second Russian socialist civil code (1964) the second chapter of the general part deals with persons.

In the current Russian civil code (1994 – 2006) the second subsection of the general part considers persons.

The same arrangement is also visible in all Czech (oslovak) civil codes following the Pandect systematization (1950, 1964, 2012).

In the first socialist Czechoslovak civil code (1950) the first chapter of the general part encompasses persons.

In the second socialist Czechoslovak civil code (1964) the second division of the general part deals with the participants of private law relationships.

In the Czech civil code (2012) the second title (of the first book comprising the general provisions) includes persons.

The discussed composition is also present in the Polish civil code (1964) – the second title of the general part refers to persons.

In the East German civil code (1975) the second chapter of the first book (including the fundamental principles of socialist private law) considers the status of citizens in private law, whereas the third chapter deals with the status of enterprises in private law.

[994] In the Saxon civil code (1863) the fourth book discusses family law

In the German BGB (1896) the fourth book regards family law.

In the Russian draft (1905) the second book concerns family law.

In the Czech civil code (2012) the second book includes family law.

In the socialist civil codes family law is extracted from the civil code.

As a result, among codes including a general part (Russia – 1922, 1964, 1994 – 2006; Czechoslovakia – 1950, 1964; Poland – 1964; East Germany – 1975) there is no book on family law in the code.

the Prussian *Landrecht* (1794). The *Landrecht* consists of two parts. Law of persons is placed at the beginning of the code, constituting the first component of the Gaius scheme (in the first part), whereas family law is arranged at the beginning of the second part[995].

In the Pandect systematization, *persona* is minimized in the system of the code and *res* prevails[996]. In bourgeois civil codes there are two possibilities for arranging family law. It may be settled in the fourth book (after the general part, law of obligations and *ius in re*) and before the law of succession (the fifth book). However, this systematization results in the neglect of *personae* in the code. This composition is present in the Saxon civil code[997] (1863), the German *Bürgerliches Gesetzbuch*[998] (1896), and in the interwar Polish draft of the civil code[999].

The second systematic pattern responds to the demotion of *persona* in the Pandect systematization. Legislators might introduce the order of the *Institutes* into their civil codes by situating family law after the general part. As a result, the first two books become equivalent to *persona* in the structure of the code.

---

995 The first title of the first part of Prussian *Landrecht* refers to persons and their rights in general *(von Personen und deren Rechten überhaupt).*

Family law is placed in the second part of *Landrecht*. The first title of the second part considers marriage. The second title deals with the mutual rights and duties of parents and children. The third title presents the rights and duties of the remaining members of the family. The fourth title includes the common family rights in general.

After family law there are regulations concerning other relationships in society – the fifth title of the second part comprises the rights and obligations of the lordships and servants.

996 *Conf.* Muscheler K., *Familienrecht*, München 2017, pp. 4 – 5.

997 In the Saxon civil code (1863) the sequence of books is: general part – *ius in re* – law of claims – family law (including guardianship law) – succession law.

998 In the German BGB (1896) the books are: general part – law of obligations – *ius in re* – family law – inheritance law.

999 The discussed arrangement can be observed in Poland two times.

First, in the arrangement of the draft of the interwar Polish civil code proposed by Ludwik Domański. According to Domański, the first book should consider private law relationships in general. That is the general part. The second and third books would be *ius in re* and law of obligations – the legislator should decide which among them should be arranged first. The fourth book would include family law and the last, fifth, inheritance law.

Domański L, *O systemie przyszłego Kodeksu Cywilnego Polskiego* [About the future system of the Polish Civil Code], Dziennik Urzędowy Ministerstwa Sprawiedliwości [Official Gazette of the Polish Ministry of Justice], Year II (1921), DziałNieurzę dowy [Unofficial Part], no. 4 – 8, p. 173.

In the socialist civil codes family law is arranged outside the civil code, but in the draft from 1960 family law was (according to the authors, operationally) introduced into the draft.

The sequence of books was: general part – ownership and other *ius in re* – law of obligations – family law – inheritance law.

Projekt Kodeksu cywilnego Polskiej Rzeczypospolitej Ludowej [Draft of the civil code People's Republic of Poland], Warszawa 1960.

The systematization mentioned here is present in the Russian draft[1000] (1905), the current Czech civil code[1001] (2012), and in the first draft of the Polish civil code published after the Second World War[1002]. Nonetheless, in this arrangement the regulations of the law of persons and family law are still located in two distinct books of a civil code. In the Pandect model, family law was extracted from the law of persons as an independent branch of private law[1003].

E) Separating family law from socialist civil codes

In socialist civil codes, family law is removed from the civil code. This systematization may also be found in bourgeois civil codes, provided that there is a connection with socialism[1004]. This composition is evident both in socialist codifications that include a general part, and in those that replicate the systematization based on the *Institutes* (Hungary – 1959). The first family code was adopted in Russia in 1917. Subsequent Russian civil codes have not included family law (1922, 1964, 1994 – 2006). This arrangement was also replicated in other socialist civil codes[1005] (Czechoslovakia – 1950, 1964; Hungary – 1959; Poland – 1964; East Germany – 1975). The composition of the law of persons in the general part is not affected by socialism.

As the first code discussed here was devised in 1917, initially the distinction of family law in Russia was related to the urgent need to settle family and marriage relationships; this point was mentioned by Jan Wasilkowski during the work undertaken on the Polish civil code (1964). As pre-revolutionary legislation was repealed immediately after the Bolshevik revolution, it was vital to regulate marriage and family relationships immediately. A civil code was implemented in Ru-

---

1000 In the Russian draft (1905) the order of the books is: general part – family law – inheritance law – *ius in re* – law of obligations.

1001 In the Czech civil code (2012) the sequence is: general part – family law – absolute property rights (*ius in re* and succession law) – relative property rights (obligations).

The Czech systematization is an attempt at finding a compromise between the Pandect systematization (general part) and the Austrian legal tradition, connected with the Gaius scheme.

1002 The draft was published in parts in DPP in 1947 – 1949.

The proposed arrangement of the books was: general part – family law – law of obligations – *ius in re* – law of succession. Inheritance law is the only book of the draft which was not published.

1003 VON LEWINSKI K., *Deutschrechtliche Systembildung im 19. Jahrhundert*, Frankfurt am Main/ Berlin/ Bern/ Bruxelles/ New York/ Oxford/ Wien 2001, p. 30.

1004 The Polish civil code (1964) adopted in the times of socialism is still binding, whereas the current Russian civil code (1994 – 2006) has both bourgeois and socialist features.

1005 Extracting family law from a civil code resembles the exclusion of obligations in the separate Code of obligations (1911) outside the Swiss civil code (1907).

Yet there is also a difference – in Switzerland the Code of obligations is treated as the last and fifth book of the civil code, underlining its position of *actiones*. The glorification of family law is connected with its isolation from the socialist civil codes, but at the same time the significance of *personae* in the system of codes, inherently associated with family law, decreases.

ssia much later: the first socialist Russian civil code was produced in 1922. The commentator Jan Wasilkowski stated that the theory of the distinction of family law from private law had not yet been proved. It is difficult to distinguish family law from inheritance law, especially as in Poland testate succession seldom occurs, and intestate succession constitutes a rule. It is widely known that family law relationships are the foundation of intestate succession[1006].

Much later this systematic pattern was associated with socialist ideology, inspired by the ideas of Marx and Engels[1007]. As a result, in socialism attempts were made to remedy the defects of bourgeois family law[1008]. The socialist perspective

---

[1006] Protokół z posiedzenia Komisji Kodyfikacyjnej – Zespół Prawa Cywilnego w dniu 16 grudnia 1956 r. o godz. 16:00 (obecni: Jerzy Marowski, Jan Wasilkowski, Henryka Dawidowicz, Jan Gwiazdomorski, Jerzy Mayzel, Kazimierz Przybyłowski, Seweryn Szer, Jan Topiński, Aleksander Wolter, Witold Bendetson, del. Ministra Sprawiedliwości, przewodniczył: Jerzy Marowski, przewodniczący Wydziału Cywilnego, protokołowałJan Winiarz), K. Kod. 90/57-65/1/2, s. 4 (numer wydrukowany na maszynie do pisania). Protokół znajduje się w teczce archiwalnej: Ministerstwo Sprawiedliwości, Departament Ustawodawczy, Wydział Prawa Cywilnego. Komisja Kodyfikacyjna. Tom I: Sesje: 16.12.1956, 30-31.01.1957, 28-31.03.1957 (kart 274). Archiwum Akt Nowych, Ministerstwo Sprawiedliwości w Warszawie, Nr zespołu: 285. Zespół1 – Kodeks Cywilny [Protokoły posiedzeń, fragment Kodeksu Cywilnego – tytuł II, lista członków Zespołu Prawa Cywilnego Materialnego Komisji, Tom I.] 1956 – 1957. Sygn. 5401.

[Minutes of the meeting of the Codification Commission – Private Law Group on 16th December, 1956, at 16:00 (present: Jerzy Marowski, Jan Wasilkowski, Henryka Dawidowicz, Jan Gwiazdomorski, Jerzy Mayzel, Kazimierz Przybyłowski, Seweryn Szer, Jan Topiński, Aleksander Wolter, Witold Bendetson delegate of the Minister of Justice, presided by Jerzy Marowski, chairman of the Private Law Department, minutes taken by Jan Winiarz), K. Kod. 90/57-65/1/2, p. 4 (the page number is written on a typewriter). The protocol is in the archival file: Ministry of Justice, Legislative Department, Department of Private Law. Codification Committee: Volume I: Sessions: 16.12.1956, 30-31.01.1957, 28-31.03.1957 (274 cards). Archive of New Files, Ministry of Justice in Warsaw, number of the unit: 285. Workgroup 1 – Civil Code.
Minutes of meetings, fragment of the Civil Code - title II, list of members of the Substantive Private Law Commission, Volume I] 1956 – 1957. File number: 5401].

[1007] Marx and Engels have claimed that a capitalist family is based on assets and money.

ENGELS F., MARKS K., *Manifest komunistyczny* [The Communist Manifesto], Warszawa 1946, p. 57.

According to Marx and Engels, capitalism removed all sentimental elements from the bourgeois family.

Ibidem, p. 39.

[1008] Members of a socialist household should be connected to each other solely by love and affection. All bourgeois remnants should be removed from a socialist family.

"The task of Soviet legislation in the field of marriage and family is the active cooperation in the final purification of family law relationships from the influence of the material calculation, liquidation of the unequal situation of a woman in life, as well as creating a communist family, in which the deepest personal human affections will be satisfied".

Zasady ustawodawstwa ZSRR i republik związkowych. Kodeks małżeński i rodzinny RFSRR [The principles of the legislation of the USSR and the union republics. The marriage and family code of RSFSR], Wrocław/ Warszawa/ Kraków/Gdańsk 1972, p. 30.

also significantly impacted the content of the family codes[1009]. Socialist jurisprudence similarly devised several reasons for justifying the isolation of family law, and for legitimizing the state and its ideological choices[1010]. The stress placed on family law and attempts to isolate family law from private law resulted in weakening *personae* in codes that included a general part, whiles imultaneously strengthening *res*. Currently, outside Russia, the arrangement discussed here is present in Poland, because the Polish civil code (1964) emerged during a socialist era[1011]. In socialist Poland the isolation of family law met with strong resistance from lawyers; in one of the published drafts, family law was included in the arrangement of one of the books[1012]. Whatever the divisions of the code might be, in Poland family law is considered to be part of private law[1013]. Currently in Poland family

[1009] Apart from the impact on systematizations, socialism also introduced new rules into family law. A socialist marriage was a civil and not a religious one – in many socialist countries that was an innovation. Marriage could be terminated by divorce. Equality of spouses was an important principle of socialist law. Additionally, the possibilities of settling matrimonial property law by spouses were strongly restricted – prenuptial agreements modifying the legislative situation of the spouses differently from the statutes did not have legal force. Besides, natural children were aligned in rights with children born in marriage.

SZER S., *Nowe prawo rodzinne* [New family law], Warszawa 1950.

[1010] In socialist legal systems family law does not constitute a part of private law (*Zivilrecht*). The socialist justification had an ideological character: in socialist legal systems family law is not connected to property law (*droit patrimonial*).

LITYŃSKI A., *Prawo Rosji i ZSRR 1917 – 1991 czyli historia wszechzwiązkowego komunistycznego prawa (bolszewików). Krótki kurs* [The law of Russia and the Soviet Union 1917 – 1991, namely the history of the all-union communist law (bolshevik). A short introduction], Warszawa 2017, p. 284.

Another argument was based on the fact that one attribute of private law is the equivalency of benefits of the parties in a private law relationship. As that is not typical for family law, this proves that family law is characterized by a different method of regulation from that of private law.

Ibidem, p. 305.

More about the relationship of the civil code and private law to family law: PIĄTOWSKI S.J. (ed.), *System prawa rodzinnego i opiekuńczego* [The system of family and guardianship law], Wrocław/ Warszawa/ Kraków/Gdańsk/Łódż 1985, pp. 16 – 24.

[1011] In the newest Czech (2012) and Hungarian (2013) civil codes family law was reintroduced into the civil codes. In Czechia the second book comprises family law, and in Hungary that is the fourth book.

[1012] The books in the draft are: general part – ownership and other *ius in re* – law of obligations – family law – law of succession.

Projekt Kodeksu cywilnego Polskiej Rzeczypospolitej Ludowej [Draft of the civil code People's Republic of Poland], Warszawa 1960.

[1013] Currently in Poland, family law is treated as a branch of private law. The isolation of family law outside the civil code does not impact the divisions of the legal science of private law.

As a result, during work on a new Polish civil code originally undertaken by Zbigniew Radwański, it was clear that family law should be reintroduced into the civil code as one of its books.

RADWAŃSKI Z. (ed.), *Zielona Księga. Optymalna wizja Kodeksu cywilnego w Rze-*

law is located in the family and guardianship code, whereas the Polish civil code encompasses the majority of private law. In order to settle numerous legal cases of family law, it is necessary to apply the provisions placed in the family and guardianship code and in the civil code simultaneously, but that does not create significant difficulties from the practical point of view.

F) East Germany (1975)

In the East German civil code, the Pandect systematization was abandoned; the East German arrangement is also an alteration of the Pandect structure. As in all other socialist civil codes, family law is located in a separate code[1014]. Regulations of *personae* present in the general part were distributed between the first book[1015] (referring to the fundamental principles of socialist private law) and the seventh book[1016] (which includes the specific provisions of the respective relationships of private law). That which could be treated as the most general content in the code is placed in the first book (status of citizens and enterprises), whereas the further institutions (particular institutions) are arranged in the seventh book – these are incapacitation and death in absentia.

Personae constitute the most general content in the arrangement of the code. This remains the same as in the typical Pandect systematization. Contrary to the German *Bürgerliches Gesetzbuch* (1896), in the East German civil code more particular institutions of *personae* are transferred to the seventh book. Those among *personae* which are most coherent with the socialist vision of a civil code in East

---

czypospolitej Polskiej [Green book. The optimal vision of the civil code of the Republic of Poland], Warszawa 2006, pp. 32 – 33.

In interwar Poland family law was supposed to be one of the books of the code.

DOMAŃSKI L, *O systemie przyszłego Kodeksu Cywilnego Polskiego* [About the future system of the Polish Civil Code], Dziennik Urzędowy Ministerstwa Sprawiedliwości [Official Gazette of the Polish Ministry of Justice], Rok II (1921), DziałNieurzę dowy [Unofficial Part] no. 4 – 8, p. 173.

1014 The reforms of family law in East Germany after the implementation of socialism are described here:

HAFERKAMP H.-P., *Wege zur Rechtsgeschichte: Das BGB*, Köln/ Wien 2022, pp. 275 – 276.

1015 In the East German civil code (1975) the second chapter of the first book (including the fundamental principles of socialist private law) considers the status of citizens in private law, whereas the third chapter deals with the status of enterprises in private law. The fourth chapter determines the rules of cooperation of citizens and enterprises.

1016 In the East German civil code the fourth chapter of the seventh book (dealing with the specific provisions of the respective relationships of private law) refers to incapacitation, death in absentia, and announcements.

The first subdivision of the fourth chapter concludes incapacitation, the second death in absentia, and the last, third, subdivision considers announcements of the invalidity of a document.

Placing the provisions on the invalidity of a document together with incapacitation and death in absentia shows almost the randomness of the East German arrangement. It was not possible to elaborate further successfully the systematization of a civil code.

Germany are citizens, enterprises, their legal status, and the rules of their cooperation. That which did not fit in the seventh book was transposed to the equivalent of an "attic" at the end of the code, in its final book. As with all other socialist codifications and the German BGB, the East German civil code does not stress *persona* in its arrangement. In East Germany, the justification for the isolation of family law outside a civil code does not vary from that which can be found in other socialist legal systems[1017].

G) Arrangement of legal persons in the researched civil codes

Finally, we come to the composition of legal persons in the systems of the analyzed codes. In codes based on the Gaius model, legal persons can be located in the book on the law of persons[1018]. If the content of the code is distributed between more books and the code follows the Gaius scheme, then legal persons can be arranged in one of its books among *personae*, at the beginning of the code[1019]. By codes that follow the Gaius model, here we mean both the first generation of codes based on the Gaius scheme, and later codifications which replicated the arrangement founded on the *Institutes* and which did not include a general part (Switzerland – 1907; Hungary – 1928, 1959, 2013). In codes comprising a general part, the precepts relevant to legal persons are placed at the beginning of the general part, in the section on persons, after natural persons[1020]. In the socialist civil

---

[1017] WESTEN K., SCHLEIDER J., *Zivilrecht im Systemvergleich. Das Zivilrecht der Deutschen Demokratischen Republik und der Bundesrepublik Deutschland*, Berlin 1984, pp. 83 – 84. More about the systematization of family law in East Germany and in the BGB (1896): *Ibidem*, pp. 687 – 689.

[1018] In the ABGB (1811) legal persons are mentioned in the fourth subdivision of the first chapter (regarding rights relating to individual qualities and relationships) of the first book on personal rights, in §§ 26 – 27.

In the Swiss civil code (1907) the second title of the first book (including law of persons) refers to legal persons.

[1019] In the current Hungarian civil code (2013) content of private law is divided into more books: introductory provisions – man as a subject of law – legal persons – family law – *ius in re* – law of obligations – succession law.

[1020] This arrangement was first applied in the Saxon civil code (1863). The second division of the general part regards persons. The second subdivision of the second division refers to legal persons (§§ 52 – 57).

In the German BGB (1896) the second title (in the first chapter referring to persons) of the general part deals with legal persons.

In the Russian draft (1905) the first division of the general part concerns persons. The second subsection of the first division includes legal persons.

In the first socialist Russian civil code (1922) the second chapter of the general part concerns the subjects of rights (persons). There is no systematic distinction into natural and legal persons, but natural persons are settled first (Articles 4 – 12) and then legal persons (Articles 13 – 19).

In the second socialist Russian civil code (1964), in the general part the second chapter refers to persons. The first subdivision of the second chapter regards citizens, and the second legal persons.

codes, the section regarding socialist organizations may be identified in the table of contents of the first book[1021].

H) Conclusions

The analysis in this section has demonstrated that *personae* are settled in the opening of the code. This systematic pattern can be observed in the first generation of codes based on the Gaius scheme (the CMBC – 1756, the CC – 1804, the ABGB – 1811) and in later codes inspired by Gaius and which do not include a general part (Switzerland – 1907, Hungary – 1928, 1959, 2013). In the codes mentioned here, matrimonial property law can be classified among *personae* (e.g. the CMBC – 1756) or among *res*, constituting the part of the law that concerns the property of an individual (*res*). In later codifications, matrimonial property law is classified among family law. *Personae* are invariably visible in the openings of all codes, including those that contain a general part. This rule also applies to socialist codifications, which modify the traditional arrangement of private law in the civil codes the most significantly. The new attempt to systematize the general part in East Germany also involved the reformulation of *personae* according to socialist ideology[1022]. The codifications thatplaced the greatest stress on *personae* in their arrangement are those that do not comprise a general part. Including a civil code in a general part inevitably changes the centre of gravity of a written law, transferring it to *res*. In the German BGB (1896) they are *actiones* (obligations), settled in the second book; however, obligations are an aspect of private law that principally concerns the assets of an individual, and not a person. What is most crucial, from the perspective of *personae* in the civil codes, is whether they are located in

In the current Russian civil code (1994 – 2006) the second subsection of the general part refers to persons. First, citizens (natural persons) are arranged in the third chapter. The fourth chapter comprises legal entities.

In the first socialist Czechoslovak civil code (1950) the first chapter of the general part discusses persons. First, natural persons are set (Articles 4 – 17), and next legal persons (Articles 18 – 21).

In the current Czech civil code (2012) the second title of the general part is about persons. The first title contains: the general provisions (the first chapter), natural persons (the second chapter) and legal persons (the third chapter).

In the Polish civil code (1964) the second title of the general part considers persons. The first subsection of the second title pertains to natural persons, and the second legal persons.

[1021] In the second socialist Czechoslovak civil code (1964) the second division of the general part examines the participants of private law relationships. The first chapter of the second division analyzes citizens, and the second chapter socialist organizations.

In the East German civil code (1975) the second chapter of the first book mentions the status of citizens in private law, and the third chapter concerns the status of enterprises in private law.

[1022] In the East German civil code (1975) the first book (on the fundamental principles of the socialist private law) composes: the status of citizens in private law (the second chapter), the status of enterprises in private law (the third chapter) and the rules of cooperation of citizens and enterprises (the fourth chapter).

the most significant element in the systematization of civil codes or not – and the reply here may be solely yes or no; there is no place for an answer in-between.

Chapter 5: Inheritance law

In the final chapter of this study, we consider the composition of inheritance law in the civil codes. The issue of settling the transmission of the material goods of a particular person after his or her death has a strong link with *ius in re*. Succession law is usually placed in a separate book. From the point of view of arranging a code as a whole, it is merely a detail, transferred from place to place. In the codes analyzed here, the law of succession is either positioned in the middle of the code or at its end. In the *Institutes* of Gaius inheritance law is included in the second book (*res*), among the different ways of acquiring ownership. In legislative reinterpretations of the Gaius model succession law is classified among *res* or *actiones*. In the civil codes, different ways of acquiring inheritance may constitute the divisions of the book on the law of succession[1023].

Inheritance law is an area of private law that exhibits the most significant differences between different jurisdictions. For the authors of the German BGB (1896) establishing a system of inheritance was a challenge, because they had to find a compromise between numerous autonomous regional systems, of which there were over one hundred[1024]. As with family law, succession law varies from other branches of private law characterized by the Pandect German systematization. Contrary to the general part, *ius in re* and the law of obligations are not abstract legal classifications; instead they concern a social sphere area involving the death of an individual[1025]. The law of succession can also be defined as the impact of family law relationships on the property of an individual in the event of his or her death[1026]. Due to its significant connection with family law and *ius in re*, inheritance law has the closest systematic links with those areas of private law. Furthermore, if a civil code includes a general part, then in applying the provisions

---

[1023] In the Polish civil code (1964) the first title (of the fourth book including the succession law) includes the general provisions. The second title: statutory succession. The third title: disposition in case of death.

[1024] LOOSCHELDERS D., OLZEN D., *Erbrecht*, Berlin/ Boston 2017, p. 3.

[1025] KOCH E., *Einleitung I: Familienrecht im System des Zivilrechts*, in: SCHMOECKEL M. (ed.), *Historisch-kritischer Kommentar zum BGB. Band IV Familienrecht §§ 1297–1921*, Tübingen 2018, p. 2.

[1026] LEHMANN H., HÜBNER H., *Allgemeiner Teil des Bürgerlichen Gesetzbuches*, Berlin 1966, p. 30.

Conf. FLOSSMANN U., KALB H., NEUWIRTH K., *Österreichische Privatrechtgeschichte*, Wien 2014, p. 363.

of the book on inheritance law it may be also necessary to use the provisions of the general part, e.g. those concerning the declaration of will. If, accordingly, a codification does not contain a general part and those provisions are transferred to the book on obligations, then the book on inheritance law preserves the systematic relationships with the law of obligations.

The law of succession regulates the legal consequences of the death of a natural person. The death of an individual results in his or her loss of legal capacity, and for this reason another legal subject enters his or her place[1027]. Inheritance law only considers the consequences of death in relation to property law[1028]. Nonetheless, the death of an individual affects all areas of private law, and for this reason not all precepts concerning inheritance law are located in the corresponding book of the code; for instance, in the BGB § 727 regulates the legal consequences of the death of a partner in a partnership[1029]. This classification results from the subject matter, which is the partnership contract[1030]. Accordingly, in the fifth book on inheritance law the BGB also contains the provisions of public law, including the regulation of probate courts[1031].

Furthermore, it must be noted that inheritance law has a strong systematic connection with family law and *ius in re*[1032]; while applying the provisions of succession law it is necessary to address the regulations of family law and *ius in re*. Inheritance law is integrally related to the acquisition of the property of an individual after his or her death. Here, the influence of Gaius's concepts is also evident: one area of private law distinguished by the Pandect German systematization involves ways of acquiring ownership. The acquisition of ownership is a wide concept, applying both to acquisition among the living and in the case of death[1033].

After these introductory remarks, we move to examining inheritance law in the systematization of the civil codes. First, we analyze the arrangement of succession

---

[1027] BROX H., WALKER W.-D., *Erbrecht*, Köln 2007, p. 1.

[1028] *Ibidem*, p. 2.

[1029] *§ 727 Auflösung durch Tod eines Gesellschafters*

(1) Die Gesellschaft wird durch den Tod eines der Gesellschafter aufgelöst, sofern nicht aus dem Gesellschaftsvertrag sich ein anderes ergibt.

(2) Im Falle der Auflösung hat der Erbe des verstorbenen Gesellschafters den übrigen Gesellschaftern den Tod unverzüglich anzuzeigen und, wenn mit dem Aufschub Gefahr verbunden ist, die seinem Erblasser durch den Gesellschaftsvertrag übertragenen Geschäfte fortzuführen, bis die übrigen Gesellschafter in Gemeinschaft mit ihm anderweit Fürsorge treffen können. Die übrigen Gesellschafter sind in gleicher Weise zur einstweiligen Fortführung der ihnen übertragenen Geschäfte verpflichtet. Die Gesellschaft gilt insoweit als fortbestehend.

[1030] *Conf.* GURSKY K.-H., *Erbrecht*, Heidelberg 1988, p. 2.

[1031] BROX H., WALKER W.-D., *Erbrecht*, Köln 2007, p. 2.

[1032] MUSCHELER K., *Familienrecht*, München 2017, p. 6.

[1033] GRUBER M., KALSS S., MÜLLER K., SCHAUER M. (ed.), *Erbrecht und Vermögensnachfolge*, Wien 2010, p. 4.

law in the civil codes based on the Gaius model. Inheritance law can be contained in a separate book[1034] (the CMBC – 1756) or it might be one of the components assembled in the most extensive of the three books[1035] (the CC – 1804, the ABGB – 1811). In codes based on the Gaius model, succession law is placed between *ius in re* and law of obligations[1036], acting as a systematic bridge between both areas[1037]. In the French arrangement inheritance law is perceived as one of the cases of succession in private law. For this reason, the law of succession in France cannot be situated in a separate book; in the exterior divisions of the CC it is evident that inheritance and other cases of succession (e.g. donation or the transfer of a thing as the result of a sale) share common systematic aspects. Furthermore, in this composition the relation between inheritance law and family law is notable. Both branches of private law are closely connected to each other, and placing the content of private law close to each branch (the result of the lack of a strict division in the arrangement of the CC) enables systematic connections to be maintained between the law of succession and matrimonial property law; this systematization could be particularly useful in the case of the death of a spouse.

[1034] In the CMBC (1756) this is the third book regarding the law of succession.

[1035] In the French CC (1804) this is the third book, including different ways of acquiring ownership, and in the ABGB (1811) that is the second book on *ius rerum*.

[1036] In the CMBC (1756) inheritance law is included in the third book. The second book refers to *ius in re,* and the last, fourth, book comprises the law of obligations.

In the CC (1804) the law of succession is placed at the beginning of the third book (on different ways of acquiring ownership).

The second book comprises goods and different modifications of ownership. The first title of the third book (on different ways of acquiring ownership) considers successions. The second title includes donations *inter vivos* and wills. The third title of the third book refers to contracts and conventional obligations in general. That is the content applying to the general part of obligations.

In the ABGB (1811) inheritance law is located after *ius in re* [the first division (on *ius in re*) of the second book on *ius rerum*, from the eighth to the fifteenth chapters]. It is arranged before the law of obligations [the second book on *ius in re*, the second division containing the personal rights].

In Austria succession is treated as the last among *ius in re*. In front of it, in the seventh chapter, servitudes are situated. As inheritance law settles the legal consequences of the death of a particular person in relation to his property, then in the code it is classified among absolute property rights.

The Austrian arrangement had a significant impact on Czech systematization.

In the current Czech civil code (2012) the law of succession is arranged together with *ius in re* in the third book on absolute property rights. The third book contains three titles. The first title of the third book: general provisions. The second title: *ius in re*. The third title: succession law.

[1037] BECKER C., *Systembildung in Europas Kodifikationen*, in: ARMGARDT M., REPGEN T. (ed.), *Naturrecht in Antike und früher Neuzeit. Symposium aus Anlass des 75. Geburtstages von Klaus Luig*, Tübingen 2014, p. 47.

In all codes preceding the Pandect systematization there was a close relationship between inheritance law and the acquisition of ownership (*res*). That is the case both in the codes based on the Gaius model (the CMBC – 1756, the CC – 1804, the ABGB – 1811) and in the Prussian *Landrecht* (1794). All were inspired by the systematization of the *Institutes* of Gaius, where inheritance law is situated among *res*, designating different ways of acquiring ownership. Both in the CMBC and in the ABGB inheritance law is classified among *res*[1038]. Austrian legal science considers the law of succession to be an absolute property right[1039]; that is the reason for the systematization of inheritance law among *ius in re*. In the CC (1804) succession law is set among *actiones*, at the opening of the third book (*actiones*), concerning different ways of acquiring ownership. In the Prussian *Landrecht* (1794) succession law is viewed as a mode of acquiring ownership, including a specification that death must occur in order for the acquisition of ownership to take effect[1040].

The Pandect systematization began a new phase in the arrangement of succession law. Contrary to its systematic predecessors, in the Pandect model inheritance law is removed from other areas of private law[1041]. In order to improve the clarity of the code, it was isolated in a separate book. Previously, that was only the case in the CMBC (1756). From that point onward, on inheritance law was arranged in a distinct book of the code[1042]. In later codes there are two main options for systematizing inheritance law. Either it can be arranged in the middle of the code, constituting a part of *res*, or it can be situated at the end of the code or close to its end.

If the Gaius scheme is adopted in the divisions of the code, inheritance law may be classified among *res*. This structure is visible both in codes that contain a general part (Russia – 1905, Czechia – 2012) and those which do not (Switzerland – 1907). In the Swiss civil code (1907) inheritance law is located in the third

---

1038 In the CMBC (1756) the second book (on *ius in re)* and third book (concerning inheritance law) constitute together *res*.

In the ABGB (1811) the law of succession is arranged in the first division (comprising *ius in re*) of the second book (on *ius rerum*), from the eighth to the fifteenth chapters.

1039 *Conf.* FLOSSMANN U., KALB H., NEUWIRTH K., *Österreichische Privatrechtgeschichte*, Wien 2014, p. 364.

1040 In the Prussian *Landrecht* (1794) the twelfth title (of the first part) includes titles of acquiring ownership arising from dispositions in the case of death.

1041 VON LEWINSKI K., *Deutschrechtliche Systembildung im 19. Jahrhundert*, Frankfurt am Main/ Berlin/ Bern/ Bruxelles/ New York/ Oxford/ Wien 2001, p. 30.

1042 This rule was broken only in Czechia (2012), due to the strong attachment to the Austrian civil code. Yet contrary to the Austrian systematization, the law of succession and *ius in re* are systematically separated from each other.

In the Czech civil code (2012), at the beginning of the third book (on absolute property rights), there is the first title, comprising the general provisions. The second title of the third book deals with *ius in re,* and the third with inheritance law.

book, after *personae* and before *ius in re*[1043]. Together with *ius in re*, succession law concerns *res*. In codes that contain a general part and which follow the sequence of the *Institutes* of Gaius (Russia – 1905, Czechia – 2012) the law of succession (with *ius in re*) is settled among *res*[1044]. In Czechia this shape is related to the influence of the Austrian model (1811), which follows the systematization of the *Institutes*.

Inheritance law can also be arranged at the end of the code, in the final book. This systematization was first implemented for in Saxony[1045] (1863) and then in Germany[1046] (1896). The German arrangement was adopted in many codes. In codes that adopt the Pandect systematization, inheritance law is often positioned at the end (or close to the end) of the written law. As succession law is connected with the death of an individual, it is settled at the end of the code. In the same way, prescription is situated at the end of the general part. Furthermore, inheritance law is more rarely used than other books included in the civil codes. These arguments justify this arrangement, which is now the most usual composition.

In socialist civil codes succession law is placed in the final book or close to the end of the code. In the socialist civil codes comprising a general part the sequence is: general part – *ius in re* / ownership – obligations – inheritance law[1047]

[1043] In the Swiss civil code (1907) the first two books contain *personae* – the first book considers the law of persons and the second book family law. The third book regards inheritance law and the fourth book *ius in re*. Those two books constitute *res*. Obligations *(actiones)* are put in the separate Code of obligations (1911).

[1044] The Russian draft (1905) consists of five books: general part – family law – inheritance law – *ius in re* – law of obligations.

The general part and family law comprise *personae*, the law of succession and *ius in re res*, and the law of obligations *actiones*.

The Czech civil code (2012) includes: general part – family law – absolute property rights – relative property rights (obligations).

In the opening of the third book (on absolute property rights) there is the first title, including the general provisions. The second title of the third book deals with *ius in re*, and the third title inheritance law.

The first two books examine *personae*. In the third book on absolute property rights *(res)* *ius in re* and law of succession are settled together. The last, fourth, book is an equivalent of *actiones*.

[1045] In the Saxon civil code (1863) the order of books is: general part – *ius in re* – law of claims – family law (including guardianship law) – inheritance law.

[1046] In the German BGB (1896) the sequence is: general part – law of obligations – *ius in re* – family law – succession law.

[1047] The first socialist Russian civil code (1922) has: general part – *ius in re* – law of obligations – succession law.

The first socialist Czechoslovak civil code (1950) contains: introductory provisions – general part – *ius in re* – law of obligations – inheritance law.

The Polish civil code (1964), impacted by socialism, includes: general part – ownership and other *ius in re* – obligations – law of succession.

The sequence in the second socialist Russian civil code from 1964 is: general principles –

(Russia – 1922, 1964, 1994 – 2006; Czechoslovakia – 1950, 1964; Poland – 1964). If a code includes a general part, then supplementary books can be added to it. Such a systematization has been applied in Russia (1964, 1994 – 2006). The law of succession can be placed before the accessory books[1048] or among the additional content placed in the code[1049]. In the Czechoslovak civil code (1964) inheritance law is located in the seventh book, prior only to the final provisions[1050]. In the East German civil code (1975) succession is situated in the sixth book, immediately before the final, seventh, book, a systematic equivalent of the general part[1051]. Interestingly, even in the socialist civil codes that modify their arrangement the most significantly (Czechoslovakia – 1964, East Germany – 1975), the systematization of inheritance law is almost identical to that found in bourgeois civil codes.

Finally, we address the place of succession law in Hungary. In Hungary there is no general part, and inheritance law is located in the final book. The sequence of the systematic components is: law of persons and family law (*personae*) – *ius in re* (*res*) – obligations and inheritance law (*actiones*). The Gaius scheme is introduced in the exterior divisions of the code, but in Hungary the composition typical of codes that contain a general part was also introduced. In codes that replicate the Gaius scheme, inheritance law is usually settled in the middle of the code, among *res*. After the German and Swiss civil codes were adopted, obligations became widely recognized as *actiones*. In Hungary, obligations and inheritance law always

---

ownership – law of obligations – copyright law – right of discovery – patent law – *succession law* – international private law.

The current Russian civil code (1994 – 2006) comprises: general provisions – right of ownership and other rights to estates – general part of obligations – particular kinds of obligations – *inheritance law* – international private law – rights to the results of intellectual activities and means of individualisation.

[1048] The current Russian civil code (1994 – 2006) includes: general provisions – right of ownership and other rights to estates – general part of obligations – particular kinds of obligations – *inheritance law* – international private law – rights to the results of intellectual activities and means of individualisation.

[1049] The second socialist Russian civil code (1964) contains: general principles – ownership – law of obligations – copyright law – right of discovery – patent law – *succession law* – international private law.

[1050] The composition in the second socialist Czechoslovak civil code (1964) is: general provisions (the first book) – socialist collective ownership and personal ownership (the second book) – personal use of flats, other units and land (the third book) – services (the fourth book) – rights and duties from other juridical acts (the fifth book) – responsibility for damage and unjust enrichment (the sixth book) – inheritance of property constituting personal ownership (the seventh book) – final provisions (the eighth book).

[1051] The order of the books in the East German civil code (1975) is: fundamental principles of socialist private law (the first book) – socialist ownership and personal ownership (the second book) – contracts relating to material and cultural life (the third book) – use of real estate for residential and recreational purposes (the fourth book) – protection of life, health and property from damage (the fifth book) – inheritance law (the sixth book) – specific provisions of the respective relationships of private law (the seventh book).

together constitute *actiones*, and inheritance law is always situated in the final book, preceded by the law of obligations[1052].

This analysis has shown that in the codes only two ways of systematizing inheritance law can be found. Its composition is either connected to the fact that it is part of *res* (private law regarding property), or it is placed at the end of the code. These systematic patterns can be found both in the codes based on the Gaius scheme or in those containing a general part. Attempts to establish socialist systematizations did not exert an impact on the place of the law of succession in the structure of the civil codes. Despite strong systematic links with *ius in re* (inheritance law may be reduced to a means of acquiring ownership in the case of the death of an individual), the law of succession is now a distinct branch of private law, arranged in a separate book of a civil code. However, given familiarity with how the systematization of the civil codes has evolved, it does not come as a surprise that formerly inheritance law was not considered a separate area of private law. It was the elaboration of the Pandect modelthat changed the systematic perception of succession law. From that point onward, the division of private law in a civil code into five books in a civil code has become standard. They are: the general part, the law of obligations, *ius in re*, family law and inheritance law. State ideology never influences the composition of inheritance law; the systematizations in the CC (1804) and in the socialist civil codes are no different to those of other codifications.

[1052] The Hungarian draft (1928) includes: law of persons and family law – *ius in re* – law of obligations – law of succession.

In the socialist Hungarian civil code (1959) there are: introductory provisions – persons – right of ownership – law of obligations – inheritance law.

Socialism did not affect the arrangement of inheritance law in the socialist Hungarian civil code (1959).

The current Hungarian civil code (2013) comprises: introductory provisions – individual as subject of law – legal persons – family law – *ius in re* – law of obligations – law of succession.

Conclusions from the study

This study shows that there are two main ways of arranging the civil codes: the Gaius model (*personae – res – actiones*), visible in the first codifications, and the Pandect systematization, elaborated by German professors of law in the 19th century. The Pandect classifications signify the divisions with in the branches of private law: general part, law of obligations, *ius in re*, family law and succession law. This categorization now provides the foundation for structuring all civil codes, regardless of whether they contain a general part or not. Civil codes that follow the sequence based on the *Institutes* are also influenced by the Pandect classifications (Switzerland and Hungary). In other jurisdictions (Germany, Russia, Czechia and Poland) a general part was incorporated into the written laws.

The introduction of socialism in private law could have affected the structure of the socialist civil codes. The main framework of ownership is the most visible sign of the influence of socialism. Socialist civil codes tend to favour the Pandect model with a general part. The impact of socialism is most notable in the area of *ius in re*, and it is insignificant in the law of obligations. In the second socialist Czechoslovak civil code (1964) and in the East German civil code (1975) a new socialist systematization was elaborated; these attempts primarily come at the expense of *ius in re* (East Germany) or the law of obligations (Czechoslovakia). In both jurisdictions, after the fall of socialism there was a return to the traditional concepts of private law.

Among the law of obligations the most important rule is the division between the general part of obligations and the particular obligations. The arrangement of the law of obligations is flexible, contrary to *ius in re*, which are regulated by a set of rigid rules. The systematization of the general part varies the least among the civil codes researched for this study. Apart from in the first codifications, family law and inheritance law are always situated in distinct books of the codes. In the socialist civil codes, family law is arranged in a separate family code.

Index of abbreviations

ABGB	Allgemeines bürgerliches Gesetzbuch
BGB	Bürgerliches Gesetzbuch
CC	Code civil
CMBC	Codex Maximilianeus Bavaricus Civilis
DPP	Demokratyczny Przegląd Prawniczy (Democratic Law Journal)
ed.	editor
e.g.	for example
i.a.	among other things
i.e.	that is
n°	number
no.	number
nos.	numéros
p.	page
pp.	pages
TPP	Transformacje Prawa Prywatnego (Transformations of Private Law)
vol.	volume

Bibliography

A) Publications in Latin letters:

1. ANGELESCO Alexandre C., *La technique législative en matière de codification civile. Étude de droit comparé*, Paris 1930
2. BAGIŃSKA Ewa, *Prawo umów konsumenckich w strukturze kodeksu cywilnego* [The shape of consumer contract law in the future civil code], TPP 2017 no. 2, pp. 5 – 21
3. BARTHOLOMEYCZIK Horst, SCHLÜTER Wilfried, *Erbrecht*, München 1975
4. BAZOVSKÝ Jean, *La codification du droit civil en Tchéco-Slovaquie*, Paris 1927
5. BECKER Christoph, *Dekalog. Podwaliny wolności* [Decalogue. The foundations of freedom], Kraków 2006
6. BECKER Christoph, *Die „res" bei Gaius – Vorstufe einer Systembildung in der Kodifikation. Zum Begriff des Gegenstandes im Zivilrecht*, Köln/ Berlin/ Bonn/ München 1999
7. BECKER Christoph, *Die Zehn Gebote. Verfassung der Freiheit*, Augsburg 2004
8. BECKER Christoph, *Persönlichkeitsrecht in der Systematik der Zivilgesetzbücher*, in: KUBIS Sebastian, PEIFER Karl-Nikolaus, RAUE Benjamin, STIEPER Malte (ed.), in: *Ius Vivum: Kunst - Internationales - Persönlichkeit. Festschrift für Haimo Schack zum 70. Geburtstag*, Tübingen 2022, pp. 925 – 938
9. BECKER Christoph, *Systematische Anlage von Zivilgesetzbüchern*, in: *Krakauer-Augsburger Rechtsstudien. Normschaffung*, HELLWEGE Phillip, SCHMIDT Reiner, SONIEWIECKA Marta, STELMACH Jerzy (ed.), Warszawa2017, pp. 13 – 38
10. BECKER Christoph, *Systembildung in Europas Kodifikationen*, in: *Naturrecht in Antike und früher Neuzeit. Symposium aus Anlass des 75. Geburstages von Klaus Luig*, ARMGARDT Matthias, REPGEN Tilman (ed.), Tübingen 2014, pp. 17 – 59
11. BECKER Christoph, *Verkauf und Übereignung der Ware bei Anton Friedrich Justus Thibaut. Kausalität oder Abstraktion des Eigentumwechsels in Römischem Recht, Kodifikationen und Pandektenlehre*, in: HATTENHAUSER Christian, SCHROEDER Klaus-Peter, BALDUS Christian (ed.), *Anton Friedrich Justus Thibaut (1772 – 1840). Bürger und Gelehrter*, Tübingen 2017, pp. 189 – 224 (together with a revised note)
12. BETTI Emilio, *Le système du code civil allemand*, Milano 1965
13. BJÖRNE Lars, *Deutsche Rechtssysteme im 18. und 19. Jahrhundert*, Ebelsbach am Main 1984
14. BLOCH Cyril, CERATI-GAUTHIER Adeline, PERRUCHOT-TRIBOULET Vincent, *L'influence de la réforme du droit des obligations sur le droit des affaires. The influence of the new French law of obligations on business law*, Paris 2018

15. BOEMKE Burkhard, ULRICI Bernhard, *BGB Allgemeiner Teil*, 2nd edition, Heidelberg/ Dordrecht/ London/ New York 2014

16. BORK Reinhard, *Allgemeiner Teil des Bürgerlichen Gesetzbuchs*, 4th edition, Tübingen 2016

17. BORKOWSKA-BAGIEŃSKA Ewa, *Kodeks w kulturze prawnej Polski* [Code in a legal culture of Poland], in: *O kulturze prawnej czasów stanisławowskich* [About the legal culture of the times of King Stanisław], Poznań 2009

18. BOUINEAU Jacques, Roux Jérôme, *200 ans de Code civil*, Paris 2004

19. BROX Hans, WALKER Wolf-Dietrich, *Erbrecht*, 22nd edition, Köln 2007

20. BRUNNER-KALMAN Vera, *Vertragsrecht und Vertragsfreiheit in der Volksrepublik Ungarn*, Zürich 1971

21. BUCHER Eugen, *Schweizerisches Obligationenrecht. Allgemeiner Teil ohne Deliktsrecht*, 2nd edition, Zürich 1988

22. BUCHHOLZ Stephan, DÖLEMEYER Barbara, *Deutschland*, in: COING Helmut (ed.), *Handbuch der Quellen und Literatur der Neueren Europäischen Privatrechtsgeschichte. Dritter Band. Zweiter Teilband: Gesetzgebung zum allgemeinen Privatrecht und zum Verfahrensrecht. Allgemeines Privatrecht: Mitteleuropa (Abschnitte 8 bis 14). Landesberichte: England, Rußland (Abschnitte 15, 16. Verfahrensrecht*, München 1982, pp. 1403 – 1773

23. CAPITANT Henri, *De la cause des obligations (contrats, engagements unilatéraux, legs)*, 2nd edition, Paris 1923

24. ČEŠKA Zdeněk (ed.), *Občanský zákoník: komentář. Díl I., (Zásady, § 1 až 221)* [Civil code: commentary. Part 1, (Principles, § 1 – 221)], Praha 1987

25. ČEŠKA Zdenek, ŠVESTKA Jiři, *Wstęp* [Introduction], in: *Kodeks cywilny, Kodeks gospodarczy, Kodeks handlu międzynarodowego Czechosłowackiej Republiki Socjalistycznej* [Civil code, Economic Code, International commercial code of the Czechoslovak Socialist Republic], Wrocław/Warszawa/ Kraków/Gdańsk/ Łódź 1981

26. CHAŁFINA R. O., *Znaczenie i istota umowy w radzieckim prawie cywilnym* [Significance and substance of contract in Soviet private law], Warszawa 1956

27. CHAŁFINA R. O., *Prawo dziedziczenia w ZSRR* [The law of inheritance in the USSR], Warszawa 1952

28. COING Helmut, *Europäisches Privatrecht. Band I. Älteres Gemeines Recht (1500 bis 1800)*, München 1985

29. CORNU Gérard, *Regards sur le titre III du livre III du Code civil "des contrats ou des obligations conventionnelles en général": essai de lecture d'un titre du code*, Paris 1977

30. CSANÁDI Gy., *Das Eigentumsrecht im ungarischen Zivilgesetzbuch*, in: EÖRSI G., *Das ungarische Zivilgesetzbuch in fünf Studien*, Budapest 1963, pp. 113 – 186

31. CZACHÓRSKI Witold, *Własność osobista w świetle konstytucji Polskiej Rzeczypospolitej Ludowej* [Personal ownership in the in view of the constitution of the People'sRepublicof Poland], Warszawa 1956

32. CZACHÓRSKI Witold, BRZOZOWSKI Adam, SAFJAN Marek, SKOWROŃSKA-BOCIAN Elżbieta, *Zobowiązania. Zarys wykładu* [Introduction to the law of obligations], 10th edition, Warszawa 2007

33. DAN BOB Mircea (ed.), *Family and inheritance in Romania*, Bucharest 2017

34. DANNEMANN Gerhard, SCHULZE Reiner, *German Civil Code. Bürgerliches Gesetzbuch (BGB). Volume I. Books 1 – 3: §§ 1 – 1296. Article-by-Article Commentary*, München 2020

35. DAVID Réné, *Le droit soviétique. Tome I. Les données fondamentales du droit soviétique*, Paris 1954

36. DESHAYES Olivier, GENICON Thomas, LAITHIER Yves-Marie, *Réforme du droit des contrats, du régime général et de la prevue des obligations. Commentaire article par article*, Paris 2018

37. DETHLOFF Nina, *Familienrecht. Ein Studienbuch*, 32nd edition, München 2018

38. DOMAŃSKI Ludwik, *Instytucje Kodeksu zobowiązań. Komentarz teoretyczno – praktyczny. Część ogólna* [Institutions of the Code of obligations. Theoretical and practical commentary. General part], Warszawa 1936

39. DOMAŃSKI Ludwik, *Instytucje Kodeksu zobowiązań. Komentarz teoretyczno – praktyczny. Część szczególna* [Institutions of the Code of obligations. Theoretical and practical commentary. Particular part], Warszawa 1938

40. DOMAŃSKI Ludwik, *O systemie przyszłego Kodeksu Cywilnego Polskiego* [About the future system of the Polish Civil Code], Dziennik Urzędowy Ministerstwa Sprawiedliwości [Official Gazette of the Polish Ministry of Justice], Year II (1921), Dział Nieurzędowy [Unofficial Part], no. 4 – 8, pp. 161 – 173

41. DOMAŃSKI Ludwik, *System Kodeksu zobowiązań* [The system of the Code of obligations], Warszawa 1934

42. DREWS Werner, HALGASCH Richard, *Erbrecht* (Grundriß Zivilrecht. Heft 9), Berlin 1978

43. DYBOWSKI Tomasz, *Ochrona własności w polskim prawie cywilnym* (rei vindicatio – actio negatoria) [The protection of the property in Polish private law (*rei vindicatio – actio negatoria*)], Warszawa 1969

44. DYBOWSKI Tomasz, *System Prawa Prywatnego. Tom 3 Prawo rzeczowe* [System of Private Law. Volume 3 *Ius in re*], 2nd edition, Warszawa 2007

45. DUGUIT Léon, *Les transformations générales du droit privé depuis le Code Napoléon*, Paris 1912

46. ECCHER Bernhard, *Erbrecht*, 4th edition, Wien 2010

47. EICHENHOFER Philipp, *Rechtsmissbrauch. Zu Geschichte und Theorie einer Figur des Europäischen Privatrechts*, Tübingen 2019

48. EISENHARDT Ulrich, *Allgemeiner Teil des BGB*, 3rd edition, Heidelberg 1989

49. ELIACHEVITCH B., *Le droit contractual dans le système du droit soviétique*, Paris 1938 (extract from *Revue trimestrielle du droit civil*, no. 38 from 1938)

50. ELISCHER David, FRINTA Ondřej, PAUKNEROVÁ Monika, *Recodification of Private Law in the Czech Republic*, in: RIVERA Julio César (ed.), *The Scope and Structure of Civil Codes*, Dordrecht/ Heidelberg/ New York/ London 2013

51. EMINESCU Yolanda, POPESCU Tudor, *Les codes civils des pays socialistes. Étude comparative*, Bucarest/ Paris 1980

52. ENGELS Fryderyk, MARKS Karol, *Manifest komunistyczny* [The Communist Manifesto], Warszawa 1946

53. EÖRSI Gyula, *Das ungarische Zivilgesetzbuch in fünf Studien*, Budapest 1963

54. EÖRSI Gyula, HARMATHY Attila (ed.), *Law and economic reform in socialist countries*, Budapest 1971

55. FENET Pierre-Antoine, *Recueil complet des travaux préparatoires du Code civil. Tome premier*, Paris 1836

56. FENET Pierre-Antoine, *Recueil complet des travaux préparatoires du Code civil. Tome sixième*, Paris 1836

57. FIEDORCZYK Piotr, *Polski kodeks rodzinny z 1950 r.: czy przełom?* [Polish family code from 1950: a turning point or not?], Zeszyty Prawnicze [Legal Notebooks] 2011 no. 2, pp. 129–151

58. FLOSSMANN Ursula, KALB Herbert, NEUWIRTH Karin, *Österreichische Privatrechtgeschichte*, 7th edition, Wien 2014

59. FROHNECKE Eberhard, *Die Rolle des ABGB in Gesetzgebung und Rechtswissenschaft des 19. Jahrhunderts*, Münster 2001

60. *Gai Instituiones. Instytucje Gaiusa* [Gai Institutiones. The Institutes], translated by Władysław ROZWADOWSKI, Poznań 2003

61. GIENKIN D. M., *Radzieckie prawo cywilne. Tom I* [Soviet private law. Volume I], Warszawa 1955

62. GIENKIN D. M, *Radzieckie prawo cywilne. Tom II* [Soviet private law. Volume II], Warszawa 1955

63. GLOS George E., *The Czechoslovak Civil Code of 1964 and Its 1982 Amendment with in the Framework of Czechoslovak Civil Law*, New York Law School Journal of International and Comparative Law, vol. 6 no. 2 1985, pp. 215–274

64. GNIEWEK Edward (ed.), *System Prawa Prywatnego. Tom 4 Prawo rzeczowe* [System of Private Law. Volume 4 *Ius in re*], 3rd edition, Warszawa 2012

65. GOŁĄB Stanisław, *Przed projektem polskiego kodeksu cywilnego* [Before the draft of the Polish civil code], Czasopismo Prawnicze i Ekonomiczne [Legal and Economic Journal] 1920, pp. 5 – 45

66. GÖHRING Joachim, POSCH Martin, *Zivilrecht. Lehrbuch. Teil 1*, Berlin 1981

67. GÖHRING Joachim, *Dienstleistungen, Gemeinschaften von Bürgern, Gegenseitige Hilfe und Schenkung* (Grundriß Zivilrecht. Heft 6), 2nd edition, Berlin 1977

68. GÖHRING Joachim (ed.), *Grundfragen des sozialistischen Zivilrechts* (Grundriß Zivilrecht. Heft 1), 2nd edition, Berlin 1978

69. GÖHRING Joachim, KURZHALS Peter, *Kauf* (Grundriß Zivilrecht. Heft 5), Berlin 1977

70. GOLDHAHN Eberhard, SCHMIDT Harald, *Konto-, Sparkonto-, Kredit – und Darlehnsverträge, Versicherungen* (Grundriß Zivilrecht. Heft 7), Berlin 1977

71. GÓRNICKI Leonard, *Zagadnienia systematyki kodyfikacji prawa cywilnego i handlowego w pracach Komisji Kodyfikacyjnej (1918 – 1939)* [The issues of the systematization of the codification of private and commercial law in the works of the Codification Committee (1918 – 1939)] Kwartalnik Prawa Prywatnego [The Quarterly of Private Law] 2004 vol. 3, pp. 623 – 664

72. GRAHAM-SIEGENTHALER Barbara, *Privatautonomie im Privatrecht – Entwicklungen und Tendenzen*, in: Zeitschrift für Schweizerisches Recht, Band 137 (2018), pp. 155 – 238

73. GRUBER Michael, KALSS Susanne, MÜLLER Katharina, SCHAUER Martin (ed.), *Erbrecht und Vermögensnachfolge*, 2nd edition, Wien 2010

74. GRZYBOWSKI Stefan, *Sprzedaż a dostawa w nowym kodeksie cywilnym* [Sales and delivery contracts in thenewcivil code], Państwo i Prawo [State and Law] 1965 vol. 10, pp. 459 – 471

75. GRZYBOWSKI Stefan, *System Prawa Cywilnego. (Tom I) Część ogólna* [System of Private Law. (Volume I) General part], Wrocław/ Warszawa/ Kraków/ Gdańsk 1974

76. GRZYBOWSKI Stefan (ed.), *System Prawa Cywilnego. (Tom III, Część 2) Prawo zobowiązań – Część szczegółowa* [System of Private Law. (Volume III, part 2) The law of obligations – particular part], Wrocław/ Warszawa/ Kraków/Gdańsk 1976

77. GURSKY Karl-Heinz, *Erbrecht*, Heidelberg 1988

78. HAFERKAMP Hans-Peter, *Georg Friedrich Puchta und die "Begriffsjurisprudenz"*, Frankfurt am Main 2004

79. HAFERKAMP Hans-Peter, *Wege zur Rechtsgeschichte: Das BGB*, Köln/ Wien 2022

80. HAIBACH Ulrike, *Familienrecht in der Rechtssprache. Die historische Entwicklung zentraler Ausdrücke des geltenden Familienrechts*, Frankfurt am Main 1991

81. HAMZA Gábor, *Enstehung und Entwicklung der modernen Privatrechtsordnungen und die römischrechtliche Tradition*, Budapest 2009

82. HATTENHAUER Hans, *Grundbegriffe des Bürgerlichen Rechts. Historisch-dogmatische Einführung*, 2nd edition, München 2000

83. HAUSMANINGER Herbert, *The Austrian Legal System*, Wien 2000

84. HEISE Arnold, *Grundriss eines Systems des gemeinen Civilrechts. Zum Behuf von Pandecten-Vorlesungen*, Heidelberg 1816

85. HUBE Romuald, *Uwagi nad systematem Kodexu cywilnego francuzkiego* [The remarks on the system of the French *Code civil*], Warszawa 1829

86. HÜBNER Heinz, *Allgemeiner Teil des Bürgerliches Gesetzbuches*, Berlin/ New York 1985

87. IGNATOWICZ Jan, *Obrót nieruchomościami miejskimi* [Municipal property trade], Zeszyty Problemowo-Analityczne [Problem-Centred and Analytical Bulletin] 1971 no. 21, pp. 5 – 74

88. IGNATOWICZ Jerzy, STEFANIUK Krzysztof, *Prawo rzeczowe* [*Ius in re*], 4th edition, Warszawa 2012

89. IGNATOWICZ Jerzy (ed.), *System Prawa Cywilnego. (Tom II) Prawo własności i inne prawa rzeczowe* [System of Private Law. (Volume II) The right of ownership and other *ius in re*], Wrocław/ Warszawa/ Kraków/Gdańsk 1977

90. JAGIELSKA Monika, *Prawo konsumenckie w przyszłym kodeksie cywilnym* [Consumer law in the prospectivecivil code], TPP 2017 no. 2, pp. 23 – 36

91. JULLIOT DE LA MORANDIÈRE Léon, *Rapport à Monsieur le Garde des Sceaux Ministre de la Justice*, (place of edition unknown) 1953

92. JUNG Peter, *Handelsrecht*, 12th edition, München 2019

93. KALETA Stefan, *Miejsce prawa rodzinnego w systemie prawa na przykładzie prawa polskiego* [The place of family law in the system of law based on the example of Polish law], Wrocław 1965 [unpublished; copy available in the library of the Faculty of Law, Administration and Economics of the University of Wrocław]

94. KANTOROVITCH Jacob, *Civil Code of Soviet Russia*, Yale Law Journal vol. 32 1922 – 1923, pp. 779 – 789

95. KEMENES B., *Die prinzipiellen Grundlagen des Vertragsystems im ungarischen Zivilgesetzbuch*, in: EÖRSI Gyula, *Das ungarische Zivilgesetzbuch in fünf Studien*, Budapest 1963, pp. 187 – 260

96. KLINKERT Johannes, OEHLER Elleonor, ROHDE Günther, *Eigentumsrecht. Nutzung von Grundstücken und Gebäuden zum Wohnen und zur Erholung* (Grundriß Zivilrecht. Heft 2), Berlin 1977

97. KNAPP Viktor (ed.), *Bibliography of Czechoslovak legal literature 1945 – 1958*, Prague 1959

98. KNAPP Viktor, LUBY Štefan, *Československé občanské právo. Druhé přepracované a doplněné vydání Schváleno výnosem ministerstva školství ČSR čj. 8.153/74-31 ze dne 26. ú nora 1974 jako vysokoškolska učebnice. Svazek 1* [Czechoslovak private law. Second, revised and extended edition. Approved by ordinance of the Ministry of Education of the Czechoslovak Socialist Republic, no. 8.153/74-31 from the 26th February 1974 as a university textbook. Volume 1], Praha 1974

99. KNAPP Viktor, LUBY Štefan, *Československé občanské právo. Druhé přepracované a doplněné vydání Schváleno výnosem ministerstva školství ČSR čj. 8.153/74-31 ze dne 26. ú nora 1974 jako vysokoškolska učebnice. Svazek 2* [Czechoslovak private law. Second, revised and extended edition. Approved by ordinance of the Ministry of Education of the Czechoslovak Socialist Republic, no. 8.153/74-31 from the 26th February 1974 as a university textbook. Volume 2], Praha 1974

100. KNAPP Viktor, *Les principes du nouveau droit civil*, Bulletin de Droit Tchécoslovaque 1951 no. 1 – 2, pp. 6 – 19

101. KNAPP Viktor, *Předmět a systém československého socialistického práva občanského* [Subject and system of the Czechoslovak socialist private law], Praha 1959

102. KNAPP Viktor, BEDŘ ICH Andres, *Učebnice občanského a rodinného práva: celostátní vysokoškolská učebnice. Svazek 1. Obecná část – Práva věcná* [Textbook of private and family law: national university textbook. Volume 1. General part – *Ius in re*], 2nd edition, Praha 1955

103. KNAPP Viktor, LUBY Štefan, BLAŽ KE Jaromír, *Učebnice občanského a rodinného práva: celostátní vysokoškolská učebnice. Sv. 2 – Závazkové právo* [Textbook of private and family law: national university textbook. Volume 2 – Law of obligations], Praha 1954

104. KNAPP Viktor, LUBY Štefan, BLAŽ KE Jaromír, *Učebnice občanského a rodinného práva: celostátní vysokoškolská učebnice. Sv. 3 – Dědické právo. Rodinnéprávo* [Textbook of private and family law: national university textbook. Volume 3 – Inheritance law. Family law], Praha 1954

105. KOCOT Wojciech, *Systematyka prawa zobowiązań umownych w przyszłym kodeksie cywilnym* [Systematics of the law on contractual obligations in the future Civil Code], Państwo i Prawo [State and Law] 2018 no. 3, pp. 82 – 110

106. KÖHLER Helmut, *BGB. Allgemeiner Teil. Ein Studienbuch*, 29th edition, München 2005

107. KONIC Henryk, *Uwagi do Projektu Kodeksu Handlowego* [Remarks on the Project of the Commercial Code], Gazeta Sądowa Warszawska [Warsaw Court Journal] 14 August 1933 no. 33, pp. 513 – 517

108. KÖTZ Hein, *Europäisches Vertragsrecht. Band I: Abschluß, Gültigkeit und Inhalt des Vertrages. Die Beteiligung Dritter am Vertrag*, Tübingen 1996

109. DE KOSCHEMBAHR-LYSKOWSKI Ignace, *Les dispositions de la loi et le droit en droit civil. Étude de droit comparé*, Varsovie 1933

110. DE KOSCHEMBAHR-ŁYSKOWSKI Ignacy, *Quelques dispositions générales d'un projet de code civile polonais*, extract from RTDC (Revue Trimestrielle de Droit Civil) 1928 no. 3, pp. 5 – 32

111. KOSCHEMBAHR-ŁYSKOWSKI Ignacy, *W sprawie kodyfikacji naszego prawa cywilnego* [In the subject of codification of our private law], Warszawa 1925

112. KRASOWSKI Krzysztof, *Próby unifikacji osobowego prawa małżeńskiego w II Rzeczypospolitej* [The attempts of unifying the personal marriage law in the Second Republic of Poland], Kwartalnik Prawa Prywatnego [The Quarterly of Private Law] 1994 no. 3, p. 467 – 502

113. KUNDERT Werner, HOLTHÖFER Ernst, DÖLEMEYER Barbara, *Schweiz*, in: COING Helmut (ed.), *Handbuch der Quellen und Literatur der Neueren Europäischen Privatrechtsgeschichte. Dritter Band. Zweiter Teilband: Gesetzgebung zum allgemeinen Privatrecht und zum Verfahrensrecht. Allgemeines Privatrecht: Mitteleuropa (Abschnitte 8 bis 14). Landesberichte: England, Rußland (Abschnitte 15, 16). Verfahrensrecht*, München 1982, pp. 1833 – 2070

114. KÜPPER Herbert, *Einführung in das ungarische Recht*, München 2011

115. KURZYNSKY-SINGER Eugenia, *Transformation der russischen Eigentumsordnung. Eine vergleichende Analyse aus der Sicht des deutschen Rechts*, Tübingen 2019

116. LAMBERT Édouard, PATOUILLET Jules, *Introduction*, in: *Les codes de la Russie Soviétique. Tome 1 Code de la famille Code civil*, Paris 1925

117. LARENZ Karl, *Methodenlehre der Rechts-Wissenschaft*, 2nd edition, Berlin/ Heidelberg/ New York/ London/ Paris/ Tokyo/ Hong Kong/ Barcelona/ Budapest 1992

118. LASSERRE-KIESOV Valérie, *La téchnique législative. Étude sur les codes civils français et allemand*, Paris 2002

119. LEHMANN Heinrich, HÜBNER Heinz, *Allgemeiner Teil des Bürgerlichen Gesetzbuches*, 15th edition, Berlin 1966

120. LIPP Martin, *Die Bedeutung des Naturrechts für die Ausbildung der Allgemeinen Lehren des deutschen Privatrechts*, Berlin 1980

121. LITYŃSKI Adam, *Prawo Rosji i ZSRR 1917 – 1991 czyli historia wszechzwiązkowego komunistycznego prawa (bolszewików). Krótki kurs* [The law of Russia and the Soviet Union 1917 – 1991 namely the history of the all-union communist law (bolshevik). A short introduction], Warszawa 2017

122. LONGCHAMPS DE BERIER Romain, *Quelques observations sur le projet franco-italien de code des obligations (Partie générale)*, Varsovie 1931

123. LONGCHAMPS DE BERIER Roman, *Uzasadnienie projektu Kodeksu zobowiązań. Z uwzględnieniem ostatecznego tekstu kodeksu. W opracowaniu głównego referent a projektu Prof. Romana Longchamps de Berier. Art. 1 – 167* [Explanation of the draft of Code of obligations. With taking into account the final text of the code. Elaborated by the main reporter of the draft Prof. Roman LONGCHAMPS DE BERIER. Articles 1 – 167], Warszawa 1934

124. LONGCHAMPS DE BÉRIER Roman, *Zasada wolności umów w projektach polskiego prawa o zobowiązaniach* [The principle of freedom of contract in the drafts of the Polish law of obligations], Lwów 1936 (extract from *Księga pamiątkowa ku czci Władysława Abrahama T. 1* [A commemorative book in honour of Władysław Abraham. Volume 1], Lwów 1930, pp. 351 – 365

125. LONGCHAMPS DE BÉRIER Roman, *Zobowiązania* [Obligations], 2nd edition, Lwów 1939

126. LOOSCHELDERS Dirk, OLZEN Dirk, *Erbrecht*, 5th edition, Berlin/ Boston 2017

127. LÜBCHEN Gustav – Adolf, *Die Stellung des Zivilgesetzbuchs in der einheitlichen sozialistischen Rechtsordnung der DDR,* Neue Justiz 1975 no. 16, p. 469 – 473

128. LÜBCHEN Gustav-Adolf, POSCH Martin, *Zivilrechtsverhältnisse mit Auslandsberührung* (Grundriß Zivilrecht. Heft 10), Berlin 1978

129. LUBY Štefan (ed.), *Le droit civil tchécoslovaque*, Bratislava 1969

130. LUBY Štefan, *Les dispositions fondamentales et les problèmes d'actualité du droit civil tchécoslovaque*, Bulletin de droit tchécoslovaque 1973 no. 1 – 2, pp. 193 – 201

131. LUBY Štefan, *La propriété personnelle des maisons de famille et des habitations*, Bulletin de droit tchécoslovaque 1973 no. 1 – 2, pp. 202 – 221

132. LUTOSTAŃSKI Kamil, *Uwagi o pracach prawodawczych w ubiegłem dziesięcioleciach w materji prawa cywilnego* [Remarks about legislative works in the previous decade in the field of private law], Gazeta Sądowa Warszawska [Warsaw Court Journal] 1928 no. 46, pp. 717 – 720

133. MACHNIKOWSKI Piotr, *Zasada swobody umów jako problem kodyfikacyjny* [The principle of freedom of contract as a codification problem], in: SAWCZUK Mieczysław (ed.), *Czterdzieści lat kodeksu cywilnego: materiały z Ogólnopolskiego Zjazdu Cywilistów w Rzeszowie (8 – 10 października 2004 r.)* [Forty years of the civil code: Materials from the National Congress of Civilists in Rzeszów (8th – 10th October 2004)], Kraków/ Warszawa 2006

134. MACIERZYŃSKA-FRANASZCZYK Elwira, *Umowy o świadczenie usług w prawie szwajcarskim* [Service contracts under the Swiss law], TPP 2014 no. 3, pp. 103 – 120

135. MADEY Marek, STELMACHOWSKI Andrzej, *Zarys prawa gospodarczego* [Introduction to economic law], Warszawa 1980

136. MALAURIE Philippe, FULCHIRON Hugues, *Droit de la famille*, 6th edition, Paris 2018

137. MENYHÁRD Attila and VERESS Emöd (ed.), *New Civil Codes in Hungary and Romania*, Budapest/ Cluj-Napoca 2017

138. MENYHÁRD Attila, *Property Law in the New Hungarian Civil Code: Key Issues*, in: *New Civil Codes in Hungary and Romania*, MENYHÁRD Attila and VERESS Emöd (ed.), Budapest/ Cluj-Napoca 2017

139. LAMETTI David, *Objects of Private Property in the Civil Code of the Russian Federation and in the Civil Code of Quebec*, Review of Central and East European Law 2005, vol. 30, no. 1, pp. 19–28

140. LEWY Marceli, *Nadużycie prawa według orzecznictwa francuskiego i prawa polskiego* [Abuse of rights according to the French jurisprudence and Polish law], Warszawa 1938

141. LEWY Marceli, *Swoboda umów i jej ograniczenia we francuskim kodeksie cywilnym z punktu widzenia społecznego* [Freedom of contract and its limitations in French civil code from a social point of view], Warszawa 1924

142. LUDWICZAK Witalis, *Umowa zlecenia* [Mandate contract], Poznań 1955

143. MACHNIKOWSKI Piotr, *Swoboda umów według art. 353 (1). Konstrukcja prawna* [Freedom of contract according too Art. 353 (1). Legal construct], Warszawa 2005

144. MEDICUS Dieter, *Allgemeiner Teil des BGB. Ein Lehrbuch*, 8th edition, Heidelberg 2002

145. MEDICUS Dieter, LORENZ Stephan, *Schuldrecht II. Besonderer Teil. Ein Studienbuch*, 15th edition, München 2010

146. MEDICUS Dieter, *Schuldrecht I. Allgemeiner Teil*, 17th edition, München 2006

147. MOUSOURAKIS George, *Fundamentals of Roman Private Law*, Berlin/Heidelberg 2012

148. MÜHLMANN Manfred, *Miete* (Grundriß Zivilrecht. Heft 4), Berlin 1977

149. MUSCHELER Karlheinz, *Familienrecht*, 4th edition, München 2017

150. NAMITKIEWICZ Jan, *Zasady prawa handlowego obowiązującego w Polsce. Prawo handlowe b. dzielnic: rosyjskiej, austryjackiej i pruskiej. Prawo wekslowe i czekowe. Prawo upadłościowe b. Królestwa Kongresowego* [Principles of the commercial law binding in Poland. Commercial law of the former districts: Russian, Austrian and Prussian. Law on negotiable instruments and law for cheques. Insolvency law of the former Congress Kingdom], Warszawa 1929

151. NOLDE Boris, *Le code civil de la République des Soviets*, Bulletin de la Société de Législation Comparée 1923 nos. 7–8–9, pp. 231–257

152. NOWICKI I. B., ŁUNC Ł. A., *Ogólna nauka o zobowiązaniach* [The general science of the law of obligations], Warszawa 1954

153. NUSSBERGER Angelika, *Einführung in das russische Recht*, München 2010

154. OHANOWICZ Alfred, GÓRSKI Józef, *Zobowiązania. Część szczegółowa* [Obligations. Specific part], 2nd edition, Warszawa/ Poznań1964

155. OPPETIT Bruno, *Essai sur la codification*, Paris 1998

156. OSAKWE Christopher, *Russian civil code annotated*, Moscow 2000

157. OVERSTAKE Jean-Francis, *Essai de classification des contrats spéciaux*, Paris 1969

158. PAŃKO Walerian, *O prawie własności i jego współczesnych funkcjach* [On ownership and its contemporary functions], Katowice 1984

159. PASHCHENKO Tatjana, *Das Recht der Handelsgeschäfte in der Russischen Föderation*, Frankfurt am Main 2003

160. PAWLOWSKI Hans-Martin, *Allgemeiner Teil des BGB. Grundlehren des bürgerlichen Rechts*, 6th edition, Heidelberg 2000

161. PECYNA Marlena, *Zakres rosyjskiej koncepcji regulacji świadczenia usług* [The Russian regulation of the services contracts], TPP 2014 no. 3, pp. 121 – 140

162. PECYNA Marlena, ZOLL Fryderyk, *Założenia projektu struktury części szczegółowej prawa zobowiązań. W poszukiwaniu nowego modelu* [The principles of the draft of the specific part of the law of obligations. In the process of searching for the new model], TPP 2012 no 1, pp. 25 – 60

163. PELLÉ Sébastien, *Les résultats: une rénovation formelle du Code civil*, in: *Quel renouveau pour le droit des contrats? Une réforme entre tradition et modern ité. Actes du colloque, Pau le 20 mai 2016*, PELLÉ Sébastien and LARRIBAU-TERNEYRE Virginie (ed.), Pau 2016, pp. 43 – 52

164. PETEV Valentin, *Sozialistisches Zivilrecht. Eine rechtsvergleichende Einführung unter Berücksichtigung der Rechte der Volksrepublik Bulgarien, der ČSSR, der DDR, der Volksrepublik Polen, der Rumänischen Sozialistischen Republik, der Ungarischen Volksrepublik und der UdSSR*, Berlin/ New York 1975

165. PIASECKI Kazimierz, *Prof. dr Viktor Knapp: "Przedmiot i system czechosłowackiego prawa cywilnego" – Praga 1959* [Prof. Dr Viktor Knapp: "The subject and system of the Czechoslovak private law" – Prague 1959], Przegląd Ustawodawstwa Gospodarczego [Review of Economic Legislation] 1960 no. 3, pp. 91 – 92

166. PIĄTOWSKI Stanisław Józef, *System Prawa Cywilnego (Tom IV). Prawos padkowe* [System of Private Law (Volume IV). Inheritance law], Wrocław/ Warszawa/ Kraków/ Gdańsk/ Łódź 1986

167. PIĄTOWSKI Józef Stanisław (ed.), *System prawa rodzinnego i opiekuńczego* [System of Family and Guardianship law], Wrocław/ Warszawa/ Kraków/ Gdańsk/ Łódź 1985

168. PISULIŃSKI Jerzy, *Das neue Zivilgesetzbuch - eine Herausforderung für den Gesetzgeber*, in: HELLWEGE Phillip, SCHMIDT Reiner, SONIEWICKA Marta, STELMACH Jerzy (ed.), Krakauer-Augsburger Rechtstudien. Normschaffung, Warschau 2017, pp. 99 – 110

169. PISULIŃSKI Jerzy, *Prawo konsumenckie w systemie prawa cywilnego* [Consumer law in the system of private law], in: SAWCZUK Mieczysław (ed.), *Czterdzieści lat kodeksu cywilnego: materiały z Ogólnopolskiego Zjazdu Cywilistów w Rzeszowie (8 – 10 października 2004 r.)* [Forty years of the civil code: Materials from the National Congress of Civilists in Rzeszów (8th – 10th October 2004)], Kraków/ Warszawa 2006, pp. 171 – 187

170. PISULIŃSKI Jerzy, *Struktura części ogólnej prawa zobowiązań (wprowadzenie do dyskusji)* [The structure of the general part of the law of obligations (introduction to discussion)], TPP 2017 no. 2, pp. 37 – 51

171. PISULIŃSKI Jerzy, *The Polish Civil Law Codification Commission Working on the Draft of the New Civil Code*, in: GRUNDMANN Stefan, GROCHOWSKI Mateusz (ed.), *European contract law and the creation of norms*, Cambridge/ Antwerp/ Chicago, pp. 97 – 107

172. PISULIŃSKI Jerzy, *W sprawie systematyki szczegółowej prawa zobowiązań (głos w dyskusji)* [On the systematics of the specific part of law of obligations (a voice in the discussion)], TPP 2012 no. 1, pp. 15 – 23

173. PLANIOL Marcel, *Traité élémentaire de droit civil conforme au programme officiel des facultés de droit. Tome deuxième*, 11th edition, Paris 1931

174. PLANK Karol, *Le droit de succession*, in: Luby Štefan (ed.), *Le droit civil tchécoslovaque*, Bratislava 1969, pp. 248 – 253

175. PÖPPERL Peter, *Quellen und System des Codex Maximilianeus Bavaricus Civilis*, Bamberg 1967

176. POSCH Martin, *Allgemeines Vertragsrecht* (Grundriß Zivilrecht. Heft 3), Berlin 1977

177. POSCH Martin, *Schutz des Lebens, der Gesundheit und des Eigentums vor Schadenszufügung* (Grundriß Zivilrecht. Heft 8), Berlin 1977

178. POSCH Willibald, *Grundzüge fremder Privatrechtssysteme*, Wien/ Köln/ Graz 1995

179. PRZYBYŁOWSKI Kazimierz, *Wpływ zmiany stosunków na zobowiązania ("Clausula rebus sic stantibus" – jej renesans w dobie współczesnej)* [The impact of the changing relationships on obligations ("Clausula rebus sic stantibus" – its renassaince in the modern era)], Lwów 1926

180. RADWAŃSKI Zbigniew, *Aktualność posłużenia się częścią ogólną kodeksu cywilnego jako instrumentu regulacji prawa prywatnego* [Actuality of using the general part of the civil code as an instrument of the regulation of private law], TPP 2010 no. 4, pp. 13 – 20

181. RADWAŃSKI Zbigniew, *Kierunki reformy prawa cywilnego* [Tendencies of thereform of private law], Państwo i Prawo [State and Law] 1987 no. 4, pp. 5 – 19

182. RADWAŃSKI Zbigniew (ed.), *System Prawa Cywilnego. (Tom III, Część 1) Prawo zobowiązań – Część ogólna* [System of Private Law. (Volume III, part 1) The law of obligations – general part], Wrocław/ Warszawa/ Kraków/Gdańsk/Łódź 1981

183. RADWAŃSKI Zbigniew, *Wstę pny projekt systematyzacji tak zwanej części szczegółowej prawa zobowiązań* [The initial draft of the systematization of the so-called specific part of the law of obligations], TPP 2012 no. 1, pp. 5 – 14

184. RADWAŃSKI Zbigniew, *Teoria umów* [Theory of contracts], Warszawa 1977

185. RADWAŃSKI Zbigniew (ed.), *Zielona Księga. Optymalna wizja Kodeksu cywilnego w Rzeczypospolitej Polskiej* [Green Book. The optimal vision of the Civil Code in the Republic of Poland], Warszawa 2006

186. RANIERI Filippo, *Europäisches Obligationenrecht. Ein Handbuch mit Texten und Materialien*, 3rd edition, Wien 2003

187. RASKAZOVA Y. Natalya, *Russian Law of Obligations: Structure, Positioning and Connection with Supra national Law*, in: SCHULZE Reiner, ZOLL Fryderyk (ed.), *The Law of Obligations in Europe. A New Wave of Codifications*, Munich 2013, pp. 139–151

188. RAY Jean, *Essai sur la structure logique du Code civil*, Paris 1926

189. REICH Norbert, *Rußland*, in: COING Helmut (ed.), *Handbuch der Quellen und Literatur der Neueren Europäischen Privatrechtsgeschichte. Dritter Band. Zweiter Teilband: Gesetzgebung zum allgemeinen Privatrecht und zum Verfahrensrecht. Allgemeines Privatrecht: Mitteleuropa (Abschnitte 8 bis 14). Landesberichte: England, Rußland (Abschnitte 15, 16). Verfahrensrecht*, München 1982, pp. 2281–2328

190. RESICH Zbigniew (ed.), *Kodeks cywilny. Komentarz. Tom 1* [Civil Code. Commentary. Volume 1], Warszawa 1972

191. RIPERT Georges, *La règle morale dans les obligations civiles*, 4th edition, Paris 1949

192. RIVERA Julio César (ed.), *The Scope and Structure of Civil Codes*, Dordrecht/ Heidelberg/ New York/ London 2013

193. ROTT-PIETRZYK Ewa, *Systematyka części szczegółowej zobowiązań a miejsce umów o pośrednictwo* sensu largo *(głos w dyskusji)* [The systematics of the specific part of the law of obligations, and the place of agency contracts *sensu largo* (a voice in the discussion)], TPP 2013 no. 1, pp. 41–72

194. ROTT-PIETRZYK Ewa, GROCHOWSKI Mateusz, *Regulacja umów o pośrednictwo w DCFR (wzorcem dla ustawodawcy polskiego?)* [Regulation of intermediation contracts in DCFR (as a pattern for the Polish legislator?], TPP 2017 no. 3, pp. 49–81

195. RÜCKERT Joachim, SEINECKE Ralf, *Methodik des Zivilrechts – von Savigny bis Teubner*, Baden-Baden 2012

196. RÜCKERT Joachim, SCHÄFER Frank L. (ed.), *Historisch-kritischer Kommentar zum BGB. Band III Schuldrecht: Besonderer Teil §§ 433–853*, Tübingen 2013

197. RULAND Yorick M., *Die Causa der Obligation. Rechtshistorische und rechtsvergleichende Perspektive nach Einführung des Nieuw Burgerlijk Wetboek in den Niederlanden*, Köln 2004

198. RYBÁRIK Karol, *Le droit d'usage personnel d'habitations*, Bulletin de Droit Tchécoslovaque 1973 no. 1–2, pp. 239–253

199. SAVATIER Réné, *Du droit civil au droit public à travers les personnes, les biens et la responsabilitécivile*, Paris 1945

200. SAVATIER Réné, *L'art de faire les lois. Bonaparte et le Code civil*, Paris 1927

201. VON SAVIGNY Friedrich Carl, *O powołaniu naszych czasów do ustawodawstwa i nauki prawa* [About the vocation of our times to the legislation and science of law], Warszawa 1964

202. SCHELLE Karel, TAUCHEN Jaromír, *A Brief Introduction to Czech Civil Law*, München 2011

203. SCHELLE Karel, VESELÁ Renata, VOJÁČEK Ladislav, TAUCHEN Jaromír, *Europäischer Kontext der Entwicklung des Privatrechts auf dem Gebiet der Tschechischen Republik (Ausgewählte Kapitel aus der Geschichte der Rechtsangleichung in Europa)*, Brno 2009

204. SCHELLEOVÁ Ilona, SCHELLE Karel, *Vývoj kodifikace občanského prava* [The evolution of the codification of private law], in: SCHELLE Karel (ed.), *Vývoj právních kodifikací. Sborník z mezinárodní vědecké konference* [The development of legal codifications. Proceedings of an international scientific conference], Brno 2004

205. SCHLOSSER Hans, *Neuere Europäische Rechtsgeschichte. Privat- und Strafrecht vom Mittelalter bis zur Moderne*, 3rd edition, München 2017

206. SCHMIDT Rolf, *Familienrecht (Ehe, Verwandtschaft, Vormundschaft, Betreuung, Pflegschaft)*, 10th edition, Hannover 2018

207. SCHMOECKEL Mathias (ed.), *Historisch-kritischer Kommentar zum BGB. Band I Allgemeiner Teil §§ 1–240*, Tübingen 2003

208. SCHMOECKEL Mathias (ed.), *Historisch-kritischer Kommentar zum BGB. Band IV Familienrecht §§ 1297–1921*, Tübingen 2018

209. SCHULIN Hermann, VOGT Nedim Peter, *Einleitung zum Obligationenrecht*, in: *Schweizerisches Obligationenrecht*, Basel 2018

210. SCHULZE Reiner, *Allgemeine Rechtsgrundsätze und europäisches Privatrecht*, in: Zeitschrift für Europäisches Privatrecht 1993, pp. 442–473

211. SCHUMAN R., *La théorie des obligations dans le projet de code civil tchécoslovaque*, Paris 1927

212. SCHWAB Dieter, *Familienrecht und Religion – ein Blick in die Geschichte*, in: MAYER Claudia, SCHWAB Dieter, GOTTWALD Peter, HENRICH Dieter (ed.), *Familienrecht und Religion – Europäische Perspektiven. Beiträge zum europäischen Familien- und Erbrecht*, Bielefeld 2019

213. SEDLÀČEK Jaromir, *La codification du droit civil en Tchécoslovaquie*, Bulletin de la Société de législation comparée avril – juin 1925, pp. 140–150

214. SEUBE Jean-Baptiste, ATTIAS Benjamin, DUMONT-LEFRAND Marie-Pierre, GOUT Olivier, LANDEL James, LOIR Romain, MAFFRE-BAUGÉ Agnès, MARLANGE Ambroise, ROUSSILLE Myriam, SOUSTELLE Philippe, TERRIER Vincent, ZATTARA-GROS Anne Franç oise, *Droit des contrats. Bilan de réforme et loi de ratification*, Montrouge 2018

215. SIEBENHAAR Eduard, SIEGMANN Georg, PÖSCHMANN Karl Magnus, *Commentar zu dem bürgerlichen Gesetzbuche für das Königreich Sachsen. Zweiter Band. Das Recht der Forderungen*, Leipzig 1869

216. SIMON Thomas, *Inhalt und rechtspolitische Bedeutung der "Einleitung" des ABGB im Kontext der Kodifikationsgesetzgebung des frühen 19. Jahrhunderts*, in: DÖLEMEYER Barbara, MOHNHAUPT Heinz (ed.), *200 Jahre ABGB (1811 – 2011): Die österreichische Kodifikation im internationalen Kontext*, Frankfurt am Main 2012

217. SKĄPSKI Józef, *Kodeks cywilny z 1964 r. Blaski i cienie kodyfikacji oraz jej perspektywy* [Civil Code from 1964. Lights and shadows of the codification and its perspectives], Kwartalnik Prawa Prywatnego [The Quarterly of Private Law] 1992 vol. 1 – 4, pp. 57 – 90

218. SKODA Diane, *La propriété dans le Code civil de la Fédération de Russie, un système entre deux traditions*, Paris 2007

219. SOŚNIAK Mieczysław, *Zasada swobody umów w prawie obligacyjnym z perspektywy schyłku XX wieku* [The principle of freedom of contract in the law of obligations from the perspective of the end of the twentieth century], Studia Iuridica Silesiana, Katowice 1985, pp. 7 – 50

220. SOŚNIAK Mieczysław, *Z zagadnieńsystematyki prawa obligacyjnego* [From the questions of the systematization of the law of obligations], in: RADWAŃSKI Zbigniew, *Studia z prawa zobowiązań* [Studies from the law of obligations], Warszawa/Poznań 1979

221. SOŚNIAK Mieczysław, *Zagadnienia typologii i systematyki umów obligacyjnych* [The problems of the typology and the systematization of the contrats], Katowice 1990

222. SOŚNIAK Mieczysław, *Zasady kodeksu cywilnego Niemieckiej Republiki Demokratycznej* [Principles of the civil code of the German Democratic Republic], in: *Kodeks cywilny Niemieckiej Republiki Demokratycznej* [Civil code of the German Democratic Republic], Wrocław/ Warszawa/ Kraków/Gdańsk 1979

223. SÓJKA-ZIELIŃSKA Katarzyna, *Kodeks Napoleona. Historia i współczesność* [The Napoleonic Code. History and present times], 2nd edition, Warszawa 2008

224. STAGL Fortunat Jakob, *Die Rezeption der Lehre vom Rechtsgeschäft in Österreich durch Joseph Unger*, Zeitschrift für Europäisches Privatrecht 2007, pp. 37 – 55

225. STELMACHOWSKI Andrzej, *Ewolucja autonomii woli* [Evolution of the autonomy of will], in: ŁĘTOWSKA Ewa (ed.), *Tendencje rozwoju prawa cywilnego* [Tendencies of the development of private law], Wrocław/Warszawa/ Kraków/ Gdańsk/ Łódź, pp. 157 – 210

226. STELMACHOWSKI Andrzej, *Istota i funkcja posiadania* [The essence and function of possession], Warszawa 1958

227. STELMACHOWSKI Andrzej, *Zarys teorii prawa cywilnego* [Introduction to the theory of private law], Warszawa 1998

228. STIEBER Miloslav, *Systematika zákoníků Střední Evropy* [Systematization of codifications in Central Europe], *Sborníkvě dprávních a státních* 1922, volume. 2 – 4, pp. 229 – 242

229. SUŁKOWSKI Józef, *Polski kodeks handlowy* [Polish commercial code], Ruch Prawniczy Ekonomiczny i Socjologiczny [Legal, Economic and Sociological Movement] 1934 vol 2, pp. 94 – 108

230. SZCZYGIELSKI Adam Daniel, *Zasady prawa handlowego Tom I. Podstawy konstrukcyjne polskiego Kodeksu handlowego. Zasady podstawowe – Czynności handlowe – Pojęcie kupca* [The principles of commercial law Volume I. The structural foundations of Polish Commercial Code. Basic principles. Commercial operations. The concept of a merchant], preface by J. NAMITKIEWICZ, Warszawa 1936

231. SZER Seweryn, *Nowe prawo rodzinne* [New family law], Warszawa 1950

232. SZOSTAK Ryszard, *Problem systematyki umów obligacyjnych w nowym kodeksie cywilnym* [The problem of the systematics of the contracts under the new Polish Civil Code], TPP 2012 no. 1, pp. 61 – 75

233. TICHÝ Luboš, *Czech and European Law of Obligations at a Turning Point*, in: SCHULZE Reiner, ZOLL Fryderyk (ed.), *The Law of Obligations in Europe. A New Wave of Codifications*, Munich 2013

234. TILL Ernest, *Wykład nauki o stosunkach obowiązkowych. II. (Część szczegółowa)* [Study on the law of obligations. II. (Particular part)], Lwów 1897

235. TYLBOR Stanisław, *Wstęp* [Introduction], in: *Kodeks cywilny R.S. F.S.R. wraz z kodeksem ustaw o małżeństwie, rodzinie i opiece* [Civil code of RSFSR with the code of bills on marriage, family and guardianship], Warszawa 1930

236. VÉKÁS Lajos, *Zivilrecht*, in: GROTHUSEN Klaus-Detlev, *Südosteuropa-Handbuch. Band V. Ungarn*, Göttingen 1984

237. DE VINCELLES Carole Aubert, *France: Position of the Law of Obligations in National and Supra national Law*, in: SCHULZE Reiner, ZOLL Fryderyk (ed.), *The Law of Obligations in Europe. A New Wave of Codifications*, Munich 2013

238. VONDRACEK Th. J., *Commentary on the Czechoslovak civil code*, Dordrecht/ Boston/ Lancaster 1988

239. VON LEWINSKI K ai, *Deutschrechtliche Systembildung im 19. Jahrhundert*, Frankfurt am Main/ Berlin/ Bern/ Bruxelles/ New York/ Oxford/ Wien 2001

240. WABNITZ Heinz-Bernd, KORBEL František, NOVOTNÝ Petr, THEISS Christian (ed.), *Einführung in das tschechische Recht*, München 2020

241. WASILKOWSKI Jan, *Kodyfikacja prawa cywilnego w Polsce* [The codification of private law in Poland], Nowe Prawo [New Law] 1950 no. 12, pp. 3 – 7

242. WASILKOWSKI Jan, *Prawo własności w PRL. Zarys wykładu* [Ownership in People's Republic of Poland. Introduction], Warszawa 1969

243. WASILKOWSKI Jan, WOLTER Aleksander, *Projekt kodeksu cywilnego (charakterystyka ogólna)* [Draft of the civil code (general profile)], Nowe Prawo [New Law] 1961 no. 12, pp. 1507 – 1536

244. WASILKOWSKI Jan, *Zagadnienie kodyfikacji jednolitego prawa cywilnego* [The problem of the codification of uniform private law], Demokratyczny Przegląd Prawniczy [Democratic Law Journal] 1947 no. 1 – 2, pp. 62 – 64

245. WASILKOWSKI Jan, *Zagadnienia ogólne nowego prawa cywilnego* [General problems of new private law], Demokratyczny Przegląd Prawniczy [Democratic Law Journal] 1946 no. 9 – 10, pp. 18 – 22

246. WASILKOWSKI Jan, *Zarys prawa rzeczowego* [An introduction to *ius in re*], Warszawa 1963

247. WEILER Frank, *Schuldrecht. Allgemeiner Teil*, 5th edition, Bielefeld 2019

248. WERTENBRUCH Johannes, *BGB. Allgemeiner Teil*, 5th edition, München 2021

249. WESENBERG Gerhard, WESENER Gunter, *Neuere deutsche Privatrechtsgeschichte im Rahmen der europäischen Rechtsentwicklung*, 3rd edition, Lahr/Schwarzwald 1976

250. WESTEN Klaus (ed.), *Das neue Zivilrecht der DDR nach dem Zivilgesetzbuch von 1975*, Berlin 1977

251. WESTEN Klaus, SCHLEIDER Joachim, *Zivilrecht im Systemvergleich. Das Zivilrecht der Deutschen Demokratischen Republik und der Bundesrepublik Deutschland*, Berlin 1984

252. WIELING Hans Josef, FINKENAUER Thomas, *Sachenrecht*, 6th edition, Berlin 2020

253. WIENIEDIKTOW A.W. (Venediktov Anatoliĭ Vasil'evich), *Państwowa własność socjalistyczna* [Socialist state ownership], Warszawa 1952

254. WINDSCHEID Bernhard, *Lehrbuch des Pandektenrechts. Erster Band*, Düsseldorf 1862

255. WINDSCHEID Bernhard, *Lehrbuch des Pandektenrechts. Zweiter Band. Erste Abtheilung*, Düsseldorf 1865

256. WINDSCHEID Bernhard, *Lehrbuch des Pandektenrechts. Zweiter Band. Zweite Abtheilung*, Düsseldorf 1866

257. WINDSCHEID Bernhard, *Lehrbuch des Pandektenrechts. Dritter Band*, Düsseldorf 1870

258. WINIARZ Jan, *Użytkowanie wieczyste* [Perpetual usufruct], Warszawa 1967

259. WISZNIEWSKI Jerzy, *System projektu kodeksu cywilnego Polskiej Rzeczypospolitej Ludowej* [System of the draft of the civil code of the People's Republic of Poland], in: *Materiały dyskusyjne do projektu kodeksu cywilnego Polskiej Rzeczypospolitej Ludowej. Materiały sesji naukowej 8 – 10 grudnia 1954 r.* [Discussive materials to the draft of the civil code of the People's Republic of Poland. Materials to the scientific session 8th – 10th December 1954], Warszawa 1955

260. WISZNIEWSKI Jerzy, *Wstęp* [Introduction], in: *Zasady ustawodawstwa cywilnego ZSRR. Kodekscywilny RFSRR* [The Principles of the Civil Legislation of the USSR. Civil code of the RSFSR], Wrocław/ Warszawa 1977

261. WOŁODKIEWICZ Witold, *Les origines romaines de la systématique du droit civil contemporain*, Wrocław/ Warszawa/ Kraków/ Gdańsk 1978

262. ZALÁN K., *Hauptprobleme des Erbrechts im ungarischen Zivilgesetzbuch*, in: EÖRSI Gyula, *Das ungarische Zivilgesetzbuch in fünf Studien*, Budapest 1963, pp. 319 – 381

263. ZIMMERMANN Reinhard (ed.), *Historisch-kritischer Kommentar zum BGB. Band II Schuldrecht: Allgemeiner Teil §§ 241 – 432*, Tübingen 2007

264. ZIMMERMANN Reinhard, *The Present State of European Private Law*, Amsterdam 2010

265. ZOLL Fryderyk, *Contract Law in the Draft of the New Polish Civil Code: Formation of Contract, Performance and Non-Performance of Obligations*, in: SCHULZE Reiner, ZOLL Fryderyk (ed.), *The Law of Obligations in Europe. A New Wave of Codifications*, Munich 2013

266. ZOLL Fryderyk, *Prawa rzeczowe na ziemiach polskich* [*Ius in re* on the Polishlands], Warszawa/ Kraków 1920

267. ZOLL Fryderyk, *Prawo cywilne opracowane głównie na podstawie przepisów obowiązujących w Małopolsce. Tom II Prawa rzeczowe i prawa rzeczowym podobne* (Private law elaborated mainly on the basis of the provisions binding in Małopolska. Volume II *Ius in re* and rights similar to *ius in re*], 3rd edition, Poznań1931

268. ŻABIŃSKI Zbigniew, *Systematyka umownych stosunków prawnych pod względem treści* [Systematization of the contractual legal relationships in terms of content], Studia Cywilistyczne [Studies in Private Law] 1972 vol. XIX, pp. 97 – 130

269. ŻABIŃSKI Zbigniew, *Wpływ poję cia rzeczy na kształtowanie się systemu prawa cywilnego* [The influence of the concept of the thing on the formation of the system of private law], Zeszyty Naukowe Uniwersytetu Jagiellońskiego [Jagiellonian University Research Bulletin] Vol. CCCXLVI. Prace z zakresu prawa cywilnego i praw na dobrach niematerialnych [Works on private law and proprietary rights in intangible assets. Vol. 1 (1974)], pp. 251 – 261

B) Publications in cyrillic letters:

1. *Братусь С. Н.*, *Предмет и система совецкого гражданского права*, Москва 1963

   BRATUS S. N., *Predmet i sistema sovetskogo grazhdanskogo prava*, Moskva 1963 [BRATUS S. N., *Subject and system of the Soviet private law*, Moskva 1963]

2. СУХАНОВ Е.А., *Вещноеправо. Научно-познавательный очерк*, Москва 2011SUKHANOV E.A., *Veshchnoye pravo. Naučno-poznavatelnyjočerk*, Moskva 2011 [SUKHANOV E.A., Ius in re. *A scientific and instructive study*, Moskva 2011]

3. СУХАНОВ Е.А. (ed.), *Российское гражданское право: Учебник: В 2-х томах. Том I. Общая часть. Вещное право. Наследственное право. Интеллектуальные права. Личные неимущественные права*, Москва 2009

   SUKHANOV E.A. (ed.), *Rossiyskoye grazhdanskoye prava: Uchebnik: V 2-kh tomakh. Tom I. Obshchaya Chast. Veshchnoye prava. Nasledstvennoyepravo. Intellektualnye prava. Lichnyye prava*, Moskva 2009

   [SUKHANOV E.A. (ed.), *Russian private law. Handbook in two volumes. Volume I. General part.* Ius in re . *Inheritance law. Intellectual rights. Personal non-property rights*, Moskva 2009]

4. СУХАНОВ Е.А. (ed.) *Российское гражданское право: Учебник: В 2-х томах. Том II. Обязательственное право*, Москва 2011

   SUKHANOV E.A., *Rossiyskoye grazhdanskoye pravo: Uchebnik: V 2-kh tomakh. Tom II. Obyazatelnojepravo*, Moskva 2011

   [SUKHANOW E.A., *Russian private law. Handbook in two volumes. Volume II. The law of obligations*, Moskva 2011]

5. Шершеневич Г.Ф., *Учебник русскаго гражданского права. Том I*, 11. издание. Москва 1914

   Shershenevich G.F., *Uchebnik russkago grazhdanskogo prava. Tom I*, 11. izdaniye, Moskva 1914

   [Shershenevich G.F., *Textbook of Russian private law. Volume I*, 11th edition, Moskva 1914]

Published sources

a) **Austria**

1. *Allgemeines bürgerliches Gesetzbuch für die gesammten deutschen Erbländer der Österreichischen Monarchie. I. Theil*, Wien 1811
2. *Allgemeines bürgerliches Gesetzbuch für die gesammten deutschen Erbländer der Österreichischen Monarchie. II. Theil*, Wien 1811
3. *Allgemeines bürgerliches Gesetzbuch für die gesammten deutschen Erbländer der Österreichischen Monarchie. III. Theil*, Wien 1811
4. *Das österreichische ABGB:Deutsch-Englisch = The Austrian Civil Code: German – English*, Wien 2013

b) **China:**

1. *Codex Iuris Civilis Reipublicae Sinicae. Zivilgesetzbuch von China. Civil Code of the Republic of China. Code Civil de la République de Chine. Chinesisch – Lateinische – Deutsche – Englische – Französische Ausgabe des Zivilgesetzbuches von 1929*, Shanghai, Zinan, Paris & Marburg 1930-34

c) **Czechoslovakia**

1. *Sně movnítisk 844. Vládnínávrhzákona, kterým se vydáváobčanskýzákoník* (Government proposal of a written law, by which the civil code is published), Praha (Státnítiskárna/ State Printing Office) 1937
2. Czechoslovak civil code from 1950 (Loi du 25 octobre 1950, No 141 du Recueil des lois de la République Tchécoslovaque, promulgée le 23 novembre 1950, entrée en vigueur le 1er janvier), annex to: Bulletin de Droit Tchécoslovaque 1951 numéro 1 – 2, pp. 151 – 224
3. [Czechoslovak civil code from 1964], *Kodeks cywilny. Kodeks gospodarczy. Kodeks handlu międzynarodowego Czechosłowackiej Republiki Socjalistycznej* (Civil code, Economic code, International commercial code of the Czechoslovak Socialist Republic), Wrocław/ Warszawa/ Kraków/ Gdańsk/ Łódź 1981
4. Czech civil code 89/2012 Sb., act of 3 February 2012, published on the website of the new Czech civil code (http://obcanskyzakonik.justice.cz/) http://obcanskyzakonik.justice.cz/images/pdf/Civil-Code.pdf, date of access: 21.09.2021

d) **France**

1. *Code civil des français. Édition originelle et seule officielle*, Paris 1804
2. *Les cinq codes. Mit gegenüberstehenden deutschen Uebersetzung von einem praktischen Juristen*, CRAMER Johann (ed.), Crefeld 1843 (including *Code civil*, *Code de procédure civile*, *Code de commerce*, *Code pénal* and *Code d'instruction criminelle*)
3. *Code civil annoté*, Paris Dalloz 2017 (including the reform of the law of obligations)

4. The law of contract, the general regime of obligations, and proof of obligations, The new provisions of the Code civil created by Ordonnance n°2016-131 of 10 February 2016 translated into English by John CARTWRIGHT, Bénédicte FAUVARQUE-COSSON and Simon WHITTAKER, accessible on the website of Trans-lex.org, https://www.Trans-lex.org/601101, date of access: 21.09.2021

e) **Germany**

1. [Codex Maximilianeus Bavaricus Civilis from 1756] *Codex Maximilianeus Bavaricus Civilis oder neu verbessert und ergänzt Chur-Bayrisches Land-Recht, Welches Alle zur bürgerlichen Rechts- Gelehrsamkeit gehörige Materien, so viel nicht schon in dem bereits Ao. 1751.respective 1753 neu-eröfneten Codice Criminali und Judicario besonders hievon enthalten ist, sowohl nach denen Gemein – als Statuarischen Rechts- Grundsätzen mit durchgängiger Applicirung der Ersten auf die Letztere, wie auch mit nöthiger Entscheid oder Supplirung deren vorhin entweder in Thesi strittig und zweifelhaft oder defectuos befundener Stellen, benebst dem am Ende beygefügten Lehen-Recht in sich begreift wohin mit Einschluß obgedacht neuer Gerichts- und Criminal-Ordnungen ein kurz, deutlich, ordentlich, und vollständiges Systema Juris Privati Universi, wie solches in hiesigen Chur-Landen dermahlen üblich und eingeführt ist, in IV. Theilen, XLIX Capitulen, Doch allerweegen in ganz natürlich und ungezwungnen Zusammenhang darstellt*, München 1756
2. [Prussian *Allgemeines Landrecht* from 1794] *Allgemeines Landrecht für die Preußischen Staaten von 1794. Textausgabe*, HATTENHAUER Hans (ed.), Frankfurt am Main/Berlin 1970
3. *Bürgerliches Gesetzbuch für das Königreich Sachsen von 1863/1865*, Darmstadt 1973
4. *Bürgerliches Gesetzbuch vom 18. August 1896. Faksimileausgabe anläßlich der Verkündung des BGB vor 100 Jahren* [Reichs-Gesetzblatt 1896, p. 195], München 1996
5. *Handelsgesetzbuch für das Deutsche Reich vom 10. Mai 1897 (mit Ausnahme des Seerechts) nebst dem Einführungsgesetze* [Reichs-Gesetzblatt 1897, p. 219], München 1902
6. *The German Civil Code. Revised Edition (as amended to January 1, 1992)*, Littleton/ Colorado 1994
7. [Civil code of the German Democratic Republic from 1975; Gesetzblatt der Deutschen Demokratischen Republik1975, Teil I Nr. 27] *Zivilrecht der Deutschen Demokratischen Republik. Zivil – und Familiengesetzbuch mit Nebengesetzen, Urheberrecht, gewerblicher Rechtsschutz, internationales Privat – und Wirtschaftsrecht, Seehandelsrecht*, BRUNNER Georg (ed.), München 1977
8. *Kodeks cywilny Niemieckiej Republiki Demokratycznej* [Civil code of the German Democratic Republic], Wrocław/Warszawa/ Kraków/Gdańsk 1979
9. Erbbaurechtsgesetz vom 15. Januar 1919 (Reichs-Gesetzblatt, p. 72, p. 122), lastly modified on 1st October 2013, Bundesgesetzblatt 2013 Teil I, p. 3719

10. Gesetz zur Modernisierung des Schuldrechts vom 26. November 2001, Bundesgesetzblatt 2001 Teil I, p. 3138

f) **Greece**

1. *Das Zivilgesetzbuch von Griechenland (1940) mit dem Einführungsgesetz*, Tübingen/ Berlin 1951

g) **Hungary**

1. [translation of one of Hungarian drafts] *Entwurf eines ungarischen allgemeinen bürgerliches Gesetzbuches*, Budapest 1901
2. [Hungarian draft from 1928, one of the main sources] *Ungarns Privatrechtsgesetzbuch. Entwurf (1928)*, Budapest 1940
3. [Hungarian civil code from 1959], *Civil Code of People's Hungarian Republic*, Budapest 1960
4. *The statutes of the Hungarian People's Republic. Civil Code of the Hungarian People's Republic*, Budapest 1982
5. *Węgierski kodeks cywilny* [Hungarian civil code], Wrocław/ Warszawa/ Kraków/ Gdańsk/ Łódź 1984
6. Hungarian civil code (2013), act V of 2013, on 11/02/2013, document published by International Trade Organization, https://www.ilo.org/dyn/natlex/natlex4.detail?p_lang=en&p_isn=96512&p_country=HUN&p_count=937&p_classification=01.03&p_classcount=4, date of access: 21.09.2021

h) **Poland**

1. [Code of obligations from 1933] *Code des obligations de la République de Pologne,* Paris 1935
2. [Code of obligations from 1933 and Commercial Code from 1934] *Das polnische Recht der Schuldverhältnisse und das polnische Handelsgesetzbuch nebst den zugehörigen Einführungsbestimmungen (Dz. U. R. P. 1933, Nr. 82, Pos. 598, 599, 600 und 601) in deutscher Übersetzung*, Poznań1934
3. [draft on *ius in re* from 1937] *Projekt prawa rzeczowego uchwalony w pierwszym czytaniu przez Podkomisję Prawa Rzeczowego Komisji Kodyfikacyjnej* [Draft on *ius in re* adopted in the firstreading of the Codification Committee Subsection on *ius in re*], *Komisja Kodyfikacyjna. Podkomisja Prawa Rzeczowego. Zeszyt 1* [Codification Committee. Subsection of *ius in re*. Volume 1], Warszawa 1937
4. *Komisja Kodyfikacyjna Rzeczypospolitej Polskiej. Podsekcja III Prawa Cywilnego. Tom I. Zeszyt 3 c* [Codification Committee of the Republic of Poland. Subsection III of Private Law. Vol. I. Issue 3 c], content: *Kodeks cywilny Rzeczypospolitej Polskiej. Księga pierwsza przepisy ogólne* [Civil Code of the Republic of Poland. The first book general provisions], Warszawa 1931
5. Dekret z dnia 11 października 1946 r. Prawo rzeczowe [Decree from 11th 1946 on *ius in re*] (Dz. U. R. P. Nr 57, poz. 320)

6. Postwar draft of a civil code, published in Demokratyczny Przegląd Prawniczy (Democratic Law Journal) [the first book (general part), published in DPP 1947 no. 12; the second book (family law), published in DPP 1948 no. 4, 6, 8, 9; the third book (obligations), published in DPP 1948 no. 10 – 12; the fourth book *(ius in re)*, published in DPP 1949 no. 1 – 3; the book including inheritance law was not published]

7. Ustawa z dnia 18 lipca 1950 r. Przepisy ogólne prawa cywilnego (Law from 18th July 1950 General provisions on private law), *Przepisy ogólne oraz przepisy wprowadzające [przepisy ogólne prawa cywilnego]* [General provisions and provisions implementing [general provisions on private law]], Warszawa 1952

8. *Projekt Kodeksu cywilnego Polskiej Rzeczypospolitej Ludowej* [Draft of the civil code of the People's Republic of Poland], Warszawa 1954

9. *Projekt kodeksu cywilnego Polskiej Rzeczypospolitej Ludowej. Tekst ustalony w wyniku dyskusji ogólnokrajowej* [Draft of the civil code of the People's Republic of Poland. Text settled as a result of the national discussion], Warszawa 1955

10. *Projekt Kodeksu cywilnego Polskiej Rzeczypospolitej Ludowej* [Draft of the civil code of the People's Republic of Poland], Warszawa 1960

11. *Projekt Kodeksu cywilnego* [Draft of the civil code], Warszawa 1961

12. *Projekt kodeksu cywilnego oraz przepisów wprowadzających kodeks cywilny* (Draft of the civil code and of the provisions introducing the civil code], Warszawa 1962

13. [Civil code from 1964] Kodeks cywilny (ustawa z dnia 23 kwietnia 1964 r., Dz. U. Nr 16, poz. 93), *Kodeks cywilny wraz z przepisami wykonawczymi i skorowidzem. Kodeks rodzinny i opiekuńczy. Prawo prywatne międzynarodowe* [Civil code with introductory provisions and index. Family and guardianship code. Private international law], Warszawa 1970

14. *Code civil de la République Populaire de Pologne*, Varsovie 1966

15. *Polnische Wirschaftsgesetze. Aktuelle Gesetztexte in deutscher Übersetzung*, Warszawa 2010 (including among others the Polish civil code)

16. *Kodeks cywilny. Kodeks rodzinny i opiekuńczy* [Civil code. Family and Guardianship Code], Warszawa 2021

17. *Projekt Księ gi pierwszej Kodeksu cywilnego wraz z uzasadnieniem* [Draft of the first book of the civil code with the justification], MACHNIKOWSKI Piotr (ed.), Warszawa 2008, text accessible online on the website of the Ministry of Justice: https://www.gov.pl/web/sprawiedliwosc/komisja-kodyfikacyjna-prawa-cywilnego

18. *Księga pierwsza kodeksu cywilnego. Projekt z uzasadnieniem* [First book of the civil code. Draft with a justification], Warszawa 2009

19. MACHNIKOWSKI Piotr (ed.), *Kodeks cywilny. Księga pierwsza. Część ogólna. Projekt Komisji Kodyfikacyjnej Prawa Cywilnego przyjęty w 2015 r. z komentarzem członków zespołu problemowego KKPC* [Civil code. First book.

General part. The draft of the Codification Committee of Private Law adopted in 2015, commented by the members of the Codification Committee of Private Law], Warszawa 2017

i) **Portugal**

1. [civil code from 1966] *Código civil português (Edição revista e actualizada)*, Coimbra 1984

j) **Russia**

1. [draft of the Russian civil code from 1905] VON SEELER Wilhelm, *Entwurf des Russischen Zivilgesetzbuches*, Berlin 1911
2. [Russian civil code from 1922] *Les codes de la Russie Soviétique. Tome 1 Code de la famille Code civil*, Paris 1925
3. *Kodeks cywilny R.S. F.S.R. wraz z kodeksem ustaw o małżeństwie, rodzinie i opiece* [Civil code of RSFSR with the code of bills on marriage, family and guardianship], Warszawa 1930
4. [Russian civil code from 1964] *Zasady ustawodawstwa cywilnego ZSRR. Kodekscywilny RFSRR* [The Principles of the Civil Legislation of the USSR. Civil code of the RSFSR], Wrocław/ Warszawa 1977
5. *Zasady ustawodawstwa ZSRR i republik związkowych. Kodeksmałż eńskii-rodzinny RFSRR* [The principles of the legislation of USSR and the union republics. The marriage and family code of RSFSR], Wrocław/ Warszawa/ Kraków/Gdańsk 1972
6. [The Russian civil code 1994 – 2006] BUTLER William E., *Civil code of the Russian Federation. Parts one, two and three*, Oxford University Press 2002
7. The civil code of the Russian Federation Part One No. 51-FZ of November 30, 1994, Part Two No. 14-FZ of January 26, 1996, Part Three No. 146-FZ of November 26, 2001 and Part Four No. 230-FZ of December 18, 2006, accessible online on the website of the World Intellectual Property Organization https://www.wipo.int/edocs/lexdocs/laws/en/ru/ru083en.pdf, date of access: 21.09.2021

k) **Switzerland**

1. *Schweizerisches Zivilgesetzbuch. Textausgabe mit Einleitung, Anmerkungen, Ausführungserlassen und Sachregister von W. Schönenberger*, Zürich 1980
2. *Schweizerisches Obligationenrecht. Textausgabe mit Einleitung, Anmerkungen, Ausführungserlassen und Sachregister von W. Schönenberger*, Zürich 1980

l) **Drafts of a European civil code** not discuss

1. DOCAN Georges P., *Code comparé des obligations. Le projet franco-italien des obligations et contrats comparé avec les codes civils français, roumain, suisse et polonais des obligations. Avec notes et renvois aux codes civils allemand et italien*, Bucureŝ ti 1937

2. LANDO Ole and BEALE Hugh (ed.), *Principles of European Contract Law: parts 1 and 2*, the Hague 2000

3. LANDO Ole (ed.), *Principles of European Contract Law: part 3*, the Hague/ London/ New York 2000

4. VON BAR Christian, CLIVE Eric and SCHULTE-NÖLKE Hans (ed.), *Principles, definitions and Model Rules of European Private Law. Draft Common Frame of Reference (DCFR). Outline Edition*, München 2009

Unpublished sources

Protokół z posiedzenia Komisji Kodyfikacyjnej – Zespół Prawa Cywilnego w dniu 16 grudnia 1956 r. o godz. 16:00 (obecni: Jerzy Marowski, Jan Wasilkowski, Henryka Dawidowicz, Jan Gwiazdomorski, Jerzy Mayzel, Kazimierz Przybyłowski, Seweryn Szer, Jan Topiński, Aleksander Wolter, Witold Bendetson, del. Ministra Sprawiedliwości, przewodniczył: Jerzy Marowski, przewodniczący Wydziału Cywilnego, protokołował Jan Winiarz), K. Kod. 90/57-65/1/2, s. 4 (numer wydrukowany na maszynie do pisania). Protokółznajduje się w teczce archiwalnej: Ministerstwo Sprawiedliwości, Departament Ustawodawczy, Wydział Prawa Cywilnego. Komisja Kodyfikacyjna. Tom I: Sesje: 16.12.1956, 30-31.01.1957, 28-31.03.1957 (kart 274). Archiwum Akt Nowych, Ministerstwo Sprawiedliwości w Warszawie, Nr zespołu: 285. Zespółl – Kodeks Cywilny [Protokoły posiedzeń, fragment Kodeksu Cywilnego – tytuł II, lista członków Zespołu Prawa Cywilnego Materialnego Komisji, Tom I.] 1956 – 1957. Sygn. 5401. [Minutes of the meeting of the Codification Commission – Private Law Group on 16th December, 1956, at 16:00 (present: Jerzy Marowski, Jan Wasilkowski, Henryka Dawidowicz, Jan Gwiazdomorski, Jerzy Mayzel, Kazimierz Przybyłowski, Seweryn Szer, Jan Topiński, Aleksander Wolter, Witold Bendetson delegate of the Minister of Justice, presided by Jerzy Marowski chairman of the Private Law Department, the minutes by Jan Winiarz), K. Kod. 90/57-65/1/2, p. 4 (the page number written on a typewriter). The protocol is in the archival file: Ministry of Justice, Legislative Department, Department of Private Law. Codification Committee: Volume I: Sessions: 16.12.1956, 30-31.01.1957, 28-31.03.1957 (274 cards). Archive of New Files, Ministry of Justice in Warsaw, number of the unit: 285. Workgroup 1 – Civil Code. [Minutes of meetings, fragment of the Civil Code - title II, list of members of the Substantive Private Law Commission, Volume I] 1956 – 1957. File number: 5401

Opracowywanie Kodeksu cywilnego. Materiały pomocnicze. Projekt Kodeksu cywilnego ZSRR, objaśnienia do projektu 1948 – 1950, Archiwum Akt Nowych, Ministerstwo Sprawiedliwości, Departament Ustawodawczy, Wydział Prawa Cywilnego, sygnatura: 2/285/0/4.2/2201 [Development of the Civil Code. Supporting materials. Draft civil code of the USSR, explanations to the draft 1948 – 1950, Archive of New Files, Ministry of Justice, Legislative Department, Private Law Department, reference number: 2/285/0/4.2/2201]

Augsburger Schriften zur Rechtsgeschichte

hrsg. von Prof. Dr. iur. utr. Christoph Becker (Universität Augsburg)

Sarah Kamm
Gemeindenutzungsrechte
Holznutzungsrechte im bayerischen Regierungsbezirk Schwaben
Seit unvordenklicher Zeit spielt für die Menschheit die Holznutzung eine entscheidende Rolle - ob als Werkstoff, als Brennstoff oder als Baustoff. Die Holznutzung ist vielseitig und nicht mehr aus dem Alltagsleben der Menschen hinwegzudenken. Zudem dienen die Wälder der Erholung und beeinflussen unser Klima.
In Deutschland übt eine abgegrenzte Gruppe von Menschen, die in Bayern häufig sogenannten Rechtler, viele Jahrhunderte alte Rechte zur Holznutzung an Gemeindewäldern bis heute aus. Diese Holznutzungsrechte sind komplex und noch vielerorts vorhanden.
Die Autorin zeigt die juristischen Besonderheiten dieser Rechte in Vergangenheit und Gegenwart auf. Sie konzentriert sich dabei auf die bayerische Gesetzgebung und das Gebiet des heutigen Regierungsbezirks Schwaben.
Bd. 42, 2023, 450 S., 64,90 €, gb., ISBN 978-3-643-15284-8

Maria Malt
Die Rechtsnachfolge in Personengesellschaften im Deutschland und im Russland des 19. Jahrhunderts
Bd. 41, 2023, 388 S., 49,90 €, gb., ISBN 978-3-643-15208-4

LIT Verlag Berlin – Münster – Wien – Zürich – London
Auslieferung Deutschland / Österreich / Schweiz: siehe Impressumsseite

Florian Schwinger
Schicksale jüdischer Rechtsanwälte in Bayerisch-Schwaben zur Zeit des Nationalsozialismus
Die Arbeit zeigt anhand der 16 in Bayerisch-Schwaben zur Zeit des Nationalsozialismus tätigen Rechtsanwälte auf, wie jüdische Anwälte im Dritten Reich verfolgt wurden. Der Autor stellt dabei das Leben der Rechtsanwälte vor dem Nationalsozialismus dar sowie die einzelnen Schritte, wie die Verfolgten aufgrund des Gesetzes über die Zulassung zur Rechtsanwaltschaft und der Fünften Verordnung zum Reichsbürgergesetz zunächst ihre wirtschaftliche Existenz und anschließend entweder durch Flucht ihre Heimat oder durch die Shoah ihr Leben verloren. Darüber hinaus geht die Arbeit auf die Entschädigungsansprüche der Anwälte und ihrer Erben nach dem Nationalsozialismus ein.
Bd. 40, 2021, 340 S., 49,90 €, gb., ISBN 978-3-643-14885-8

Das Augsburger Stadtrecht von 1156
Eine zweisprachige Ausgabe des Augsburger Stadtrechts von 1156 mit Erläuterungen. Herausgegeben von Christoph Becker und Matthias Ferber
Das in lateinischer Sprache verfasste Augsburger Stadtrecht von 1156 zählt zu den ältesten überlieferten mitteleuropäischen Stadtrechten. Seine Entstehung ist mit der Entwicklung des römischen Rechts zum gemeineuropäischen Recht verbunden. Zugleich ist es früher Ausdruck der Idee kommunaler Selbstverwaltung. Die vorliegende zweisprachige Edition erschließt Text und Entstehungsumstände. Sie geht aus einem gemeinsamen Forschungsprojekt von Universität Augsburg und Gymnasium bei Sankt Stephan Augsburg hervor.
Bd. 39, 2021, 144 S., 19,90 €, gb., ISBN 978-3-643-14806-3

Maximilian Schatz
Entwicklung und Zukunftsperspektive der Unternehmensrestrukturierung
Ein historischer Vergleich zwischen den Vereinigten Staaten von Amerika und Deutschland
Sowohl die Weltwirtschafts- und Finanzkrise im Jahr 2008 als auch die COVID-19-Pandemie im Jahr 2020 beweisen, dass in Krisensituationen ein funktionierendes nationales Insolvenzrecht für Unternehmen von immenser Bedeutung ist. Das deutsche Insolvenzrecht befindet sich angesichts der europäischen Richtlinie über Restrukturierung und Insolvenz im Wandel. Der Gesetzgeber muss einen präventiven Restrukturierungsrahmen in das Gesetz einfassen. Der Autor beleuchtet anhand der aktuellen Gesetzeslage in Deutschland und den Vereinigten Staaten von Amerika, welche Gestaltungsmöglichkeiten bestehen.
Bd. 38, 2020, 402 S., 49,90 €, gb., ISBN 978-3-643-14782-0

Nicola Birk
Die Gestaltung von Grundstücksübertragungen in der Reichsstadt Augsburg und in der Territorialstadt Neuss
Bd. 37, 2024, 244 S., 39,90 €, gb., ISBN 978-3-643-14781-5

Iring Christopeit
Ius Gentium. Zur Entwicklung internationalen Rechts
Eine Untersuchung von Rechtssubjekten, Rechtsobjekten und Normprinzipien
Bd. 36, 2021, 312 S., 44,90 €, gb., ISBN 978-3-643-14773-8

LIT Verlag Berlin – Münster – Wien – Zürich – London
Auslieferung Deutschland / Österreich / Schweiz: siehe Impressumsseite

Dominik Lutz
Zusammenbrüche in der deutschen Textilwirtschaft
Krisen und Insolvenzverfahren in Produktion und Einzelhandel unter Konkursordnung, Vergleichsordnung und Insolvenzordnung
In den 1950er Jahren war die Textilproduktion mit fast einer Million Beschäftigten einer der wichtigsten Teile des produzierenden Gewerbes in Deutschland. Seitdem erlebte die Textilproduktion einen dauernden Strukturwandel mit zahlreichen Krisen und Insolvenzen. Seit den 1990er Jahren befindet sich auch der deutsche Bekleidungseinzelhandel in einem dauerhaften Strukturwandel, der zu zahlreichen Krisen und Insolvenzen geführt hat. Dieses Buch zeigt Verlauf und Ursachen des Strukturwandel in beiden Wirtschaftszweigen und geht anhand von Gerichtsakten ausführlich auf wichtige Gesamtvollstreckungsverfahren ein.
Bd. 35, 2021, 452 S., 54,90 €, gb., ISBN 978-3-643-14771-4

Caren Hertfelder
Der betrügerische Fallit in Mittelalter und Neuzeit
Zivil- und strafrechtliche Bestimmungen wider vorsätzliches gläubigerschädigendes Entziehen von Vermögenswerten vor und in der Insolvenz
Seit jeher versuchen manche Schuldner angesichts ihrer drohenden oder schon eingetretenen Insolvenz, ihr Vermögen dem Zugriff der Gläubiger zu entziehen. Die Reaktionsmöglichkeiten des Rechts hierauf sind vielfältig: Dem Schuldner und seinen Helfern drohen Erstattungspflichten, Haftung, strafrechtliche Sanktionen und der Ausschluss von Rechtswohltaten. Ausgehend vom römischen Recht über das italienische Stadtrecht des Mittelalters und die deutschen Partikularrechte in Mittelalter und Neuzeit bis hin zu den heutigen Regelungen legt die Autorin die Entwicklung dieser über die Jahrhunderte sich stetig verfeinernden Bestimmungen dar. Ein Schwerpunkt der Arbeit liegt dabei im Augsburger Recht.
Bd. 34, 2020, 412 S., 54,90 €, gb., ISBN 978-3-643-14635-9

Christoph Becker (Hrsg.)
Themen der Zeit
Vortragsveranstaltungen der Juristischen Gesellschaft Augsburg als rechtsgeschichtlicher Spiegel. Eine Dokumentation aus 30 Arbeitsjahren
Die Juristische Gesellschaft Augsburg, im Jahre 1988 mit der Zielsetzung eines Gedankenaustauschs zu rechtlichen Fragen jeglicher Art gegründet, nahm im Jahre 1989 ihren Veranstaltungsbetrieb auf. Drei Jahrzehnte später weisen mehrere hundert durchgeführte Vortragsabende, Diskussionen, Mittagsgespräche und andere Veranstaltungen die Gesellschaft mit ihren Damen und Herren Referenten, Diskutanten und Gästen als Zeitzeugin aus.
Der Herausgeber ließ in zwei Seminaren der Wintersemester 2017/2018 und 2018/2019 die nachwachsende Generation sich mit Themen der zurückgelegten Zeit und ihren Akteuren auseinandersetzen. Daraus entstand der vorliegende Band als Dokumentation jüngster Rechtsgeschichte und ihrer Reflexion.
Bd. 33, 2020, 428 S., 69,90 €, gb., ISBN 978-3-643-14630-4

Fabian Reiter
Zwischen Gläubigerbefriedigung und politischer Opportunität
Die Umgehung und Beeinflussung des Insolvenzverfahrens in der neueren deutschen Geschichte bis zur Gegenwart
Bd. 32, 2020, 248 S., 39,90 €, gb., ISBN 978-3-643-14614-4

LIT Verlag Berlin – Münster – Wien – Zürich – London
Auslieferung Deutschland / Österreich / Schweiz: siehe Impressumsseite

Bettina Wirth-Duncan
Rechtsberatung in der römischen Antike
Von der Ehrentätigkeit zum Beruf
Die Autorin untersucht die Entwicklung der Rechtsberatung im Laufe der römischen Antike. Ausgehend von der Königszeit zeichnet sie das Bild eines Rechtsberatungswesens, das sich über die Jahrhunderte hinweg bis zum Erlass des Corpus Iuris Civilis im Jahr 533 n. Chr. allmählich professionalisierte: Von einer zunächst ehrenvollen, auf sozialen Bindungen beruhenden Beratungstätigkeit, die der Aristokratie vorbehalten war und für deren Erfüllung es zwar Anerkennung, nicht aber einen Lohn gab, hin zu einer bezahlten Rechtsdienstleistung, die durch verbandlich organisierte Berufsträger erbracht wurde.
Bd. 31, 2020, 312 S., 49,90 €, gb., ISBN 978-3-643-14319-8

Stefan Müller
Aktiengesellschaften des 19. Jahrhunderts
Familienunternehmen zwischen Kapitalbedarf und Einflusswahrung
Statistiken zeigen, dass etwa neun von zehn Unternehmen der deutschen Privatwirtschaft in Familienhand sind. Jedoch sind weite Teile im Bereich der Familienunternehmen noch gänzlich unerforscht. Die Forschungen in diesem Bereich werden unter anderem dadurch erschwert, da Familienunternehmen regelmäßig nur spärliche Informationen über sich herausgeben.
Dieses Werk widmet sich der Umwandlung von Familienunternehmen in eine Aktiengesellschaft. Dabei konnte auf originale Archivunterlagen von Familienunternehmen zurückgegriffen werden. Bei den ausgewählten Familienunternehmen handelt es sich um die namhaften Betriebe Siemens, MAN und Momm.
Bd. 30, 2018, 280 S., 49,90 €, gb., ISBN 978-3-643-14049-4

Christoph Becker (Hrsg.)
Persönlichkeitsrecht und Persönlichkeit des Rechts
Gedächtnisschrift für Heinz Hübner (1914 – 2006)
Heinz Hübner (1914 – 2006), Universitätsprofessor für Bürgerliches Recht, Handelsrecht und Römisches Recht in Köln, wäre im Jahre 2014 einhundert Jahre alt geworden. Im Jahre 2016 jährte sich sein Tod zum zehnten Male. Die beiden Daten gaben den Anlaß zu dieser Gedächtnisschrift.
Der Band enthält Angaben zu Lebenslauf und Werken Hübners, einen bislang unpublizierten Vortrag Hübners über Friedrich II. von Hohenstaufen sowie sechs noch zu seinen Lebzeiten aus verschiedenen Ländern übersandte Beiträge zu einem unvollendet gebliebenen rechtshistorisch-rechtsvergleichenden Forschungsvorhaben über den Schutz des Persönlichkeitsrechts.
Bd. 29, 2017, 344 S., 59,90 €, gb., ISBN 978-3-643-13413-4

Catherine Jilek
Priorität im bayerischen Konkurs seit der Frühen Neuzeit
Bd. 27, 2015, 262 S., 39,90 €, gb., ISBN 978-3-643-12991-8

Sebastian Bachmann
Rudolf Callmann
Leben und Wirken eines jüdischen Wettbewerbs- und Kartellrechtsexperten im 20. Jahrhundert
Bd. 26, 2015, 424 S., 44,90 €, gb., ISBN 978-3-643-12963-5

LIT Verlag Berlin – Münster – Wien – Zürich – London
Auslieferung Deutschland / Österreich / Schweiz: siehe Impressumsseite

Christoph Becker; Peter Fassl (Hrsg.)
Die Höheren Kommunalverbände in Deutschland – Modell der Zukunft
Tagung vom 19. bis zum 21. März 2014 im Schwäbischen Bildungszentrum Irsee
Bd. 25, 2018, 352 S., 44,90 €, gb., ISBN 978-3-643-12919-2

Sabrina Birnbaum
Konkursrecht der frühen Augsburger Neuzeit mit seinen gemeinrechtlichen Einflüssen
Bd. 24, 2014, 264 S., 44,90 €, gb., ISBN 978-3-643-12685-6

Alexander Flechsig
Frühneuzeitlicher Erfindungsschutz
Eine Untersuchung unter besonderer Berücksichtigung der Reichsstadt Augsburg
Bd. 23, 2013, 232 S., 34,90 €, br., ISBN 978-3-643-12213-1

David Georg
Gesellschafterdarlehen in der Insolvenz
Die Entwicklung seit Schaffung des GmbH-Gesetzes im Jahre 1892
Bd. 22, 2011, 280 S., 34,90 €, gb., ISBN 978-3-643-11099-2

Abdellatif Dakkak
Der Kaufvertrag im marokkanischen und im deutschen Recht
Eine rechtsvergleichende Untersuchung unter Berücksichtigung des islamischen Rechts
Bd. 21, 2011, 216 S., 39,90 €, gb., ISBN 978-3-643-10988-0

Markus Antonius Mayer
Der Kauf nach dem Augsburger Stadtrecht von 1276 im Vergleich zum gemeinen römischen Recht
Bd. 20, 2009, 208 S., 24,90 €, gb., ISBN 978-3-643-10370-3

Ökonomie und Recht – Historische Entwicklungen in Bayern. 6. Tagung der Gesellschaft für Bayerische Rechtsgeschichte am 4. und 5. Juli 2008 in Augsburg
Herausgegeben von Christoph Becker und Hans-Georg Hermann im Auftrag der Bayerischen Gesellschaft für Rechtsgeschichte. Gewidmet Dr. Hans Schlosser, emeritiertem Universitätsprofessor in Augsburg, zur Vollendung seines 75. Lebensjahres am 29. Juli 2009
Bd. 19, 2009, 208 S., 34,90 €, gb., ISBN 978-3-643-10116-7

Peter M. Bauer
Der Insolvenzplan
Untersuchungen zur Rechtsnatur anhand der geschichtlichen Entwicklung
Bd. 18, 2009, 424 S., 54,90 €, gb., ISBN 978-3-643-10115-0

Evelyn Bezler
Die Bedeutung des Stammkapitals für die GmbH
Eine rechtswissenschaftliche Untersuchung anhand der Entstehungs- und Entwicklungsgeschichte der GmbH, der dogmatischen Grundlagen und der praktischen Funktion des Stammkapitals
Bd. 17, 2009, 272 S., 24,90 €, br., ISBN 978-3-643-10114-3

LIT Verlag Berlin – Münster – Wien – Zürich – London
Auslieferung Deutschland / Österreich / Schweiz: siehe Impressumsseite

Sascha Spiegel
Einführung der Gesellschaft mit beschränkter Haftung in das deutsche und Schweizer Recht
Bd. 16, 2010, 176 S., 29,90 €, gb., ISBN-CH 978-3-643-90001-2

Sabrina Rückert
Die Einführung der obligatorischen Buchführung
Eine rechtshistorische Untersuchung über die Anfänge und die Entwicklung des Bilanzrechts in Frankreich und Deutschland
Bd. 15, 2009, 216 S., 34,90 €, gb., ISBN 978-3-643-10003-0

„Consvetvdines almae Reipublicae Augustanae" von Matthaeus Laimann und Georg Tradel mit „Notwendigs Bedenckhen" von Georg Tradel
Eine Zusammenstellung Augsburger Stadtrechts mit einer Denkschrift zu seiner Reform vom Ende des sechzehnten Jahrhunderts (Handschrift der Staats- und Stadtbibliothek Augsburg 2° Cod. Aug. 168). Herausgegeben und bearbeitet von Christoph Becker
Bd. 14, 2009, 136 S., 29,90 €, gb., ISBN 978-3-8258-1859-3

Birgit Susanne Müller
Kreditgenossenschaften in Bayern
Eine rechtsgeschichtliche Untersuchung der Kreditvergabe, der Kreditsicherung und der Kreditabwicklung von den Anfängen bis 1914
Bd. 13, 2009, 400 S., 54,90 €, gb., ISBN 978-3-8258-1809-8

Michael Pils
Die rechtsgeschichtliche Entwicklung der Brandstiftung
Ein Beitrag zum Umgang mit Gefahren
Bd. 12, 2010, 624 S., 79,90 €, br., ISBN 978-3-8258-1538-7

Heinrich Gottfried Wilhelm Daniels
Vorlesungen des Herrn Geheimen Staatsraths Daniels über das Statutar Recht von Khur Köln Stadt Köln und Jülich und Berg, im Jahre 1800 zu Köln gehalten. Eine Vorlesungsnachschrift (Universitäts- und Stadtbibliothek Köln 5 P 233). Herausgegeben und bearbeitet von Christoph Becker
Bd. 11, 2009, 120 S., 24,90 €, gb., ISBN 978-3-8258-1497-7

Volker von Danckelmann
Aus- und Absonderung im deutschen Konkursrecht
Eine Untersuchung über die Entwicklung des Verständnisses von Verwaltung und Verwertung fremdrechtbelasteter beweglicher Sachen und Immobilien im deutschen Konkursrecht seit 1855
Bd. 10, 2008, 368 S., 44,90 €, gb., ISBN 978-3-8258-1431-1

Peter Kreutz
Romidee und Rechtsbild in der Spätantike
Untersuchungen zur Ideen- und Mentalitätsgeschichte
Bd. 9, 2008, 384 S., 44,90 €, gb., ISBN 978-3-8258-1423-6

Nicole Reisinger-Selk
Heinrich Gottfried Wilhelm Daniels (1754 – 1827)
Leben und Werk – Ein Jurist in drei Zeitaltern
Bd. 8, 2008, 376 S., 39,90 €, gb., ISBN 978-3-8258-1281-2

Christiane E. Vollmershausen
Vom Konkursprozess zum Marktbereinigungsverfahren
Das deutsche Konkursverfahren vom Jahr 1700 bis heute – Eine exemplarische Untersuchung
Bd. 7, 2007, 392 S., 39,90 €, gb., ISBN 978-3-8258-0819-8

Katharina von Ciriacy-Wantrup
Familien- und erbrechtliche Gestaltungen von Unternehmen der Renaissance
Eine Untersuchung der Augsburger Handelsgesellschaften zur frühen Neuzeit
Bd. 6, 2007, 400 S., 39,90 €, gb., ISBN 978-3-8258-0357-5

Silke Pettinger
Vermögenserhaltung und Sicherung der Unternehmensfortführung durch Verfügungen von Todes wegen
Eine Studie der Frühen Augsburger Neuzeit
Bd. 5, 2007, 296 S., 29,90 €, gb., ISBN 978-3-8258-0076-5

Hans-Peter Philipp Anlauf
Vorgänger der Restschuldbefreiung nach heutigem Insolvenzrecht
Von der landwirtschaftlichen Entschuldungsgesetzgebung der Weimarer Republik über die NS-Schuldenbereinigung zur heutigen Restschuldbefreiung
Bd. 4, 2006, 480 S., 34,90 €, gb., ISBN 3-8258-9170-4

Christian Strasser
Der Aufstand im bayerischen Oberland 1705 – Majestätsverbrechen oder Heldentat?
Eine Untersuchung der Strafprozesse gegen die Anführer der in der „Mordweihnacht von Sendling" gescheiterten Erhebung
Bd. 3, 2005, 352 S., 29,90 €, br., ISBN 3-8258-8623-9

Stephan Schill
Der Einfluß der Wettbewerbsideologie des Nationalsozialismus auf den Schutzzweck des UWG
Bd. 2, 2004, 112 S., 14,90 €, br., ISBN 3-8258-8235-7

Michael Spann
Der Haftungszugriff auf den Schuldner zwischen Personal- und Vermögensvollstreckung
Eine exemplarische Untersuchung der geschichtlichen Rechtsquellen ausgehend vom Römischen Recht bis ins 21. Jh. unter besonderer Berücksichtigung bayerischer Quellen
Bd. 1, 2004, 336 S., 29,90 €, gb., ISBN 3-8258-7718-3